STRATEGIC PUBLIC FIN

Strategic PUBLIC Finance

STEPHEN J. BAILEY

palgrave
macmillan

First published 2004 by
PALGRAVE MACMILLAN
Houndmills, Basingstoke, Hampshire RG21 6XS and
175 Fifth Avenue, New York, N.Y. 10010
Companies and representatives throughout the world

PALGRAVE MACMILLAN is the global academic imprint of the Palgrave Macmillan division of St. Martin's Press, LLC and of Palgrave Macmillan Ltd. Macmillan® is a registered trademark in the United States, United Kingdom and other countries. Palgrave is a registered trademark in the European Union and other countries.

ISBN 0–333–92221–2

This book is printed on paper suitable for recycling and made from fully managed and sustained forest sources.

A catalogue record for this book is available from the British Library.

Library of Congress Cataloging-in-Publication Data

Bailey, S. J. (Stephen James), 1951–
    Strategic public finance / Stephen J. Bailey.
        p. cm.
    Includes bibliographical references and index.
    ISBN 0–333–92221–2 (pbk.)
        1. Finance, Public. 2. Finance, Public—OECD countries. I. Title.

HJ141.B24 2004
352.4—dc21   2003054755

Editing and origination by Aardvark Editorial, Mendham, Suffolk

10 9 8 7 6 5 4 3 2 1
13 12 11 10 09 08 07 06 05 04

Printed and bound in Great Britain by
Creative Print & Design (Wales), Ebbw Vale

Contents

List of Figures		ix
List of Tables		xi
List of OECD Data Sources		xii
Preface		xiii
Acknowledgements		xiv

1 Philosophical and Analytical Frameworks for Public Finance **1**
Introduction 1
What is 'public finance'? 3
Philosophical underpinnings of public finance 5
Public finance under Libertarianism 7
Public finance under Neo-Liberalism 8
Public finance under Collectivism 9
Overview of the three political philosophies 10
The Neo-Liberal resurgence 11
Globalisation, political philosophy and public finance 14
Eclecticism and pragmatism in public finance 16
An analytical framework for studying public finance 19
Conclusions 22

2 Property Rights and Public Finance **26**
Introduction 26
Spending public finance in the public interest 26
Property rights and the public interest 29
The legitimacy of property rights 35
Using property rights to categorise public and private services 36
Property rights, market valuations, wider social benefits
and public finance 43
Public finance versus public provision 44
Wider social benefits and public finance 45
Rights, access, efficiency and equity 47
Conclusions 50

3   The Relative Scale of Public Finance   **53**
       Introduction   53
       What are the public finance/GDP ratios?   54
       Interpreting the public finance/GDP ratios   57
       What are the actual proportions of public finance within GDP?   59
       What determines the share of public finance within GDP?   68
       Why do the four public finance/GDP ratios fluctuate from year to year? 72
       Why have some of the public finance/GDP ratios displayed
           a long-term rising trend?   73
       Testing the theories against the evidence   77
       Is a rising long-term trend in public finance/GDP ratios a cause
           for concern?   79
       What is the optimum proportion of public finance within GDP?   80
       Conclusions   84

4   Spending Public Finance   **86**
       Introduction   86
       Spending public finance in accordance with the 4Es   87
       Upon what is public finance actually spent?   90
       Does public spending secure value for money?   105
       By what means can public finance be disbursed?   106
       Additionality in public finance   108
       Identifying and measuring additionality   110
       Maximising the additionality of public finance   113
       Conclusions on additionality   115
       Cost containment   116
       Forms of cost containment   119
       Conclusions on cost containment   125
       Tax expenditures   125
       Conclusions   128

5   Raising Public Finance   **131**
       Introduction   131
       From what sources can public finance be raised?   132
       How is public finance raised in practice?   150
       What is the optimum combination of the different sources
           of public finance?   158
       Conclusions   159

6 Beneficial and Adverse Effects of Public Finance **163**
Introduction 163
Assessing the impact of public finance on the economy 164
Evidence of crowding out 170
Assessing the impact of public finance on society 172
Is concern about excessive public finance justified? 176
Conclusions 177

7 Structural Gaps in Public Finance **179**
Introduction 179
Why structural gaps in the public finances are a cause for concern 179
Evidence of structural gaps: financial indicators 180
Evidence of structural gaps: non-financial indicators 204
The causes of structural gaps: pragmatic explanations 206
The causes of structural gaps: discipline-specific explanations 207
A comprehensive theory of structural gaps: the logic of
    collective action 209
Exacerbation of structural gaps 213
How to eliminate and avoid structural gaps 217
Conclusions 220

8 Strategic Issues for Local Public Finance **223**
Introduction 223
Strategic issues for local government service responsibilities 224
Strategic issues for local government size and structure 227
Strategic issues for the financing of local governments 231
Strategic issues for the control of local government spending 234
Strategic issues for central financing of local governments 235
Conclusions 241

9 Vouchers as an Alternative Public Service Funding System **243**
Introduction 243
An empirical typology of vouchers 244
A conceptual typology of vouchers 248
A general model of vouchers 251
Perspectives for analysing arguments for and against vouchers 253
Dimensions and characteristics of vouchers 262
Rights and responsibilities of vouchers 265

The new definition of vouchers   267
Vouchers and the new public management   268
Conclusions   269

10   Conclusions – A Strategy for Public Finance   **272**
Introduction   272
What lessons are to be learnt from this study of public finance?   272
A strategy for public finance   280
Conclusion – the holistic nature of public finance   283

Index   285

List of Figures

3.1   Government expenditure as a percentage of GDP: OECD versus
        EU and large economies   62
3.2   Government expenditure as a percentage of GDP: OECD versus
        Europe and non-European nations   62
3.3   Taxation as a percentage of GDP: OECD versus EU and large
        economies   67
3.4   Taxation as a percentage of GDP: OECD versus Europe and
        non-European nations   67
3.5   Total OECD expenditure versus taxation   68

4.1   Social security transfers as a percentage of GDP: OECD versus
        Europe and non-European nations   96
4.2   Social security transfers as a percentage of GDP: OECD versus
        EU and large economies   96
4.3   Government final consumption as a percentage of GDP: OECD
        versus EU and large economies   100
4.4   Government final consumption as a percentage of GDP: OECD
        versus Europe and non-European nations   100
4.5   Government capital expenditure as a percentage of GDP: OECD
        versus EU and large economies   104
4.6   Government capital expenditure as a percentage of GDP: OECD
        versus Europe and non-European nations   105

5.1   Taxes as a percentage of GDP: OECD averages   151
5.2   Personal income tax as a percentage of GDP: OECD versus EU and
        large economies   152
5.3   Personal income tax as a percentage of GDP: OECD versus Europe
        and non-European nations   153
5.4   Social security contributions as a percentage of GDP: OECD versus
        EU and large economies   153
5.5   Social security contributions as a percentage of GDP: OECD versus
        Europe and non-European nations   154
5.6   Tax on goods and services as a percentage of GDP: OECD versus
        EU and large economies   155
5.7   Tax on goods and services as a percentage of GDP: OECD versus
        Europe and non-European nations   155
5.8   Property tax as a percentage of GDP: OECD versus EU and
        large economies   156
5.9   Property tax as a percentage of GDP: OECD versus Europe and
        non-European nations   156

5.10   Tax on corporate income as a percentage of GDP: OECD versus
        EU and large economies   157
5.11   Tax on corporate income as a percentage of GDP: OECD versus
        Europe and non-European nations   157

9.1   Vouchers in the private and public sectors   245
9.2   A conceptual typology of vouchers   249
9.3   A simplified voucher model   251
9.4   A local government voucher model   252
9.5   Characteristics of a service voucher   263
9.6   Rights and responsibilities of vouchers   266

List of Tables

1.1 A simplified taxonomy of philosophical principles for public finance   6
1.2 Alternative philosophical interpretations of the 4Es   20

3.1 Government expenditure as a percentage of GDP   59
3.2 Taxation as a percentage of GDP   64

4.1 Current disbursements of government as a percentage of GDP   91
4.2 Social security transfers as a percentage of GDP   94
4.3 Government final consumption as a percentage of GDP   97
4.4 Government capital expenditure as a percentage of GDP   101

5.1 Sources of public finance   132

6.1 Social security contributions less social security transfers   174

7.1 Total government expenditure minus total taxation (percentages of GDP)   181
7.2 Total government expenditure minus total taxation revenue (summary)   185
7.3 Comparison of surpluses and deficits (total government expenditure minus tax) (percentage of GDP)   186
7.4 Total government current expenditure minus total taxation revenue (percentage of GDP)   187
7.5 Total current expenditure minus total taxation revenue (summary)   190
7.6 Comparison of surpluses and deficits (current expenditure minus tax) (percentage of GDP)   191
7.7 Central government debt (percentage of GDP)   193
7.8 Changes in the central government debt/GDP ratio   194
7.9 Changes in capital expenditure/GDP ratio   195
7.10 Percentage point changes in the capital expenditure/GDP ratio and the central government debt/GDP ratio, 1990 versus 1999   197
7.11 Consumer price index (percentage change from previous year)   198
7.12 Real long-term interest rates   201

8.1 Total number of local authorities 1950 and 1992   229
8.2 Population size of local authorities 1990   230
8.3 Sources of municipal funding (percentages)   232
8.4 Municipal expenditure relative to GDP and GGE   238
8.5 Intergovernmental transfers (percentages of total municipal resources)   239

9.1 Perspectives for analysing vouchers   254

List of OECD Data Sources

OECD (1979) *Economic Outlook July 1979* (Paris: Organization for Economic Co-operation and Development).

OECD (1981) *Revenue Statistics 1965–1980* (Paris: Organization for Economic Co-operation and Development).

OECD (1983a) *Economic Outlook December 1983* (Paris: Organization for Economic Co-operation and Development).

OECD (1983b) *Historical Statistics 1960–1981* (Paris: Organization for Economic Co-operation and Development).

OECD (1985) *Historical Statistics 1960–1983* (Paris: Organization for Economic Co-operation and Development).

OECD (1987) *Revenue Statistics 1965–1986* (Paris: Organization for Economic Co-operation and Development).

OECD (1992a) *Historical Statistics 1960–1990* (Paris: Organization for Economic Co-operation and Development).

OECD (1992b) *Revenue Statistics 1965–1991* (Paris: Organization for Economic Co-operation and Development).

OECD (1993) *Taxation in OECD Countries 1990* (Paris: Organization for Economic Co-operation and Development).

OECD (1995) *Historical Statistics 1960–1994* (Paris: Organization for Economic Co-operation and Development).

OECD (1996) *Revenue Statistics 1965–1995* (Paris: Organization for Economic Co-operation and Development).

OECD (1997) *Revenue Statistics 1965–1996* (Paris: Organization for Economic Co-operation and Development).

OECD (1999) *Historical Statistics 1960–1997* (Paris: Organization for Economic Co-operation and Development).

OECD (2000) *Historical Statistics 1970–1999* (Paris: Organization for Economic Co-operation and Development).

OECD (2001a) *Central Government Debt Statistical Yearbook 1980–2000* (Paris: Organization for Economic Co-operation and Development).

OECD (2001b) *Economic Outlook December 2001* (Paris: Organization for Economic Co-operation and Development).

OECD (2001c) *Historical Statistics 1970–2000* (Paris: Organization for Economic Co-operation and Development).

OECD (2001d) *Revenue Statistics 1965–2000* (Paris: Organization for Economic Co-operation and Development).

Preface

Strategic Public Finance is written so as to be intelligible to non-specialist readers. Its focus being on strategic issues in public finance, the book covers the main alternative political philosophies underpinning public finance, the theoretical impact of collective choices and public finance on property rights, its relative scale in developed countries, spending and raising public finance, potential beneficial and adverse effects of public finance, structural gaps, strategic local public finance, potential use of vouchers to distribute public finance and a strategy for public finance.

The analysis of time-series data relating to all OECD countries makes the book particularly relevant for the European, North American, Australasian, and Asian markets. It is suitable for multidisciplinary undergraduate and taught postgraduate degree programmes focusing on social policy, social sciences, the welfare state, public administration, politics, public policy and so on. It is especially suitable for the increasingly large number of public sector employees taking Master of Business Administration (MBA) degree programmes.

In adopting a strategic overview of public finance, the reader should consult the further readings listed at the end of each chapter for more detailed analysis of policy and practice.

Acknowledgements

Chapter 9 was written jointly with Pekka Valkama and previously published in *Public Policy and Administration* vol. 16 no. 1 Spring 2001, pages 32–58. It is incorporated into this volume with permission of both the joint authors and the journal.

The Division of Economics and Enterprise (Glasgow Caledonian University) financed the employment of Lisa Fingland as a research assistant to collect, tabulate and present graphically the OECD data used in Chapters 3, 4, 5, 6 and 7.

OECD and Council of Europe data are reproduced with permission of those two organisations.

1 Philosophical and Analytical Frameworks for Public Finance

INTRODUCTION

This book considers the nature of public finance and its symbiotic relationship with economy and society. It considers:

- its philosophical underpinnings
- the nature of the services it finances
- its relative scale
- how it is spent
- how it is raised
- its possible beneficial and adverse effects
- its sustainability
- the appropriate governmental level of decision-making
- the means by which it can be disbursed
- an optimal strategy for public finance.

Examination of each of these aspects of public finance is set within an analytical framework based on equity, efficiency, economy and effectiveness. The intended outcome of this examination is to provide an understanding of the multidisciplinary nature of public finance. It is not the preserve of any one discipline, despite the fact that the great majority of academic texts providing detailed examinations of the rationale for public finance have been written by economists. One such economist defines public finance as 'the field of economics that analyses government taxation and spending policies' (Rosen 1999, page 536). Essentially the same definition is adopted by other economists (for example Hyman 1999, page 5) though, in practice, most simply do not define 'public finance'. However, '[public finance] is something of a misnomer, because the fundamental issues are not financial (that is, relating to money). Rather the key problems relate to the use of real resources. For this reason, some authors prefer the label "public sector economics" or simply "public economics"' (Rosen page 4).

In treating public finance as a branch of economics and presenting it as such in textbooks, the subject is immediately made inaccessible to the vast majority of undergraduate and postgraduate students. One such text bravely

1

acknowledges a criticism by one of its reviewers, namely 'death by diagrams' (Cullis and Jones 1998, preface). Moreover, economists themselves are often unclear about what parts of their discipline fall within the subcategory of public finance, as would be made clear by an examination of the contents pages of the books in the reading list at the end of this chapter. Traditionally, however, economists have limited their study of public finance to microeconomics, in particular using economic theory to examine how governments can and should affect the use of a country's productive resources (labour, capital, land and entrepreneurship) to promote the welfare of its citizens. Other treatments of public finance take the form of highly technical considerations of individual taxes, government borrowing and debt, the financing of local and regional governments and so on.

Not surprisingly, therefore, public finance is often regarded as a highly technical, esoteric subject, comprehensible to only an enlightened minority of economists, practitioners and fiscal federalists. This is unfortunate because a clear understanding of the nature of public finance is an essential underpinning for an understanding of many of the key public policy debates in both developed and developing countries. Even economics students often have a poor understanding of those debates because their view of public finance has been so heavily influenced by the abstract approach adopted by economists.

Therefore, the aim of this book is to provide a multidisciplinary, broad-based appreciation of the nature and scope of public finance. In its broadest terms, public finance is an essential (but often neglected) foundation for the study and practice of social policy, public management, economics and other applied social sciences. Too often, those who study or work in the public sector have an insufficient understanding of the extremely broad nature of public finance. There never seems to be enough money for public services. Service practitioners and service clients often believe that more money being made available from national and/or local taxes would necessarily lead to enhanced service provision and improved social welfare. When more money is not made available, disgruntled practitioners and clients often regard the cause as ideological or due to 'the dead hand of finance'. This blinkered understanding arises because of the failure to comprehend the strategic underpinnings of public finance.

Whilst knowledgeable of fine detail, practitioners often neglect the strategic foundations of public finance, being 'unable to see the wood for the trees'. The imperative of having to make the system of public finance work leaves little time for reflection on the nature and scope of public finance. Such reflection is crucial for the development of a sustainable strategy for public finance.

In considering the strategic underpinnings of public finance, this book is written for the non-specialist layperson. Its objective is to provide a clear and unambiguous understanding of the ongoing public policy debates relating to public finance and, in particular, to the bullet points listed above. That understanding culminates in the last chapter which provides a strategy for public finance.

WHAT IS 'PUBLIC FINANCE'?

One may initially think that the meaning of 'public finance' is perfectly clear, being money raised and spent by the state: raised from taxes and spent on services in promoting the public interest, particularly in terms of benefiting the poor. This 'tax and spend' model of public finance is, in fact, a severely distorted perception. It is distorted for three reasons:

■ taxation is not the only source of public finance
■ public finance is not spent only on public services or welfare payments
■ 'the public interest' is conceptually vague and meaningless in practical terms.

A comprehensive definition of public finance would have to encompass the following characteristics:

■ it is money raised from a wide variety of sources by the state and its agencies
■ including taxes, sales, fees, charges, borrowing, lotteries, donations and bequests, payments in kind and so on
■ disbursed within the public sector, and often in the private and voluntary sectors
■ to individuals, families, companies and service organisations
■ both at home and abroad
■ spent in the form of welfare payments, subsidies, grants, wages and salaries, rents, insurance premiums, interest and amortisation payments on public debt, international transfers, humanitarian aid, payments for construction projects, equipment and other inputs from private sector companies.

Thus, *public finance* 'comprises any revenues or expenditures passing through state budgets, derived from whatever source and however spent'. The essential point is that finance has to be accounted for within governmental budgets for it to qualify as public finance. Therefore, any revenues or expenditures not passing through governmental budgets cannot be defined as public finance. The sources and uses of revenues are therefore *not* the defining features of public finance. Recent moves towards more 'entrepreneurial government', namely paying more attention to raising (rather than simply spending) money from a plurality of sources, can be accommodated within this definition of public finance. It matters not how the money is raised, whether from taxes, charges, licence fees, lotteries or the other sources noted above. What matters is that, irrespective of their source, those revenues are recorded in local, regional, central or federal government accounts. Likewise, it does not matter how or on what those revenues are spent, expenditures are treated as public finance if and only if they pass through state budgets.

This definition resolves imponderables regarding the treatment of revenues and expenditures that could arguably be treated as public finance, for example so-called tax expenditures (see Chapter 4) and that part of finance within 'public–private partnerships' (also known as 'private finance initiatives') not provided by governments or state agencies. Such definitional questions are now resolved because, having defined public finance, any revenues or expenditures not included therein therefore become defined as private finance by default. Thus *private finance* 'comprises any revenues or expenditures *not* passing through state budgets, irrespective of their source and howsoever spent'.

The difference between public and private finance can be illustrated using several examples. Expenditures on over-the-counter medicines are classified as public finance in respect of that part of spending supported by publicly funded exemptions and concessions, the remaining part of expenditure not so supported being classified as private finance because it does not enter public accounts. Similarly, spending on private sector leisure services supported by publicly funded vouchers is categorised as public finance but any top-up payments funded by the users of private sector leisure services themselves are categorised as private finance (see Chapter 9). If, however, those vouchers had been exchanged for use of municipal leisure services, both forms of finance would enter the public accounts and so be treated as public finance. Spending on domestic energy such as electricity and gas is classified as public finance if that energy is provided by state-owned industries but as private finance if those industries are not state-owned. Central, federal, regional or local government subsidies for domestic energy consumption are categorised as public finance irrespective of whether they are paid to state-owned organisations, private sector companies or mutual organisations.

Thus, on the basis of these definitions, there is a clear, mutually exclusive, distinction between public and private finance. It would be a mistake, however, to believe that that distinction is based solely upon accounting rules. Two prior decisions have to be made before an item of revenue or expenditure is recorded in the public accounts:

■ citizens have rights to receive particular services deemed essential for their livelihoods, for example access to education and/or health services
■ the state should make financial provision in order for those rights to be secured.

Where no such rights exist (whether explicit or implicit), then no public finance is required. Where such rights do exist, the amount of public finance required to secure them will then depend upon operational decisions about service provision. There are two main options for service delivery:

■ Direct provision by the state
■ The state enables services to be provided by the private and/or voluntary sectors.

Public finance will generally be greater when direct state provision occurs compared with when the state enables them to be provided by the non-state sector. In the latter case the state pays (either citizens or service providers) the minimal amount of subsidy required to enable those deemed to be in need of services to receive them. Only the subsidy enters the state budget, not the total amount spent on the service(s). This was made clear by the leisure vouchers example above.

Thus whether or not an item of revenue or expenditure enters the public accounts ultimately depends upon public policy decisions about citizens' rights to services and how access to those services should be enabled. These public policy decisions reflect the dominant political philosophy within any one country. It is necessary, therefore, to examine the philosophical underpinnings of public finance.

PHILOSOPHICAL UNDERPINNINGS OF PUBLIC FINANCE

There is a long-lived tradition of philosophical discourse regarding the need for government, beginning with the ancient Greek philosophers (Socrates, Plato and Aristotle) three or four centuries BC. Today, political philosophy remains a vibrant subject for debate in considering the relationship between the citizen and the state. This relationship crucially impinges on the nature and scope of public finance. Any text purporting to deal with public finance must pay attention to its philosophical underpinnings but, in fact, most do not. Very few of the texts listed in the 'Further Reading' section below address philosophical underpinnings, the most notable exception being Barr 1998.

Three broad categories of political philosophy are outlined in Table 1.1. Philosophers may be dismayed by their reductionist nature, as they are gross simplifications of complex philosophical propositions. Each category contains different strands of arguments that have developed over the centuries. These strands overlap at the margins, such that there are no clear categorical boundaries between them. However, detailed analysis of these different political philosophies is not necessary for the purposes of this book, bearing in mind that they are only intended to illustrate how differing political philosophies impinge upon public finance.

The intention of the categorical summary provided by Table 1.1 is to make clear to readers that public finance is about much more than just money. In fact, it is about political philosophy. It reflects the constitutional and cultural relationship between individual citizens and their governments at national, regional and local levels. It reflects the rights and responsibilities of individual citizens, not just for their own livelihoods but also for those of their families, neighbourhoods and local, regional and national communities.

It is sometimes problematic to attempt to classify individual writers in terms of one or other of these political philosophies, precise interpretation of

Table 1.1 A simplified taxonomy of philosophical principles for public finance

	Libertarian[1]	Neo-liberal	Collectivist
	Classical liberal theory	Modern liberal theory	Civic theory
Defining features	Autonomy of the individual	Primacy of the individual	Mutual dependence
	Unregulated markets	Modified markets	Reject markets
	Negative rights only[2]	Negative plus limited positive rights	Full positive rights[3]
	Laissez-faire state	Enabling state	Provider state
	Capitalism[4]	Mixed economy[5]	Socialism[6]
Beliefs	The state is corruptible	The state is a necessary evil	Benevolent state
	Taxation is confiscation	Taxation for efficiency	Taxes for social aims
	Moral hazard/dependency culture	Promote human capital	Build social capital
	No moral case for equality	Equality of opportunity	Equality of outcome
	Private property rights are inviolable	Property rights reflect policy aims	Property is theft
General implications	No such thing as society	Weak conception of society	Society emphasised
	Private enterprise guarantees rights	Modified market rights	State confers rights
	Individuals are consumers not citizens	Individuals primarily consumers	Citizens firstly
	Depend on charity and active citizen	State supplements charity/voluntary action	State replaces charity
Implications for the public sector	Minimal state	Heavily constrained state	Expansive state
	Enforces only negative rights[7]	Some limited positive rights[8]	Full positive rights[9]
	Private sector provision of public services	Private or public sector provision	Public sector provision
	Minimal welfare state ('safety net' only)	Conditional welfare state	Unconditional welfare
	Private insurance	Public plus private insurance	Public insurance
Implications for public finance	Minimal public finance	Restrained public finance	Unrestrained public finance
	Private spending replaces public spending	Seek additionality of public spending	Public replaces private spending
	Minimise 'burden of taxation'	Tax 'bads' not 'goods' for efficiency	Redistributive taxes for equity
	Regressive taxes	Proportional taxes	Progressive taxes
	Borrowing and public debt very limited	Borrowing/debt for efficiency purposes	Borrowing/debt for welfare

Notes:

1. The term 'Libertarian' is used to denote classical liberal theory in order to distinguish it from modern liberal theory, here referred to as 'Neo-liberal' in order to avoid confusion
2. Freedom from coercion, interference, discrimination
3. Social and economic rights
4. An economic system based on the private ownership of the means of production, distribution and exchange
5. An economic system in which the public and private sectors coexist side by side
6. An economic system in which the means of production, distribution and exchange are owned collectively by the community, usually through the state
7. Via system of justice: police, courts, prison and so on
8. To education, health care, culture and so on
9. Social justice

their arguments being open to dispute. Bearing this caveat in mind, Libertarian viewpoints were developed in the eighteenth and nineteenth centuries by Hume, Smith, Bentham and Mill and hence are regarded as classical liberal theory. The most extreme form of Collectivist thinking was developed by Marx in the twentieth century, communist theory being subsequently further developed by neo-marxists. Neo-Liberal views were expounded in the twentieth century and so are regarded as modern liberal theory. However, the range of views within the Neo-Liberal category of political philosophy is potentially very wide, reflecting different interpretations of 'primacy of the individual', 'limited positive rights', 'enabling state', 'mixed economy', 'modified markets' and other such terms in Table 1.1. Put simply, the Libertarian and Collectivist political philosophies are much more absolutist and hence much clearer in terms of their beliefs than is the variable spectrum of Neo-Liberal philosophy.

The broad strategic implications of these philosophical foundations of public finance are now discussed separately for each political philosophy. The more precise implications for spending, taxation and other sources of public finance are considered in more detail in following chapters.

PUBLIC FINANCE UNDER LIBERTARIANISM

Libertarians believe strongly in 'individual responsibility', the state only intervening to protect citizens from coercion, interference and discrimination. The state therefore should only provide services protecting those 'negative rights', namely the system of justice and the associated law, order and protective services such as the police, courts, prisons, probation and rehabilitation services. There is therefore only minimal need for public finance.

For Libertarians there is no such thing as social justice: a person's life chances are simply the result of market outcomes. Those outcomes may be fortunate for some and unfortunate for others but they are not unfair. They merely reflect one's innate abilities to earn one's livelihood through individual flair, initiative and hard work. Charitable giving and charitable work (rather than state action) should be relied upon to help those who are unfortunate in lacking innate abilities for self-support.

There is therefore no moral case for equality, no such thing as society, no need for the modern welfare state, no need for public finance (other than for law and order and, perhaps, to relieve destitution). Instead the private sector can and should be relied upon to provide individuals and their households with the services they are willing and able to pay for. Private finance is therefore the dominant form of finance, dispensing almost completely with the need for public finance.

Even if well intentioned, government intervention is counterproductive. It stifles individual initiative, destroys the culture of charitable giving and charitable work, creating instead a 'dependency culture'. Individuals, families and communities become unnecessarily dependent upon the state support for their livelihoods. They lose the ability to provide for themselves an adequate standard of living. Dependency is exacerbated by 'moral hazard' whereby people change their behaviour as a consequence of being insured, being less cautious in their attitudes and responses to risk.

For example, in being protected by a publicly financed social insurance scheme, individuals may fail to provide for themselves and their families (for example against sickness and old age) because they believe they can rely on the state in times of need. Even worse, they may fail to act responsibly in terms of living healthy lifestyles because they know the state will care for them if the worst happens. Thus smokers may believe they have a right to free publicly funded health care even though they have contributed to their own smoking-related illnesses, the prospect of free care encouraging them to be reckless with their health. Perversely, therefore, people may believe they have a right to public finance simply because they have paid taxes. The very payment of taxes therefore creates the need for more taxation.

Likewise, governments cannot be trusted to act responsibly. The state is corruptible, public patronage being used to serve the interests of those who work in government or who can benefit the government. Benevolent patronising governments are bad enough but corrupt ones are even worse. Governments grow for their own sake as well as for (or even instead of) those they are meant to serve (see Chapter 2).

Put simply, the best role for the state is 'laissez-faire'. The best thing the state can do is get out of the way of private enterprise and leave 'markets' to do what they are best at, namely generating private finance in the form of profits and incomes. Government intervention creates the need (and the incentive) for further intervention in a vicious circle. Public finance goes out of control as the state has increasingly to confiscate (that is, tax) people's incomes and wealth in order to finance ever higher levels of public expenditure (see Chapters 6 and 7). In contrast, individual responsibility creates less need for state action, encourages further private sector provision and so progressively reduces the need for government intervention and public finance in a virtuous circle of self-help and self-improvement through private finance.

PUBLIC FINANCE UNDER NEO-LIBERALISM

Like Libertarians, Neo-Liberals emphasise individual responsibility. However, they believe that market outcomes may be unjust because not everyone has the same opportunity to earn one's livelihood through flair, initiative and hard work. Therefore the state should ensure that everyone has the same opportunity to secure an adequate standard of living. Thus some 'limited positive rights' should be ensured by the state creating 'equality of opportunity'.

These positive rights include an education sufficient to make people employable, a health service to keep them fit for work, a jobs market free from social, racial, gender or age discrimination, and a social security system to help those who cannot reasonably be expected to support themselves because of disability or old age. Thus there is need for fairly substantial amounts of public finance.

Nevertheless, there are strict limits to government intervention in economy and society. One's *rights* to state assistance are matched with *responsibilities* for self-sufficiency. The state's role is to *enable* people and families to look after themselves, rather than being the first port of call in times of need. Thus positive rights are strictly limited by making eligibility for state support conditional upon acting responsibly, for example by undertaking training and subsequently seeking employment. The state enables people to invest in themselves, building their 'human capital' to secure equality of opportunity. Equality of outcome will not, however, be achieved. This is because, even though there is no discrimination, people's innate abilities, flair and work effort will vary and this should be rewarded through differential (but nonetheless fair) outcomes.

Hence, although Neo-Liberals have a conception of society, it is not all-embracing: there is still an emphasis on the primacy of the individual. The emphasis is on what the individual can do for the state, not what the state can do for the individual. Whilst governments are generally well intentioned and competent, there is an acceptance of the need to avoid an expansive and self-serving state sector. Thus the need for intervention should always be questioned on pragmatic grounds, namely whether public intervention makes markets work better or worse. Put simply, the role of the state should be restricted to an 'enabling state', enabling people to provide for themselves and their families through paid employment in the private sector rather than become dependent on welfare handouts. The state should concentrate on creating equality of opportunity but not of outcome, removing discrimination and arbitrary disadvantage. Thus, there are limits to government intervention. Hence, public finance should *complement* private finance, not *replace* it.

PUBLIC FINANCE UNDER COLLECTIVISM

Collectivist philosophy does not accept the concept of the autonomous individual. Each individual is part of a 'community' and cannot function without it. Mutual dependence requires collective rather than individualised provision to meet 'social needs'. People have full (rather than limited) positive rights as citizens, not just negative rights as consumers. Only the benevolent and omniscient state can provide for such extensive social and economic rights. Thus markets have to be directly controlled (that is, collectivised, not just modified) by the state. In the extreme case, state control is intended to ensure 'equality of outcome' (not just of opportunity). However, not even the most interventionist states have sought complete equality of outcome, if only because it is most likely impractical. In practice, therefore, the objective is much greater equality of outcome than could be achieved by either unrestrained or modified markets. Under collectivism, private property rights are replaced by 'social ownership' and the building of social (rather than private) capital. Private profit must not be at the expense of social welfare.

Hence, the state is expansive, becoming all-encompassing through highly progressive taxes used to finance the comprehensive public provision of goods and services in delivering the 'unconditional welfare state'. Only by such means can 'social justice' be achieved. A person's livelihood must be guaranteed by the state because free markets cannot be relied on to deliver socially acceptable standards of living for all social groups.

The state cannot simply stand back to leave markets to allocate resources by chance, as is the case under the laissez-faire state of Libertarianism. Nor should it rely on equality of opportunity to secure socially acceptable outcomes because those outcomes cannot be guaranteed by the enabling state of Neo-Liberalism. Instead, the state must be the 'provider state', itself providing a fully comprehensive range of public services in accordance with its assessment of the need for service of each and every citizen. The resulting social benefits more than compensate for any concerns about dependency cultures, moral hazard, incompetent state or corrupt state. These concerns are generally misplaced and are blown out of all proportion by Libertarians and Neo-Liberals.

Thus, under the Collectivist political philosophy, public finance is unrestrained, fully funding public services in accordance with need. State planning is seen as more effective than either unrestrained or modified markets in delivering the economic growth underpinning social welfare. Thus, social (rather than simply economic) welfare is the modus operandi of public finance and it can best be delivered by skewing taxes and public services in favour of disadvantaged low-income groups in order to obviate all such institutionalised and class-based disadvantage. Hence, public finance completely *replaces* private finance.

OVERVIEW OF THE THREE POLITICAL PHILOSOPHIES

The three categories of political philosophy outlined above clearly have fundamentally different implications for the degree to which governments should intervene in the economy and society. They hold radically different views of the nature of citizenship, rights, responsibilities and equity and, in particular, the constitutional relationship between the state and the individual citizen. Just how far is it legitimate for the state to seek to control or influence the everyday lives and behaviours of its citizens and to raise the necessary finances from them?

Notwithstanding such fundamentally different political philosophies, one common theme is that they all recognise the benefits of economic growth. Growth of national output is seen as essential for improved individual and/or social welfare in the longer term. Obviously, the three philosophies differ fundamentally in terms of the most effective way of achieving economic growth, that is, whether by unrestrained, modified or collectivised markets. Nevertheless, state intervention (or lack of it) is concerned with economic efficiency as well as equity.

The Libertarian, Neo-Liberal and Collectivist political philosophies clearly relate to differing views of the legitimacy and effectiveness of public finance. Libertarians argue that private interests should take precedence over public interests and that the state has no right to redistribute incomes and wealth in pursuit of irrelevant and unsustainable notions of social justice. Collectivists argue the opposite case, rejecting market outcomes and taking the view that individuals belong to a civic community whose interests are safeguarded by the collective provision of services. Whilst these two diametrically opposed extreme political philosophies have been very influential in past centuries, Neo-Liberalism has arguably been the more influential political philosophy in terms of more recent social, political and economic reforms in most countries.

THE NEO-LIBERAL RESURGENCE

The long-term changes in the relative scale of public finance analysed in Chapter 3 can only be understood by appreciating the changing balance between the three political philosophies in influencing public policy-making. At the risk of oversimplifying and overgeneralising a complex and constantly shifting balance of political philosophy in the westernised world, the twentieth century saw shifts:

■ from the pre-1940s Libertarian end of Neo-Liberalism
■ towards the Collectivist end during the following several decades
■ returning to the Libertarian end of Neo-Liberalism during the 1980s and 90s.

The Great Depression of the 1930s led to substantial levels of unemployment in Western economies. It apparently demonstrated the failure of free markets to promote the public interest, contrary to the writings of Adam Smith (a famous eighteenth-century Scottish economist and philosopher). Thus developed countries adopted more interventionist stances, in general accepting arguments by Keynes, Galbraith and other contemporary economists that governments could and should use public finance (that is, government expenditures, borrowing and taxation) to modify market behaviour in order to promote full employment and so promote the public interest. Most developed countries adopted a Keynesian approach towards the management of the economy, seeking to maintain the totality of demand for goods and services so as to create and sustain full employment.

They did this by varying their levels of public finance as follows:

- by borrowing so as to spend their way out of prolonged recession or temporary cyclical economic downturn
- by raising more public finance than was spent so as to minimise any inflationary consequences of full employment.

They also used public finance to fund comprehensive schemes of social insurance covering loss of earnings due to unemployment, sickness and retirement, the state acting as a cradle-to-grave 'safety net'.

Keynesian economic policies seemed to work from the late 1940s through to the early 1970s. However, it became increasingly difficult for governments to use public finance to maintain full employment. Public finance began to account for an ever-increasing proportion of national income in most developed countries as public expenditures, public borrowing, public debt and taxation rose inexorably.

The growth of the relative scale of public finance in the second half of the twentieth century (see Chapter 3) reflected the then general presumption that 'the state knows best' what is in the interests of its citizens. This assumption of state benevolence, superior knowledge and far-sightedness provided the constitutional and sociopolitical rationale for the growth of the 'all-powerful state'. Citizens are obliged to pay compulsory taxes and to consume services over which they have typically had little say as individual users (as distinct from voters). Compulsion of the individual by the state was the foundation of the growth of the welfare state in almost all developed economies, most notably after 1945 (see Chapter 4). The perceived solution was for the state to promote and redistribute prosperity through compulsory levies on its citizens and industries and through the direct provision of services.

Whilst Collectivists regarded such developments as socially beneficial, others regarded them as potentially disastrous. George Orwell's novels foresaw a nightmare of all-pervasive state control of the minutiae of our everyday lives, the 'Big Brother' state deciding how the citizen should be raised, their jobs, their sex lives, even their thoughts. Although the most extreme predictions of his novel *1984* (written in 1948) had not transpired by the year of the title, it was still generally regarded by Libertarians and more right-wing Neo-Liberals as a thoroughly undesirable portent.

The near universal acceptance of the success of high levels of state intervention began to break down in many developed countries from the mid-1970s onwards. The rapid economic growth rates of the 1945–70 period could not be sustained. Sharp fluctuations in economic activity coincided with bouts of inflation, rising rates of unemployment, rapid deindustrialisation and loss of manufacturing jobs, deficits in international trade, rising public sector borrowing and debt, increasingly high proportions of incomes and expenditures taken by taxation, and increasing dependence on the welfare state. This apparently demonstrated the 'impotent state', namely the failure of governments to control markets in seeking to promote the public interest.

The general acceptance of the all-powerful state and its ability to solve economic and social problems began to break down. Solutions to socioeconomic problems became less obvious, as societies became increasingly multicultural, family, household and labour market restructuring occurred, and with increasing emphasis on numeracy, literacy and other human capital skills appropriate for growing service sectors.

This led to a resurgence of Neo-Liberal arguments that states were growing out of control, increasingly seeking to control the lives of their citizens and stifling economic prosperity by both excessive regulation of the market economy and high taxes making work and enterprise less worthwhile. Neo-Liberals blamed the 1930s Great Depression on governments, not on markets. They argued that governments had restricted international trade by imposing taxes and quotas on imports of other countries' exports. This led to the fall in world trade and prosperity

Friedman and other neo-classical economists argued that Keynesian economic policies were bound to fail because governments simply cannot control the level of economic activity (and hence employment) by varying the levels of public finance. They argue that growth of the public sector is at the expense of the private sector, public expenditure replacing private expenditure through confiscatory taxes. Moreover, they argue that, in stifling work and enterprise, high taxes do not simply lead to a substitution of public finance for private finance, they actually reduce the total level of (public and private) finance. Thus Neo-Liberals such as Hayek and Friedman argue that cradle-to-grave welfare states are counterproductive in making economies less productive by crowding out the private sector: public finance *crowds out* private finance (see Chapter 6).

Hence, according to the Neo-Liberal argument, public finance creates greater equality in the distribution of incomes by 'levelling down' in making the mass of people poorer on average than they would have otherwise been without that state intervention. Neo-Liberals argue that the prosperity of free markets 'trickle down' to the poorest groups in society by creating jobs, a 'levelling-up' process that benefits the poor without requiring government intervention. Hence, by reducing their intervention in the market economy, governments would actually be working in the public interest.

An increasing distrust of politicians and bureaucrats developed alongside the profound restructuring of economy and society. Not only were governments increasingly seen not to have all the answers, they were also increasingly seen as being composed of elites who often pursued their own self-interests rather than the welfare of those they were supposed to serve (see Chapter 8).

■ Mancur Olson explained the rise and decline of nations by means of social rigidities at national level caused by self-serving powerful elites ('distributional coalitions') which he argued reduce wealth creation by preventing rapid and efficient adaptation to changing conditions, thus leading to 'institutional sclerosis'.

■ J. K. Galbraith argued that the distribution of power, rights and economic resources reinforce producer power within the planning system, allowing control of nominally competitive markets and ensuring the survival of existing firms.

■ Niskanen and others developed the theory of 'self-serving bureaucracies', whereby public sector bureaucrats pursue their own self-interest rather than the public interest once some minimum level of performance acceptable to governments has been achieved. Hence, the view that (national, regional and local) governments promote the public interest is naive.

The Neo-Liberal arguments became widely accepted within the developed world during the 1980s and 90s. Whilst the Libertarian and Collectivist schools have been very influential at a philosophical level, it is the Neo-Liberal school that has been most influential for public policy. The resurgence of Neo-Liberalism was arguably an inevitable result of globalisation.

GLOBALISATION, POLITICAL PHILOSOPHY AND PUBLIC FINANCE

Globalisation is an ongoing process, not a one-off event. It refers to a cumulative process of increasing internationalisation of trade and financial and investment markets. This has arisen as a result of:

■ deregulation (for example removal of import tariffs and quotas and other trade restraints)

■ improved communications, most notably transport of goods by air and development of e-commerce (that is, the purchase of goods and services over the Internet).

Globalisation has been associated with a move away from Collectivist states (that is, communism and socialism) and towards a greater degree of capitalism within more Neo-Liberal mixed economies. These terms are expanded on below:

■ *Socialism*, an economic system in which the means of production, distribution and exchange are owned collectively by the community, usually through the state and in which income is distributed according to work. Hence, unlike totalitarianism (that is, a dictatorial one-party state regulating every facet of life), socialism is consistent with democratic systems of government. Nevertheless, the wishes of the minority are overridden by those of the majority through central government planning. Market-driven outcomes are simply unacceptable. In effect, there is not such thing as 'the free market' or 'free enterprise'. Equity and community are of overriding importance. Profitability is simply not an issue.

- *Communism*, a classless society in which private property has been abolished and in which income is distributed according to need (as assessed by the state) rather than according to work (under socialism) or according to work and ownership of property rights (under capitalism). In Marxist theory, socialism is a transitional stage in the development of a society from capitalism to communism.
- *Capitalism*, an economic system based on the private ownership of the means of production, distribution and exchange. Also known as 'free enterprise' and 'free markets', it requires unfettered free-market economies, free of government restrictions. Government intervention is minimal, restricted only to that which is essential in order to facilitate economic activity through enforcement of laws of contract. No welfare state exists, services such as education and health being purchased and provided privately and personal and household incomes being solely dependent upon one's earnings and other market-derived incomes. In effect, there is no such thing as 'society' in terms of welfare planning to achieve equitable outcomes. The distributions of income, wealth and life chances between individuals and their households are determined solely by market outcomes. Equity is simply not an issue.
- A *mixed economy*, an economic system in which the public and private sectors coexist side by side. The balance between the public and private sectors within economy and society varies along a continuum approaching capitalism at one end and socialism at the other. Towards the middle of this continuum, equity and community rank equal in importance with profitability and individualised consumerism. Markets and society complement each other in a symbiotic relationship whereby, within democratically determined limits, profits can be used to pursue social aims and state provision of social services such as education and health care can be used to underpin and facilitate efficient markets. There are such things as society and markets, just as there is individual liberty within communities.

Broadly speaking, the Libertarian philosophy requires a pure capitalist economy. The Collectivist philosophy in its purest form requires a wholly centrally planned economy (either communism or socialism). The Neo-Liberal philosophy requires a mixed economy in which the public and private sectors coexist and which is therefore characterised by a variable mix of free enterprise and state planning.

The closest approximations to a centrally planned economy are the former Soviet Union (that is, the Union of Soviet Socialist Republics), namely Russia and its former satellite states (dissolved in 1991), (the People's Republic of) China, Cuba and (the People's Republic of) North Korea. China joined the World Trade Organization in 2001, reflecting its growing desire to trade within the global economy. The closest approximation to a pure capitalist economy was the former British Crown Colony of Hong Kong (returned to Chinese control in 1997). Most other countries fall within the mixed economy category, the USA being closer to the capitalism end of the spectrum, Scandinavian countries closer to the socialist end of the spectrum, Western European countries being at intermediate points on that spectrum.

In general, however, the greater degree of capitalism has been associated more with a shift in mixed economies towards the capitalist end of the spectrum than with the collapse of communism or socialism. Nevertheless, both events have occurred as nation states have increasingly 'rolled back the frontiers of the state'. They have done this by selling state industries and other assets, by liberalising markets through the abolition of statutory monopolies, by contracting out the provision of public services to private sector and voluntary sector organisations, and by forming public–private partnerships and other types of private finance initiative. Referred to generically as 'privatisation', withdrawal of the state as a direct provider of services and its transformation into the enabling state has occurred in almost all developed and developing countries. That withdrawal has been most profound in social and economic terms in the 'transition economies' of Central and Eastern Europe, in transition from centrally planned to free-market economies.

Thus, whilst the philosophical debate rages on, there seems to be an international trend towards the more free-market end of Neo-Liberalism, as countries try to help markets work better whilst not going so far as to withdraw completely from ensuring positive rights. Instead, those positive rights have become more limited (most notably in Scandinavian countries) and been made more conditional (most notably in the Anglo-American culture).

ECLECTICISM AND PRAGMATISM IN PUBLIC FINANCE

The bulk of the population in any one country may take a more eclectic than ideological view of public finance. Many people would accept that the minimal state of pure Libertarianism is impractical in modern society. Indeed, many would argue that economic development (that is, the transformation from an agricultural, through industrial, to postindustrial service economy) depends critically on state intervention. Thus governments often provide 'physical capital' (that is, the infrastructure of roads, railways, water supply, sanitation and so on) in the early stages of industrial development and human capital (that is, through education, training, health care and so on) in the later stages of urbanised development. Many people believe that economic development simply could not take place if public finance was restricted to the minimalist state providing only for negative rights.

Likewise, many people would accept that the all-encompassing state of the pure Collectivist political philosophy is impractical in a modern society. Indeed, many would argue that the wants and needs of citizens and consumers are so diverse and developing so rapidly that the state simply cannot comprehend them, let alone provide for them. The state does not have the knowledge or wherewithal to provide for increasingly cosmopolitan, multicultural and affluent societies. Many people believe that attempting to meet the needs and wants of such societies through public finance would be ineffective and extremely wasteful.

For most people, the choice between alternative political philosophies is perhaps likely to be influenced by the experience of their application to public policy. As a matter of practicality, it is no use believing in a political philosophy that either doesn't work at all or can no longer work as socioeconomic conditions change. Similarly, one's position on the spectrum of Neo-Liberalism (whether more towards the free-market or controlled market ends) may be dependent upon one's experience of policy in practice. Idealism may have to be tempered by pragmatism.

Indeed, people may not even be schooled in alternative political philosophies and may fail to distinguish between them in categorically exclusive terms. Moreover, the above analysis made clear that Neo-Liberalism is located along a spectrum of ideology between the extremes of Libertarianism to Collectivism. To the extent that governments are democratically elected and respond to the wishes of the electorate, the ideologies of political parties are necessarily tempered by the need to win votes. The casting of those votes may reflect citizens' demands for services more than a particular political philosophy. It is possible for a citizen to believe in minimal state intervention and yet be unwilling to agree to a reduction in the public services used by his or her household. Ideology is tempered by self-interest. People's behaviour is not always in accordance with their principles.

Put simply, there are limits to how far ideology can be implemented in a democratic state. Governments face political opposition in pluralist political systems and must constantly respond to criticisms from opposition parties about too much or too little state intervention. Even a government broadly Neo-Liberal in its economic and social programmes may still accept the need for a predominantly publicly financed health service. Thus what voters want and how governments use public finance may be more eclectic than ideological.

Moreover, the public finances may be heavily influenced by the pragmatism of policy-making and policy implementation. Political parties inherit public expenditure programmes from previous governments when they take office and so the extent to which they can implement their ideologies immediately upon taking up office is severely limited. For example, a newly elected Libertarian government replacing a previous Collectivist government will find it difficult to fully implement its ideology of minimal state intervention and minimal public finance.

It is not possible immediately to replace Collectivist principles by Libertarian principles (see Table 1.1). Privatisation of state assets through sale to the private sector may take many years to implement fully, especially if private property rights have to be re-established in legal terms before assets can be sold. Moreover, the market sector may lack the financial, managerial and technological capacity to provide those services. Likewise, public services cannot simply be withdrawn overnight if there is no alternative private or voluntary sector provision for citizens to fall back on. Dependency cultures are difficult to overcome in the short term. Charges for public services cannot be introduced overnight as a replacement of tax finance. Reform of public finance is therefore problematic. At the very least, it will have to continue refinancing the debt created by borrowing used to underpin expansionist welfare states under a previous Collectivist government.

Whilst replacement of a Collectivist by a Libertarian government would appear to be an unlikely extreme categorical shift, the radical restructuring of Central and Eastern European economies and societies during the 1990s after the collapse of the former Soviet Union is a case in point. Even a more modest shift along the ideological spectrum from a less to a more Neo-Liberal ideological outlook will be subject to many of the same constraining factors noted above. Thus some political scientists argue that political party ideology is less important than the inheritance of past expenditure programmes in explaining what governments actually do with public finance (as distinct from what they say they will do as party rhetoric). This is especially likely to be the case in democratic systems whose governments are subject to fairly regular changes in party control.

A citizen may be predisposed to a particular political philosophy. Nevertheless, he or she may accept that there are practical limitations on the extent to which that philosophy can be reflected in the public finances. Most people would seem to agree that ideology cannot be pursued at all costs. They may adopt a 'pick and mix' approach to public finance in terms of its strategic role, total amount, sources, uses, the rights of its recipients, the incentives it creates and the conditions attached to its receipt. Most Libertarians accept (perhaps begrudgingly) the need for a welfare safety net to avoid destitution. Many Collectivists agree that citizens cannot simply choose to live off state handouts when they could reasonably be expected to support themselves and their families. Put simply, Collectivism is not a scrounger's charter. For many voters, it may be that what matters is what works or, at least, what seems to work. Many people may accept that being humanitarian and paternalistic is counterproductive if it creates a strong dependency culture. Within limits, the state 'has to be cruel to be kind'.

Thus the pragmatism of government and the eclecticism of voters may severely constrain the extent to which particular political philosophies shape the public finances at any one point in time. Pragmatism and eclecticism are likely to be influenced over time by developments in economy and society. For example, the relatively recent and rapid development of service sectors in modern economies has massively expanded job opportunities for all groups in society. The traditional dependence of families upon male heads of household as the sole breadwinner has progressively disappeared in most developed countries. The shift from heavy industrial jobs requiring manual strength towards office employment requiring more intellectual abilities led to sharp increases in the proportion of the population receiving post-school education and also of women in paid employment. Higher proportions of physically disabled people are now able to work in office-type environments. There are more opportunities for part-time and casualised employment. Family structures are becoming increasingly fluid. Personal mobility (and so access to employment) has increased enormously as transport infrastructures have developed. Rates of self-employment have increased in many developed countries.

Socioeconomic changes have increased the ability of people to support themselves through work in increasingly educated, skilled, meritocratic, less paternalistic societies. The increasing complexity of modern economies means that governments are increasingly less able to make the 'right choices' (if ever they could) on behalf of their citizens. This shift has profound implications for the role of the state and so for public finance. It was noted above that some developed countries have introduced a shift from unconditional welfare payments to those dependent upon recipients undertaking training, education or work experience programmes with a view to reducing their dependence on state handouts. Thus, in many countries, the expression of state paternalism has shifted from 'workless welfare' to 'work-based welfare'. Increasing capacity in the private sectors of many countries means that governments no longer have to be direct providers of public services. An increasing customer focus in the private sector brought about by increased competition is paralleled by similar developments in the public sector. Such changes in the ability of people to make decisions for themselves and to have those decisions validated by the market sector have arguably led to a Neo-Liberal resurgence in many countries.

AN ANALYTICAL FRAMEWORK FOR STUDYING PUBLIC FINANCE

An analytical framework is necessary for the study of public finance. Such a framework can be derived from the three political philosophies described above. They implicitly provide operationally relevant objectives in terms of their differing interpretations of equity, efficiency, economy and effectiveness. The new public management literature has paid increasing attention to the need to secure economy, efficiency and effectiveness in use of public finance, referring to them as 'the 3Es'. Social policy activists have emphasised equity issues, the '4th E'. Table 1.2 provides a summary integration of the 4Es with the defining features, beliefs and implications of the three categories of political philosophy summarised in Table 1.1.

Table 1.2 recapitulates some of the philosophical propositions considered above. It demonstrates the ambiguous meanings of each of the 4Es, each philosophical viewpoint having a fundamentally different interpretation of them.

'Efficiency' as defined by Libertarians is the ability of free markets to minimise the costs of producing the goods and services demanded by consumers and also to minimise their prices. This requires efficiency at the level of the individual firm (that is, minimum production costs) and at the level of the economy (that is, goods and services are produced in the quantities consumers are willing to buy). In this way 'market efficiency' enables consumers to maximise their consumption of commodities within the limits of their incomes and wealth. Any use of public finance beyond that necessary to aid the functioning of markets by securing property rights (that is, negative rights) is inefficient. Collectivists simply do not accept market-based concepts of efficiency, arguing that efficiency can only be defined in social terms. 'Social efficiency' is concerned with community benefits, not private benefits. It avoids the social costs of unemployment and other market failures whilst ensuring the social benefits of equal educational, health and other outcomes. Neo-Liberals agree that persistent unemployment, industrial dereliction, inadequate services and other market-driven economic inefficiencies must be avoided. However, this does not mean that the state should adopt the Collectivist solution based on creating jobs directly, nationalising land and providing

Table 1.2   *Alternative philosophical interpretations of the 4Es*

	Libertarian	Neo-Liberal	Collectivist
Efficiency	Very narrow concept: market efficiency	Modified market efficiency: qualified by the public interest	Very broad concept: social efficiency
Equity	Judged in terms of free-market welfare outcomes: reward for effort and talent	Judged in terms of work-based welfare: rights and responsibilities	Judged in terms of social welfare: vertical equity and social needs
Economy	Secured by restricting government intervention to safeguard only negative rights	Secured by only pursuing equality of opportunity through modified markets	Not a relevant concept when meeting collective needs through equality of outcome
Effectiveness	Best achieved by laissez-faire, freeing markets to maximise productivity and profits and relying on trickle down to poor groups of the benefits of economic growth	Limiting markets' maximising behaviour where necessary to avoid market failure whilst recognising the possibility of government failure	Best achieved by eschewing markets' maximising behaviour in favour of government intervention to secure socially acceptable outcomes

services directly to achieve efficiency. Instead, the Neo-Liberal state achieves efficiency by enabling the creation of employment opportunities and investment potential, modifying inefficient markets to remove the barriers to jobs and investment caused by market failure. Thus the Neo-Liberal conception of efficiency is 'modified market efficiency'.

'Equity' is defined by Libertarians solely in terms of rewards or other outcomes delivered by the market system reflecting the aptitudes, abilities and application of people to generate income and profits. Hence, equity is the same as market welfare. Collectivists simply do not accept that markets can deliver equitable outcomes and believe that there must be extensive government intervention, using the public finances to secure 'social welfare' in terms of socially acceptable outcomes. This requires redistribution of income from rich to poor through taxation and public expenditure (that is, 'vertical equity'). Neo-Liberals accept the equity of market outcomes in principle but believe that unregulated markets may not afford everyone the opportunity to benefit from work. Thus there may be a need for government intervention to ensure that people in similar circumstances have the same opportunities (that is, 'horizontal equity') through work-based welfare, not unconditional handouts to those who choose not to support themselves and their dependants.

'Economy' refers to minimising the cost of government intervention. At an operational level, economy refers to minimising the costs of inputs and processes for a given range and level of services. This 'operational economy' is the meaning adopted in the new public management literature and is common to the three political philosophies. At a strategic level, economy is achieved by avoiding wasteful provision of public services, in terms of unwanted or unnecessary outputs and/or outputs that are ineffective in terms of delivering objectives set in terms of outcomes. For Libertarians, this 'strategic economy' in the use of public finance is best achieved by minimal state intervention, only that amount of public finance which is absolutely necessary to ensure negative rights. For Collectivists strategic economy is simply not a relevant concept since public finance should be at whatever level is necessary to secure collective needs and full positive rights. For Neo-Liberals, operational and strategic economy in achieving (limited) positive rights is best achieved by an enabling state modifying market processes so that they operate efficiently. For example, markets for labour can be made more efficient by subsidising low-paid jobs and/or retraining for the long-term unemployed, instead of simply giving them unemployment benefits over the long term. Likewise, energy markets can be made more efficient by taxing polluting activities in order to reduce their scale and so reduce the associated costs of ill health and environmental degradation. This avoids the state having to pay for treatment of those adverse effects that would otherwise have been caused by the higher level of pollution. By such means, strategic economy in the use of public finance is secured in being the minimum amount necessary to modify (rather than replace) markets. Any other level of public finance is unnecessary and wasteful.

'Effectiveness' is defined by Libertarians as 'market outcomes', leaving markets to do what they are best at, namely generating profits and economic growth. As already noted, the economic welfare resulting from laissez-faire is assumed to trickle down to all social groups. Government attempts to generate profits are bound to fail simply because the state does not have the requisite entrepreneurial skills and business acumen. Laissez-faire therefore limits government intervention to negative rights. Any other level of intervention is doomed to be ineffective in its use of public finance. Collectivists judge effectiveness in terms of 'social outcomes'. They argue that markets are ineffective as a means of delivering socially acceptable outcomes in terms of service provision and redistribution. Securing them requires copious amounts of public finance. Neo-Liberals accept the need to abandon laissez-faire when market processes lead to substantial social and environmental costs. However, just as laissez-faire may be ineffective because markets sometimes fail, so might government intervention because governments may fail too. Indeed, 'government failure' may be greater than 'market failure'. Thus there should be a presumption against government intervention unless it is incontrovertibly beneficial, namely where it improves the functioning of markets. Hence, government intervention has to be justified on a case-by-case basis if public finance is to be used effectively.

It is clear that any attempt to define equity, efficiency, economy and effectiveness in absolutely unambiguous and indisputable terms is doomed to failure. Any one writer's definitions of each of the 4Es necessarily reflects his or her political philosophy, even if that person's philosophy is ill-defined. Ideally, those who write about the 4Es should make their political and philosophical positions explicit. This analytical framework will be used in subsequent chapters to examine public finance.

CONCLUSIONS

Public finance is about much more than just money. It crucially reflects the dominant political philosophy of a country or region. Hence, whilst public finance has been defined as any revenues or expenditures passing through state budgets, those financial flows reflect the relationship between the citizen and the state. That relationship differs between the Libertarian, Neo-Liberal and Collectivist political philosophies. Ultimately, therefore, political philosophy (albeit tempered by pragmatism) determines the levels of government expenditures and revenues from taxation, borrowing and other sources.

Hence, there is no clear consensus about the appropriate role and functions of public finance. Libertarians would restrict public finance to securing negative rights only; Neo-Liberals to these plus limited positive rights; Collectivists setting no limits on the role and functions of public finance. Expressed in more philosophical terms, the role and functions of public finance are to:

■ Allow autonomous citizens to exercise full individual responsibility for their own standard of living whilst remaining totally free of state control (Libertarian role)
■ Enable responsible citizens to have the potential to secure an adequate standard of living by affording equality of opportunity in the marketplace (Neo-Liberal role)
■ Guarantee protected citizens adequate standards of living through direct state control of their everyday lives in terms of access to and outcomes of state-provided services (Collectivist role).

Clearly, the role of public finance is not first and foremost the provision of services (a practitioner's perspective), nor the redistribution of incomes and wealth (a social policy activist's perspective), nor the rectification of failed private sector markets (an economist's perspective). Instead, the role of public finance is to underpin the citizen–state relationship. The role of public finance is therefore first and foremost a constitutional role, its other perceived roles having only subservient status. Thus the role and functions of public finance give effect to the constitutional relationship between state and citizen, that is, primacy of the citizen or the state. Public finance is used to secure the positive and/or negative rights of citizens arising from that fundamental constitutional relationship. Thus taxes and other sources of public revenues finance the provision of services, redistribute incomes and wealth and offset market failures to degrees consistent with the fundamental constitutional relationship between state and citizen.

In reflecting political philosophy, public finance is clearly not the sole preserve of any one discipline such as economics. Instead, the study of public finance has to be undertaken within a multidisciplinary perspective if it is to result in a comprehensive understanding of the subject.

This book attempts to provide such a multidisciplinary approach by adopting an analytical framework much broader than that traditionally used by economists. Whilst efficiency defined in terms of maximum economic welfare is a powerful analytical tool for the study of public finance, so too are equity, economy and effectiveness. The definition of equity, efficiency, economy and effectiveness is problematic. The precise definition of each of the 4Es is different for each of the three broad categories of political philosophy.

Therefore the study of public finance provided by any text will definitely not yield definitive answers to frequently posed questions such as whether public expenditure, taxation and borrowing are too large, too small or just about right. Such questions can only be addressed by giving qualified answers couched in terms of each of the three political philosophies. What is an acceptable level of public finance for Neo-Liberals will be deemed excessive by Libertarians and insufficient by Collectivists.

Recently there seems to have been a shift in the scale of public finance deemed acceptable by most countries, reflecting a move towards the Libertarian end of the philosophical scale and away from the Collectivist end. Collectivist approaches towards the organisation of economy and society have waned globally as communist regimes collapsed, their constituent parts becoming economies in transition away from central planning and towards capitalism. Even less extreme forms of Collectivism, such as socialism, appear to have been on the wane as ruling political parties increasingly adopted Neo-Liberal policies, most notably privatisation and work-based welfare.

Thus, perceptions of public finance have changed radically over the course of the last century, initially being couched in free-market Libertarian terms, supplanted by paternalistic cradle-to-grave Collectivist terms and now increasingly reconfigured in Neo-Liberal terms. In the economies in transition the shift has been from one political philosophy to another, from Collectivism to Neo-Liberalism. Elsewhere, the shift has arguably been one of degree rather than category, a shift along the Neo-Liberal spectrum from more state intervention to less, from state ownership of assets to privatisation, from unconditional state support to conditional welfare, from the direct-provider state to the enabling state.

The categorical shift of political philosophy led to substantial falls in the relative scale of public finance in the transition economies. In contrast, the much more modest shift for westernised countries had a much more limited impact on the relative scale of public finance. These differential outcomes for the relative scale of public finance are the subject of the following chapter.

REFERENCES

Cullis, J. and Jones, P. (1998) *Public Finance and Public Choice: Analytical Perspectives* (second edition) (Maidenhead: McGraw-Hill).

Hyman, D. N. (1999) *Public Finance: A Contemporary Application of Theory to Policy* (sixth edition) (Orlando: Harcourt Brace).

Rosen, H. S. (1999) *Public Finance* (fifth edition) (Boston: McGraw-Hill).

FURTHER READING

Bailey, S. J. (2002) *Public Sector Economics: Theory, Policy and Practice* (second edition) (Basingstoke: Palgrave Macmillan).

Barr, N. (1998) *The Economics of the Welfare State* (third edition) (Oxford: Oxford University Press).

Connolly, S. and Munro, A. (1999) *Economics of the Public Sector* (Harlow: Prentice Hall).

Friedman, M. and Friedman, R. D. (1980) *Free to Choose: A Personal Statement* (New York: Secker and Warburg).

Galbraith, J. K. (1970) 'Economics as a System of Belief' *The American Economic Review* vol. 60, no. 2, pp. 469–78.

Hayek, F. A. (1944) *The Road to Serfdom* (London: Routledge).

Hayek, F. A. (1948) *Individualism and Economic Order* (Chicago: Chicago University Press).

Hayek, F. A. (1959) *The Counter-Revolution of Science* (Indianapolis: Liberty Press).

Hayek, F. A. (1960) *The Constitution of Liberty* (London: Routledge).

Hayek, F. A. (1982) *Law, Legislation and Liberty* (London: Routledge).

Hayek, F. A. (1988) *The Fatal Conceit* (London: Routledge).

Jackson, P. M. (1993) *The Foundations of Public Finance Volumes I and II* (Cheltenham: Edward Elgar).

Jha, R. (1998) *Modern Public Economics* (London: Routledge).

Musgrave, R. A. (2000) *Public Finance in a Democratic Society Volume III: The Foundations of Taxation and Expenditure* (Cheltenham: Edward Elgar). [Chapter 1 'The Role of the State in Fiscal Theory'. Also published in P. B. Sorensen (1998) *Public Finance in a Changing World* Basingstoke: Macmillan – now Palgrave Macmillan].

Musgrave, R. A. and Musgrave, P. B. (1989) *Public Finance in Theory and Practice* (New York: McGraw-Hill).

Olson, M. (1965) *The Logic of Collective Action: Public Goods and the Theory of Groups* (Cambridge MA: Harvard University Press).

Olson, M. (1982) *The Rise and Decline of Nations: Economic Growth, Stagflation and Social Rigidities* (New Haven: Yale University Press).

Ott, A. F. (2002) *The Public Sector in the Global Economy: From the Driver's Seat to the Back Seat* (Cheltenham: Edward Elgar).

Pigou, A.C. (1999) *A Study in Public Finance: A. C. Pigou Collected Economic Writings Volume 7* (Basingstoke: Macmillan – now Palgrave Macmillan). [First published 1928].

Roth, T. P. (2002) *The Ethics and Economics of Minimalist Government* (Cheltenham: Edward Elgar).

Schokkaert, E. (2001) (editor) *Ethics and Social Security Reform* International Studies on Social Security Volume 7 (Aldershot: Ashgate).

Sharman, L. (2001) *Holding to Account: The Review of Audit and Accountability for Central Government* ('The Sharman Report') (London: HM Treasury).

Smith, A. (1776) *An Inquiry into the Nature and Causes of the Wealth of Nations* Edited by Campbell, R. H. and Skinner, A. S. (1982) (Indianapolis: Liberty Fund).

Stiglitz, J. E. (2000) *Economics of the Public Sector* (third edition) (New York: Norton).

Winer, S. L. and Shibata, H. (2002) (editors) *Political Economy and Public Finance: The Role of Political Economy in the Theory and Practice of Public Finance* (Saarbrucken: International Institute of Public Finance).

2 Property Rights and Public Finance

INTRODUCTION

Chapter 1 raised the question as to whether public finance is always strictly necessary and whether private finance could be used in whole or in part to provide public services. Such questioning is the main purpose of this chapter. It makes clear that public finance and private finance are not necessarily mutually exclusive. Indeed, it will demonstrate that public and private finance can be used to complement each other in the provision of many public services in securing positive and/or negative rights.

Irrespective of whether public and/or private finance is used to fund service provision, one could go further and question whether some so-called public services should be provided by the public sector at all. It has long been a commonly held belief that public services must be provided by the public sector. Recently, however, it has been increasingly recognised that public services could be provided by the private and/or not-for-profit sectors consistent with governments' social and economic objectives. The private sector comprises profit-seeking companies and other enterprises. The not-for-profit sector includes charities, voluntary organisations and independent trusts.

In other words, the provision of public services can be enabled by the state, as distinct from being directly provided by it. A shift from 'direct provision' to enabling services to be provided by the private and not-for-profit sectors is based on a reconfiguration of 'property rights'. Such a reconfiguration will clearly affect the relative scale of public finance (see Chapter 3). It will be shown that enabling governments can transform public property rights into private property rights without making services any less public. What is public is the *policy* relating to citizens' access to the service, not its provision or the particular structure of property rights used to provide it. Public ownership of the inputs and processes necessary for the provision of services is not necessary for outputs and outcomes to be consistent with public policy objectives. Put simply, public property rights are not necessary to secure the public interest.

SPENDING PUBLIC FINANCE IN THE PUBLIC INTEREST

Most people would accept that public finance should be used (that is, raised as well as spent) to promote the public interest, securing outputs and outcomes

26

serving the community as a whole. However, as noted in Chapter 1, 'the public interest' is a very nebulous concept. Being vague and amorphous, 'the public interest' is open to a wide range of differing philosophical interpretations and the concept may be abused or hijacked to serve the interests of particular sections of society and economy. For example, a majority of the population could exploit a minority by taxing them more heavily than the rest of the population, justifying that exploitation in terms of 'the public interest'. Alternatively, a politically and economically powerful elite (that is, a minority) could exploit a majority so as to benefit themselves, for example levying taxes on all the population whilst disproportionately concentrating the provision of services on that elite.

Bearing such caveats in mind, the public interest can be defined in terms of the 4Es analytical framework developed in Chapter 1. Here, the strategic use of public finance would be directed towards achieving greater equity, efficiency, economy and effectiveness. Notions of equity, efficiency, economy and effectiveness changed in many countries as part of the Neo-Liberal resurgence (noted in Chapter 1), and so therefore has the perception of the public interest.

■ *Equity* was discussed in Chapter 1 in terms of market welfare (the Libertarian interpretation of equity), social welfare (the Collectivist interpretation) and work-based welfare (the Neo-Liberal interpretation). It was noted that, as service sectors develop, people and households may be more able to support themselves rather than rely solely on state handouts, the state providing training opportunities to help people gain employment and emphasising their responsibility to do so, that is, work-based welfare. Under this interpretation of equity, the focus of equity shifts from more equal outcomes to more equal opportunities. The meaning of social justice is therefore rebalanced, there being less emphasis on a more equal distribution of income and wealth for its own sake and more on one that reflects merit and desert. Property rights therefore also have to be rebalanced accordingly, being made more conditional upon merit and desert.

■ *Efficiency* was discussed in Chapter 1 in terms of market efficiency (the Libertarian interpretation of efficiency), social efficiency (the Collectivist interpretation) and modified market efficiency (the Neo-Liberal interpretation). Modified market efficiency requires maximisation of the social and economic benefits arising directly as a result of the use of public finance which, in turn, requires the value of additional benefits to be not less than the additional costs (both direct and indirect) of public finance. Besides the direct financial costs of public finance, use of public money for one purpose pre-empts its use for other socially productive uses of that money either by governments or taxpayers, so incurring an indirect cost in terms of a lost opportunity (that is, an 'opportunity cost'). Moreover, unnecessarily high levels of taxation and/or borrowing may have potentially adverse effects on incentives to work and invest, the resulting lost outputs constituting a potentially profound indirect cost (see Chapter 6). The Neo-Liberal resurgence led to greater attention being paid to the potential disincentive effects resulting from the use of public finance, emphasising the need to pay more attention to market efficiency. Many countries considered how best to make markets work better by reconfiguring property rights (less public, more private).

■ *Economy* was discussed in Chapter 1 in terms of operational economy and strategic economy. The Neo-Liberal resurgence led to increasing attention being paid to both categorisations of economy. For operational economy, the main initiatives have been increased use of competitive contracting for the provision of inputs and the management of public services (for example the EU's public procurement initiative) and greater decentralisation of management processes (for example within local governments). This reform made property rights more contestable through markets. For strategic economy, the main initiatives have been increased 'subsidiarity', exercising government powers and associated property rights at the lowest possible level of government (see Chapter 8). In more generic terms, improved operational and strategic economy require avoidance of 'deadweight subsidy', defined as any disbursement of public finance greater than the absolute minimum necessary for a policy outcome to be achieved. Operational economy requires 'cost containment', whilst strategic economy requires 'net additionality' in the use of public finance (see Chapter 4).

■ *Effectiveness* was discussed in Chapter 1 in terms of market outcomes (the Libertarian interpretation) and social outcomes (the Collectivist interpretation). Effectiveness requires the trade-offs between equity, efficiency and economy to be minimised. For example, increased equity may come at a cost to the nation as a whole by reducing the size of the 'economic cake' available for redistribution in pursuit of equity. It would be misguided to pursue only one whilst ignoring the other two. The Neo-Liberal resurgence (see Chapter 1) led to increasing attention being paid to the possibility that government intervention may be ineffective or even counterproductive, that is, when government failure is greater then market failure. Hence, the reconfiguration of property rights ultimately must reflect *both* market failure and government failure.

Thus, 'the public interest' is not a static concept. Its meaning has changed over recent times with increasing emphasis on personal responsibilities as well as rights, market efficiency, the need to economise the use of public funds, and the wisdom of restricting government intervention to core functions (that is, policy-making and enabling equality of opportunity).

PROPERTY RIGHTS AND THE PUBLIC INTEREST

The theoretical basis for the reinterpretation of the public interest in Neo-Liberal terms is 'property rights theory'. It was noted in Chapter 1 that Libertarians, Neo-Liberals and Collectivists have different perceptions of rights in terms of negative and positive rights. It was also noted that they have radically different views of property rights, Libertarians regarding them as inviolable, Collectivists regarding them as theft and Neo-Liberals adopting a less absolutist view.

Property rights relate to the exploitation of economic resources for monetary benefit. In formal legalistic terms 'property rights' refers to the ability to possess, use and dispose of any tangible (for example land) or intangible (for example copyright) thing of value. Thus 'property' is not restricted to tangible products such as land or durable goods such as cars. It also refers to intangible items of value, such as intellectual property relating to knowledge (for example the invention of new drugs for medical purposes) or the amenity derived from environmental resources (for example use of a river for fishing, boating, swimming and so on.). The ability to enforce property rights has to be set down in law, otherwise anyone could commandeer property without it being regarded as theft, fraud or other such criminal activity.

Like the law, property rights are social constructs subject to differing interpretations and to change over time. They defend the interests of specific individuals or groups and therefore reflect 'natural rights', 'human rights' and 'moral rights'. In being able to enforce them using legal mechanisms, property rights create exclusivity and are alienable. In contrast, natural rights are said to be inalienable and common to all (for example the right to freedom from oppression or to justice). Clearly, the shift from one structure of property rights to another necessarily changes (perhaps reinforces) the distribution of social, political and economic power.

Property rights relate not just to 'private' property but also to 'common' property (that is, available to all) and 'sovereign' (that is, state) property. There has been a long-standing philosophical debate about the relative merits of common and private property rights. Over 2000 years ago the Greek philosopher Aristotle argued that individuals care more for that which is their own and less for that which is common, an argument echoed down the centuries by St Thomas Aquinas and others. That debate is reflected by the three political philosophies. It will be seen to hold profound implications for the services that should (or should not) be provided by the public sector and so also have profound implications for how public finance should be raised and for which services it should be used to support.

The Collectivist theory of property rights

Collectivists argue that sovereign and common property rights should be the sole form of property rights. They argue that common and sovereign property rights are a means of codifying the mutual obligations of the members of a community. Only by denial of exclusive private property rights can full positive rights be provided for.

Collectivists argue that the state provision of education, health and other services is essential for the good of the community. In particular, they rely on the argument that such services generate wider social benefits and so should be financed from public funds in order to promote the public interest. Those social benefits are essential for society to function. They also argue that state provision of public services generates a sense of community identity, binding citizens together through a shared mutual interest.

Notwithstanding the indeterminacy of 'the public interest,' many people would probably accept the argument that public finance is needed to support services benefiting the community and to tax those actively damaging the community. Many would probably also accept the argument that the provision of high-profile public services gives municipalities a strong sense of identity, a well-rehearsed argument for strengthening the powers of local government consistent with the European Charter of Local Self-Government (see Chapter 8). Such services generally yield collective (as distinct from purely personal) benefits. For example, it is widely accepted that education yields substantial social benefits in providing an educated workforce, generally accepted to be a prerequisite of economic growth. Therefore, in providing money for state education, public finance promotes the public interest. Likewise, a publicly financed health service facilitates higher GDP by facilitating a fit and healthy workforce and ensures that the poor are not excluded from it because of inability to pay. Caring for the sick and infirm is a clear sign of mutual dependence and a social or collective conscience.

Private sector education and health services are feasible. However, many people would accept the argument that, in making their own provision for health and education services, individual citizens would not take into account these wider social benefits, with the result that the public interest would not be secured fully. For example, many parents would not wish to pay for college and university education for their children, perhaps not even pay for school education. This would be seriously disadvantageous for the employment prospects of such children in their adult years and could inhibit economic growth due a shortage of appropriately educated and skilled labour. Thus, school education is usually compulsory. However, compulsion can probably only work as long as parents are not charged directly for the education of their children. Hence, public finance is almost invariably used to make school education free of any direct charge.

Put simply, the Collectivists' view is that using public finance to provide education, health and other public services free at the point of use secures the collective or public interest, collective property rights providing the foundations for a fully inclusive society and so guaranteeing full positive rights. Markets for private property simply cannot achieve this.

The Libertarian theory of property rights

Libertarians argue the opposite case to Collectivists, namely that virtually all tangible and intangible property should be subject to private property rights. This is because, as noted in Chapter 1, they reject totally the notion of positive rights, only sanctioning negative rights. Libertarians argue that collective ownership is inevitably self-defeating, making the collective worse off rather than better off. Rather than generating wider social benefits, Libertarians argue that state ownership of the nation's resources results in social costs.

They illustrate this argument with a simple example, namely the 'tragedy of the commons'. The argument is that common pasture will be overgrazed, resulting in tragedy for everyone. Overgrazing occurs because an individual herder grazing an additional animal on the pasture gains more from the value of the addition to his or her stock than is lost due to the increased intensity of grazing, which is shared with all other herders. Hence, rational herders seeking to maximise the value of their stock will increase the sizes of their herds on the common pasture even though, ultimately, all will be ruined. The Libertarian's solution is to privatise the commons, converting common property rights into private property rights. The owner can then exclude the excessive stock and so prevent overgrazing, thus avoiding the tragedy of the commons and so safeguarding the public interest.

The tragedy of the commons is paralleled in modern times by:

■ overfishing leading to the collapse of fish stocks, this being the rationale for the EU's licensing of fishing rights and controlling the size of fishing fleets by decommissioning fishing boats.

■ damage to the natural environment caused by pollution from industry, agriculture and the domestic sector, this being the rationale for the EU's controls on pollution of watercourses and its bathing water, drinking water and urban waste water directives.

■ overuse of wilderness areas by the public, for example many feet trampling plant life and many visitors destroying the very sense of wilderness they came to see, this being the rationale for controls on the numbers of visitors to national parks in Canada and New Zealand.

■ erosion of the fabric of sites of national heritage, again due to too many trampling feet, this being the justification for admission charges or other means of controlling visitor numbers.

The reforms in these four bullet points have made property rights more private and less public. However, the introduction of private property rights is only one way of avoiding the tragedy of the commons. The underlying problem is 'open access' to the resource. Common property rights do not necessarily require open access, as made clear by the above examples of licensing, regulation, rationing and charging. The first three responses generate little or no revenue and yet incur substantial costs. In contrast, charging raises revenue to at least partially offset costs. In the tragedy of the commons example, each member of the collective could be charged for use of the commons, the level of the charge per additional animal being set just high enough to prevent deterioration of the grazing. The advantage of this method of rationing is that it generates revenues for the community to use for socially beneficial purposes (for example improving the amenity). Property rights are formalised but they are not privatised. Instead, they control access so as to conserve or sustain the amenity.

The Libertarian response is that tragedy will still occur because preferences for environmental resources are not registered and valued in market transactions. They cannot be registered and valued because they cannot be traded, in turn because no one has exclusive property rights over them. If resources cannot be valued they cannot be used efficiently. Thus the natural environment is severely damaged by pollution even though it is generally regarded to be an undesirable outcome and even though various regulatory controls are in place. Hence, lack of private property rights leads to market failure which, in turn, leads to the inefficient use of a nation's resources.

Put simply, the Libertarian view is that markets cannot work efficiently if private property rights are not established, consumers' preferences cannot be taken account of and so collective or sovereign property rights ultimately result in tragedy, making people worse off rather than better off.

The Neo-Liberal theory of property rights

The Neo-Liberal resurgence has been associated with a shift from state property and common property to private property, most notably through privatisation and demutualisation respectively. Like Libertarians, they argue that a nation's resources cannot be used efficiently if they cannot be valued in monetary terms. Scarce resources would be used wastefully if they were free or undervalued. Neo-Liberals argue that the shift towards private property rights facilitates and encourages greater efficiency (for example of privatised energy or water companies) by allowing for the accumulation of profits from the ownership and use of property. They argue that this result occurs irrespective of the institutional framework or cultural context within which private property rights are introduced. The solution to environmental problems therefore is to establish a market for environmental amenities, such as watercourses, ecosystems, natural habitats and landscape, so that they can be valued *directly*. Market systems require private property rights.

However, Neo-Liberals accept that it may not always be possible to establish market systems based on private property rights. Rather than reverting to the Collectivists' concept of social need, Neo-Liberals argue that the next best solution is to value environmental amenities *indirectly* by inference from proxy goods for which markets exist. For example, the higher values of residential properties benefiting from an environmental amenity (such as a lake abutting their boundaries) provides a proxy measure of the value of that amenity. Where proxy goods do not exist, such amenities could still be valued indirectly by asking individuals to put values on them. They could be asked how much they would be *willing to pay* to prevent deterioration of an environmental amenity (for example pollution of a lake or river) or how much they would be *willing to accept* in compensation for such an unwelcome event. These are referred to as 'contingent valuation methods' because they assume a given contingency.

Unfortunately, these two methods have been found to yield different valuations for the same contingency and so may be unreliable as measures of value. Moreover, both direct and indirect valuation of environmental amenities necessarily prioritises the preferences of high-income groups over low-income groups. This is because the former have a greater ability to pay than the latter. Collectivists consider this to be unethical and also argue that such valuations ignore the preferences and needs of future generations. Whilst such valuation methods certainly can be criticised in these terms, Neo-Liberals argue that even crude valuations are better than none at all because otherwise the tragedy of the commons occurs.

Nevertheless, Neo-Liberals accept that markets and proxy goods may underestimate both the social and personal value of education, health care, environmental amenities and so on. In that case, markets fail to secure socially and economically optimal levels of such services. This does not, however, mean that they accept the Collectivists' community benefits rationale for services being provided free to users. Neo-Liberals argue that many activities yield wider social benefits in creating economic prosperity and social welfare, but this does not necessarily mean that they should all be fully subsidised by public finance. For example, it was noted above that Collectivists argue that a healthy workforce underpins economic growth and thus justifies a publicly financed health service. But long-term improvements in health and life expectancy owe more to ongoing improvements in nutrition and housing standards than to the provision of short-term health care. Should the 'wider social benefits' argument therefore be used to justify using public finance to subsidise housing, food and, more generally, 'healthy' lifestyles? Perhaps, but many countries do not subsidise housing and food costs. In fact many countries levy VAT on 'healthy' as well as 'unhealthy' foods and private sector profit-making health and fitness facilities are well established. Besides, fashions for particular foods, sports and leisure activities may be much more influential than subsidised prices in encouraging healthy lifestyles.

Similarly, education yields personal as well as social benefits, for example by increasing an individual's potential lifetime earnings and quality of life. On average, higher levels of education are associated with higher levels of earnings from employment and, consequently, with higher savings and other forms of personal wealth. In principle, people could be expected to pay for services such as education and health in direct proportion to the personal benefits they confer on the user. However, Neo-Liberals also accept that people are likely to underestimate those personal benefits because of:

■ *Lack of information.* Individuals may not have sufficient information about the future benefits arising from education and health care to enable them to make wise investment decisions (that is, in terms of building up their human capital and making adequate provision for health insurance).
■ *Myopia.* Even if they were fully informed about the balance between personal costs and benefits, they may discount those future benefits too heavily when comparing them with current costs. Put simply, people may live primarily for the present to the neglect of their future welfare.
■ *Lack of appreciation of risk.* Whilst, on average, most people live into old age and require medical care during their lives, not everyone does. People may adopt the 'it will never happen to me' syndrome and so believe that making provision for possible ill health and old age is a waste of money.

Put simply, ignoring wider social benefits together with undervaluation of personal benefits due to lack of accurate information, myopic assessments and relaxed attitudes to risk may lead to insufficient or suboptimal consumption of services. It may therefore be necessary to use public finance to supplement private finance so as to increase the consumption of such services. Hence, rather than simply providing such services free at the point of use from within the public sector (the Collectivists' solution) the Neo-Liberals' solution is to use a combination of public and private finance, preferably subsidising production by the private (market) sector.

The Collectivists' line of argument leaves unresolved what the minimum levels of services should be: there could be too much or too little service made available (that is, government failure) depending on the rather arbitrary decisions of politicians and bureaucrats regarding the amount of public finance to be made available. On the other hand, the Libertarians' dependence on laissez-faire is likely to result in suboptimally low levels of education, health and other services because free markets ignore social benefits and may understate individual preferences, thus resulting in insufficient private finance being made available (that is, market failure). In contrast, Neo-Liberals argue that it is possible, in principle, to determine the optimal levels of services by taking explicit account of such undervaluations and, hence, determine the optimal combination of private and public finance. The optimal balance between these two sources of finance reflects the balance between private benefits and social benefits. By such means, modified market efficiency is achieved.

Put simply, the Neo-Liberal view is that whilst markets may fail, such failure is partial rather than absolute. Therefore, the solution is not to abandon private property rights altogether but instead to strengthen them in order to help markets work better in accordance with the public interest.

THE LEGITIMACY OF PROPERTY RIGHTS

Libertarians and Collectivists clearly have fundamentally different views about the legitimacy of property rights. It is arguable, however, that the choice between private property and collective property rights is not necessarily a mutually exclusive one.

Without private property rights, some forms of socially beneficial property would simply not exist. For example, without such legal protection there would be no incentive for private sector pharmaceutical companies to spend money researching and developing new drugs. With private property rights a pharmaceutical company can protect its intellectual property rights by patenting any new drugs it develops. A patent is granted by the state to an inventor assuring that person (or company) the right to use and sell that product or process during a specified period of time. This allows the inventor the opportunity to recover the costs incurred in creating that invention (for example developing a new drug) and to earn profits. Patents therefore encourage the expansion of knowledge by turning it into a tradable commodity for a specified period of time. Thus legislation can allow intangible things of value to be traded in much the same way as tangible items.

However, some scientists argue that scientific knowledge should not be subjected to private property rights, these being inconsistent with the open communication of scientific knowledge which is essential for scientific progress. Just because intellectual property rights can be enforced in law does not necessarily mean that they should be. The practical solution to this ethical problem is that patented knowledge becomes common property upon expiry of the patent period. Ideally, that period will be of the minimum duration sufficient to encourage a socially optimal level of research and development into new products, processes, treatments and so on.

The ethical problem remains, however, namely that subjecting scientific knowledge to private property rights means that those who are excluded from the benefits of that knowledge may suffer intolerable consequences. Nothing highlights this ethical issue more vividly than the denial by pharmaceutical companies of the use by poor African countries of their patented drugs used in the treatment of Aids. Many African countries' populations are being decimated by Aids-related deaths but they are too poor to pay for the drugs, resulting in huge loss of life. In this case, private property rights could be regarded as in breach of natural, human and moral rights.

Similar ethical arguments apply to the patenting of genes, for example leading to the denial by Western agribusiness corporations of the right of farmers in developing countries to save some of the seed from the patented crop for replanting next year. The patenting of seeds made resistant to disease and pests requires farmers wishing to replant the crop to purchase new seed from the companies holding the patent. Nevertheless, it is arguable that, without private property rights secured through patents, these more efficacious drugs and seeds would never have been developed in the first place.

The debate boils down to a question of which is more unethical: to deny or inhibit scientific progress of benefit to future generations by destroying or constraining the incentives provided by private property rights, or to temporarily restrict access by the current generation to what progress has already been made? Both outcomes are unethical but a choice has to be made nonetheless.

Likewise, conferring private property rights on environmental and natural resources may be regarded as unethical in allowing the current owners to deplete those resources and so deny their use by future generations. This particular problem can be addressed by instituting 'usufruct', namely the right to use and derive profit from a property belonging to another, provided that property remains uninjured or undiminished in any way. Thus, whilst retaining collective property rights, the collective (for example the state) would allow private sector exploitation of, say, a fish stock, watercourse, wilderness area or heritage site, but restrict the use of that resource to a level that is sustainable in the long term. The reforms described in the last four bullet points above instituted usufruct. By such means, future generations may also benefit from such resources. The ethical position underpinning usufruct is that only 'use rights' are morally legitimate, not 'ownership rights'.

Clearly, patents are a means of gaining the social benefits of private property rights without forgoing collective property rights in the long term. Likewise, usufruct is a means of avoiding the tragedy of the commons associated with collective property rights. Hence, different combinations of private and collective property rights and of use rights and ownership rights may be appropriate for different circumstances and at different times. Property rights need not necessarily be fixed for all time. The Neo-Liberal resurgence led to a shift away from collective to private property rights. Also use rights were increasingly constrained to sustainable levels for renewable natural resources such as fish stocks, forestry and even the atmosphere (that is, via 'emissions trading' under the United Nation's 1997 Kyoto Protocol).

The fact that many countries privatised their state assets over the last several decades makes clear that property rights are indeed social constructs as, therefore, is the public sector. What is public can easily become private and vice versa. Clearly, such a reconfiguration of property rights has had a profound impact on the relative scale and composition of the public sector and therefore on public finance.

USING PROPERTY RIGHTS TO CATEGORISE PUBLIC AND PRIVATE SERVICES

The implications of the above discussion for the public sector and public finance can be made clear by using the concept of property rights to categorise goods and services. This clarification can be achieved by distinguishing between:

- Pure public goods and services (henceforth referred to as 'pure public goods')
- Pure private goods and services (henceforth referred to as 'pure private goods')
- Mixed goods and services (henceforth referred to as 'mixed goods').

The concept of 'pure public goods' will be used to determine which goods and services can only be financed by the public sector. Thus, a minimum size for the public sector can be determined and therefore so can a minimum need for public finance in promoting the public interest. The concept of 'pure private goods' will likewise be used to determine which goods and services can be wholly financed by private finance without any need for public finance. The concept of 'mixed goods' will be used to demonstrate the *complementary* use of public and private finance in promoting the public interest.

Pure public goods

Pure public goods are defined as goods and services with the following characteristics:

- property rights are completely unenforceable
- there is no need to enforce property rights in order to ensure sustainable use of that property.

For example, an environmental organisation incurring costs in persuading governments and/or companies to reduce atmospheric pollution cannot restrict the resulting benefits (for example improved health and amenity) to those who contribute to its costs (that is, via membership fees and voluntary contributions and bequests). In such cases, the environmental benefits are *non-excludable* because property rights are completely unenforceable. In this case it is simply not possible to establish property rights and so the private sector market system cannot operate. Beneficial property rights simply cannot be specified in legal terms and so it is impossible for any one person, company or other such legal entity to prevent any other person or company from benefiting and so access to those benefits cannot be denied. Enforcement of property rights is unnecessary, however, because any number of people can benefit from that environmental improvement, one person's benefit not detracting from any other person's benefit. The service is *non-rival* in use and so there are no scarcity or congestion characteristics that would otherwise require use of the service to be regulated so that its use be sustainable. Being *both* non-excludable and non-rival, 'the benefits of pure public goods cannot be privatised because they are pure community-level services'.

National defence and the system of justice are examples of services whose property rights are unenforceable and which need not be enforced to ensure sustainable use. They afford all citizens protection (against enemy incursions and crime respectively). No citizen can be excluded from that protection, nor can they exclude themselves by rejecting the service. For example, conscientious objectors or pacifists cannot exclude themselves from the benefits of military deterrence. The same characteristics apply to consumer protection, environmental health, public health and food safety services. Thus everyone has unlimited sustainable access to the benefits of those services, not as a matter of right but rather as a matter of fact.

This means that a private provider would not be able to cover the costs of providing these services. For example, an individual buying a nuclear weapons system to deter attack by a hostile country could not compel fellow nationals to pay for the protection thus provided. Hence, the costs of national defence can only be covered by public finance. The same conclusion about the sole dependence on public finance applies for the other examples of pure public goods listed above.

The question remains about the particular form of public finance, in particular whether the service should be financed by taxation or charges. 'Charges' would only be appropriate if either the costs of providing the service could be attributed to particular individuals or if the benefits each person received could be measured. However, it is not possible to attribute service costs to particular individuals because the service is inexhaustible (that is, non-rival in use) and once it is provided to one citizen it is provided to all. Similarly, it is not possible to quantify how much each individual benefits from the service because benefit cannot be measured in financial terms, there being no provision by market systems and so no market price that can be used to value the service. Individual citizens could simply be asked to express in monetary terms the amount of benefit they enjoy. However, once they realise that their valuations would be matched directly by the charge levied on them, they would have a strong incentive to understate their willingness to pay for the service, even claiming it was of zero value. The same caveat applies to willingness to accept measures of value (see above). In effect, individual citizens would have an incentive to take a 'free ride' at the expense of other citizens, therefore being dubbed 'free riders', more colloquially known as 'freeloaders'. Hence, user-charges are not an appropriate means of financing this category of services and decisions about how much of a pure public good to produce and of what quality that output should be can only be determined collectively (for example by the state).

Instead, compulsory levies in the form of taxes are the most appropriate source of public finance for pure public goods. Put simply, individual citizens have to be compelled to pay for purely collective services once governments decide that they should be provided. The question then arises as to what form of taxation should be used.

'Flat-rate poll taxes' would be most appropriate if it is thought that each citizen benefits equally from the service. Alternatively, if it is thought that the greatest benefit is derived by those with most to lose (in terms of income and wealth) due to war or crime, then 'proportionate or progressive taxes on income and wealth' would be the most appropriate source of taxation. This could also be consistent with any 'redistribution of income and wealth' objectives. It may, however, be inconsistent with moral prerogatives in respect of philosophical notions of natural justice or commutative justice. Consumer protection may be more appropriately financed by 'taxes on expenditures' on the grounds that those who spend the most derive the most benefit from the service. Whichever tax is appropriate, in principle it should be limited to raising only the amount of revenue necessary for provision of the pure public good with which it is associated. This implies the 'earmarking' (that is, 'hypothecation') of taxes.

Besides the nature of the tax most appropriate for raising public finance to pay for the provision of pure public goods, there is also a question about the 'originator' of the tax. The 'community' benefiting from such services may be the national, regional, or local community depending on how far the benefits extend. In the case of defence, the community is the nation state and so the tax originator should be central or federal government. The other five examples above may have benefits only or predominantly at local and/or regional level. For example, smokeless zones (in respect of fuels for heating houses and so on) benefit specific urban areas and so the costs of policing them are most appropriately borne by municipal taxpayers in those areas. The same applies to environmental health services relating to policing hygiene standards in food shops and restaurants. Thus, although completely unenforceable property rights provide a justification for public finance, they do not necessarily require finance from national taxation (see Chapter 8).

In summary, the essential characteristics of pure public goods are that they are services for which property rights are completely unenforceable and which need not be enforced in order for their beneficial use to be sustainable. Thus decisions about whether, how much and what quality of output to produce can only be taken collectively. *Everyone can and does benefit without limitation or exception* because pure public goods are *non-excludable and non-rival* in use. Since they *cannot be depleted*, there is no constraint imposed by scarcity and therefore no rationale for attempting to control access through user-charges which, in practice, are unenforceable. Instead, taxes are the most appropriate source of public finance, though whether flat-rate, or related to income, wealth or expenditure depends on the nature of the service. The strictly limited number of examples of services discussed above demonstrates that most of the services conventionally provided by the public sector are not pure community-level services. Those examples broadly correspond to the services justified by Libertarians on the basis of negative rights (see Chapter 1).

Pure private goods

Pure private goods are the polar opposite of pure public goods. They are defined as goods and services with the following characteristics:

- property rights are completely and wholly enforceable
- property rights must be enforced for the good or service to be provided on a sustainable basis.

As long as property rights can be fully enforced, the owner can exclude others from using or otherwise benefiting from that property. This means that the owner can sell the property or charge others for its use. Those who are unwilling or unable to pay can be prevented from benefiting from the property. Thus exclusion is possible and so the private market sector can operate, being able to recover the costs of provision of pure private goods by levying charges (that is, market prices) on the users (that is, consumers) of such goods and services. Moreover, pure private goods are characterised by 'scarcity' in terms of having a strictly limited capacity. Hence, one person's use of the good or service does preclude use by others. Therefore, pure private goods do *not* benefit everyone without limitation or exception, meaning they are individualised outputs, not community-level services. Instead, they are *excludable and rival* in use: *they only benefit those who own or pay for them.*

Thus private sector providers can recover the costs of providing such goods and services and so their provision becomes sustainable. For example, owners of domestic, commercial and industrial properties can prevent others from occupying them unless they agree to pay rent. Similarly, those who do not pay the entrance fee levied by a private sector leisure company can be excluded from admission and so from use of the facility. Likewise, those who do not pay for cosmetic surgery can be excluded by a private sector clinic. In each of these examples the good or service is *excludable*: property rights are fully enforceable. Each is also *rival* in use because there is only a limited amount of occupational space, places and treatment facilities available.

These services therefore have a finite capacity, meaning that they *can be depleted*. In other words, there is a constraint imposed by scarcity: in such cases a service can be completely exhausted. Thus access to pure private goods has to be controlled in order to match capacity with use and so ensure sustainability. Property rights can easily be conceptualised and enforced. Non-nationals, non-residents and non-payers can all be excluded from benefiting from the service and they can be rejected by those unwilling to pay. Therefore, the most appropriate means of financing these services is using private finance derived from user-charges. Public finance is neither necessary nor appropriate for pure private goods.

There are many other examples of goods and services that the private sector can provide and recover costs. These include energy supply, postal services, repair services for cars and other consumer durables, legal services relating to the sale or purchase of one's house, restaurant meals, plumbing and electrical services, all forms of insurance, transport services, leisure services, cleaning and catering services, residential care services, and many educational (for example teaching English as a foreign language) and medical services (for example cosmetic surgery). Water and sewerage services are typically provided by the public sector in European countries and, whilst proper disposal and treatment of sewage is essential for public health, nothing demonstrates the rival and exclusive use of water better than droughts and the increasing popularity of bottled mineral water. Put simply, water is a tradable commodity and it can be completely financed by user-charges levied by private sector providers (as is the case in the USA and England).

Clearly, almost all goods and services display elements of exclusion and rivalry in use. However, to be categorised as a pure private good, they must be *both* excludable and rival in use. It has to be emphasised that excludability means that the 'benefits' of pure private goods are restricted to those who use or consume them.

Mixed goods

The characteristics of mixed goods contain elements of both pure public goods and pure private goods. There are two categories of mixed goods:

- property rights can be enforced but need not be for sustainable use
- property rights cannot be enforced and this prevents sustainable use.

The first category of mixed goods includes those that are *excludable but non-rival* in use. Thus private property rights can be fully enforced. Therefore private finance can fully cover the costs of provision of this type of mixed good by charging citizens using it and so it is sustainable. Moreover, the service can be directly valued according to the willingness to pay expressed by its users. An example is a non-terrestrial (that is, satellite) television company where any number of people are capable of receiving those satellite transmissions but where reception is limited to those renting or buying the receiver (that is, satellite dish) from the company.

The second category of mixed goods includes those that are *rival but non-excludable* in use. These do need support from public finance if they are to be provided. This is because property rights cannot be enforced, providers cannot cover costs, its use is therefore unsustainable and it cannot be directly valued because user-charges cannot be levied. An example is a municipal or regional country park where charging for admission would be inordinately expensive due to the need to build fences but the park can become congested, eroded or otherwise damaged as a result of overuse. It may be possible to raise finance from park visitors and to control access (at least in part) by charging for car parking and/or charging for guided tours. Thus public finance may be raised from an excludable good or service that is complementary to the non-excludable mixed good. In their own terms, however, rival but non-excludable mixed goods require use of public funds to enforce property rights so as to control access and ensure collective welfare is secured by sustainability in the use of resources. Similarly, sustainable use of the environment requires public finance for policing pollution and enforcing compliance with legislation. Pollution control based on a polluter-pays policy raises public finance by taxing those activities causing pollution. This justification for public finance does not necessarily depend upon a particular view of natural rights or human rights, namely the right not to be polluted (and so the right not to have to suffer adverse health consequences for somebody else's benefit). Such a right would seem to be equivalent to that of protection against crime and so fall within the negative rights category. Clearly negative rights are based on ethical considerations in much the same way as human or natural rights.

Technological factors may affect enforcement of property rights and changing technology could lead to a change in the categorisation of a service. This has occurred, for example, in the case of television transmissions that, as just noted, are mixed goods, in being excludable but non-rival in use. The pure public goods argument has traditionally been used in justifying public sector broadcasting of radio and television signals. This public service has been financed in many countries by taxation or a licence fee paid by owners of television-receiving equipment (that is, a television set, video recorder, personal computer with a broadcast card and so on.). Licence fees are suitable where policing payment of the fee is not prohibitively expensive, for example in developed countries having comprehensive property registers. Like taxation, the revenues raised by the licence fee are categorised as public finance (see Chapter 1). In comparison, private television transmission companies have typically covered their costs by advertising other companies' products and charging them a fee.

However, since television transmissions are now technologically excludable by means of the decoding or specialist reception equipment required for reception of signals, private sector television broadcast companies can cover their costs by a mixture of user-charges and advertising revenues, that is, by private finance. There is therefore no longer a need for public finance to support transmission companies. Whilst there may be a need for public finance to support commercially non-viable programmes that governments consider should be made and broadcast to promote the public interest, it is the programme maker that should be subsidised, not the transmission company. Public sector broadcasters could be privatised and required to cover their costs by advertising and/or by introducing charges for new receiver technologies (for example digital reception equipment).

PROPERTY RIGHTS, MARKET VALUATIONS, WIDER SOCIAL BENEFITS AND PUBLIC FINANCE

Property rights theory has been used to determine what conditions are necessary for the efficient provision of goods and services, namely using market valuations directly to determine supply. Public finance is required for the provision of pure public goods and for that category of mixed goods characterised by non-excludability and rival use. This is because the failure of property rights means that markets fail to put an accurate valuation on a nation's resources and so they cannot be used efficiently on a sustainable basis.

In principle, public finance is not required for pure private goods or for that category of mixed goods characterised by excludability and non-rival use. This is because, in principle, markets can be relied upon to put an accurate valuation on a nation's resources and so they can be used efficiently. However, even in these two cases markets may fail to provide accurate valuations. This is the case when:

■ people underestimate the personal benefits of service consumption due to lack of information, myopia or lack of appreciation of risk, as already noted above
■ people ignore the benefits or costs accruing to others arising out of their consumption of a mixed good.

An example of the second case is when governments wish to encourage inoculation against contagious diseases so that everyone benefits from the reduced incidence of disease, even those who are not inoculated. Compulsory inoculations would infringe individual liberty and 100 per cent coverage of inoculations is not necessary on medical grounds (that is, for control of the contagion). Hence, governments typically prefer to encourage them by subsidising their take-up. However, this does not necessarily mean that inoculations should be fully subsidised and so free to recipients. There is clearly a private benefit to recipients who, in many cases, are affluent and so could be expected to pay at least some of the cost (for example those taking foreign holidays in areas with prevalent contagious diseases). Thus a complementary mix of public and private finance should be used to provide the optimal level of collective protection that would otherwise not be achieved. This complementary financing clearly does not provide a rationale for the state to finance all the production costs or take over (that is, nationalise) the production of the drug.

Thus, public finance is required for efficiency purposes when:

■ markets fail to exist due to difficulties in enforcing property rights
■ markets exist but, whilst accurately valuing goods and services in terms of how much consumers are willing to pay, nonetheless fail to provide accurate valuations of the personal benefits of consumption and/or also fail to provide measures of the wider social benefits arising from that consumption.

The use of property rights to categorise services has made clear when public finance is necessary for efficiency purposes. The 'failure of property rights' rationale broadly corresponds with the Libertarian negative rights justification for public finance in that both identify pure public goods. This justification for the public financing of services is profoundly distinct from the 'wider social benefits' argument resorted to by Collectivists because, whilst markets can and do exist for most of the services yielding wider social benefits, they simply cannot exist for pure public goods.

Ultimately, the failure of property rights and the 'wider social benefits' arguments can be subsumed within the 'market failure' rationale for public finance, in that both cases mean that markets fail to maximise economic and social welfare. The market failure rationale also encompasses the 'underestimation of the personal benefits' case.

Thus, in summary, market failure can occur because of:

■ the failure of property rights
■ the failure of actual or potential consumers to fully appreciate the personal benefits of goods services
■ the failure to take account of benefits or costs incurred by those other than the immediate consumer.

Whether public finance is actually necessary to deal with market failure is an empirical question. The answer depends upon just how great is the degree of market failure and just how effectively public finance can be used to offset the lack of private finance caused by market failure. Clearly, governments themselves do not have perfect information about the degree of market failure and the effectiveness of intervention. It is possible that intervention may increase (rather than decrease) the degree of market failure.

The Neo-Liberal resurgence (see Chapter 1) has been based on the premise that government intervention has often been counterproductive, actually increasing the degree of market failure by further constraining market forces. Hence, Neo-Liberals adopt a much more qualified view than either Libertarians or Collectivists in judging whether failure of property rights and the inaccuracy of market valuations necessarily require public finance. Neo-Liberals believe that there are more effective ways of dealing with market failure than throwing public money at the problem. On efficiency grounds, they argue that it is more effective to help markets work better by strengthening private property rights and competitive market forces wherever possible. Public finance should only be used as a last resort and, even then, only when the ensuing benefits are greater than the direct and indirect costs of raising and spending public finance.

PUBLIC FINANCE VERSUS PUBLIC PROVISION

It must be emphasised that none of the market failure justifications for public finance necessarily require public property rights to replace private property rights in respect of the inputs and processes necessary to produce outputs. Many services currently provided by the public sector can be (and often are) provided by the private sector. Both forms of provision exist in many countries. In most developed countries, municipal leisure and cultural services provide activities also available in the private sector. There are many examples of private (and voluntary) sector sports clubs, gymnasiums, museums and galleries. Many countries have both public and private hospital and other medical services, and over-the-counter medicines and alternative therapies proliferate. Some countries have private as well as (or instead of) public sector universities. Private tuition out of school hours is fairly common in many countries. So-called 'public transport' is often provided by private sector operators, particularly bus and taxi services. There are private as well as public libraries and information services and private as well as public energy and water and sewerage companies.

Even compulsory services such as school education do not necessarily require direct provision by the state. Private and voluntary (including religious) sector educational companies/organisations exist in many countries. Likewise, compulsory health insurance (whether through premiums paid to a private company or taxes paid to the state) does not preclude private provision of medical services.

Public sector provision is not even necessary for pure public goods. National defence relies on private armaments companies and defence equipment, information technology systems, barracks and even training can all be privatised. Whilst the system of justice is also a pure community-level service, the private sector can build, own and even manage prisons, police stations, law courts, detention centres and so on. As for crime prevention, there are many examples of private security firms and many households provide for their own protection using burglar alarms and so on. In other words, even if a service is a pure public good, at least part of the means by which it is provided can be based on private property rights.

Even when property rights are retained within the public sector, they can be managed under contract by the private sector, for example prisons, hospitals, municipal housing, residential care of elderly people and even schools.

Thus, whilst Collectivists regard public provision as the underpinning of the collective ethos, it cannot be justified by the market failure rationale, not even for pure collective goods and services. Put simply, 'public finance does *not* require public provision'.

WIDER SOCIAL BENEFITS AND PUBLIC FINANCE

The 'wider social benefits' argument used by Collectivists does not provide a robust categorisation of services that should be supported by public finance.

The provision of education to children may indeed benefit the economy as a whole, but so do other services for which it would be difficult to justify use of public finance. For example, well-maintained cars are safer not just for the driver but also for other road users who would otherwise be injured or killed in accidents resulting from lack of maintenance of brake systems and so on. However, few people would use this as the justification for public finance being used to subsidise car repair and maintenance services or for public provision of the service. What it does justify is that the safety of vehicles be made a legal requirement and that public finance be spent policing it.

Hence, trying to justify the public financing of services only on the grounds of wider social benefits leads to no clear categorisation of services, since all the examples in the preceding paragraphs can be said to benefit society in some way or other. If the aim is to maximise social welfare (however defined), then, in principle, the use of public finance must satisfy the 4Es of equity, economy, efficiency and effectiveness. In general, this would require public finance to be spent only when the additional social benefits exceed (or at least equal) the additional social costs of using it (in terms of financial, opportunity and other costs).

In practice, the wider social benefits of publicly financed education, health and other such key public services are rarely as clear cut as Collectivists would argue. For example, the 'wider social benefits' argument for education assumes a direct and positive relationship between rising levels of educational achievement and rising rates of economic growth. This assumption is questionable on both theoretical and empirical grounds:

■ *It assumes that there are only positive social consequences arising out of increases in the public financing of education.* However, increasing public provision financed by taxation may have adverse effects in terms of moral hazard, infringement of individual liberty, crowding out and disincentive-to-work effects and the creation of a dependency culture. For example, moral hazard occurs if parents take no interest in the education of their children precisely because of the provision of compulsory state education. Such lack of parental interest may be seen as an abrogation of parents' responsibilities to their children. Moreover, public services are not free; they incur an opportunity cost by denying other beneficial uses of those taxed incomes and expenditures. At the very least, such adverse consequences result in the net social benefits of higher levels of education being less than the gross social benefits. At worst, they result in net social costs, the direct and indirect social costs being greater than the social benefits of extra educational provision.

■ *Empirical evidence does not prove conclusively that improving the level of education will necessarily lead to greater economic prosperity.* Rather than more education leading to more prosperity, economic growth resulting from other causal factors may simply allow prosperous countries to spend more on education. Statistical association between two events does not prove causation from one to the other. Indeed, it has been argued that very rapid expansion of university education in some countries has reduced standards of undergraduate education and/or has led to an over-supply of graduates. Put simply, it is argued that universities have enrolled increasing numbers of students not able to benefit from university-level education and that many graduates are employed in jobs for which a university education is not necessary.

These arguments are highly controversial. In turn they make largely non-testable assumptions: for example, that universities have had to compromise their standards and that the number of jobs requiring graduate skills is fixed and exogenous of the supply of graduates. Suffice it to say, therefore, that the 'wider social benefits' case for increased provision of education and other services cannot be taken for granted in justifying the continuing expansion of state education. It may be the case that some minimal level of education is necessary to foster economic growth but beyond that level the benefits of increasing provision may diminish increasingly rapidly and the costs (both direct and indirect) may rise progressively faster.

Therefore, categorisation of public services in 'wider social benefits' terms is of doubtful validity and simply not robust enough to justify the conventional distinction between the public and private sector provision of services. As already noted, even where public finance is justified, such beneficial goods and services do not have to be produced by the public sector itself. The relevant policy-making questions concern:

- precisely how much should be spent on each public service
- how any extra spending should be financed (that is, from the private or public purse)
- how those services should be provided.

RIGHTS, ACCESS, EFFICIENCY AND EQUITY

Notwithstanding the above analysis, it could be argued that the philosophical argument is not about the categorisation of services per se but about access to them. The negative and positive rights categorisations are concerned with the rights of citizens to access various services. Nevertheless, the distinction between positive and negative rights is value-laden and arbitrary. Moreover, to argue that citizens have rights to access particular services provides no guidance as to the level of access.

It is commonly argued by Collectivists that access to services can only be guaranteed by denial of private property rights. But does collectivisation of property rights guarantee access for everyone? As noted above, the tragedy of the commons occurs not because of collective property rights but, instead, because of unrestricted access. In effect, in destroying or otherwise damaging the facility, open access ultimately denies access to all. The examples given above were overgrazed common pastures, fish stocks depleted to extinction, pollution of open-access watercourses, and destruction of wilderness areas and heritage sites as a result of too many visitors.

Public services as well as environmental facilities can be destroyed or severely damaged by unrestricted access. For example, parents can be expected to want to send their children to schools achieving high educational standards for their pupils. If there were no controls on pupil intake, such schools would be oversubscribed, typically resulting in a lowering of educational standards because of overcrowded accommodation, excessively high pupil–teacher ratios, shortages of teaching materials and equipment and so on. Thus, most countries control access to individual state schools, selecting pupils for each school on the basis of area of residence (that is, proximity to the school), examination results, occupational class of parents and so on. Similarly, access to family doctors may be controlled by requiring patients to make appointments which allow sufficient time for proper medical examination. Access to hospitals may be controlled by 'gatekeeper' general practitioners acting as a referral service, controlling citizens' access to hospital surgeons on the basis of professionally assessed medical need. In these examples, unrestricted access would lead to a deterioration of service quality due to gross overcrowding, there being insufficient time or other resources to deal effectively with service clients.

In practice, the availability and quality of public sector services such as health is rarely uniform across a country as a whole. Structural disparities in the need for and availability of services arise as a result of difficulties in changing the allocation of financial resources for individual services in accordance with the changing need for services. Thus, for example, changing demographic structures and totals create surplus medical and educational capacity in some areas (for example cities and regions whose populations are falling) and shortages in others (for example those whose urban and regional economies are growing). The resulting mismatches in need and capacity result in geographical variations in service availability, made evident, for example, by longer waiting times for medical treatments in some areas than in others. This leads to complaints of a 'postcode lottery' in access to public services. In such cases, state property rights and state service provision does not lead to equality of access. In fact, they may actually increase inequality of access by restricting people to the service providers in their congested areas notwithstanding the surplus capacity in other areas.

Hence, collectivisation of property rights does not necessarily secure access to a service, even when the service is free at the point of use. Access may be restricted or denied in such cases by the poorer quality of service resulting from overcrowding. Justification of poor quality of service by providers may rely on the fact that it is free at the point of use. Service users may begrudgingly accept this justification. Although the service may be highly valued by the state and by actual and potential service users, being free at the point of use means that public finance is not generated in accordance with valuation and use. Thus poor service quality (including shortage of service capacity) cannot be rectified. This outcome of uncontrolled property rights helps to explain the 'private affluence–public squalor' typology observed in some countries (see Chapter 7).

Public sector museums provide another example of collective property rights not necessarily securing access. Collections of heritage and other artefacts began in most countries as a private sector initiative, private collectors amassing their own collections. Private collectors often bequeath their collections to the state in the belief that the state will preserve them and allow public access. Paradoxically, however, conversion of private property to public property often results in only very limited access, many state and municipal museums having insufficient space to put all (or even the majority) of their collections on display to the public. Those museums often feel obliged to retain donated collections (rather than sell them to raise public finance for conservation of their other artefacts) and yet do not have sufficient finance to display or even conserve them. The more successful a museum is in attracting such bequests, the more subsidies it needs to accommodate, conserve and insure them and the more difficulties it faces in ensuring access. Many state museums resort to storing the larger part of their collections in warehouses, resulting in less rather than more access compared with private sector museums which typically charge for admission and so can raise additional finance.

As already noted, Libertarians and Neo-Liberals argue that it is extremely difficult, if not impossible, to put values on resources in the absence of private property rights and so it is not possible to use resources efficiently to promote economic and social welfare. Nonetheless, it was also noted above that there may still be problems of valuation even with private property rights, for example when the current generation's use of a natural resource denies use (that is, access) by future generations. Of course, this also applies to collective property rights. In this example, the solution is not to change property rights from private to public but, instead, to impose usufruct (explained above). Usufruct does not require public finance and so avoids any of the potential adverse effects related to use of that finance. Likewise, where markets for private property rights fail to value resources accurately, the efficiency solution is to help markets work better by levying taxes (for example on polluting activities) and paying subsidies (for example for rail or bus transport) rather than direct state control. For Neo-Liberals, the solution to market failure is the discriminating use of public finance, not the indiscriminate use of public property rights.

Equity issues are also often used to justify collective property rights. It is often argued that market systems result in affluence for some and poverty and deprivation for others and that only state provision of public services can secure equitable (if not complete equality of) outcomes. In effect, this argument is that uncontrolled market systems result in an inequitable distribution of private property rights and the resulting income and wealth that they confer upon their owners. Again, however, the solution is not collectivisation of property rights but rather improving access to private property by poor or otherwise deprived groups. Again, access can be facilitated by public finance, as distinct from public property rights. Use of public finance for equity purposes is dealt with in more detail in Chapter 4.

CONCLUSIONS

This chapter has demonstrated the conditions under which public finance is necessary to promote the public interest by supporting the provision of services. However, it has also made clear that it is insufficient (and perhaps disingenuous) to use 'in the public interest' without clarification or qualification. That term denotes an extremely vague (and, at times, contentious) concept. This was illustrated by examining the public interest in terms of the 4Es, making clear that the 'public interest' does not facilitate robust decisions about which services should be supported by public finance nor about how they should be provided.

Hence, an attempt was made to develop a rigorous classification of services based on the concept of property rights. Consideration of the degree to which property rights are enforceable and sustainable allowed a distinction to be drawn between pure public goods, pure private goods and mixed goods. It was concluded that, in principle, public finance is required for efficiency purposes only for pure public goods and for rival but non-excludable mixed goods. In practice, however, use of public finance in such cases may exacerbate rather than ameliorate market failure and so the working rule is that its use should be restricted to the most severe forms of market failure, namely where sustainable provision by means of private finance is simply not possible.

It has also been made clear that justifying the use of public finance neither justifies public property rights nor public sector provision of services. Almost all so-called 'public services' are capable of being provided by the private sector to socially optimal levels as long as public finance is used to complement private finance where market failure occurs. Therefore, to say that *all* public services must be publicly owned and *fully* funded by public finance is based on an incomplete logic. Very few public services are pure community-level services and even those that are pure public goods can be provided largely (if not solely) on the basis of private property rights. Likewise, to say that all services yielding social benefits must be provided by the public sector is based on a gross overgeneralisation of the nature of a pure community-level service.

In short, it is not self-evident that all or most of the services currently provided by the public sectors of many countries should be largely or wholly supported by public finance or that they should be provided by the public sector itself. This suggests that the relative scale of both the public sector and public finance is higher than necessary to secure the particular levels of negative and positive rights thought appropriate in individual countries. The next chapter considers how to assess the relative scale of public finance.

FURTHER READING

Barzel, Y. (1997) *Economic Analysis of Property Rights* (second edition) (Cambridge: Cambridge University Press).

Brenner, C. (1998) *Intellectual Property Rights and Technology Transfer in Developing Country Agriculture: Rhetoric and Reality* OECD Development Centre Technical Papers No 133 (Paris: Organisation for Economic Co-operation and Development).

Coase, R. H. (1960) 'The Problem of Social Cost' *Journal of Law and Economics* vol. 3, no. 1, pp. 1–44.

Correa, C. M. (2000) *Intellectual Property Rights, the WTO and Developing Countries: The TRIPS Agreement and Policy Options* (London: Zed Books).

D'Auria, G., Tynan, N., Gillespie, C. and Thomas, J. (1999) *Property Rights and the Environment* IEA Studies on the Environment No. 13 (London: Institute of Economic Affairs).

Demsetz, H. (1967) 'Towards a Theory of Property Rights' *American Economic Review* vol. 57, pp. 347–59.

Drahos, P. and Mayne R. (2002) (editors) *Global Intellectual Property Rights: Knowledge, Access and Development* (Basingstoke: Palgrave Macmillan).

Dutfield, G. (2002) *Intellectual Property Rights, Trade and Biodiversity* (London: Earthscan).

Furubotn, E. G. and Pejovich, S. (1974) *The Economics of Property Rights* (Cambridge, MA: Ballinger Publishing).

Gordon, W. J. and Watt, R. (2003) (editors) *The Economics of Copyright: Developments in Research and Analysis* (Cheltenham: Edward Elgar).

Hardin, G. (1968) 'The Tragedy of the Commons' *Science* vol. 162, pp. 1243–8.

McKean, M. A. (1992) 'Success on the Commons: A Comparative Examination of Institutions for Common Property Resource Management' *Journal of Theoretical Politics* vol. 4, pp. 247–81.

Mortazavi, R. (1997) 'The Right of Public Access in Sweden' *Annals of Tourism Research* vol. 24, no. 3, pp. 609–23.

OECD (2001) *Policies to Enhance Sustainable Development* (Paris: Organisation for Economic Co-operation and Development).

O'Neill, J. (2001) 'Property, Care and Environment' *Environment and Planning C: Government and Policy* vol. 19, pp. 695–711.

Ostrom, E. (1990) *Governing the Commons: The Evolution of Institutions for Collective Action* (Cambridge: Cambridge University Press).

Thomson, K. (2002) *Treasures on Earth: Museums, Collections and Paradoxes* (London: Faber and Faber).

Tooley, J. (1998) *Education Without the State* (London: Institute of Economic Affairs).

Tooley, J. (2001) *The Global Education Industry: Lessons from Private Education in*

Developing Countries (second edition) (London: Institute of Economic Affairs).

Towse, R. (2002) (editor) *Copyright in the Cultural Industries* (Cheltenham: Edward Elgar).

Towse, R. and Holzhauer, R. (2002) (editors) *The Economics of Intellectual Property* (Cheltenham: Edward Elgar).

Webster, C. (2003) *Property Rights, Planning and Markets: Managing Spontaneous Cities* (Cheltenham: Edward Elgar).

West, E. G. (2001) (editor) *Education and the State: A Study in Political Economy* (third edition) (Indianapolis: Liberty Fund).

3 The Relative Scale of Public Finance

INTRODUCTION

Alternative philosophies for public finance were developed in Chapter 1. Those philosophies clearly have implications for the scale of public finance relative to the economy as a whole. However, philosophical stances alone cannot tell us whether public finance is too great, too small or just right. Their guidance is couched in strategic rather than precise terms. Whilst the Libertarian philosophy argues the case for less state intervention and the Collectivist philosophy for more, they do not provide precise guidance for the relative scale of public finances. Thus, even in respect of negative rights, Libertarians do not say precisely how much should be spent on law and order and so on. Clearly, the greater the protection against crime afforded to the citizen the greater the cost. But how great should that protection (and therefore cost) be? This indeterminacy of scale is exacerbated in the case of Neo-Liberal and Collectivist philosophies, since they provide little guidance as to the levels of public finance necessary for services yielding limited and full positive rights respectively.

Thus, Chapter 2 used property rights theory to consider which types of services definitely do need public finance if they are to be provided at all. It also considered other categories of services that may need greater or lesser amounts of public finance if they are to maximise social and economic efficiency and so welfare. It demonstrated that need for public finance does not necessarily require the replacement of private property rights by public property rights. Thus, to the extent that public finance and public property rights have become synonymous, the relative scale of public finance will be greater than is necessary to secure the desired mix of negative and positive rights.

Measures of scale must be constructed before the relative scale of public finance in any one country can be assessed. This chapter demonstrates the need to be concerned with more than just the relative size of public expenditure within the economy. It outlines the factors and processes that both affect and are affected by the various components of public finance. In so doing it demonstrates the symbiotic relationship between economy, society, political philosophy and the state of the public finances.

WHAT ARE THE PUBLIC FINANCE/GDP RATIOS?

The ratio between public finance and gross domestic product (GDP) is a measure of the proportion of total output in a country accounted for by the government sector. The relative sizes of the public and private sectors have recently been major issues of public policy in most countries. In particular, the resurgence of Neo-Liberalism (noted in Chapter 1) highlighted the possible adverse effects of a growing dependency culture.

GDP is not the only possible denominator but is thought to be the most accurate measure of the relative scale of public finance within the domestic economy. Gross national product (GNP) could also be used. A country's GDP is less than its GNP by the amount of earnings from overseas investments by its companies and citizens. Typically, therefore, the public finance ratio would be smaller for GNP than for GDP in developed countries. However, foreign earnings fluctuate from year to year due to changing rates of exchange between the home currency and the currencies of the countries where those investments have been made. They also fluctuate as the levels of economic activity in those countries fluctuate. Hence, the ratio of public finance to GDP is the more reliable indicator of the relative scale of public finance in terms of the domestic economy.

The public finance/GDP ratio most often referred to is the proportion of public expenditure within GDP. There are, however, four public finance/GDP ratios:

- public expenditure/GDP ratio
- tax/GDP ratio
- public sector borrowing/GDP ratio
- public sector debt/GDP ratio.

The 'public expenditure/GDP ratio' provides an indication of the balance between public sector and private sector provision. A ratio of, say, 40 per cent indicates that the public sector provides two-fifths of national output whilst the private sector provides three-fifths. It therefore provides an indication of the degree to which governments intervene in the economy and society in attempting to influence the availability and consumption of services such as education and health care. The discussion in Chapter 1 made clear that Collectivists favour very high public expenditure/GDP ratios, possibly greater than 70 per cent. Libertarians favour very low ratios, possibly less than 10 per cent. Neo-Liberals favour fairly low ratios, somewhere around 30 per cent being broadly representative.

Since public expenditure has to be financed, the higher the public expenditure/GDP ratio, the higher the tax/GDP ratio and/or the public sector borrowing/GDP ratio. Public sector borrowing in any one financial year necessarily leads to a rise in the public sector debt/GDP ratio. The only significant qualifications to these interdependencies are revenues from charges for use of public services (that is, user-charges) and from the sale of state assets to the private sector (see Chapter 5). User-charges are relatively minor and privatisation receipts are finite. Ultimately, therefore, the higher the public expenditure/GDP ratio, the greater the tax/GDP, borrowing/GDP and debt/GDP ratios.

The 'tax/GDP ratio' provides an indication of the extent to which the state appropriates citizens' incomes directly from employment, interest, dividends, capital gains and wealth or indirectly by taxing subsequent expenditure. The conventional wisdom is that no one likes paying taxes and the old adage is that there are only two certainties in life: payment of taxes and death. As noted in Chapter 1, high tax/GDP ratios are indicative of excessive government intervention for Libertarians and Neo-Liberals. For Collectivists, however, they are indicative of a strong cultural commitment amongst citizens to a relatively large public sector in general and welfare state in particular.

The 'public sector borrowing/GDP ratio' reflects the excess of public expenditure over public sector revenue. It can be affected by either or both of the following:

- *investment in long-lived physical infrastructure* such as roads, schools, and hospitals. Borrowing spreads costs over the successive generations benefiting from use of that infrastructure. In this way those who benefit bear the costs, consistent with 'intergenerational equity'.
- *the extent to which the current generation of taxpayers is living at the expense of future generations of taxpayers.* Intergenerational inequity results if borrowing (rather than current taxes or charges) is used to finance the consumption of services benefiting only the current generation, future generations ultimately having to foot the tax bill.

Public sector investment in physical infrastructure is only acceptable to Libertarians in exceptional circumstances, namely in delivering negative rights (see Chapter 1). Thus whilst Libertarians approve of such capital expenditures as those on government offices, courts, prisons and police stations, they do not approve of public sector capital expenditures on cultural and leisure facilities, libraries, schools and hospitals. Neo-Liberals accept a greater level of public sector investment may be necessary to deliver limited positive rights related to equality of opportunity. However, both Neo-Liberals and Libertarians believe that the private sector can and should play the major role in providing a country's physical infrastructure, for example rail and air transport, tolled roads and motorways, privately run hospitals and schools and so on. Thus, these political philosophies require the borrowing/GDP ratio to be small to very small respectively. In contrast, a high public sector borrowing/GDP ratio is acceptable to Collectivists if it helps promote social welfare and, in particular, equality of outcome.

Whatever the political philosophy, the public sector borrowing/GDP ratio will fall:

■   if those investments increase GDP by more than the costs of their provision. For this to happen, public sector investment must increase significantly the productive potential of the economy, for example by providing improved transport infrastructure.

■   if current income and current expenditure are in balance over the economic cycle, that is, as the economy moves from recession to recovery (see below). This is because GDP rises over the longer term as economic growth occurs. In this way the current generation lives within its financial means.

Thus borrowing does not get out of control (that is, become unsustainable in terms of the tax base) as long as governments adopt 'full-cycle balanced budgets'. Whilst governments may borrow to finance current expenditure in order to boost total spending in the economy and so (in theory) help their economies out of a recession, they must match those budget deficits with budget surpluses once the recession is over so that borrowing can be repaid.

The problem with this strategy is that it is difficult to determine the duration of the economic cycle (see below) and so difficult to ensure that borrowing is repaid within that cycle. Thus a more prudential strategy would be to adopt the 'golden rule'. This rule stipulates that borrowing by the public sector should not exceed its net capital spending (that is, gross capital spending less any revenues from the sale of state assets). Put simply, borrowing should not be used to finance current expenditure and should only be used to finance that part of capital expenditure not funded by capital receipts.

The European Union's (EU) requirement for its member states adopting the single currency (the euro) is that general government net borrowing (that is, gross borrowing less repayments of loans) should be no more than three per cent of GDP. Referred to as the 'Maastricht deficit', this is thought to be the maximum level of borrowing consistent with avoiding inflation and so safeguarding the value of the euro. Higher levels of borrowing may lead to inflation to the extent that the totality of spending in an economy exceeds the domestic production of goods and services. Prices therefore rise as a result of excess demand, the euro losing some of its purchasing power.

The 'public sector debt/GDP ratio' is a measure of the unavoidable commitment of public finance to paying the annual interest on that debt and also repaying over a period of years the original sums borrowed. Ultimately, therefore, the higher the public sector debt/GDP ratio the greater the prior claim on public finance. Repaying debt pre-empts use of public funds for other purposes, for example improving the provision of education and health care. These opportunity costs are additional to the financial costs of debt.

Libertarians and Neo-Liberals believe that, like taxation and borrowing, very high levels of public sector debt relative to GDP indicate unwarranted government intervention in the economy. They also believe that debt is highly undesirable on moral grounds and that governments, like households, should live within their financial means. Collectivists believe that public sector debt, like borrowing, is a means of pursuing social welfare in being necessary for financing public services when tax or other revenues are not immediately available. The EU's condition for member states adopting the euro is that the level of gross public debt should not exceed 60 per cent of GDP. Referred to as the 'Maastricht debt ratio', this is thought to be the maximum sustainable level of debt above which countries lose control of their public finances and so compromise the stability of the single currency union.

INTERPRETING THE PUBLIC FINANCE/GDP RATIOS

Whilst the four public finance/GDP ratios are clearly interlinked, they provide strategically different measures of the relative scale of public finance within national economies and strategically different implications for public policy. Any one measure gives only a partial indication of that scale, such that historical and international comparisons of a given ratio are likely to be seriously misleading. A number of examples aid appreciation of this point:

■ *A very stable tax/GDP ratio in a given country over the previous decade.* This suggests that governments of that country have prevented a rise in the ratio and so have the public finances closely under control. However, the capped tax/GDP ratio may have been achieved only by a substantial increase in very long-term public sector borrowing, such that the consequential rise in the tax/GDP ratio has merely been postponed.

■ *A secular rise in the public expenditure/GDP ratio of a given country over several decades.* This does not necessarily indicate comparable increases in any or all of the tax/GDP, borrowing/GDP or debt/GDP ratios. Instead, it may have been (at least partially) financed by progressively much greater use of charges for public services.

■ *An international comparison of public expenditure/GDP ratios across a group of countries made for a single year* is almost completely useless simply because it does not indicate trends in that ratio.

■ *An international comparison of public expenditure/GDP ratios over several years* is still not a particularly useful indicator of trends because it fails to recognise that all the public finance/GDP ratios necessarily fluctuate from year to year as economic activity fluctuates (see below). Those countries' economic fluctuations may not be synchronised, so that the public finance/GDP ratios are not strictly comparable at a given point or points in time.

■ *An international comparison of the public expenditure/GDP ratio over the medium to long terms* is heavily qualified because it gives no indication of the means by which public expenditures are financed across the group of countries being compared. Whilst trends and levels of the public expenditure/GDP ratio may be very similar for a group of countries, there may still be substantive differences in the levels and trends of the other public finance ratios.

Put simply, expenditure is only half of the picture of public finance: the other half is revenue. Any time-series or cross-sectional data relating to public finances must be interpreted with great caution. The main generic caveats are:

■ *data may only be partial* and thus not provide a comprehensive picture of public finance
■ *data is frequently subject to more than one interpretation*, especially if it is partial in nature
■ *conclusions are strongly influenced by choice of the base year*, radically different conclusions perhaps being reached using a different start year for the data series, for example at a different stage of the economic cycle
■ *conclusions are strongly influenced by the other countries chosen for comparison*, this caveat being of greater import the smaller the number of those countries
■ *conclusions drawn from data are applicable only to the period and/or countries to which they relate* and should not be used as the basis of blanket generalisations relating to other countries and periods
■ *data may not be standardised and so not truly or precisely comparable.* This caveat applies notwithstanding the increasing international standardisation of data series produced by organisations such as the Organisation for Economic Co-operation and Development, the International Monetary Fund and the World Bank. Definitional discrepancies are inevitable for any data series, particularly those provided for periods of several or more decades and/or for developed, developing and transition economies
■ *public finance data cannot provide an appreciation of the political philosophy underpinning the state sector*, cultural and historical contexts varying over time for each country.

Ultimately, therefore, data does not 'speak for itself' despite the frequent use of that colloquialism. This warning must be taken on board when examining the public finance ratios in the following section.

WHAT ARE THE ACTUAL PROPORTIONS OF PUBLIC FINANCE WITHIN GDP?

The public expenditure/GDP ratio

Table 3.1 reveals a slow and fairly steady rise in the government expenditure/GDP ratio during the 1960s for the OECD countries as a whole from 29 per cent in 1960 to just over 31 per cent in 1969, a rise of only two percentage points. During the 1970s the OECD ratio rose by six percentage points, being between 37 and 38 per cent of GDP during the second half of that decade. The ratio then exceeded 40 per cent during the first half of the 1980s, falling back to 37 per cent by the end of that decade. The ratio exceeded 40 per cent in only one year during the 1990s but fell below 37 per cent in only one year,

Table 3.1   *Government expenditure as a percentage of GDP*

	1960	1961	1962	1963	1964	1965	1966	1967	1968	1969	1970	1971	1972	1973	1974	1975
Australia	22.1	23.7	23.5	23.3	23.7	25.6	25.6	26.3	25.1	25.1	25.5	26.3	26.3	26.7	26.7	32.3
Austria	32.1	32.3	33.6	34.7	38.2	37.9	38.3	40.5	40.6	40.3	39.2	39.7	39.8	41.3	41.9	46.1
Belgium	30.3	29.8	30.5	31.5	30.8	32.3	33.5	34.5	36.3	36.1	36.5	38.0	38.8	39.1	39.4	44.5
Canada	28.9	30.0	30.0	29.5	28.9	29.1	30.1	32.1	33.0	33.5	35.7	36.6	37.2	36.0	37.4	40.8
CzechRepublic																
Denmark	24.8	27.1	28.1	28.6	28.4	29.9	31.7	34.3	36.3	36.3	40.2	43.0	42.6	42.1	45.9	48.2
Finland	26.8	26.0	27.4	29.2	30.5	31.3	32.5	33.4	33.4	31.8	31.3	32.1	32.5	31.2	32.2	36.3
France	34.6	35.7	37.0	38.0	38.4	38.5	39.0	39.0	40.3	39.6	38.9	38.3	38.3	38.5	39.7	43.5
Germany	32.4	33.8	35.6	36.4	36.1	36.7	36.9	38.8	39.2	38.8	38.7	40.1	40.8	41.5	44.6	48.9
Greece	17.4	17.4	18.4	18.7	19.8	20.6	21.5	23.6	23.5	22.5	22.4	22.8	22.0	21.1	25.0	26.7
Hungary																
Iceland	28.2	24.0	23.9	26.0	27.6	28.4	28.4	32.2	33.8	30.2	29.6	32.6	33.6	35.5	36.6	38.7
Ireland	28.0	29.7	29.5	30.5	31.8	33.1	33.6	34.8	35.2	36.6	39.6	40.5	38.8	39.0	43.0	46.6
Italy	30.1	29.4	30.5	31.1	31.8	34.3	34.3	33.7	34.7	34.2	34.2	36.6	38.6	37.8	37.9	43.2
Japan		17.4	19.0	19.3	19.1	20.0	20.3	19.3	19.3	19.3	19.4	20.8	21.8	22.1	24.5	27.3
Korea																
Luxembourg	30.5	30.3	32.2	32.1	32.3	33.3	35.0	37.5	37.3	34.1	33.1	36.3	37.0	35.7	36.1	48.9
Mexico																	
Netherlands	33.7	35.4	35.6	37.6	37.8	38.7	40.7	42.5	43.9	44.4	46.0	48.0	48.6	49.3	51.5	56.6
NewZealand																	
Norway	29.9	29.7	31.5	33.1	33.1	34.2	34.8	36.4	37.9	39.9	41.0	43.0	44.6	44.6	44.6	46.6
Poland																	
Portugal	17.0	19.3	18.8	20.3	20.4	20.1	20.3	20.9	20.9	20.9	21.6	21.3	22.7	21.3	24.7	30.3
SlovakRepublic																	
Spain		13.0	12.8	13.0	18.8	19.6	19.6	21.1	21.3	21.7	22.2	23.6	23.2	23.0	23.1	24.7
Sweden	31.1	31.0	32.4	34.7	35.0	36.1	38.3	40.1	42.8	43.1	43.7	45.8	46.6	45.1	48.5	49.3
Switzerland	17.2	18.0	18.5	18.6	19.3	19.7	20.1	20.4	20.7	21.8	21.3	21.9	21.9	24.2	25.5	28.7
Turkey			18	19.1	20.5	20.6	20.6	21.0	21.9	23.1	21.9	22.1	22.5			
UK	32.4	33.4	34.2	35.6	33.9	36.4	35.6	38.5	39.6	41.5	39.3	38.1	39.8	40.7	44.9	46.4
United States	27.5	29.0	28.9	28.9	28.4	27.9	29.2	31.2	31.3	30.9	32.3	32.3	32.0	31.3	32.9	35.6
Total OECD	**29.0**	**27.7**	**28.1**	**28.5**	**28.5**	**28.9**	**29.6**	**30.8**	**31.2**	**31.1**	**31.6**	**32.2**	**32.6**	**32.6**	**34.5**	**37.6**
Standard deviation	*5.4*	*6.4*	*6.9*	*7.2*	*6.6*	*6.8*	*7.0*	*7.5*	*7.9*	*7.9*	*8.2*	*8.5*	*8.7*	*8.5*	*8.7*	*8.9*

continued

Table 3.1 *continued*

	1976	1977	1978	1979	1980	1981	1982	1983	1984	1985	1986	1987	1988	1989	1990	1991
Australia	32.8	34.1	33.4	32.9	33.3	34.0	36.4		38.5	38.0	37.7	36.3	33.4	32.4	33.2	34.7
Austria	46.9	46.8	49.7	48.9	48.9	50.3	50.4		50.8	50.3	51.3	51.7	50.8	49.3	48.8	49.9
Belgium	45.1	46.6	47.9	49.4	51.2	55.7	56.2	56.3	62.8	57.1	56.3	54.3	52.2	50.5	50.4	51.5
Canada	39.4	40.3	40.8	39.3	40.9	41.8	46.0	46.8	46.8	45.2	44.6	43.2	42.5	43.0	45.7	48.9
CzechRepublic																
Denmark	47.8	48.9	50.6	53.2	56.2	60.0	60.9		60.3	59.3	55.7	57.3	54.2	54.3	53.6	54.5
Finland	37.3	38.6	38.2	37.4	37.2	38.1	39.9	40.3	43.4	42.3	43.3	43.8	42.7	41.0	44.4	52.7
France	44.0	44.2	45.2	45.5	46.4	49.1	50.8	51.5	52.0	51.9	51.2	50.2	49.9	48.9	49.5	50.0
Germany	48.0	48.0	47.7	47.6	48.4	49.2	49.4	48.6	48.1	45.6	45.0	45.3	44.9	43.5	43.8	44.2
Greece	27.4	29.0	29.9	29.7	30.5	36.8	37.6	38.3	40.2	43.8	42.9	43.1	41.4	43.1	47.4	43.8
Hungary																
Iceland	33.9	34.0	34.4	35.2	34.4				33.7	35.3	37.3	34.3	39.0	41.5	39.0	40.1
Ireland	46.3	44.3	44.9	47.7	51.9	54.6			54.0	50.7	50.6	48.1	45.4	39.2	39.9	41.3
Italy	42.2	42.5	46.1	45.5	46.1	51.4	54.9	57.4	47.1	49.7	49.6	49.4	49.5	50.3	52.9	54.0
Japan	27.9	29.0	31.1	31.6	32.4	34.5	34.4	34.8	32.9	29.4	29.6	30.0	29.4	28.9	30.5	30.3
Korea										17.6	16.9	16.0	16.2	17.3	18.3	19.4
Luxembourg	49.7	52.7	51.8	52.8	54.3				51.8	51.7	51.0				41.3	43.3
Mexico																
Netherlands	56.6	54.6	55.9	58.0	59.5	61.2	63.6		61.0	51.9	52.0	53.3	51.3	48.9	49.4	49.5
NewZealand											51.8	48.1	49.1	47.5	48.1	45.3
Norway	48.5	50.1	52.3	50.9	48.9	48.5	48.7	48.9	46.3	41.5	45.4	47.7	49.5	49.1	49.7	50.6
Poland																
Portugal	35.1	35.2	36.4	35.8	25.2	42.5			44.4	39.9	40.3	38.9	37.5	36.7	39.6	42.0
SlovakRepublic																
Spain	26.0	27.5	29.3	30.5	32.4	34.1	36.6		39.3	39.7	40.6	39.6	39.0	40.7	41.6	42.7
Sweden	52.2	58.0	59.7	61.0	62.1	65.1	66.8		63.5	60.4	58.6	54.8	55.2	55.1	55.9	58.9
Switzerland	30.2	30.4	30.2	29.9	29.3	28.9	30.1	30.8	31.4	31.0	30.5	30.1	30.5	30.2	30.9	32.5
Turkey																
UK	45.6	43.7	43.3	43.1	45.1	47.8	47.3	47.2	49.8	51.3	51.1	40.5	38.1	37.3	39.1	41.1
United States	34.5	33.4	32.8	33.0	35.0	35.3	37.7	38.1	35.5	33.8	34.2	33.9	32.9	32.8	33.6	34.2
Total OECD	**37.2**	**37.1**	**37.6**	**37.7**	**39.0**	**40.6**	**42.2**	**41.6**	**41.0**	**38.7**	**38.8**	**37.9**	**37.1**	**36.8**	**37.9**	**38.6**
Standard deviation	*8.8*	*8.9*	*9.2*	*9.6*	*10.6*	*10.4*	*10.7*	*8.4*	*9.7*	*10.4*	*9.9*	*9.8*	*9.5*	*9.2*	*8.9*	*9.0*

continued

being forecast to remain at 37 per cent during the first few years of the new millennium.

The rise in the OECD public expenditure/GDP ratio above 40 per cent was associated with falls in GDP during the economic recessions of the early 1980s (some sharp falls) and early 1990s (less severe falls) in major countries. Nevertheless, the ratio in the late 1990s was almost ten percentage points higher than in the early 1960s. Clearly, the relative scale of public expenditure had increased substantially over the 40-year period, rising much faster than GDP.

Of course, some countries had ratios higher than the OECD average and some below. Government expenditure exceeded 40 per cent of GDP in the EU as a whole every year from 1974 onwards, exceeding 50 per cent in 1982, 1983 and 1993. The situation was much the same during the 1990s in the three EU accession countries for which data is available (that is, the Czech Republic,

Table 3.1 *continued*

	1992	1993	1994	1995	1996	1997	1998	1999	2000	2001*	2002*	2003*
Australia	36.4	36.5	35.6	35.7	34.9	33.7	33.3	32.9	32.6	33.3	33.2	32.9
Austria	50.5	53.3	52.6	52.5	52.0	49.8	50.1	49.5	47.9	47.9	47.5	46.6
Belgium	51.5	53.0	51.1	50.2	50.1	48.6	48.0	47.4	46.7	46.3	46.0	45.7
Canada	49.9	48.7	46.3	45.0	43.1	40.5	40.2	38.7	37.7	37.8	38.6	38.4
CzechRepublic		43.9	44.8	43.9	43.2	42.6	41.5	43.9	45.8	46.6	48.5	46.2
Denmark	55.5	58.1	58.0	56.6	56.3	54.4	53.4	51.8	49.9	49.4	49.6	49.4
Finland	57.7	59.1	57.5	54.3	54.0	51.3	48.1	47.1	43.9	44.6	45.3	44.5
France	51.7	53.9	53.8	53.5	53.8	52.8	52.1	51.8	51.0	50.8	50.9	50.4
Germany	45.0	46.2	45.9	46.3	47.3	46.5	46.0	46.2	43.3	45.7	46.2	45.2
Greece	45.9	48.1	46.0	54.6	52.4	50.8	50.7	52.1	52.3	51.0	50.5	49.7
Hungary		59.8	63.4	56.2	53.2	52.2	53.1	50.0	48.2	48.1	48.0	48.2
Iceland	40.5	40.4	39.9	39.2	38.6	37.2	37.7	39.1	38.5	39.9	40.3	39.7
Ireland	41.7	41.3	41.1	38.0	36.4	34.2	32.2	31.9	29.3	30.0	30.9	31.2
Italy	53.2	55.4	52.7	51.1	51.3	48.5	47.3	46.7	44.4	45.3	44.7	44.7
Japan	31.0	32.8	33.3	34.4	34.9	33.8	34.8	35.9	36.6	36.9	37.4	37.4
Korea	20.6	20.1	19.7	19.3	20.7	21.5	24.1	23.3	23.1	24.6	25.1	24.9
Luxembourg	43.6	44.3	42.4	43.3	43.3	40.8	40.0	40.1	38.1	39.3	40.5	40.1
Mexico						20.0	18.8	45.8				
Netherlands	50.0	49.9	47.6	47.7	45.6	44.4	43.4	43.3	41.6	41.3	41.6	41.4
NewZealand	44.8	41.4	39.3	38.6	37.6	38.4	39.5	39.0	38.6	38.9	39.9	40.0
Norway	52.0	51.0	49.9	47.6	45.4	43.8	46.3	45.8	40.8	40.8	42.4	41.5
Poland		54.3	49.4	47.0	46.1	45.6	43.8	43.4	43.8	46.1	46.1	45.9
Portugal	42.6	44.2	42.7	41.3	41.6	40.0	40.2	40.6	40.8	40.7	40.0	39.7
SlovakRepublic						56.3						
Spain	43.9	47.2	45.1	44.0	42.8	41.2	40.6	39.6	38.8	38.1	38.1	37.9
Sweden	64.3	67.5	64.8	61.9	59.9	58.0	55.5	55.1	52.7	52.9	53.0	52.8
Switzerland	34.9	36.7	33.7	33.5	34.2							
Turkey												
UK	43.0	43.2	42.6	42.2	40.7	38.9	37.7	37.1	37.0	38.4	39.4	39.8
United States	34.8	34.1	33.1	32.9	32.4	31.4	30.5	30.2	29.9	30.4	31.2	30.6
Total OECD	**39.5**	**40.3**	**39.4**	**39.2**	**39.0**	**37.3**	**36.8**	**37.5**	**36.6**	**37.2**	**37.7**	**37.3**
Standarddeviation	*9.4*	*10.0*	*9.9*	*9.2*	*8.8*	*9.3*	*9.2*	*7.6*	*7.4*	*7.1*	*6.9*	*6.7*

* Projection

Notes: Government expenditure consists of current disbursements, gross capital formation and purchases of land and intangible assets. The weighted averages have been calculated based on the weightings provided in OECD (2001b)

Sources: OECD (1983a) Table R8; OECD (1985) Table 6.5; OECD (1999) Table 6.5; OECD (2001b) Annex Table 28

Hungary and Poland, no data being available for the Slovak Republic or Turkey). Figure 3.1 makes clear the increasing disparity between these two groups of countries (even more so for those in the Eurozone) and the OECD average over the period as a whole.

The highest ratios occurred in Sweden, ratios exceeding 50 per cent of GDP every year from 1976 to 1999, and likewise Denmark from 1978. In Sweden, ratios exceeded 60 per cent at the end of the 1970s, early 1980s and early 1990s, approaching 70 per cent at the height of recession in 1982. The ratio also exceeded 60 per cent in Denmark and Netherlands (1981–84) and Hungary (1994). In sharp contrast, although rising over the period as a

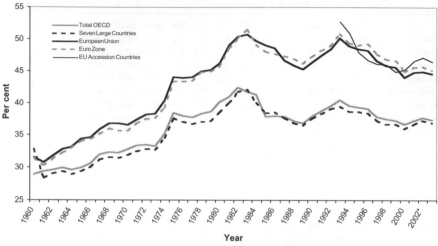

Note: Seven large countries are Canada, France, Germany, Italy, Japan, the UK and the USA. EU accession countries are the Czech Republic, Hungary, Poland, the Slovak Republic and Turkey

Figure 3.1 Government expenditure as a percentage of GDP: OECD versus EU and large economies

Source: Table 3.1

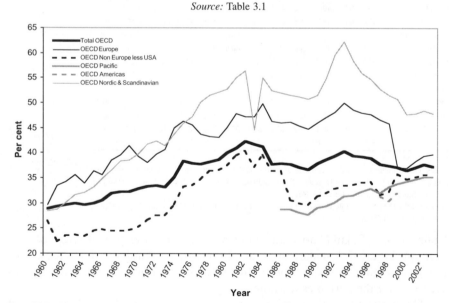

Note: OECD Europe includes all European countries who are OECD members. OECD non-Europe less USA consists of Australia, Canada, Japan, Korea, Mexico and New Zealand. OECD Pacific is Australia, Japan, Korea and New Zealand; OECD Americas is Canada, Mexico and the USA; OECD Nordic and Scandinavian is Denmark, Finland, Iceland, Norway and Sweden

Figure 3.2 Government expenditure as a percentage of GDP: OECD versus Europe and non-European nations

Source: Table 3.1

whole, the government expenditure/GDP ratio never reached 40 per cent in Australia, Japan, Switzerland, or the USA. In Korea, the ratio never exceeded 25 per cent.

Clearly, the scale of public finance as measured by the government expenditure/GDP ratio is twice as great in some countries than in others. Nevertheless, the general picture is one of a fluctuating rise from between a quarter and a third at the beginning of the 1960s to between a third and two-fifths at the end of the millennium. It has to be noted, however, that the trend for the OECD 'weighted average' is driven by Canada, France, Germany, Italy, Japan, the UK and the USA (see Figure 3.1), these seven large countries together constituting a combined weighting of over three-quarters of the average over the period. Notwithstanding the influence of France, Germany and the UK increasing that average, Figure 3.2 makes clear that the relative scale of public finance in European countries has consistently been much greater than the OECD average, at least until the very late 1990s. The graph also makes clear that the relative scale of public finance has consistently been much greater in European countries than in non-European countries, although there is convergence towards the end of the 1990s. The reasons for convergence are discussed in Chapter 7.

Table 3.1 also shows that the standard deviation ended the period at almost the same level at which it started after rising particularly sharply during the early 1980s (a rise indicating a greater dispersal of data around the 'unweighted average'). Nonetheless, the spread between the high and low outliers increased substantially during the early and middle part of the period.

The tax/GDP ratio

It could reasonably be expected that the trend in the tax/GDP ratio would be very similar to that of the government expenditure/GDP ratio. Certainly, the ratio was higher at the end of the period than at the beginning (see Table 3.2). However, the rise in the tax/GDP ratio (by 6.7 percentage points) was significantly less than the rise in the government expenditure/GDP ratio (8.6) comparing 1965 and 1999 (tax data only being available since 1965). In between those years, there was clearly a marked difference in the growth of the two ratios:

- during the second half of the 1960s the tax/GDP ratio grew more than the expenditure/GDP ratio (3.6 and 2.2 percentage points respectively)
- during the 1970s the tax/GDP ratio grew by less than half the rise in the expenditure/GDP ratio (2.8 and 6.1 percentage points respectively)
- during the 1980s the tax/GDP ratio rose whereas the expenditure/GDP ratio fell (plus 2.0 and minus 2.2 percentage points respectively)
- during the 1990s the tax/GDP ratio again rose whilst the expenditure/GDP ratio again fell (by plus 1.8 and minus 0.4 percentage points respectively).

Table 3.2   *Taxation as a percentage of GDP*

	1965	1966	1967	1968	1969	1970	1971	1972	1973	1974	1975	1976	1977	1978
Australia	23.8	23.9	24.7	24.5	25.3	25.5	26.0	25.0	26.6	28.6	29.1	29.7	29.7	28.9
Austria	34.6	35.4	35.3	35.3	35.8	35.7	36.5	37.1	37.6	38.4	38.5	38.5	39.4	41.8
Belgium	31.2	33.3	34.0	34.8	35.0	36.0	36.2	36.4	37.4	38.3	41.1	41.5	42.8	44.1
Canada	25.9	27.6	28.8	29.6	32.0	32.0	31.2	31.8	31.3	33.9	32.9	32.5	31.8	31.6
CzechRepublic														
Denmark	30.1	32.7	33.1	36.2	35.7	40.2	43.4	42.7	42.0	44.0	41.1	40.9	41.3	42.9
Finland	30.1	31.4	32.3	32.6	31.1	32.1	33.6	33.8	34.5	33.7	38.2	39.9	39.5	36.4
France	35.0	34.8	35.2	35.4	36.3	35.6	35.1	35.3	35.7	36.3	37.4	35.4	39.5	39.6
Germany	31.6	32.2	32.2	32.1	33.9	32.8	33.2	34.7	36.3	36.3	36.7	36.7	37.9	37.6
Greece	20.6	22.2	23.3	24.3	24.4	24.3	24.4	24.6	23.2	24.0	24.6	27.3	27.6	27.9
Hungary														
Iceland														
Ireland	26.0	28.1	28.9	29.1	29.8	31.2	32.4	31.1	31.5	32.1	32.5	36.1	35.2	33.9
Italy	27.3	27.0	28.0	28.8	28.2	27.9	28.7	28.5	26.3	28.3	29.0	30.3	30.9	31.3
Japan	18.1	17.6	18.0	17.7	18.2	19.7	20.0	20.7	22.5	23.0	21.1	21.6	22.6	24.3
Korea														
Luxembourg	30.8	30.7	30.9	29.8	30.2	31.9	34.1	34.9	35.2	36.4	43.6	44.3	49.0	50.3
Mexico														
Netherlands	35.5	37.0	38.1	38.8	39.1	39.1	41.7	42.5	43.7	44.4	45.8	45.4	46.3	47.0
NewZealand	24.3	25.1	24.9	24.7	24.8	26.4	26.8	28.4	28.0	31.4	30.0	30.1	32.7	30.8
Norway	33.2	34.5	36.5	37.6	39.1	39.2	42.4	44.8	45.2	44.7	44.8	48.2	47.2	48.4
Poland														
Portugal	18.6	19.1	19.9	19.9	20.7	23.2	22.9	22.6	22.1	22.6	24.8	29.0	27.5	26.5
SlovakRepublic														
Spain	14.7	13.7	17.2	16.4	16.9	17.2	17.4	18.4	19.0	18.2	15.6	15.6	21.5	22.7
Sweden	35.6	36.4	37.6	39.8	40.8	40.9	41.6	43.0	42.2	43.2	44.2	48.5	50.8	51.4
Switzerland	20.7	21.5	21.6	22.6	23.7	23.8	23.5	23.9	26.3	27.3	29.6	31.2	31.6	31.6
Turkey	14.9	15.1	16.1	15.9	17.2	17.6	19.4	19.1	19.6	17.9	20.7	21.2	21.7	21.3
UK	30.8	32.0	33.1	34.8	36.6	37.5	35.3	34.0	31.9	35.4	36.1	35.7	35.5	34.0
United States	26.5	26.9	28.1	27.5	30.1	30.1	28.8	29.6	29.7	30.2	30.2	29.3	30.3	30.2
Weighted averages	**26.1**	**26.5**	**27.4**	**27.3**	**28.9**	**29.1**	**28.7**	**29.3**	**29.5**	**30.3**	**30.3**	**30.1**	**31.2**	**31.4**
Standard deviation	*6.5*	*6.9*	*6.8*	*7.2*	*7.3*	*7.2*	*7.6*	*7.8*	*7.8*	*8.0*	*8.4*	*8.6*	*8.6*	*8.9*

continued

Hence, the two ratios give radically different measures of changes in the relative scale of public finance, especially in the short to medium term. As will be explained in more detail below, recessions tend to cause the public expenditure/GDP ratio to rise (spending on unemployment benefits rises as GDP falls) but the effect on the tax/GDP ratio is muted (tax receipts fall as profits, incomes and expenditures fall). Thus, there is much more variability in the expenditure/GDP ratio given the recessions of the early 1980s and 90s. The comparisons of 1980 with 1989 and 1990 with 1999 are clearly much less satisfactory for the expenditure/GDP ratio than for the tax/GDP ratio, the recessions making those years not fully comparable for either ratio. This emphasises both the need to take a long-term approach and to consider all years, any one year possibly being unrepresentative. This is facilitated by Figures 3.3 and 3.4.

Table 3.2 continued

	1979	1980	1981	1982	1983	1984	1985	1986	1987	1988	1989	1990	1991	1992
Australia	25.8	27.5	27.9	28.3	27.5	29.0	29.1	30.0	29.9	29.6	29.4	29.4	27.7	27.2
Austria	41.4	39.8	41.0	39.8	39.4	41.2	41.9	41.9	41.5	41.5	40.4	40.4	40.9	42.4
Belgium	44.7	42.5	42.5	44.2	44.4	45.5	45.8	45.5	46.0	44.5	42.8	43.1	43.2	43.3
Canada	31.0	32.5	34.3	33.9	33.9	33.7	33.6	34.3	35.7	35.0	35.9	36.6	37.3	37.0
CzechRepublic														
Denmark	44.1	43.9	43.7	42.8	44.8	46.1	47.4	49.3	50.0	50.4	49.3	47.1	46.9	47.3
Finland	35.0	36.2	38.1	37.0	36.8	38.4	40.0	41.6	39.6	42.3	42.6	44.7	46.1	45.9
France	41.2	40.6	40.9	41.9	42.6	43.6	43.8	43.4	43.8	43.1	42.9	43.0	43.2	43.1
Germany	37.3	33.1	32.7	32.6	32.4	32.5	32.9	32.7	32.9	32.7	33.3	32.6	36.8	37.7
Greece	27.7	24.2	24.3	27.5	27.9	28.6	28.6	30.0	30.5	27.6	26.7	29.3	29.4	30.4
Hungary													45.9	45.7
Iceland		28.9	29.9	30.2	27.8	29.4	28.1	28.1	28.6	31.2	32.1	31.0	31.2	32.0
Ireland	33.8	31.4	32.5	33.9	35.3	36.1	35.0	35.8	36.0	37.2	33.9	33.5	34.1	34.4
Italy	31.0	30.4	31.6	33.8	35.8	34.9	34.4	35.9	36.1	36.7	37.8	38.9	39.3	41.7
Japan	24.8	25.7	26.2	26.5	27.0	27.2	27.5	28.2	29.5	29.9	30.2	30.7	29.9	28.2
Korea		17.7	17.5	17.7	18.2	17.2	16.9	16.5	16.9	17.0	18.0	19.1	18.7	19.4
Luxembourg	46.2	39.8	41.2	42.3	44.6	43.2	44.4	42.7	42.3	41.1	39.7	40.5	39.5	38.8
Mexico		16.2	15.7	16.0	17.9	17.4	17.0	16.2	17.2	16.6	17.2	17.3	17.3	17.6
Netherlands	47.4	43.4	42.8	43.1	44.2	42.6	42.4	43.1	45.6	45.7	43.1	42.8	45.3	44.9
NewZealand	31.2	33.0	33.9	34.6	32.3	32.5	33.6	33.9	37.1	36.5	39.1	38.0	36.6	37.0
Norway	46.1	42.7	44.4	43.6	42.5	41.7	43.3	45.5	43.7	43.1	41.3	41.8	41.8	41.0
Poland													37.2	38.2
Portugal	25.8	24.4	25.9	26.5	28.0	27.5	26.9	28.4	26.8	28.6	29.2	29.4	30.6	32.7
SlovakRepublic														
Spain	23.3	22.9	24.1	24.3	26.1	27.3	27.6	29.3	31.2	31.4	33.1	33.0	33.3	34.3
Sweden	50.3	47.5	48.9	47.9	48.5	48.1	48.5	50.8	53.5	52.8	53.3	53.6	51.9	49.5
Switzerland	31.1	28.9	29.0	29.7	30.4	30.6	30.2	31.3	31.1	31.4	30.8	30.6	30.3	30.8
Turkey	20.8	17.9	19.0	18.4	17.2	14.3	13.4	17.5	10.0	17.0	10.7	20.0	21.0	22.4
UK	34.0	35.2	36.7	39.1	37.5	37.7	37.6	38.0	37.0	37.0	36.4	35.9	35.2	34.7
United States	31.3	27.0	27.5	27.2	25.6	25.5	26.1	25.9	27.1	26.8	27.0	26.7	26.8	26.6
Weighted averages	**31.9**	**29.0**	**29.6**	**29.8**	**29.5**	**29.5**	**29.8**	**30.1**	**30.9**	**30.8**	**31.0**	**31.0**	**31.5**	**31.4**
Standard deviation	*8.6*	*8.8*	*8.9*	*8.8*	*8.9*	*9.2*	*9.4*	*9.6*	*9.5*	*9.5*	*9.0*	*8.8*	*8.7*	*8.4*

continued

As was the case for government expenditure (see Figure 3.1), Figure 3.3 shows that the EU (and within that the Eurozone) countries have again been significantly above the OECD average in terms of their tax/GDP ratio. Whilst the accession countries also exceed the OECD average they have been much below the EU's tax/GDP ratios, whereas they were very close to and sometimes above the EU government expenditure/GDP ratios. Figure 3.4 shows that, as for government expenditure, European countries exceeded the OECD averages for tax/GDP ratios, non-European countries again being below the average.

Figures 3.3 and 3.4 also make clear the much steadier rise in the tax/GDP ratio over the period as a whole than in the government expenditure/GDP ratio (Figures 3.1 and 3.2). This is confirmed by comparing the standard deviation data in Tables 3.1 and 3.2. The standard deviations for both sets of data in

Table 3.2   continued

	1993	1994	1995	1996	1997	1998	1999
Australia	27.4	28.7	29.4	30.2	29.9	29.8	30.6
Austria	42.7	42.6	41.6	43.5	44.3	44.2	43.9
Belgium	43.9	45.4	44.8	45.0	45.6	45.9	45.7
Canada	36.6	36.6	36.6	37.2	38.0	38.3	38.2
CzechRepublic	42.9	41.3	40.1	39.3	38.6	38.1	40.4
Denmark	48.8	49.9	49.4	49.9	49.8	49.5	50.4
Finland	44.6	46.6	44.9	47.3	46.1	45.9	46.2
France	43.3	43.7	44.0	45.0	45.2	45.1	45.8
Germany	37.9	38.1	38.2	37.4	37.0	37.0	37.7
Greece	30.9	31.2	31.7	31.8	33.4	35.7	37.1
Hungary	46.5	44.0	42.4	40.7	39.0	38.8	39.2
Iceland	31.2	30.6	31.2	32.4	32.2	34.1	36.3
Ireland	34.4	35.5	32.8	32.9	32.2	31.7	32.3
Italy	44.2	41.4	41.2	42.7	44.2	42.5	43.3
Japan	28.1	27.1	27.9	27.8	27.9	26.8	26.2
Korea	19.9	20.4	20.5	21.4	22.7	22.9	23.6
Luxembourg	41.6	41.9	41.7	43.1	41.4	41.1	41.8
Mexico	17.7	17.2	16.6	16.6	17.5	16.5	16.8
Netherlands	45.2	43.0	41.9	41.5	41.9	40.9	42.1
NewZealand	36.9	37.3	38.0	36.1	36.4	35.5	35.6
Norway	40.1	41.3	41.5	41.5	42.4	43.4	41.6
Poland	42.4	40.4	39.6	39.4	38.8	37.6	35.2
Portugal	31.0	31.8	32.5	32.2	32.8	33.5	34.3
SlovakRepublic						37.1	35.3
Spain	33.5	33.5	32.8	32.6	33.6	34.1	35.1
Sweden	48.4	48.7	47.6	49.8	51.2	51.6	52.2
Switzerland	31.9	32.7	33.1	33.9	33.5	34.6	34.4
Turkey	22.7	22.2	22.6	25.4	27.9	28.4	31.3
UK	33.3	33.9	35.1	35.0	35.2	37.1	36.3
United States	26.9	27.3	27.6	27.9	28.3	28.8	28.9
Weighted averages	**31.7**	**31.7**	**31.9**	**32.1**	**32.5**	**32.6**	**32.8**
Standard deviation	*8.6*	*8.5*	*8.1*	*8.2*	*7.9*	*7.7*	*7.7*

Notes: Data not available prior to 1965. The weighted averages
have been calculated based on the weightings in OECD (2001b).
Taxation includes all taxation levied by government on income,
social security, payroll and salaries, property, goods and services
and other minor taxes
Source: OECD (1981) Table 3; OECD (2001d) Table 3

these two tables rose over the period as a whole, peaked in the 1980s and were
closely matched at both the beginning and end of the period. Nevertheless, the
measures of dispersion around the average were greater for expenditure than
for tax in the 1970s and 80s. Figures 3.3 and 3.4 also make clear that there has
been little change in the rising trend for the tax/GDP ratio, despite the displacement caused by the early 1980s recession. In contrast, Figures 3.1 and
3.2 suggest that the previously rising trend in the government expenditure/
GDP ratio reversed at the start of the 1980s, in European countries at least.

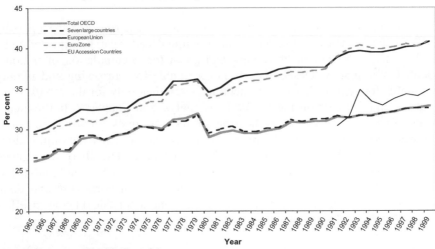

Note: Groups are as defined in Figure 3.1

Figure 3.3 Taxation as a percentage of GDP:
OECD versus EU and large economies
Source: Table 3.2

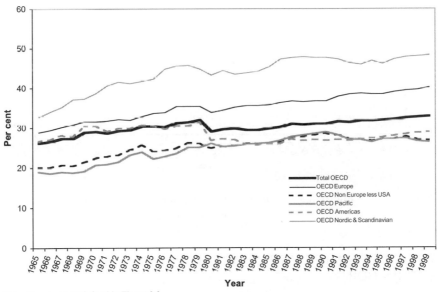

Note: Groups are as defined in Figure 3.2

Figure 3.4 Taxation as a percentage of GDP: OECD
versus Europe and non-European nations
Source: Table 3.2

The public sector borrowing/GDP and public sector debt/GDP ratios

The smaller rise in the tax/GDP ratio over the full period and the opposite movements in the two ratios during intervening decades can be expected to be reflected in government borrowing and so in the accumulation of national debt. Unfortunately, OECD data is not available for borrowing and is only available for central government debt and even then only for the 1990s. Central government debt during the 1990s is analysed in Chapter 7. In the meantime, Figure 3.5 gives an indication of the (at times growing) disparity between government expenditure and tax revenues and hence the implications for borrowing and debt for the OECD as a whole. The sharp divergence between the expenditure and tax ratios between the mid-1970s and mid-1980s can only have been accommodated by an increase in borrowing and debt, other sources of income (such as user-charges and asset sales) being insufficiently flexible to bridge the yawning gap.

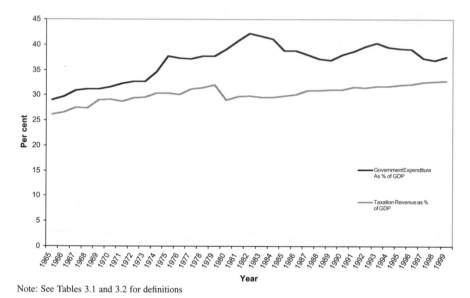

Note: See Tables 3.1 and 3.2 for definitions

Figure 3.5 Total OECD expenditure versus taxation
Sources: Tables 3.1 and 3.2

WHAT DETERMINES THE SHARE OF PUBLIC FINANCE WITHIN GDP?

The four public finance/GDP ratios vary as a result of changes in both the numerator and denominator. For example, the public expenditure/GDP ratio will rise if:

- public expenditure rises whilst GDP remains constant
- public expenditure is unchanged but GDP falls
- public expenditure rises faster than GDP.

Changes in the four ratios occur either as a deliberate act of government (for example a sharp rise in public expenditure financed by a combination of increased borrowing, debt and taxation) or as a result of fluctuating economic activity. In the latter case, the ratios tend to rise as an economy moves from a highly prosperous state of full employment into a looming recession. This occurs if similar events happen amongst the home country's trading partners, with the result that its exports of manufactured goods fall as consumers in those other countries reduce their expenditures on imports. The resulting rise in unemployment in the home country automatically leads to increased public spending on welfare benefits. Workers made redundant by manufacturing companies register themselves as unemployed with the appropriate government offices and consequently claim unemployment-related social security benefits. Thus public expenditure rises automatically as GDP falls and so the ratio rises.

Recession also leads to a fall in tax revenues. This is because incomes, profits and expenditures fall during a recession as companies sell fewer products and as workers lose their jobs or opportunity to work overtime. The impact on the tax/GDP ratio depends on which falls fastest: tax revenues or GDP.

Unless the government of the home country immediately cuts the levels and/or eligibility for those unemployment benefits or has a substantial budget surplus from which to finance those increased payments of social security, it has to borrow from the private sector by selling government bonds. Hence, public sector borrowing increases and so, consequently, does public debt as GDP falls. Thus, their respective ratios to GDP rise as a result. The borrowing/GDP ratio is likely to rise particularly sharply because, typically, public sector borrowing is the relatively small residual of two very large sums: public expenditure and government revenues. Hence, even a small percentage rise in public expenditure combined with a small percentage fall in tax and other revenues leads to a large percentage rise in government borrowing. Likewise, the impact on the debt/GDP ratio will tend to be less than on the borrowing/GDP ratio simply because the stock of public sector debt is usually very large relative to the flow of government borrowing.

The effect on the tax/GDP ratio tends to be less marked because, whilst the movements of public expenditure, borrowing and debt are in the opposite direction to that of GDP, both tax revenues and GDP move in the same direction (in this example, fall). The outcome for the ratio (that is, whether it rises, falls or remains constant) depends on just how highly progressive is the system of taxation. At one extreme, a tax structure composed largely of flat-rate poll taxes unrelated to incomes, profits and expenditures would see a sharp rise in the tax/GDP ratio because tax revenues would remain largely unchanged as GDP fell. At the other extreme, a highly progressive tax system, taking large proportions of high incomes, profits and expenditures and low proportions of low incomes, profits and expenditures, would see its tax take fall sharply as GDP fell, such that the rise in the tax/GDP ratio would be limited.

In general, during times of economic prosperity, the faster the growth of GDP, the lower each of the four public finance ratios. This is more likely to be the case the more public expenditure is used to finance economically productive investments and the smaller any disincentive-to-work and disincentive-to-enterprise effects of taxation (see Chapter 6). Economically productive investments could include not just those in physical infrastructure (for example in transport systems to facilitate the movement of goods) but also those in human capital (for example using borrowing to finance training in vocational skills required by companies). In both examples, public expenditure leads to a rise in GDP greater than the monetary value of that public expenditure. This could lead to a subsequent increase in tax revenues derived from the increased incomes and profits facilitated by economically productive investments.

The three essential conditions for the public expenditure/GDP ratio to fall are that:

1. public expenditure does not directly replace private expenditure (otherwise the ratio would rise since GDP would remain constant)
2. no disincentive-to-work and enterprise effects occur as a result of that expenditure or its financing (otherwise GDP would fall and so the ratio would rise)
3. public sector investments improve the productive potential of the economy by a much greater monetary amount than their total financing costs.

The third condition reflects the fact that public expenditure is less than GDP in mixed economies. Thus, the proportionate impact on public expenditure of a given increase in that spending is greater than the proportionate impact on GDP. A simple example illustrates this point, assuming that the first two conditions are met.

Assume GDP is 1000 billion euros, of which public expenditure is 500 billion. Thus, the public expenditure/GDP ratio is 0.5. Now assume public expenditure increases by 10 billion euros, that is, 2 per cent. However, GDP only increases by 1 per cent, from 1000 billion to 1010 billion euros. The public expenditure/GDP ratio is now 0.505 (that is, 510 divided by 1010). GDP would have to rise to 1020 billion euros for the ratio to remain at 0.5 and to more than that if the ratio was to fall. Thus, in order for the ratio to remain stable or fall, GDP would have to rise by at least the *rate of increase* in public expenditure. This means that if the public sector accounts for *half of GDP*, then every extra euro (or other currency unit) of public expenditure must be matched by an extra euro of private expenditure if the public expenditure/ GDP ratio is not to rise.

If the public sector accounts for *less than half of GDP*, it must attract additional private expenditure of an amount greater than the additional public expenditure for the ratio to remain constant or fall. The above example can be modified slightly to illustrate this point. GDP is still 1000 billion euros, but public expenditure is now 400 billion, increasing to 410 billion. So GDP would have to rise to 1025 billion for the ratio to remain at 0.4, meaning private sector expenditure has to rise by 15 billion.

If, however, the public sector accounts for *more than half of GDP*, it has only to attract additional private expenditure of an amount somewhat less than the extra public expenditure in order that the public expenditure ratio does not rise. Again modifying the example, GDP equals 1000 billion euros, public expenditure is now 600 billion, increasing to 610 billion. So GDP would have to rise to only 1017 billion for the ratio to remain at 0.6, meaning private sector expenditure has to rise by only 7 billion.

These examples are broadly representative of the range of ratios in Table 3.1. They emphasise the need to ensure that public expenditures are spent as productively as possible. If governments of mixed economies are to increase public expenditure whilst reducing (or, at least, avoiding a rise in) their public expenditure/GDP ratios, they must ensure that the extra public expenditures 'lever in' additional private sector expenditure through highly productive public sector investments in human and physical capital. This at least partly accounts for the increasing emphasis in many countries on a complementary mix of public and private finance (see Chapter 5). Ironically, those countries with a predominant state sector will generally find it easier to reduce the public expenditure/GDP ratio whilst still increasing public expenditure in absolute terms, as made clear by the above examples.

However, social security benefits are simply cash transfers from the tax-payer to the beneficiary via the social security budget. They therefore do not add directly to GDP because they do not lead to increased public sector pro-curement of goods and services. Instead, spending power is simply transferred from taxpayer to beneficiary. The only exception to this rule is when receipt of social security benefits is made conditional upon the recipient undertaking vocational training or taking subsidised employment, GDP rising in both cases. Typically, a substantial proportion of social security budgets is accounted for by state pensions, retired pensioners clearly not having to train or work as a condition of receipt of their pensions. Thus, in general, the greater the unconditional redistribution of income through the tax and social security systems, the greater the impact on both the public expenditure/GDP ratio and the tax/GDP ratio. Countries wishing to restrain any rise in those ratios should therefore ensure that:

- public expenditure is as economically productive as possible
- as many welfare payments as possible are conditional upon recipients taking part in retraining and/or paid work.

WHY DO THE FOUR PUBLIC FINANCE/GDP RATIOS FLUCTUATE FROM YEAR TO YEAR?

The example in the preceding section demonstrated why the four public finance/GDP ratios tend to rise as an economy moves into a downturn or recession. The opposite outcome occurs as an economy moves from recession, through recovery and into a state of full employment.

Working through the preceding example in reverse, the home country's GDP rises as economic prosperity amongst its trading partners leads to increased exports by the home country. As companies recruit more workers to produce those exports, incomes, profits and expenditures rise, tax revenues rise, income-related social security expenditures fall and the government's budget moves from deficit (that is, expenditures greater than revenues) towards surplus (that is, revenues greater than expenditures). The move from deficit to surplus allows borrowing to be reduced and ultimately public debt to be repaid. The public expenditure/GDP ratio is likely to fall dramatically and the borrowing/GDP ratio fall spectacularly as an economy moves out of a period of very high unemployment and very low national output as unemployment-related social security payments fall and as GDP rises.

Hence, the four public finance ratios fall, in the tax/GDP case because tax revenues rise more slowly than GDP even under a highly progressive tax structure. Fluctuations in the public finance/GDP ratios therefore occur from year to year as economies move through the four phases of the economic (or trade) cycle, namely downturn, recession, recovery and boom. These fluctuations occur under 'policy constant' scenarios, namely where governments do not attempt to offset those fluctuations by manipulating public expenditure, taxation and borrowing.

Fluctuations in the public finance/GDP ratios will be regular as long as the trade cycle has a regular periodicity and as long as the government adopts a 'policy constant' stance. A regular periodicity occurs if the duration of each of the four phases of the economic cycle remains constant. It is not self-evident, however, that the economic cycle has such a regular periodicity, booms and recessions sometimes being prolonged or, in other cases, relatively short. In practice, the world economy is frequently subject to violent economic shocks, such as major natural disasters, war or other such crisis, with the result that world trade is disrupted and so is the economic cycle (assuming one actually exists).

Changes in government policy also affect the public finance/GDP ratios. Instead of simply standing back under a 'policy constant' scenario, most governments adjust their policies in the light of unforeseen economic events. For example, EU member states seeking to ensure that their public finances remain consistent with the Maastricht deficit and Maastricht debt ratios may have to adopt a 'policy variable' stance. This will especially be the case if they are already close to being in breach of those ratios and their borrowing and debt rise sharply during a recession. In this case, they would have to introduce a programme of public expenditure cuts and tax increases.

In summary, there are three causes of fluctuations in the public finance/GDP ratios:

1. The economic cycle
2. Economic shocks not associated with the economic cycle
3. Discretionary government changes to the public finances.

WHY HAVE SOME OF THE PUBLIC FINANCE/GDP RATIOS DISPLAYED A LONG-TERM RISING TREND?

A rising long-term trend in any public finance/GDP ratio such as the public expenditure/GDP ratio is one that extends beyond the rise during the downturn and recession phases of the economic cycle. However, the possible long-term influences on public expenditure may not be clearly distinguished from short-term factors. For example, military conflict or increased international tension typically leads to higher military and defence expenditures in the short term. Unless they are fully financed by higher taxes, from a contingency fund, or by public expenditure cuts elsewhere, such increased expenditures lead to higher levels of public borrowing and public debt. Ongoing interest payments and debt repayments lead to higher public expenditures in the medium to long term, say over decades.

The *public expenditure/GDP* and *tax/GDP ratios* for developed countries revealed long-term growth during the second half of the twentieth century, as made clear above. What was not made clear, however, was the simultaneous rise in GDP. Total GDP for all OECD countries more than doubled in real terms (that is, after taking account of inflation) between 1960 and 1977 and almost doubled again between 1978 and 1999. Given the very substantial growth in GDP over the full period, public expenditure and tax revenues have clearly grown enormously in real terms.

The *public sector debt/GDP ratio* only displays a long-term trend if there is a long-lasting as well as consistent differential between the growth rates of the public expenditure/GDP and public revenue/GDP ratios, as already noted. The debt/GDP ratio rises if public expenditure is greater than revenues (reflecting long-term borrowing to fund the resultant budget deficit) and falls in the reverse case (reflecting use of revenues from the budget surplus to repay debt). In all countries the bulk of public sector revenues is derived from taxation (see Chapter 5). Hence, the trend in the debt/GDP ratio mostly reflects the difference between the public expenditure/GDP and tax/GDP ratios (see Chapter 7).

The *public sector borrowing/GDP ratio* only shows a long-term trend if there is a persistent and growing gap between public expenditure and public sector revenues. In simply being the residual between public expenditures and public revenues, public sector borrowing typically displays great variability from year to year rather than a long-term trend.

Many analysts have sought to explain the rising trend in the public expenditure/GDP ratio. There is a two-stage approach:

1. develop a theory of the growth of public expenditure
2. test that theory against the evidence.

This approach assumes that public expenditure effectively determines the other components of public finance, most notably taxation, borrowing and debt. Thus *expenditure determines finance*. In this case the primary decision is how much to spend, the amount of public finance raised depending on that decision. This is (somewhat misleadingly) referred to as the 'spend and tax model' of public finance. In fact the opposite may be the case, whereby *finance determines expenditure*. In this case governments only spend what revenues they can raise from taxation, borrowing, user-charges and so on. This is referred to as the 'tax and spend model', again rather misleading because taxation is not the only source of public sector revenues. There may of course be a two-way (rather than one-way) influence between spending and revenues.

There are many alternative theories of the growth of public expenditure, the proof or refutation of which is exceedingly difficult in practice (as will be discussed below). Specifically, theories can attempt to explain:

■ the totality of public expenditure
■ the individual components of public spending
■ the growth of expenditures.

The theories focus on either or both the demand for and supply of public services, in each case either individually or in aggregate.

Demand-side theories of public expenditure:

■ *Voters' preferences for the quantity and quality of public services.* Demand for education services tends to grow with incomes, such that it is theorised that, at any one point in time, demand will generally be greater the greater the voters' incomes. This does not necessarily mean that more affluent societies value education for its own sake. It may instead reflect an economy's transition from agricultural production, through industrial and manufacturing output, to services, the necessary levels of educational and skill requirements rising as economies move from primary through secondary to tertiary sectors. This sectoral shift has also been associated with the increasing participation of women in the labour force, whose demands for education have also grown over time. More affluent populations typically demand higher levels of health care, law and order and other public services, as well as education.

■ *Voters' preferences for redistribution of incomes.* Those preferences seem to be greater the greater the proportion of the population eligible to vote, the franchise generally being extended over historical time from higher income to lower income groups. Non-propertied classes, women, younger age groups have more to gain from redistribution. Having the power to vote allows them to achieve greater redistribution in their favour.

■ *Risk aversion.* Even though, at any one point in time, voters do not benefit from a more equal distribution of income, they may nevertheless favour higher state benefits for other groups because they expect to fall into one of those groups at some time in the future (for example becoming elderly).

■ *Pressure groups.* Voter-citizens may vote for the expenditures benefiting their own particular interest groups. For example, retired people vote or agitate for higher state pensions, concessions and exemptions from charges for public transport and public leisure services, and increased provision of health care services for the elderly. Rising proportions of the elderly within the demographic structures of many countries boost the 'grey vote'. Such rising demands are enhanced by the increasing numbers and proportions of affluent elderly groups, able to pay the extra tax costs of services from their occupational pensions and greater wealth accumulated from life savings and owner-occupied housing.

■ *Urbanisation.* Demand for services such as public transport and law and order seem to be greater the greater the degree of urbanisation, in these two cases because of increasing congestion and crime respectively.

Supply-side theories of public expenditure:

■ *The preferences of politicians and bureaucrats.* Their jobs and career prospects are generally enhanced by greater programme expenditures. This possibility would be largely pre-empted by 'direct democracy', where voters meet to vote on each and every expenditure programme. It would, however, be facilitated by 'representative democracy' because voters do not have the opportunity to vote on each expenditure item. Instead, voters choose from amongst many political parties, each offering different manifestos in competing for votes. Thus voters express their preferences for expenditures only indirectly and only in terms of the totality of public expenditure, not that on individual programmes. Representative democracy is the most common form of political representation.

■ *Fiscal illusion.* Governments hide the true tax costs of public expenditures by levying largely 'invisible' taxes on goods or by allowing inflation to progressively reduce the real value of tax allowances. Hence, voter-tax-payers do not realise just how expensive public sector services are and so demand too many of them. They underestimate the cost because they do not realise just how much they are paying in taxes to finance those services. Many taxes are 'hidden' in retail prices (for example VAT) and so people think private sector goods and services are much more expensive than they really are and that public sector goods and services are much less expensive than they really are. Thus demand for public sector outputs rises whilst that for private sector outputs falls. In principle, when voting for higher public expenditure, voters should also take account of the tax element of retail prices as the cost of public sector services. If they fail to do this, then they demand more public expenditures than they otherwise would have done.

■ *The structure of government.* Public spending may be influenced by the institutions of government. In being supposedly more closely accountable to voters, largely self-financing local governments should be less prone to higher public expenditures than a highly centralised (that is, 'remote') national government structure. However, fiscal illusion may be exacerbated at the local level by high levels of intergovernmental grants being paid by national and/or regional governments to local governments. In such cases the local tax cost of municipal services substantially understates the true cost, such that demand for municipal services is greater than if local taxation fully financed their costs (but see Chapter 8).

■ *The productivity differential hypothesis.* This states that the productivity of labour rises faster in the private sector than in the public sector. Both sectors compete with each other to hire workers and so the public sector has to match the levels of pay in the private sector. Higher rates of pay can be financed by productivity improvements in the private sector by replacing labour with capital (that is, plant and machinery). Scope for such substitution is heavily constrained in the public sector because machines cannot replace doctors and teachers and so on. Thus the cost of public sector services rises relative to those of the private sector. Normally, the increased relative cost of public services would be expected to lead to reduced demand. However, if demand and supply are insensitive to costs, then public expenditures rise. In fact, it is not self-evident that private sector services are any more amenable to greater capital intensity in their production than are public sector services. Indeed, it can be argued that, in fact, productivity has risen rapidly in the public sector as a result of cost-containment initiatives (see Chapter 4).

Demand- and supply-side influences on public expenditure may not be clearly separable and may be confused with each other. For example, higher public employment may be associated with higher public expenditure, not because bureaucrats favour higher public expenditures on the supply side, but because both may simply reflect voter preferences on the demand side. Thus, greater demand for public health services requires employment of more doctors and nurses. Nevertheless, that demand may in part be influenced by arguments by medical staff regarding the need for more health expenditures. In general, the greater the proportion of the population employed in the public sector, the greater the self-serving demand for public expenditure from public sector employees and members of their households.

TESTING THE THEORIES AGAINST THE EVIDENCE

Testing the validity of a theory typically relies on 'number crunching', using large amounts of data relating to long periods of time (several decades or more). Empirical testing is qualified by data problems. Generic data problems were discussed above. In particular, data may vary over time in its reliability and consistency as data collection methods and definitions vary, making historical comparisons difficult for any one country. Such data difficulties are compounded by comparative studies of more than one country. Whilst it may be expected that data problems diminish over time, as statistical methods improve and standardisation occurs across countries, other developments may compromise data consistency and reliability. An example is the growth of the so-called 'black economy', where economic activity is hidden from the authorities and so is unrecorded – for example incomes from employment may not be declared in order illegally to avoid payment of tax and loss of state benefits.

The apparent refutation of a theory may reflect inadequacies of the available data more than the theory. Even when data corroborates a theory, corroboration does not prove the validity of a theory in all circumstances for any one country or in all countries. It is not unusual for more than one theory to be corroborated by empirical testing, suggesting that many theories may be partial (rather than comprehensive) explanations of the rising share of public expenditure within GDP. Theories may be partial in the sense that they are based on a single academic discipline. For example, economic theories of public expenditure growth necessarily neglect political, institutional, cultural, sociological and other influences on public expenditure. On the other hand, political theories ignore economic factors (such as the incomes of voters). Theories may even be partial within the remit of a single discipline, only considering, for example, factors influencing the demand for public services whilst ignoring those influencing their supply.

Clearly, given the myriad factors influencing public expenditure, it is extremely difficult to identify a common set of factors applicable in all countries over all periods of time. Some of these factors may be stable influences, for example the incomes of voters and the costs of public services relative to private sector outputs. Other factors may be unstable or have no discernible impact, such as the political ideology of the government. In this example, a change of government would have no impact (or an unstable impact), if the

incoming government were effectively bound by the inheritance of past commitments made by the outgoing government. This would be the case, for
example, if the outgoing government had signed legally binding defence-
procurement contracts with manufacturers of armaments.

Thus, despite a massive amount of empirical testing of alternative theories, no single theory provides a satisfactory explanation of the long-term
growth of public expenditures across the generality of countries. Nevertheless,
it would clearly be grossly misleading to conclude that public expenditures
solely reflect voter preferences, since there are clearly supply-side as well as
demand-side influences on spending. Voter demand could only be decisive
under either direct democracy or truly representative democracy.

The search for one or more robust explanatory variables explaining the
growth of public expenditure is, in a sense, a chimera based on a rather mech-
anistic view of public expenditure determination. Certainly, in the short term,
public expenditure is influenced by the numbers of welfare claimants and the
ideology of the government of the day. In the long term, public spending is
clearly influenced by what voters can afford to pay in taxes (and charges for
services, if levied). But being able to afford to pay taxes is not the same as
willingness to pay for public services. That willingness is influenced by the
ongoing public debate on the relative roles of governments and markets, state
and citizen. This includes the degree to which individuals can expect to be
supported by the welfare state and broader socioeconomic developments
affecting perceptions of the minimum levels and standards of service required
in increasingly sophisticated economies.

In more technical (rather than philosophical) terms, the indeterminate
nature of the factors influencing public expenditure in the long term reflects
the fact that explanatory variables are not clearly separable and mutually
exclusive of each other. For example, voter preferences and party ideology are
interdependent of each other through the influence of public debate. That
debate is also affected by exogenous factors such as the scope for innovation
in providing public services, crises, new expensive-to-treat diseases, closer
economic and political ties between countries and so on.

All that can reasonably be concluded is that:

■ public expenditure is influenced by myriad factors
    ■ whose relative or absolute influence may not be the same in all countries
    ■ whose influence may not even be stable in any one country
    ■ whose influence differs in the short, medium and long terms.

Nevertheless, there seem to be three broad groups of factors influencing
public expenditures:

1. *economic variables* such as voters' incomes, the relative costs of public
   services, unemployment and so on

2. *political variables*, including the political ideology of the government of the day and the influence of various pressure groups, including public sector employees
3. *structural variables* such as demographic structure, industrial restructuring, the degree of urbanisation and so on.

IS A RISING LONG-TERM TREND IN PUBLIC FINANCE/GDP RATIOS A CAUSE FOR CONCERN?

As noted above, Libertarians and Neo-Liberals are concerned about the growth of the state, believing it should provide only negative rights (Libertarians) or negative and very strictly limited positive rights (Neo-Liberals), otherwise leaving citizens to spend their own money.

The ethical issue revolves around precisely when does government become so big in terms of economy and society that it overrides individual liberty to an excessive degree? The assumption is that governments are better able than the individual to plan the provision of services to promote the latter's welfare. If governments are not, in fact, able to make the right decisions, or if they make decisions serving their own interests rather than those of individuals and/or the community of citizens, then ethical issues are exacerbated. Moreover, is it fair for the state to take money from people who have earned it through their own hard work and enterprise and give it to people who may have done little to help themselves? This may be just as inequitable as doing nothing to help those who cannot help themselves.

There are also technical economic issues in addition to those of ethics and equity. As already noted, it is arguable that excessive levels of public expenditure, taxation and borrowing destroy or substantially inhibit economic incentives to work and enterprise. What is the point of working if one can live almost as well off generous state benefits when compared with what is left from earned income after paying high levels of income tax? Thus Libertarians and Neo-Liberals fear that adverse outcomes will be created:

■ high taxes destroy the incentive for enterprise and self-reliance
■ high welfare payments and service levels create a dependency culture.

The thesis that the growth of the state is at the expense of the private sector raises cause for concern about the long-term rise in public finance/GDP ratios. The thesis found considerable political support in developed countries during the later twentieth century. It was increasingly recognised that government intervention may be counterproductive in making more difficult the achievement of economic and social goals. As already noted in Chapter 2, government failure may be more profound than market failure. Hence, in such a case, the state should restrict itself to undertaking core functions (for example strategic policy-making). It should allow or enable the private sector to provide as many public sector services as possible by 'rolling back the frontiers of the state' via privatisation and, even more fundamentally, 'reinventing government' in terms of how it achieves its strategic objectives. Governments should 'steer rather than row', providing strategic direction but in most cases not providing services themselves. Instead, they enable the provision of services by the non-state sector (that is, the private and voluntary sectors). The state becomes the enabling state rather than the provider state. Those services which do not depend on the state for their survival can be privatised. Others can be provided by private sector companies under competitive contracting regimes. This scenario is referred to as the shift 'from government to governance'. In other words, government intervention should be the last (not the first) resort.

WHAT IS THE OPTIMUM PROPORTION OF PUBLIC FINANCE WITHIN GDP?

Even though a rising long-term trend in the public finance/GDP ratios may be a cause for concern, it is not clear at which point they pass the optimum proportion of GDP. Optimum proportions can be determined by referring to:

- the Libertarian, Neo-Liberal and Collectivist philosophies outlined in Chapter 1
- the property rights theory of Chapter 2.

Addressing the question as to whether governments get too big can be further facilitated by distinguishing between four models of public finance. Two broad models were referred to above, namely the tax and spend model and the spend and tax model. There are two variants of each type of model.

Tax and spend models of public finance

These are the 'fiscal exchange' and 'fiscal transfer models'. They can be categorised as 'tax and spend models' of public finance, in that citizens first decide how much they are willing to pay in taxes and so determine the levels of public spending on services:

- *The fiscal exchange model of public finance.* The defining characteristic of this model is that the state only raises and uses public finance to provide the levels of services chosen by citizens to secure their democratically determined negative and/or positive rights. Voter-citizens make tax and other such payments in exchange for services. This model therefore ensures the primacy of the rights of the citizen versus those of the state.

This state of affairs was championed by the likes of John Stuart Mill and Thomas Paine, who believed that the criterion of virtue is the individual's freedom from state control. It is also consistent with the classical liberal tradition of the likes of Aristotle, St Thomas Aquinas and John Locke, who emphasised the primacy of the individual. Aristotle's view of government, for example, was 'the art of governing free men'. This defines the constitutional relationship between the state and the individual. In principle, it is consistent with Libertarianism because it protects the citizen from coercion by the state. However, pure individualism is only possible in abstract constitutional or economic models of public finance. In particular, there is no concept of institutions or stakeholders' political power. In practice, individuals must defer to the outcome of elections, whether under majority voting or proportional representation. They are therefore bound by the decisions of the majority or largest minority (that is, where a first-past-the-post majority voting system results in a government with less than 50 per cent of votes cast). Thus, it is possible for a dominant group of voters to dictate the levels of service received (or not received) by a minority. This may not be a significant problem for the rights of the individual as long as that minority is not the same in respect of all decisions determined by the particular voting system in operation.

■ *The fiscal transfer model of public finance.* The defining characteristic of this model is that the majority uses public finance to redistribute income and wealth (inclusive of the value of public services) between individuals and groups within society. There are two alternative approaches. First, the utilitarian philosophy of Jeremy Bentham, James Mill and others seeking the greatest good for the greatest number. Second, the communist philosophy of 'from each according to ability to each according to need'. Each of these Collectivist political philosophies requires the maximisation of total benefit, welfare or utility without regard to distribution of benefits and burdens. Here, the criterion of virtue is utility or social welfare (not freedom from state control). However, utilitarianism cannot handle utility tradeoffs between individuals or groups and it is not possible to define and measure 'the greatest good', 'need' and 'ability' in any objective sense because there is no single aggregate measure of social welfare. Moreover, not all in society are equal in terms of power or status. Again, there is the possible majority exploitation of minorities. Maximising 'the greatest good' and meeting needs can be used to justify inequity and exploitation.

Spend and tax models of public finance

These are the 'despotic benevolent' and 'leviathan models'. They can be categorised as 'spend and tax models', in that the state first decides how much it wants to spend and then taxes citizens accordingly:

■ *The despotic benevolent model of public finance.* The defining characteristic of this model is that the state knows better than citizens what is in their interests. Citizens lack information and/or the ability to understand/ process it. The state is assumed to be in a better position to make decisions because of superior knowledge and decision-making abilities. Hence it uses public finance to protect citizens from the cradle to the grave (via subsidies). Here, the criterion of virtue is well-intentioned government intervention at the level of the individual (that is, neither individual liberty nor the greatest good). The paternalist state pursues maximisation of welfare of *individual* citizens. However, as already noted, paternalism may create a dependency culture by crowding out individual responsibility and enterprise. Thus paternalism may be at the cost of *collective* welfare (that is, smaller cake for everyone). Hence, intervention may be counterproductive in terms of both individual and collective welfare.

■ *The leviathan model of public finance.* The defining features of this model are that governments grow like mythical monsters (leviathans) because they are fallible, misrepresentative of voters and possibly even untrustworthy. Thus the leviathan model denies the despotic benevolent model of public finance:

   ■ *Governments are incompetent.* They simply cannot be trusted to make the right decisions for citizens. They also suffer a lack of information and/or ability to understand and process it. There is too much irrelevant information, not enough relevant data. Governments' mistakes are big and in one direction, whereas individuals' mistakes are small and many are offsetting. Government mistakes inevitably require a lot more public finance in attempting to rectify them.

   ■ *Governments are misrepresentative.* The idealised view of democracy by Rousseau, J. S. Mill and others simply does not hold in practice. Active and ongoing deliberative participation in political life simply does not take place. There is instead a democracy of infrequent passive participation, usually limited to casting one's vote (if at all) at election time. Active participation is confined to a small minority that is often unrepresentative of society in general. Power is 'brokered' by a largely closed political class that underrepresents working classes, poor, ethnic groups, women and so on. The powerful minority raises more public finance than the generality of citizens would prefer, taxing all citizens and using the resultant public finance to provide services disproportionately benefiting middle-income groups who would otherwise pay for their own consumption of services (see Chapter 7).

   ■ *Governments are untrustworthy.* Here the state serves those who work in it, not just (or not even) the citizen. Instead, it seeks protection of public employees, especially professional groups (that is, not just the low-paid, unskilled, excluded groups). These are the self-serving politicians and bureaucrats noted above.

The leviathan model of public finance is therefore anti-populist, incompetence, sleaze and corruption disadvantaging the majority of citizens. Hence, the populist criterion of virtue is benign scepticism. It adopts an eclectic rather than philosophical approach to public finance, believing that on balance there should be a presumption against government intervention and public finance.

These four models of public finance can be summarised in terms of what they say about the virtues of public finance:

■ to maximise individual freedom from state control (consistent with Libertarianism)
■ to secure the greatest good for the greatest number (consistent with Collectivism, whether in terms of utility or social welfare)
■ to protect the interests of the individual in a paternalistic way (consistent with Neo-Liberalism's equality of opportunity)
■ to recognise benign scepticism towards all government actions (political philosophy tempered by pragmatism).

Individual liberty relates to freedom from control or restriction; having the power to choose, think and act for oneself. Libertarianism is consistent with capitalism, which interprets liberty as freedom to buy and sell property rights (for example the right to sell one's labour, to retain the resulting income and to use it to purchase goods and services). Thus, under capitalism, liberty is defined exclusively in economic terms. Collectivists define liberty solely in political terms, the liberty to enjoy a socially acceptable standard of living, free from exploitation by uncontrolled market systems, namely under socialism (or communism). Whereas capitalism and socialism define liberty in mutually exclusive ways, liberty within a mixed economy relates to a trade-off between economic and political rights, government intervention supposedly securing the optimal point of trade-off. The Neo-Liberal acceptance of equality of opportunity is essentially an acceptance of limited political rights.

In practice, it is virtually impossible to prove irrefutably that government intervention makes things better, worse or has no net impact. This is because of methodological difficulties in trying to establish the 'counterfactual', that is, what would have happened in the absence of government intervention (see Chapter 4). Therefore, it is not possible to determine the optimum public finance/GDP ratio. Nevertheless, there is the distinct possibility that the side effects of the 'cure' (that is, government action) may be worse than the symptoms of the 'disease' (that is, profit-seeking activities lacking a social conscience). Hence, there should be a presumption against intervention unless absolutely necessary.

Clearly, the optimum proportion of public finance within GDP depends crucially on ideological and philosophical considerations. It is not simply a technical question regarding:

- either the point at which crowding in turns into crowding out (see Chapter 6)
- or a particular public finance/GDP ratio.

CONCLUSIONS

The analysis of OECD data made clear that the relative scale of public finance increased substantially over the last 40 years of the twentieth century, rising much faster than GDP. The OECD average government expenditure/GDP ratio rose from between a quarter and a third of GDP at the beginning of the 1960s to between a third and two-fifths at the end of the millennium. That ratio is twice as great in some countries than in others. Whilst the expenditure/GDP ratio fluctuated widely about its rising trend, the tax/GDP ratio displayed a much steadier rise, the latter ratio being consistently (and sometimes substantially) less than the former. Thus the two ratios give radically different measures of the relative scale of public finance and the speed with which that scale changes, especially in the short to medium term. It is therefore inadvisable to rely on a single measure of the relative scale of public finance.

This chapter has also made clear that the relative scale of public finance within economy and society is not simply a technical financial issue. Nor is it simply an economic issue. Instead, the relative scale of public finance can only be appreciated through a broad multidisciplinary perspective, meaning that it is not valid to assert that the level of public finance in any one country is either too high or too low relative to its GDP. The same conclusion relates to whether there is cause to be worried about rising trends in the four public finance/GDP ratios, and whether there is such a thing as an optimum proportion of public finance within GDP.

The Libertarian, Neo-Liberal and Collectivist philosophies provide no practical guidance in respect of the optimal level of public finance, whether in absolute terms or relative to GDP. All this philosophical categorisation of rights indicates are the types of services that should (or should not) be supported by public finance. They cannot themselves explain the rising trends in the four public finance ratios. This is because they philosophise about negative and positive rights rather than about entitlements to particular levels of service and they do not consider how negative and positive rights change over time in the light of the economic, social and political restructuring that accompanies economic growth.

Property rights theory relating to market failure provides a more objective approach to assessing the optimum level of public finance but, ultimately, its practical use in policy-making is severely constrained by the difficulties in identifying and measuring both direct and indirect costs and benefits. However, the spend and tax and tax and spend models of public finance make clear that the focus on the relative scale of public finance is too narrow since much broader issues of constitutional legitimacy have to be considered.

Whatever that relative scale, efficacy in the use of public finance depends crucially on how it is raised and spent. The next two chapters will demonstrate that whether the impact of public finance is adverse or beneficial depends more on how it is raised and spent than on the proportion of GDP for which it accounts. In other words, public policy has historically been too concerned with the relative size of public finance and not concerned enough with the means by which it is raised and spent. That misdirection of concern has only recently been recognised.

FURTHER READING

Bailey, S. J. (2002) *Public Sector Economics: Theory, Policy and Practice* (Basingstoke: Palgrave Macmillan) [Chapter 3 on theories of public sector growth].

Borcherding, T. E. (1985) 'The Causes of Government Expenditure Growth: A Survey of the US Evidence' *Journal of Public Economics* vol. 28, pp. 359–82.

Connolly, S. and Munroe, A. (1999) *Economics of the Public Sector* (Harlow: Prentice Hall).

Gemmell, N. (editor) (1993) *The Growth of the Public Sector: Theories and International Evidence* (Aldershot: Edward Elgar).

Lybeck, J. A. and Henrekson, M. (editors) (1988) *Explaining the Growth of Government* (Amsterdam: North-Holland).

McNutt, P. A. (2002) *The Economics of Public Choice* (second edition) (Cheltenham: Edward Elgar) [Chapter 4 on the growth of government].

Moisio, A. (2000) *Spend and Tax or Tax and Spend: Evidence from Finnish Municipalities during 1985–1992 and 1993–1999.* Paper presented at the Nordic Conference on Local Public Finance (Helsinki: Government Institute for Economic Research).

Musgrave, R. A. (2000) *Public Finance in a Democratic Society Volume III: The Foundations of Taxation and Expenditure* (Cheltenham: Edward Elgar) [Chapter 19 'When is the Public Sector too Large?'].

Payne, J. E. (1998) 'The Tax-Spend Debate: Time Series Evidence from State Budgets' *Public Choice* vol. 95, pp. 307–20.

4 Spending Public Finance

INTRODUCTION

The definition of public finance developed in Chapter 1 made clear that public finance is not only spent on public services. It is also often used to subsidise private sector outputs, for example agricultural production, coal and steel. Moreover, public finance is not the sole source of finance used to support public sector services, private finance being an integral part of public–private partnerships for example. Furthermore, what services constitute the public sector varies between countries. Therefore, public finance is not synonymous with the public sector and it should not be taken for granted that the current system of public finance in any one country is necessarily the most efficacious means of spending public money.

Most governments and citizens would agree with the need to make the best possible use of public finance. This can be taken to mean that it should secure as much additional spending on services and activities as possible and avoid wasteful use of public money. Such requirements reflect the following factors:

- at any one time, public finance is finite, there being a limit on the extent to which governments can raise finance from their citizens in order to provide services
- public finance may simply replace private finance. Increasing the amount of public finance may lead to reductions in private finance that would otherwise have been spent on the same activity or service. Thus, rather than complementing private finance, public finance may replace private finance
- not only may incremental public finance secure little if any additional benefits for the service or activity it is meant to support, it may even reduce aggregate social welfare. This could be the case if raising additional public finance required higher taxes on people and companies and/or higher interest rates for increased public sector borrowing. Higher taxes and borrowing costs could deter (crowd out) private sector activity and so lead to a net fall in national output and the associated economic and social welfare (see Chapter 6).

Hence, steps must be taken to ensure that public money is used to provide truly beneficial services, minimising costs and securing maximum additional spending. The need to raise public finance (and any unwelcome consequences) can be reduced if systems are put in place to ensure 'value for money' spent. This chapter therefore considers how value for money might be achieved in strategic terms. In doing so, it is helpful to re-examine economy, efficiency, effectiveness and equity (the 4Es).

SPENDING PUBLIC FINANCE IN ACCORDANCE WITH THE 4ES

A strategy for the spending of public finance has to look afresh at which services and activities it is to support and how it is disbursed. Libertarians, Neo-Liberals and Collectivists have different views about what constitutes strategically wasteful and unnecessary provision of public services. As noted in Chapter 1, Libertarians regard any level of service in excess of that necessary to secure negative rights as unnecessary and wasteful. Neo-Liberals and Collectivists also take account (to different extents) of positive rights.

Chapter 2 set the Libertarian, Neo-Liberal and Collectivist philosophies within the property rights framework in attempting to categorise services according to their need for public finance. It made clear that public finance does not necessarily require public provision of the services it supports. These philosophies facilitate an examination of public finance in strategic but not operational terms. Hence, use of the 4Es to examine the spending of public finance does not bias the analysis in favour of a particular philosophy because each philosophy has a different conception of each of equity, efficiency, economy and effectiveness (see Chapters 1 and 2).

Economy is defined in terms of strategic economy and operational economy. 'Strategic economy' is achieved when public finance meets clearly defined and operationally relevant objectives relating to positive and/or negative rights. Irrespective of the political philosophy underpinning those objectives, public finance is unlikely to be used economically if objectives are operationally vague or simply not set at all. 'Operational economy' refers to the minimisation of the costs of inputs and processes. This managerial interpretation of economy requires minimisation of the costs of inputs and processes for a given range and level of services. 'Cost minimisation' is considered in detail below.

Efficiency is not necessarily achieved by economy. Even if operational and strategic economy is achieved, public money could still be wasted in providing unnecessary, unwanted or underused services. Spare capacity may exist in many public services, for example when demographic change and migration result in surplus school places in particular localities or areas and when poor quality results in underused cultural venues and sports facilities. In such cases public money may be being wasted maintaining underutilised services when it could be better spent elsewhere, as either public or private spending. Thus, efficiency requires not only removal of 'organisational slack' at the level of the service provider (in achieving operational economy) but also the maximisation of 'economic welfare' arising from both public and private finance. Thus, in these terms, public finance should not replace private finance if it is at the cost of reduced economic welfare. Ideally, public finance should complement (rather than replace) private finance so as to create net additional economic welfare. This 'economic additionality' is considered in detail below.

Equity is concerned with the distribution of the costs and benefits of public finance, distributional issues being largely ignored by economic welfare. Thus, 'social welfare' can be regarded as a broader concept than economic welfare in also considering distributional issues. In effect, distributional issues are subsumed within the political philosophy debates regarding the extent (if any) of positive rights (see Chapter 1). However, equity also relates to the rights of those who provide public finance and the responsibilities of those who receive it. Whatever the notions of negative and positive rights and the degree of vertical and horizontal equity being sought in the raising and spending of public finance, it could be considered inequitable for those providing public finance if their financial sacrifice was in vain. This would be the case if their payment of taxes secured little in the way of improved outcomes for social welfare. This 'social additionality' is considered in detail below.

Effectiveness can be subdivided into two forms: cost-effectiveness and outcome-effectiveness. 'Cost-effectiveness' results from *economy* in the purchase of inputs and *efficiency* in the translation of those inputs into outputs of a given quality. Hence, cost-effectiveness is secured if both operational and strategic economy are achieved. 'Outcome-effectiveness' results when a cost-effective service delivers its outcome objectives in maximising economic and social additionality. 'Outcome additionality' is considered in detail below.

Ultimately, value for money requires both cost-effectiveness and outcome-effectiveness to be achieved. Value for money is therefore a much broader concept than that implied by the '3Es' of financial audit (that is, economy, efficiency and effectiveness). It also has to take account of equity. Outcome-effectiveness is an extremely broad concept that extends far beyond specific public service programmes to which value for money is normally confined. Outcome-effectiveness adopts a holistic perspective regarding the impact of raising and spending public finance, that impact crucially impinging on economic and social welfare at the level of the whole economy and society (this is considered further in Chapters 5 and 6).

Thus, in order for public finance to be used to best effect and value for money to be achieved in its broadest sense, objectives must be set in terms of:

- specifying the desired additional outcomes from the raising and spending of public finance (that is, outcome additionality)
- identifying the additional outputs necessary to achieve those additional outcomes
- ensuring public finance is truly additional to private finance that would otherwise have been spent on those outputs (that is, 'output additionality')
- ensuring that outputs deliver outcomes as efficiently as possible (that is, cost-effectiveness)

- ensuring that services are produced at least cost whilst maintaining their quality (that is, operational economy)
- constantly reviewing the pattern of spending to ensure that it is still required to fulfil outcome objectives.

Only policy-makers can address the first and last bullet points above. They require explicit and well-informed decisions about which services are to be supported by public finance (ideally using the classification in Chapter 2 based on the enforceability or otherwise of property rights). Strictly speaking, the second and third bullet points require research into the effectiveness of outputs in delivering the outcomes required by policy-makers and whether public finance is truly additional to private finance. An example is whether publicly funded skills training actually increases the chance of unemployed unskilled people getting jobs. This would not be the case if publicly funded training did not provide skills relevant for employers, there were simply no jobs available or the public funds simply replaced private funds that would otherwise have been spent on training and job creation.

The research required to determine whether or not outcome and output additionality are both achieved is particularly problematic (see below). In the absence of robust research results, policy-makers may simply specify the outputs they believe will deliver their chosen outcomes and assume that public finance is wholly or substantially additional to private finance. The remaining two bullet points (concerned with cost-effectiveness and operational economy) are the responsibility of practitioners.

It is clear that minimisation of input and process costs is necessary but not sufficient to ensure value for money in the public finances. Public finance would still be wasted if unnecessary or unwanted outputs are being produced, resulting in excess capacity. Likewise, public finance would be wasted if those outputs did not achieve the desired outcomes. Three examples are provided:

- *Provision of midday meals for school children.* Municipalities may minimise the costs of those meals and produce the required output of meals and yet still fail to provide the required levels of nutrition for school children. This would be the case if they provide a nutritionally unbalanced diet (for example 'junk foods') or if children simply do not eat the meals they are served (that is, 'plate waste').
- *Residential care of the elderly.* Residential care homes may provide low-cost, good quality accommodation, diet and medical and nursing services and yet not provide for the social needs of their clients (for example in terms of social and educational activities). Put simply, their elderly clients may be left to vegetate.
- *School performance.* A school's performance is ultimately judged in terms of the educational enhancement of each pupil's intellectual capacity (that is, critical faculties), this human capital enabling individuals to live a

useful and meaningful life in the modern economy and society. Improvements in school examination results do not necessarily indicate greater capacity building in human capital. They may simply indicate that examinations are being made easier to pass and/or that teachers are simply coaching pupils to pass examinations rather than build intellectual capacity.

In short, public finance can only be judged in terms of the net beneficial outcomes it secures. Net benefit is the gross benefit minus the costs (both direct and indirect) incurred in securing it. Public finance would be wasted if it merely replaced private spending that would otherwise have taken place and thus had no impact on service outputs and outcomes. Public provision of services such as education, health, sports, the arts and national heritage could partially or wholly replace private provision of those services and activities, having little or no effect in terms of additionality of service outcomes.

UPON WHAT IS PUBLIC FINANCE ACTUALLY SPENT?

Chapter 3 analysed data on total government expenditure, noting its increasing share of GDP in developed countries. That increase conflated a number of broad expenditure categories, namely current and capital expenditures and, within current expenditure, spending on services and spending on transfers.

Table 4.1 provides data on current disbursements, the OECD defining this as consisting mainly of final consumption expenditures by government itself (mainly on service provision), social security transfers to households, subsidies to businesses and interest on the public debt. The table shows that, in terms of the OECD average, current expenditure accounted for less than a quarter of GDP at the beginning of the 1960s, rising fairly steadily to over a third of GDP by the mid-1970s and, likewise, to 37 per cent of GDP by 1981. Thereafter, the ratio stayed between 37 and 39 per cent for all years except 1997 (36.1 per cent).

Whilst the OECD average never quite reached 40 per cent of GDP (1999 data being incomplete), some countries exceeded 50 per cent over extended periods. These countries were Belgium (all years 1981–96), Denmark (1980 onwards), the Netherlands (all years 1975–94) and Sweden 1977 onwards. Sweden was the only country in which current disbursements of government exceeded 60 per cent of GDP (in fact in eight years, three in the 1980s and five in the 1990s). Finland exceeded 50 per cent between 1991 and 1997 and Italy in 1983 and between 1992 and 1994. Greece exceeded 50 per cent in 1990, 1995 and 1996. Other countries reached 50 per cent in one or two years only, namely Austria (1993), Canada (1992), France (1996) and Ireland (1985 and 1986). Korea and Mexico had the lowest ratios (below 20 per cent in the 1990s) and Japan (below 30 per cent until 1998).

Within current expenditures, Table 4.2 shows social security transfers, whilst Table 4.3 shows government final consumption. Social security transfers

Table 4.1 Current disbursements of government as a percentage of GDP

	1960	1961	1962	1963	1964	1965	1966	1967	1968	1969	1970	1971	1972	1973	1974
Australia	18.9	20.1	19.8	19.7	19.9	21.3	21.6	22.2	21.3	21.5	21.8	22.5	22.7	23.1	25.5
Austria	25.5	25.8	27.3	28.4	31.2	31.4	31.9	33.3	33.8	34.1	33.1	33.4	32.9	33.3	34.6
Belgium	28.4	27.7	28.2	28.9	27.8	29.8	30.6	31.4	32.9	32.9	33.0	34.0	34.9	35.8	36.4
Canada	25.4	26.1	25.9	25.5	25.2	25.0	25.8	27.8	29.1	29.8	32.2	32.7	33.5	32.4	33.6
CzechRepublic															
Denmark	21.4	23.4	24.2	24.9	24.5	25.7	27.3	29.4	31.3	31.1	34.6	37.4	37.6	37.8	41.2
Finland	21.7	21.6	22.8	24.4	25.2	25.8	27.2	28.1	28.4	27.4	27.3	28.1	28.2	27.0	28.3
France	30.9	31.9	32.9	33.5	33.4	33.7	33.6	34.0	35.4	35.1	34.7	34.3	34.2	34.8	35.9
Germany	28.1	28.6	29.5	30.6	29.7	30.8	31.3	33.7	34.2	33.3	32.6	33.8	35.1	36.1	38.8
Greece	17.4	17.4	18.4	18.7	19.8	20.6	21.5	23.6	23.5	22.5	22.4	22.8	22.0	21.1	25.0
Hungary															
Iceland	23.3	19.9	19.3	20.5	21.6	20.7	20.8	24.3	24.9	21.8	21.7	24.2	24.8	27.3	26.7
Ireland	24.7	25.9	25.4	25.8	26.6	27.6	28.5	29.1	29.5	30.3	34.2	34.8	34.0	34.1	37.2
Italy	26.2	25.5	26.5	27.5	28.2	30.6	30.7	30.0	31.0	30.6	30.2	33.1	35.0	34.4	34.4
Japan	13.6	12.9	13.4	13.9	13.8	14.2	14.2	13.8	13.8	13.6	14.0	14.8	15.5	15.7	18.1
Korea															
Luxembourg	25.5	25.7	27.3	28.6	28.0	29.6	31.1	33.6	32.8	30.3	28.6	30.9	31.4	29.6	30.0
Mexico															
Netherlands	28.6	29.3	30.1	32.3	32.4	33.5	35.3	36.9	37.8	38.6	40.2	42.2	43.3	44.3	46.8
NewZealand															
Norway	26.4	26.4	28.0	29.2	29.0	30.3	30.8	32.0	33.6	35.2	36.5	38.3	39.6	39.9	40.0
Poland															
Portugal	15.2	17.6	18.0	17.5	17.5	17.7	17.8	18.6	18.6	18.2	19.5	19.1	19.9	19.5	22.7
Spain	13.7	13.0	12.8	13.0	15.0	15.8	15.8	17.1	17.8	18.0	18.8	19.7	19.7	19.7	19.8
Sweden	26.9	26.9	27.9	29.2	29.0	30.2	32.0	33.5	35.9	36.6	37.2	39.8	40.8	40.2	43.8
Switzerland	17.2	18.0	18.5	18.6	19.3	19.7	20.1	20.4	20.7	21.8	21.3	21.9	21.9	24.2	25.5
Turkey			13.8	13.9	15.3	15.5	15.1	15.4	15.5	16.9	16.4	17.4	18.0		
UK	20.7	30.6	31.1	31.1	30.1	30.9	31.4	33.3	33.7	33.0	33.2	32.7	34.4	34.2	38.8
United States	25.0	26.6	26.5	26.3	25.9	25.4	26.6	28.5	28.9	28.7	30.3	30.2	30.3	29.7	31.2
Total OECD	**23.7**	**24.4**	**24.5**	**24.8**	**24.6**	**24.9**	**25.6**	**26.8**	**27.3**	**27.1**	**27.9**	**28.4**	**28.9**	**29.0**	**30.9**
Standard deviation	*5.2*	*5.4*	*5.9*	*6.2*	*5.8*	*6.1*	*6.4*	*6.7*	*7.1*	*7.1*	*7.4*	*7.7*	*7.9*	*7.6*	*7.8*

continued

Table 4.1 *continued*

	1975	1976	1977	1978	1979	1980	1981	1982	1983	1984	1985	1986	1987	1988	1989
Australia	27.5	28.7	30.2	29.7	29.4	30.1	30.7	32.8		35.1	35.4	35.2	33.6	32.2	32.1
Austria	38.6	40.1	40.4	43.3	42.9	42.8	44.0	45.1	45.5	45.1	46.0	46.7	47.4	46.0	45.2
Belgium	41.2	41.7	43.4	44.8	46.2	47.7	52.3	53.0	53.5	59.2	59.2	59.0	57.6	55.1	53.5
Canada	36.8	35.9	36.9	37.5	36.3	37.8	38.8	42.4	43.0	43.3	43.6	43.2	42.3	41.6	41.9
CzechRepublic															
Denmark	43.5	43.2	44.7	46.4	48.9	52.2	55.6	57.1	58.2	57.7	56.4	53.4	55.0	56.9	57.0
Finland	31.4	33.3	34.4	34.3	33.7	33.3	34.3	35.8	36.1	36.2	37.9	38.5	38.4	35.8	34.9
France	39.2	39.7	40.8	42.0	42.3	43.0	45.8	47.3	48.2	48.7	48.8	48.1	47.6	46.7	45.8
Germany	43.3	42.6	42.7	42.6	42.3	42.8	44.3	44.8	44.4	44.1	43.9	43.3	43.7	43.5	42.0
Greece	26.7	27.4	29.0	29.9	29.7	30.5	36.8	37.6	38.3	40.2	43.7	42.9	44.8	45.2	46.4
Hungary															
Iceland	28.3	25.2	25.0	27.4	28.5	27.6				26.3	27.8	27.5	27.5	30.5	31.6
Ireland	41.3	41.6	39.8	40.1	42.4	46.0	48.3			49.6	50.5	50.3	49.6	47.6	41.5
Italy	38.3	38.0	38.5	41.7	41.0	41.5	46.4	49.3	51.5	44.9	45.3	45.9	45.5	45.8	47.0
Japan	20.9	21.6	22.5	23.3	24.2	25.4	26.5	27.2	28.1	27.0	26.6	26.9	26.9	26.2	25.5
Korea															
Luxembourg	41.3	42.5	46.2	45.1	45.4	45.7				45.2	45.4	45.0			
Mexico															
Netherlands	51.0	51.5	50.3	51.8	53.5	54.1	55.6	58.3		55.7	54.8	54.4	55.4	53.7	51.7
NewZealand															
Norway	41.8	43.8	45.3	47.2	46.6	44.8	45.0	45.5	45.9	43.4	43.0	46.7	47.9	49.8	50.9
Poland															
Portugal	27.2	30.9	30.8	31.8	31.0	33.7	37.4			38.5	39.4	40.4	39.1	39.0	37.6
Spain	21.2	22.8	23.7	26.2	27.7	29.2	30.3	31.8		34.6	36.6	36.2	35.8	35.5	
Sweden	45.1	48.0	53.1	54.5	55.4	57.3	60.1	61.7		59.6	60.9	59.6	58.1	57.1	57.2
Switzerland	28.7	30.2	30.4	30.2	29.9	29.3	28.9	30.1	30.8	31.4	31.0	30.5	30.1	30.5	30.2
Turkey															
UK	40.6	40.5	39.4	39.5	39.7	41.8	44.0	44.4	44.3	44.1	43.4	42.4	40.9	38.6	37.7
United States	33.6	33.1	32.1	31.3	31.5	33.5	34.1	36.5	36.9	34.7	35.3	35.8	35.3	34.7	34.6
Total OECD	**33.7**	**33.7**	**33.7**	**34.0**	**34.2**	**35.6**	**37.1**	**38.8**	**39.1**	**38.0**	**38.3**	**38.3**	**38.0**	**37.3**	**37.0**
Standarddeviation	*8.2*	*8.2*	*8.5*	*8.6*	*8.9*	*9.1*	*9.6*	*10.1*	*8.5*	*9.6*	*9.4*	*9.1*	*9.4*	*9.2*	*9.1*

continued

Table 4.1   continued

	1990	1991	1992	1993	1994	1995	1996	1997	1998	1999
Australia		34.4	34.7	35.1	34.7	34.5	33.6	32.4	31.9	
Austria	44.9	47.1	47.7	50.3	49.7	49.7	49.4	47.6	47.5	47.3
Belgium	53.1	52.5	52.3	53.4	51.5	50.9	50.9	49.2	48.5	48.0
Canada	44.0	49.4	50.7	49.8	47.4	46.1	44.5	42.5	42.5	
CzechRepublic		40.2	39.3	39.3	36.6	36.8	37.4			
Denmark	56.5	55.6	56.2	58.8	58.7	57.3	56.8	55.1	54.2	52.9
Finland	37.5	50.7	56.1	58.4	56.4	53.7	53.0	50.7	47.6	46.4
France	46.2	46.0	47.3	49.8	49.3	49.2	50.0	49.8	48.6	48.5
Germany	42.6	41.6	42.7	44.1	44.2	44.9	46.2	45.5	44.8	44.8
Greece	50.9	40.1	41.6	44.0	44.4	51.4	50.3	48.4	48.2	48.3
Hungary										
Iceland	31.5	33.7	34.8	34.9	34.4	35.1	34.0			
Ireland		40.7	41.1	40.6	39.5	36.8	35.2	33.6	31.1	29.1
Italy	48.1	49.6	51.8	53.1	51.1	49.3	49.2	47.4	45.7	45.0
Japan	26.2	25.0	25.5	26.4	27.1	28.5	28.3	28.7	30.0	
Korea		14.3	14.9	14.9	14.5	14.3	14.8	15.1	17.1	
Luxembourg		39.1	39.1	40.0	39.1	39.8	40.2	38.6	38.1	38.0
Mexico				16.7	17.4	18.7	17.7	17.6	17.0	
Netherlands	51.7	54.8	55.4	55.6	53.0	47.4	45.9	44.7	43.7	43.2
NewZealand										
Norway		48.1	49.5	49.0	47.9	45.6	43.7	41.8	44.3	43.9
Poland		49.3	52.2	51.5	45.7	44.2	42.2	41.4	39.6	
Portugal		39.7	39.9	41.3	40.6	39.6	39.4	38.2	37.8	38.6
Spain		38.8	40.7	43.6	42.4	41.5	41.1			
Sweden	59.1	60.2	64.3	64.1	62.8	60.6	59.6	57.5	56.3	55.0
Switzerland	30.7	30.6	32.6	33.7	33.8	33.6	34.3	34.7	34.2	
Turkey										
UK	38.1	40.0	42.0	42.3	41.3	41.5	40.0	39.2	39.2	37.7
United States		36.0	35.9	35.2	34.2	34.2	33.6	32.7		
Total OECD	**39.4**	**37.6**	**38.3**	**38.1**	**37.4**	**37.3**	**37.0**	**36.1**	**37.9**	**44.0**
Standarddeviation	*9.7*	*10.4*	*10.7*	*12.0*	*11.4*	*10.8*	*10.7*	*10.5*	*10.3*	*6.5*

Note: Current disbursements comprises final consumption expenditures, social
security transfers to households, subsidies and interest on the public debt
Source: OECD (1985) Table 6.4; OECD (1992a) Table 6.4; OECD (2000)
Table 6.4

Strategic Public Finance

Table 4.2 *Social security transfers as a percentage of GDP*

	1960	1968	1971	1972	1973	1974	1975	1976	1977	1978	1979	1980	1981	1982	1983
Australia	5.7	5.1	5.7	6.3	6.4	7.4	8.8	9.3	9.6	9.3	8.9	8.8	9.1	10.1	
Austria	10.4	15.9	15.6	15.4	15.3	15.5	16.9	17.7	17.9	19.4	19.3	19.0	19.5	19.8	20.1
Belgium	11.3	14.0	14.2	14.9	15.4	15.9	18.8	19.3	20.1	20.4	20.9	21.0	22.7	22.6	23.3
Canada	8.0	7.3	8.7	9.4	9.0	9.3	10.2	10.0	10.4	10.6	9.8	10.1	10.0	11.8	12.5
CzechRepublic															
Denmark	7.4	10.8	11.2	11.4	11.1	12.0	13.8	13.5	14.1	14.9	15.4	16.6	17.8	18.0	17.8
Finland	5.1	7.5	7.7	7.9	7.4	7.7	8.3	9.0	9.8	10.0	9.2	8.7	8.9	9.7	10.3
France	13.6	17.0	17.1	17.3	17.7	18.3	20.4	20.7	21.4	22.3	22.7	23.2	24.6	25.7	26.1
Germany	12.0	13.7	12.9	13.4	13.5	14.6	17.5	17.3	17.2	16.8	16.5	16.5	17.2	17.6	17.2
Greece	5.3	8.4	8.0	7.6	6.8	7.1	7.4	7.7	8.5	9.2	8.8	9.2	11.0	12.8	13.4
Hungary															
Iceland	7.1	9.0	9.5	10.2	11.3	10.3	10.5	10.0	9.9	10.6	10.9	11.1			
Ireland	5.5	6.5	9.5	9.3	10.2	11.4	12.7	12.7	11.7	11.4	11.4	12.7	13.7		
Italy	9.8	12.6	13.1	13.9	13.8	13.7	15.6	15.6	15.2	16.5	15.7	15.8	17.7	18.5	19.6
Japan	3.8	4.5	4.8	5.2	5.2	6.2	7.8	8.5	9.0	9.5	10.0	10.2	10.8	11.2	11.5
Korea															
Luxembourg	11.6	15.3	15.3	15.9	14.8	14.1	19.9	20.7	22.6	22.4	22.2	22.8			
Mexico															
Netherlands		16.2	18.5	19.6	20.3	21.6	24.0	24.3	23.7	24.5	25.3	25.8	26.8	28.5	
NewZealand															
Norway	7.6	10.5	13.0	13.7	13.9	13.3	13.6	13.9	14.1	15.0	15.5	14.4	14.5	15.0	15.4
Poland															
Portugal	2.9	3.1	3.2	4.2	4.6	5.3	8.6	11.6	10.8	10.1	9.5	10.6	11.5		
Spain	2.3	8.1	9.4	9.4	9.6	9.5	10.3	11.1	11.7	13.2	14.5	15.0	16.2	16.3	
Sweden	8.0	10.6	12.1	12.6	12.2	14.3	14.2	15.1	16.7	17.5	17.6	17.8	18.4	18.5	
Switzerland	5.7	7.5	8.3	8.3	10.1	10.6	12.5	13.2	13.3	13.2	13.0	12.7	12.4	13.2	13.4
Turkey		1.3	1.8	1.9											
UK	6.9	8.7	8.4	9.3	8.9	9.5	9.9	10.4	10.8	11.2	11.2	11.5	12.9	13.9	13.7
United States	5.1	6.4	8.5	8.6	8.8	9.8	11.4	11.2	10.7	10.2	10.3	11.2	11.3	12.1	12.1
Total OECD	**6.7**	**8.3**	**9.3**	**9.7**	**9.9**	**10.7**	**12.4**	**12.5**	**12.5**	**12.6**	**12.7**	**13.2**	**13.8**	**14.5**	**14.1**
Standard deviation	*3.1*	*4.3*	*4.3*	*4.4*	*4.1*	*4.1*	*4.6*	*4.6*	*4.7*	*4.8*	*5.1*	*5.1*	*5.2*	*5.3*	*4.7*

continued

Table 4.2   continued

	1984	1985	1986	1987	1988	1989	1990	1991	1992	1993	1994	1995	1996	1997	1998	1999
Australia	9.8	9.5	9.4	9.2	8.6	8.7		8.3	8.5	8.8	8.6	8.6	8.6	8.2	8.0	
Austria	20.0	20.4	20.5	21.1	20.4	20.0	19.9	17.8	18.1	19.5	19.6	19.5	19.5	18.9	18.6	18.6
Belgium	25.6	25.0	24.6	24.7	23.8	23.1	22.7	16.6	16.7	17.1	16.8	16.6	16.6	16.3	16.0	15.7
Canada	12.1	12.2	12.3	12.1	11.9	11.8	12.6	13.2	14.4	14.6	13.8	13.2	13.0	12.5	12.6	
CzechRepublic									12.9	11.8	11.7	11.4	11.7	12.5		
Denmark	17.0	16.3	15.5	16.2	17.3	18.2	18.4	18.4	18.9	19.8	21.2	20.4	19.8	18.9	18.2	17.7
Finland	10.2	10.8	11.0	10.9	9.5	9.0	10.0	18.6	22.5	24.0	23.8	22.2	21.5	19.9	18.4	17.9
France	21.8	22.1	21.9	21.6	21.5	21.2	21.4	17.3	17.7	18.5	18.4	18.5	18.7	18.8	18.4	18.4
Germany	16.5	16.2	15.9	16.2	16.1	15.7	15.3	15.7	16.3	17.4	17.7	18.1	19.3	19.3	18.9	18.9
Greece	14.0	14.8	14.9	15.6	15.7	15.9	16.0	14.6	14.5	14.8	14.8	15.1	15.4	15.6	15.6	15.8
Hungary												15.8	13.9	13.1	13.6	
Iceland	4.4	4.7	4.6	4.9	5.4	5.6	5.4	6.2	6.7	7.0	6.8	7.0	6.6			
Ireland	16.1	16.5	17.0	16.5	16.0	14.1		12.0	12.4	12.2	12.1	11.3	11.0	10.5	9.8	9.6
Italy	16.7	17.2	17.2	17.3	17.4	17.6	18.0	18.3	19.3	19.5	19.5	19.0	16.9	17.3	17.0	17.4
Japan	11.0	10.9	11.2	11.6	11.4	11.0	11.5	10.8	11.3	11.9	12.5	13.4	13.5	13.7	14.6	
Korea								2.2	2.3	2.3	2.3	2.1	2.4	2.6	3.2	
Luxembourg	22.1	22.0	21.8					15.4	15.6	16.2	16.0	16.5	16.4	15.7	15.4	15.1
Mexico									1.2	1.3	1.2	1.2	1.3	1.4		
Netherlands	27.5	26.1	25.9	26.5	25.9	25.4	26.3	26.0	26.4	26.6	25.4	15.3	14.8	13.9	13.0	12.6
NewZealand	13.7	13.7	13.7	13.6	13.4	13.3	15.4									
Norway	15.0	14.8	15.9	16.4	18.1	19.0		16.4	17.1	16.9	16.4	15.8	15.2	14.7	15.5	15.5
Poland								17.9	20.0	19.9	18.8	18.1	18.0	17.7	17.3	
Portugal	10.9	10.8	11.6	12.4	12.5	12.1		11.9	12.5	13.9	13.9	11.7	11.8	11.7	11.7	11.8
Spain	16.0	16.0	15.6	15.3	15.3			16.8	17.5	18.4	17.9	17.2	17.2			
Sweden	17.6	18.2	18.4	18.7	19.5	19.5	19.7	21.1	23.4	23.3	22.8	21.3	20.3	19.6	19.3	18.9
Switzerland	14.1	13.7	13.6	13.6	13.8	13.4	13.4	9.0	10.0	11.2	11.1	11.2	11.8	12.5	11.9	
Turkey																
UK	14.0	13.9	14.1	13.3	12.3	12.0	12.2	14.0	15.6	16.0	15.7	15.4	14.9	14.4	13.7	13.5
United States	11.0	11.0	11.0	10.8	10.6	10.8		12.2	12.9	13.0	12.8	13.0	12.9	12.6		
Total OECD	**13.6**	**13.6**	**13.6**	**13.6**	**13.4**	**13.2**	**15.3**	**13.4**	**14.1**	**14.1**	**14.1**	**14.0**	**13.9**	**13.7**	**14.3**	**16.4**
Standarddeviation	*5.2*	*5.1*	*5.0*	*4.9*	*4.9*	*5.0*	*5.1*	*5.1*	*5.3*	*6.0*	*5.9*	*5.2*	*5.1*	*4.8*	*4.8*	*2.9*

Note: Social security transfers consists of social security benefits, social security grants and unfunded employee welfare benefits paid by general government

Data is not available for 1961–67, 1969 or 1970

Sources: OECD (1985) Table 6.3; OECD (1992a) Table 6.3, OECD (2000) Table 6.3

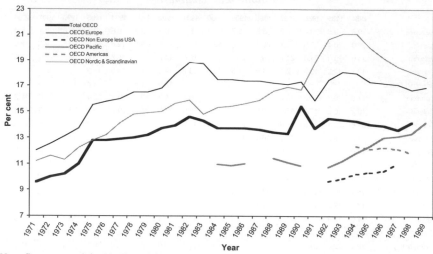

Note: Groups are as defined in Figure 3.2

Figure 4.1 Social security transfers as a percentage of GDP:
OECD versus Europe and non-European nations
Source: Table 4.2

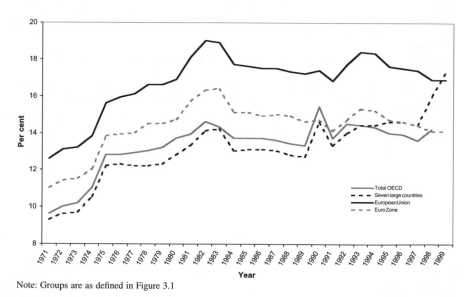

Note: Groups are as defined in Figure 3.1

Figure 4.2 Social security transfers as a percentage of GDP:
OECD versus EU and large economies
Source: Table 4.2

for the OECD as a whole rose from single figures during the 1960s into double figures in the early 1970s, remaining in double figures thereafter. Whilst understandably rising during the recessions of the early 1980s and 1990s (to 14 per cent of GDP in each recession), the OECD average ratios fell back only marginally during the subsequent economic recoveries, remaining almost a percentage point higher after each recession than before it. Thus there seems to have been a 'ratchet effect' for social security transfers: they rise during downturns in economic activity but do not fall back fully to previous levels as downturns turn into recovery. As a general rule, social security transfers were consistently and significantly higher than the OECD average in European countries (especially in the EU) and less in non-European countries (see Figures 4.1 and 4.2). Korea and Mexico are notable for their very small ratios when data is available. Australia and Iceland are also notable for their single figure ratios (Table 4.2).

Table 4.3 *Government final consumption as a percentage of GDP*

	1960	1961	1962	1963	1964	1965	1966	1967	1968	1969	1970	1971	1972	1973	1974
Australia	11.2		10.0	9.7	10.3	11.0	11.6	12.3	12.5	12.1	12.2	12.5	12.6	13.0	15.5
Austria	13.0		12.8	13.3	13.3	13.4	13.7	14.6	14.8	15.1	14.7	14.8	14.6	15.1	15.8
Belgium	12.4		12.3	13.0	12.5	12.8	13.1	13.5	13.6	13.6	13.4	14.1	14.5	14.5	14.7
Canada	13.4		15.2	14.9	14.9	14.9	15.5	16.5	17.3	17.6	19.2	19.2	19.1	18.5	18.1
CzechRepublic															
Denmark	13.3		15.2	15.4	15.6	16.3	17.1	17.8	18.6	18.9	20.0	21.3	21.3	21.3	23.4
Finland	11.9		12.6	13.5	13.6	13.8	14.5	15.1	15.5	14.7	14.7	15.2	15.3	15.0	15.2
France	14.2		13.3	13.4	13.3	13.1	13.0	13.0	13.5	13.3	13.4	13.4	13.2	13.2	15.4
Germany	13.4		14.6	15.5	14.8	15.2	15.5	16.2	15.5	15.6	15.8	16.9	17.1	17.8	19.3
Greece	11.7		11.6	11.0	11.7	11.7	11.8	13.0	12.9	12.7	12.6	12.5	12.2	11.5	13.8
Hungary															
Iceland	10.6		8.2	8.8	8.7	8.7	8.8	9.6	10.0	9.5	9.7	10.0	10.4	10.1	16.2
Ireland	12.5		12.5	12.7	13.3	13.6	13.6	13.4	13.4	13.5	14.6	15.2	15.3	15.7	17.2
Italy	12.0		13.1	13.9	14.3	15.1	14.9	14.4	14.5	14.2	13.8	15.5	16.1	15.5	13.8
Japan	8.0		7.8	8.0	7.9	8.2	8.0	7.7	7.4	7.3	7.4	8.0	8.2	8.3	9.1
Korea															
Luxembourg	9.8		10.9	12.2	10.8	10.9	11.4	11.9	11.8	10.9	10.7	11.7	11.9	11.3	11.5
Mexico															
Netherlands	12.6		13.9	14.7	14.8	14.8	15.2	15.5	15.2	15.3	15.6	16	15.9	15.6	16.2
NewZealand	10.5		11.3	10.9	11.0	12.5	13.8	12.7	12.9	12.5	13.2	12.9	12.9	12.8	14.7
Norway	12.9		14.0	14.3	14.5	15	15.5	16.1	16.6	16.8	16.9	17.9	18.2	18.2	18.3
Poland															
Portugal	10.5		12.9	12.3	123.0	12	12.1	13.1	13.1	12.9	13.8	13.5	13.4	12.8	14.1
SlovakRepublic															
Spain	8.3		7.2	7.5	7.3	7.4	7.7	8.4	8.2	8.3	8.5	8.6	8.6	8.6	10.0
Sweden	16		16.7	17.3	17.2	17.8	18.9	19.6	20.6	20.8	21.4	22.5	22.7	22.7	23.4
Switzerland	8.8		10.1	10.5	10.4	10.5	10.4	10.3	10.4	10.5	10.5	10.9	10.9	11.2	11.6
Turkey	10.5		11.1	11.0	12.1	12.4	12.1	12.3	12.6	12.4	12.9	13.4	12.1	12.5	13.0
UK	16.4		17.0	16.9	16.4	16.8	17.1	17.9	17.6	17.2	17.6	17.8	18.4	18.2	20.0
United States	16.6		17.9	17.7	17.5	17.1	18.1	19.3	19.2	18.8	19.2	18.5	18.4	17.8	18.1
Total OECD	**13.6**		**14.3**	**14.4**	**15.0**	**14.3**	**14.8**	**15.4**	**15.3**	**15.1**	**15.4**	**15.5**	**15.5**	**15.3**	**16.0**
Standarddeviation	*2.3*		*2.8*	*2.8*	*22.6*	*2.8*	*3.0*	*3.1*	*3.3*	*3.4*	*3.6*	*3.7*	*3.7*	*3.7*	*3.6*

continued

Table 4.3 *continued*

	1975	1976	1977	1978	1979	1980	1981	1982	1983	1984	1985	1986	1987	1988	1989
Australia	15.4	16.0	16.3	16.7	15.9	17.6	17.8	18.4	18.8	18.5	18.5	18.8	17.8	17.1	16.5
Austria	17.2	17.6	17.4	18.3	18.1	18.0	18.5	18.9	18.9	18.6	18.9	19.0	18.9	18.5	18.2
Belgium	16.4	16.5	16.8	17.5	17.6	17.8	18.6	18.0	17.5	17.0	17.1	16.8	16.2	15.2	14.5
Canada	20.0	19.7	20.3	20.1	19.3	19.2	19.4	21.1	21.0	20.1	20.1	19.9	19.3	19.0	18.9
CzechRepublic															
Denmark	24.6	24.1	23.9	24.5	25.0	26.7	27.8	28.2	27.4	25.9	25.3	23.9	25.2	25.7	25.5
Finland	17.1	18.1	18.5	18.3	17.9	18.1	18.7	19.0	19.4	19.4	20.4	20.7	20.8	20.1	19.7
France	14.4	14.6	14.7	15.0	14.9	18.1	18.8	19.3	19.5	19.6	19.4	18.9	18.8	18.5	18.0
Germany	20.5	19.9	19.6	19.7	19.6	20.2	20.7	20.6	20.2	20.0	20.1	19.9	20.0	19.7	18.9
Greece	15.2	15.1	16.0	15.9	16.3	16.4	18.0	18.3	18.8	19.5	20.4	19.4	19.6	20.0	20.5
Hungary															
Iceland	11.1	11.0	11.0	11.5	11.7	16.4	16.6	17.4	17.6	16.1	16.9	17.2	17.7	18.6	18.8
Ireland	18.6	18.2	17.2	17.3	18.4	19.9	19.9	19.8	19.3	18.7	18.6	18.8	17.7	16.4	15.3
Italy	15.4	14.8	15.3	15.9	16.2	14.7	16.0	16.0	16.4	16.3	16.4	16.2	16.7	16.9	16.7
Japan	10.1	9.9	9.9	9.7	9.8	9.8	9.9	9.9	9.9	9.8	9.6	9.7	9.5	9.2	9.2
Korea															
Luxembourg	14.9	14.8	16.0	15.6	15.8	16.7	17.4	16.4	15.8	15.4	15.7	15.7	16.9	16.3	15.9
Mexico															
Netherlands	17.4	17.2	17.4	17.7	18.1	17.9	17.8	17.7	17.5	16.6	16.2	16.0	16.4	15.8	15.3
NewZealand	14.8	13.8	15.4	16.5	15.7	17.9	17.8	17.6	16.8	16.0	16.2	16.2	16.4	16.6	16.5
Norway	19.3	20.0	20.2	20.4	19.5	18.8	19.1	19.4	19.4	18.6	18.5	19.8	20.7	21.0	21.0
Poland															
Portugal	15	13.7	14.0	13.9	13.9	14.5	15.0	14.9	15.1	15.0	15.5	15.4	15.2	16.0	16.1
SlovakRepublic															
Spain	9.2	9.8	10.0	10.4	10.9	13.3	13.9	14.1	14.6	14.4	14.7	14.7	15.1	14.8	15.2
Sweden	23.8	24.9	27.5	27.9	28.3	29.1	29.4	29.3	28.7	27.8	27.6	27.2	26.5	25.8	25.9
Switzerland	12.6	13.2	13.0	12.9	12.9	12.7	12.7	13	13.4	13.4	13.3	13.1	12.8	13.0	13.1
Turkey	12.3	12.7	13.5	13.5	13.6	10.2	13.4	11.5	12.6	10.8	11.4	11.7	12.4	12.0	16.0
UK	21.8	21.4	20.3	19.9	19.8	21.2	21.8	21.7	21.7	21.5	20.8	20.8	20.3	19.7	19.4
United States	19.1	18.7	18.2	17.7	17.6	17.6	17.5	18.4	18.4	18.0	18.4	18.7	18.6	18.3	17.9
Total OECD	**16.9**	**16.6**	**16.5**	**16.3**	**16.3**	**16.6**	**16.9**	**17.3**	**17.4**	**17.0**	**17.2**	**17.2**	**17.1**	**16.8**	**16.6**
Standard deviation	*4.0*	*4.0*	*4.1*	*4.1*	*4.1*	*4.3*	*4.2*	*4.3*	*4.1*	*4.0*	*3.9*	*3.7*	*3.7*	*3.7*	*3.6*

continued

Table 4.3 continued

	1990	1991	1992	1993	1994	1995	1996	1997	1998	1999
Australia	17.1	19.9	19.8	19.2	18.9	18.7	18.3	18.2	18.2	18.8
Austria	18.0	19.2	19.6	20.4	20.5	20.4	20.3	19.7	19.6	19.8
Belgium	14.3	21.0	21.0	21.5	21.4	21.5	21.8	21.3	21.2	21.4
Canada	19.8	24.1	24.6	24.0	22.7	21.7	20.9	19.8	19.7	19.0
CzechRepublic		22.6	21.5	21.9	21.6	19.9	19.9	19.9	19.0	19.7
Denmark	25.2	25.7	25.8	26.8	25.9	25.8	25.9	25.6	25.8	25.7
Finland	21.1	24.8	25.4	24.3	23.4	22.8	23.2	22.4	21.7	21.5
France	18.0	22.5	23.1	24.5	24.1	23.9	24.2	24.2	23.5	23.7
Germany	18.4	19.2	19.8	19.9	19.7	19.8	19.9	19.5	19.1	19.0
Greece	21.2	14.2	13.7	14.3	13.8	15.3	14.5	15.2	15.3	15.0
Hungary		25.2	26.0	28.0	25.7	23.6	22.0	21.9	21.7	21.4
Iceland	18.8	20.4	21.0	21.5	21.4	21.9	21.8	21.5	22.1	22.9
Ireland	15.7	17.4	17.8	17.6	17.4	16.4	15.8	15.2	14.5	14.0
Italy	17.3	20.3	20.1	19.9	19.1	17.9	18.1	18.2	18.0	18.1
Japan	9.1	9.0	9.2	9.4	9.5	9.8	9.7	9.7	10.2	10.3
Korea		10.5	10.8	10.5	10.2	9.7	10.2	10.1	11.0	10.1
Luxembourg	16.3	17.4	17.4	17.1	16.7	17.7	18.2	17.3	16.8	17.7
Mexico		9.1	9.9	11.0	11.6	10.5	9.6	9.9	10.4	10.0
Netherlands	14.8	23.7	24.4	24.8	24.1	24.0	23.1	22.9	23.0	23.2
NewZealand	16.7	17.0	17.0	15.6	14.5	14.5	14.5	15.1	15.3	15.8
Norway	21.0	21.2	22.1	21.8	21.5	20.9	20.3	19.9	21.4	21.2
Poland		21.9	20.7	19.5	16.5	16.8	16.4	16.0	15.4	15.1
Portugal	16.7	18.2	18.2	18.9	18.5	18.6	18.9	19.2	19.2	20.0
SlovakRepublic										
Spain	15.2	17.5	18.5	19.0	18.3	18.1	17.9	17.6	17.5	17.3
Sweden	27.1	27.5	28.2	28.4	27.4	26.3	27.1	26.5	26.7	26.9
Switzerland	13.3	14.5	14.8	14.5	14.5	14.3	14.6	14.1	14.0	13.6
Turkey	19.4	12.4	12.9	13.0	11.0	10.3	11.0	12.0	12.7	16.2
UK	19.9	20.8	21.2	20.6	20.1	19.8	19.4	18.4	18.2	18.4
United States	18.1	17.2	16.8	16.2	15.6	15.3	15.0	14.6	14.3	14.2
Total OECD	**16.8**	**17.1**	**17.2**	**17.1**	**16.6**	**16.3**	**16.1**	**15.9**	**15.8**	**15.8**
Standarddeviation	*3.7*	*4.9*	*4.9*	*5.0*	*4.8*	*4.7*	*4.6*	*4.4*	*4.3*	*4.4*

Sources: OECD (1983a) Table R6; OECD (1985) Table 6.2; OECD (1992a)
Table 6.2, OECD (2000) Table 6.2

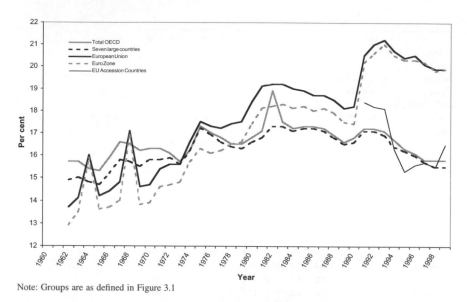

Note: Groups are as defined in Figure 3.1

Figure 4.3   Government final consumption as a percentage of
GDP: OECD versus EU and large economies
Source: Table 4.3

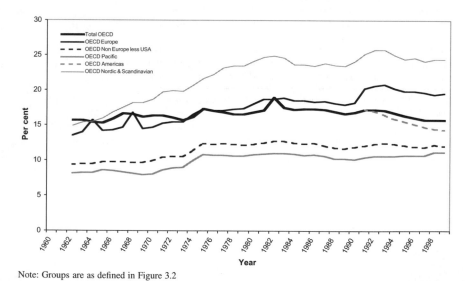

Note: Groups are as defined in Figure 3.2

Figure 4.4   Government final consumption as a percentage of
GDP: OECD versus Europe and non-European nations
Source: Table 4.3

Compared with social security transfers, Table 4.3 shows that government final consumption has accounted for a more stable proportion of GDP. The OECD average was 13.6 per cent in 1960, 15.8 per cent in 1999, peaking at 17.4 per cent in 1983, never having fallen below 15 per cent after 1967. As a general rule, government final consumption was less than the OECD average in European countries (especially the EU) before the mid-1970s but above it thereafter, whereas non-European countries were below that average throughout the period (see Figures 4.3 and 4.4). Moreover, whilst the OECD average displays a downward trend after 1982, European countries (and especially the EU) display a rising trend.

In sharp contrast with total current expenditure, Table 4.4 shows that *capital* expenditure has displayed no rising trend, accounting for 21 per cent of GDP at both the beginning and end of the period, reaching a peak of 23.5

Table 4.4 *Government capital expenditure as a percentage of GDP*

	1960	1961	1962	1963	1964	1965	1966	1967	1968	1969	1970	1971	1972	1973	1974
Australia	24.8		24.5	24.7	25.9	27.4	27.0	26.2	26.2	26.2	25.9	26.2	24.3	22.9	23.5
Austria	25.0		25.8	26.1	26.4	27.4	27.9	26.6	25.7	25.1	25.9	27.9	30.2	28.5	28.4
Belgium	19.3		21.3	20.7	22.4	22.4	22.9	22.9	21.5	21.3	22.7	22.1	21.3	21.4	22.7
Canada	22.6		20.5	20.5	22.0	23.5	24.5	23.2	22.6	21.4	20.8	21.8	21.7	22.4	23.7
CzechRepublic															
Denmark	21.6		23.1	22.0	24.5	24.1	24.1	24.2	23.4	24.6	24.7	24.2	24.6	24.8	24.0
Finland	28.3		26.7	24.8	24.6	26.0	26.0	24.6	23.1	23.4	25.9	27.3	27.7	28.7	29.8
France	20.9		21.4	22.1	22.9	23.3	23.7	23.8	24.3	23.4	23.4	23.6	23.7	23.8	25.8
Germany	24.3		25.6	25.6	26.6	26.1	25.4	23.1	22.4	23.3	25.5	26.1	25.4	23.9	21.6
Greece	19.0		20.1	19.2	21.0	21.6	21.7	20.3	23.2	24.6	23.6	25.2	27.8	28.0	22.2
Hungary															
Iceland	29.6		24.0	27.5	28.3	25.9	27.2	30.6	31.6	24.5	23.8	29.2	27.8	29.4	32.1
Ireland	14.4		17.9	19.5	20.5	21.4	19.8	20.1	20.9	23.3	22.7	23.6	23.7	25.3	24.6
Italy	26.0		23.7	24.0	22.2	19.3	18.8	19.5	23.4	21.0	21.4	20.4	19.8	20.8	25.9
Japan	29.0		32.9	31.5	31.7	29.9	30.4	32.1	33.2	34.5	35.5	34.3	34.2	36.4	34.8
Korea															
Luxembourg	20.9		26.1	29.9	33.5	28.0	26.6	23.3	22.1	21.7	23.5	28.4	28.2	27.4	24.6
Mexico															
Netherlands	24.1		24.5	23.8	25.5	25.1	26.2	26.3	26.9	24.6	25.8	25.9	23.7	23.1	21.9
NewZealand	21.3		19.7	20.1	21.4	21.9	21.9	20.3	19.6	19.6	20.8	20.6	22.3	22.6	27.5
Norway	29.0		29.2	29.5	27.9	28.2	28.7	29.7	26.9	24.3	26.5	29.7	27.7	29.3	30.5
Poland															
Portugal	23.2		22.4	23.7	22.8	22.8	25.1	26.6	22.2	22.6	23.2	24.7	27.1	26.8	26.6
SlovakRepublic															
Spain	20.4		19.2	19.4	20.7	21.7	22.0	22.3	26.0	23.2	23.2	21.2	22.2	23.6	28.4
Sweden	22.1		23.1	24.2	24.6	24.7	24.8	24.8	23.3	23.2	22.5	22.0	22.2	21.9	20.9
Switzerland	24.8		28.8	30.0	30.7	28.7	27.4	26.0	25.6	25.8	27.5	29.2	29.7	29.4	27.6
Turkey	16.0		15.1	14.4	14.6	14.6	15.9	16.4	17.3	17.4	18.6	17.0	20.2	20.1	18.6
UK	16.4		16.8	16.6	18.2	18.2	18.2	18.7	19.5	18.3	18.5	18.3	18.3	19.4	20.9
United States	18.0		17.6	17.9	18.1	18.8	18.6	17.9	18.1	18.2	17.6	18.1	18.7	19.1	18.6
Total OECD	**21.6**		**22.0**	**22.0**	**22.4**	**22.3**	**22.3**	**22.1**	**22.7**	**22.6**	**22.8**	**22.8**	**23.0**	**23.5**	**23.5**
Standard deviation	*4.2*		*4.3*	*4.5*	*4.5*	*3.8*	*3.7*	*4.0*	*3.7*	*3.4*	*3.6*	*4.2*	*4.0*	*4.1*	*4.1*

continued

Table 4.4   *continued*

	1975	1976	1977	1978	1979	1980	1981	1982	1983	1984	1985	1986	1987	1988	1989
Australia	23.2	23.1	22.8	22.8	22.2	24.2	25.9	25.4	22.9	22.9	24.7	24.3	23.7	24.1	25.0
Austria	26.7	26.0	26.7	25.6	24.7	25.7	25.4	23.2	22.4	22.2	22.6	22.8	23.1	23.8	24.2
Belgium	22.5	22.1	21.7	21.7	20.8	21.1	18.6	17.3	16.2	16.0	15.6	15.7	16.0	17.7	19.5
Canada	24.0	23.1	22.7	22.2	22.6	23.5	24.4	21.9	20.2	19.2	19.9	20.3	21.3	22.2	22.8
CzechRepublic															
Denmark	21.1	23.0	22.1	21.7	20.9	18.8	15.6	16.1	16.6	17.2	18.7	20.8	19.7	18.1	17.8
Finland	31.0	27.7	26.6	23.4	22.8	25.5	25.3	25.3	25.5	23.8	23.9	23.4	23.8	25.2	27.7
France	23.3	23.3	22.3	21.4	21.5	23.6	22.1	21.4	20.2	19.3	19.3	19.3	19.8	20.6	21.1
Germany	20.4	20.2	20.3	20.8	21.9	22.6	21.6	20.4	20.4	20.0	19.5	19.4	19.4	19.6	20.3
Greece	20.8	21.2	23.0	23.9	25.8	24.2	22.3	19.9	20.3	18.5	19.1	18.5	17.2	17.5	19.2
Hungary															
Iceland	32.1	28.6	28.0	25.4	24.5	25.3	24.4	24.3	21.5	21.0	20.5	18.7	19.7	18.9	18.5
Ireland	22.6	24.8	24.9	28.6	31.4	28.6	29.7	26.5	23.1	21.4	19.0	18.0	16.5	16.7	18.2
Italy	20.6	20.0	19.6	18.7	18.8	24.3	23.9	22.3	21.3	21.0	20.7	19.7	19.7	20.1	20.2
Japan	32.4	31.3	30.5	30.8	32.1	31.6	30.6	29.5	28.6	27.7	27.5	27.3	28.5	29.9	31.0
Korea															
Luxembourg	27.8	24.5	25.3	23.9	24.6	27.1	25.4	25.6	21.2	20.0	17.7	22.1	25.6	26.9	23.4
Mexico															
Netherlands	20.9	19.3	21.1	21.3	21.0	21.0	19.2	18.2	18.2	18.6	19.2	20.1	20.2	21.3	21.7
NewZealand	27.2	25.0	22.0	20.2	17.8	20.6	23.6	24.6	24.2	24.9	25.8	22.0	21.4	19.4	20.2
Norway	34.2	36.3	37.1	31.8	27.7	24.8	28.0	25.5	25.7	26.0	22.0	28.3	28.0	29.2	27.5
Poland															
Portugal	25.9	25.1	26.5	27.9	26.8	28.6	30.8	31.1	29.2	23.6	21.8	22.1	24.2	26.8	26.4
SlovakRepublic															
Spain	23.3	21.8	21.0	19.9	18.9	22.5	22.1	21.6	20.9	19.0	19.2	19.5	20.8	22.6	24.2
Sweden	20.9	21.2	21.1	19.4	19.8	19.7	18.5	18.3	18.3	18.2	18.9	18.1	18.9	19.7	21.5
Switzerland	24.0	20.6	20.7	21.4	21.8	23.8	24.1	23.1	23.3	23.4	23.8	24.2	25.3	26.6	27.5
Turkey	20.8	23.1	24.4	21.9	20.8	16.0	19.6	19.6	18.6	18.5	21.1	24.0	25.2	24.0	22.8
UK	19.5	18.9	17.9	18.0	18.0	18.0	16.2	16.1	16.0	17.0	17.0	16.9	17.6	19.1	20.0
United States	17.0	17.2	18.3	19.5	19.8	19.1	18.6	17.2	17.2	18.0	18.1	17.8	17.3	17.1	16.6
Total OECD	**21.7**	**21.4**	**21.6**	**21.9**	**22.2**	**22.5**	**21.9**	**20.8**	**20.3**	**20.3**	**20.3**	**20.2**	**20.4**	**20.8**	**21.1**
Standarddeviation	*4.5*	*4.2*	*4.21*	*3.7*	*3.8*	*3.7*	*4.2*	*4.0*	*3.6*	*3.0*	*2.9*	*3.2*	*3.5*	*3.9*	*3.7*

continued

Table 4.4 continued

	1990	1991	1992	1993	1994	1995	1996	1997	1998	1999
Australia	23.1	20.9	21.5	22.0	23.3	22.4	22.7	23.5	23.8	23.8
Austria	24.3	24.2	23.7	23.2	23.5	23.3	23.3	23.5	23.5	23.7
Belgium	20.3	21.5	21.3	20.5	20.0	20.2	20.2	20.6	20.9	21.3
Canada	21.4	19.4	18.5	17.7	18.4	17.3	17.5	19.4	19.6	19.8
CzechRepublic		24.1	27.9	28.4	28.7	32.0	31.8	30.8	28.3	26.4
Denmark	17.7	19.1	17.0	17.1	17.3	18.6	18.6	19.4	20.2	19.7
Finland	26.3	24.4	19.9	16.4	15.5	16.3	17.0	18.0	18.7	18.8
France	21.2	22.0	20.9	19.4	19.1	18.8	18.5	18.0	18.3	19.0
Germany	21.2	23.8	24.0	23.0	23.1	22.4	21.8	21.4	21.3	21.3
Greece	19.7	22.6	21.3	20.3	18.6	18.6	19.5	20.0	21.6	22.5
Hungary		22.0	20.9	19.9	21.2	20.0	21.4	22.2	23.6	23.8
Iceland	19.4	21.0	19.2	17.4	17.0	16.7	20.2	20.9	24.6	22.8
Ireland	19.1	17.1	16.9	15.5	16.5	17.2	18.8	20.3	21.9	23.4
Italy	20.2	21.0	20.5	18.4	18.0	18.3	18.3	18.1	18.4	18.9
Japan	32.2	31.4	30.5	29.5	28.6	28.5	29.5	28.6	26.8	26.1
Korea		39.0	37.0	36.2	36.0	36.7	36.8	35.1	29.8	28.0
Luxembourg	25.3	25.4	22.7	24.2	20.7	21.7	20.3	20.1	19.2	22.4
Mexico		18.7	19.6	18.6	19.4	16.2	17.9	19.5	20.9	21.0
Netherlands	21.5	21.8	21.4	20.5	20.0	20.3	21.1	21.4	21.7	22.3
NewZealand	19.8	16.0	16.5	18.3	20.3	21.0	21.3	20.2	19.2	19.5
Norway	18.9	20.6	19.9	20.4	20.7	20.7	21.3	23.0	25.0	22.2
Poland		19.5	16.8	15.9	17.9	18.6	20.7	23.5	25.1	26.2
Portugal	26.4	24.3	23.2	21.6	21.7	21.9	22.4	23.9	24.7	24.9
SlovakRepublic										
Spain	24.6	25.2	23.1	21.0	21.0	22.0	21.6	21.9	22.9	24.2
Sweden	20.7	20.8	18.3	15.3	15.1	15.5	15.7	15.2	16.0	16.8
Switzerland	27.1	25.5	23.0	21.6	22.0	21.4	20.2	19.6	20.0	19.9
Turkey	22.7	23.8	23.6	26.5	24.6	23.8	25.1	26.4	24.6	21.8
UK	19.2	17.9	16.5	15.8	15.8	16.3	16.6	16.7	17.4	17.8
United States	16.1	16.2	16.2	16.7	17.3	17.7	18.2	18.6	19.2	19.9
Total OECD	**21.0**	**21.5**	**21.0**	**20.6**	**20.7**	**20.7**	**21.1**	**21.2**	**21.2**	**21.4**
Standard deviation	*3.6*	*4.6*	*4.5*	*4.7*	*4.5*	*4.7*	*4.6*	*4.2*	*3.3*	*2.8*

Sources: OECD (1983a) Table R3; OECD (1985) Table 6.8; OECD (1992a) Table 6.8; OECD (2000) Table 6.8

per cent in 1973 and never falling below 20 per cent. Thus, having been 91 per cent of current expenditure in 1960, capital expenditure was not much more than half of current expenditure during the 1990s. There was also much less variability amongst countries in the capital expenditure/GDP ratio (the standard deviation range being 2.8 to 4.7) than in the current expenditure/GDP ratio (the standard deviation range being 5.2 to 12.0). Interestingly, Figures 4.5 and 4.6 show a reversal of the usual situation depicted above. Except for the EU accession countries, European countries (and especially the EU) have been fairly consistent in having capital expenditure/GDP ratios below the OECD average, whereas non-European countries have been consistently above that average (except OECD Americas, dominated by the USA, during the 1990s). This reversal of the usual scenario reflects a number of factors:

- the smaller GDPs in some (but by no means all) non-European OECD countries and EU accession countries
- the importance governments attach to capital expenditures as they attempt to foster economic growth to catch up with the OECD average (see Chapter 3)
- the perceived need amongst EU member states to constrain capital expenditures to control emergent structural gaps in the public finances (see Chapter 7).

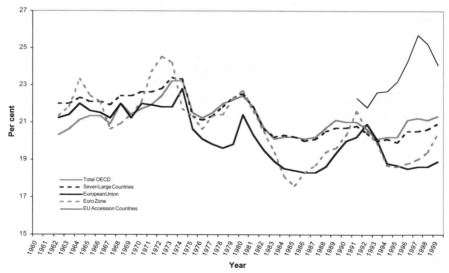

Note: Groups are as defined in Figure 3.1

Figure 4.5 Government capital expenditure as a percentage of
GDP: OECD versus EU and large economies

Source: Table 4.4

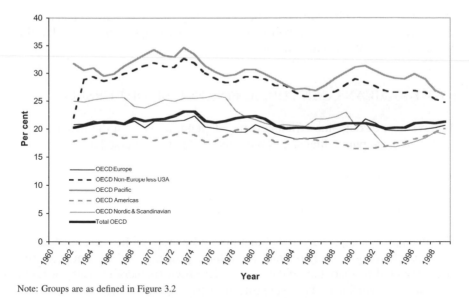

Note: Groups are as defined in Figure 3.2

Figure 4.6 Government capital expenditure as a percentage of
GDP: OECD versus Europe and non-European nations
Source: Table 4.4

DOES PUBLIC SPENDING SECURE VALUE FOR MONEY?

Ongoing expenditure programmes are typically the result of past (rather than
current) decisions, attention usually focusing on incremental expenditures
from year to year. Hence, there is a substantial degree of inheritance in public
expenditure programmes. Radical approaches requiring annual reviews of
decisions about which services are to be produced and at what levels and qualities (for example zero-based budgeting) have generally not been adopted,
perhaps partly because of resistance by distributional coalitions (see Chapter
1). Thus, there has been a general failure to consider outcome-effectiveness in
any rigorous way.

In practice, most countries produce public services without a clear specifi-
cation of the objectives they are meant to achieve. Objectives tend to be written in such vague terms that they are of little practical use for the evaluation of
services. In such cases, it is obviously difficult to determine whether services
are actually being used by those groups for whom they are primarily intended.
Even where service objectives are made explicit enough to be useful for evaluation studies, there is often little attempt to ensure that service provision
actually fulfils them. For example, proponents of cultural services such as
museums and galleries often claim that these services seek to maximise access
for low-income groups and yet they often fail to monitor the socioeconomic

characteristics of their visitors. In such cases they cannot be sure that access is maximised. As noted above, badly targeted services represent poor value for money in terms of outcome-effectiveness.

BY WHAT MEANS CAN PUBLIC FINANCE BE DISBURSED?

Achievement of outcome efficiency may depend, in part, on the mechanisms used to allocate public finance. Public finance can be disbursed to:

- service providers
- service users
- both service providers and service users.

The analysis of Chapter 2 showed that public finance can be used most effectively by helping to clarify and strengthen property rights. Thus, public finance should be disbursed either to service providers, service users or both, according to whichever best supports property rights in delivering as efficiently and effectively as possible the outcome objectives underpinning the use of public finance.

Disbursement to providers can be on the basis of agreed inputs, processes, outputs, outcomes or any combination of these four stages of service production. As already noted, outcomes (such as those of education and training services) are difficult to define, monitor and measure. Hence, the usual approach is to disburse public finance on the basis of inputs (for example numbers of teachers or trainers), processes (for example numbers of school or training places) and outputs (for example numbers of academically qualified or trained clients produced). An outcome proxy may be used such as payment by mission of service provider. Thus, central, federal or state governments may wish universities to widen access, drawing proportionately more students from lower socioeconomic groups (that is, from low-income households living in areas of multiple deprivation). More simply, instead of paying public funds to universities simply on the basis of student numbers (full-time equivalents), those funds could be weighted according to the socioeconomic group from which they are drawn. For example, students from 'lower' socioeconomic groups could attract more funding than those from 'higher' socioeconomic groups, the difference in funding perhaps reflecting the differential need for educational resources necessary to achieve a given educational outcome.

Disbursement to service users can simply be in the form of cash. Disbursing money directly to welfare recipients and others allows markets to measure preferences by putting values on property rights (see Chapter 2). In general, allowing market systems to provide for the preferences of consumers, according to their willingness to pay for goods and services, maximises economic welfare. Thus, in principle, it is better to give public finance directly to, say, high need and/or low-income target groups so that they can spend cash benefits in accordance with their own preferences.

However, it was noted in Chapter 2 that markets may fail due to problems associated with lack of information about the benefits of service use, myopia and lack of appreciation of risk. Welfare payments as cash may therefore not be spent on the services intended by the policy-maker. In such cases, publicly financed consumption subsidies would have to be tied directly to the consumption of particular services. This does not mean, however, that the subsidy should be tied to particular service providers. In principle, public finance should not be given directly to the service provider because:

- subsidising service providers does not allow service clients to express preferences regarding their favoured provider
- guaranteeing the income of the service provider provides little incentive for that provider to cater for the preferences of service users
- in such cases there is likely to be a deterioration of service quality, for example in the form of a highly standardised service unresponsive to the needs or wants of individual service users. Service providers may adopt a 'take it or leave it' attitude, service clients having little alternative but to accept poorer quality service, service providers justifying this because it is free at the point of use. The policy-maker's intended outputs and outcomes are compromised in such cases
- unnecessarily high service costs are also likely to occur if the service provider has a statutory or de facto monopoly because there is no incentive for the service provider to economise on inputs and processes.

Put simply, the performance of the organisation deteriorates if its income is guaranteed. The result is increasing levels of organisational slack in the form of unnecessarily high costs and poorer quality of output. The solution in such a case is to allow service users to go to alternative service providers (that is, 'exit' the current provider) and/or give them an effective say (that is, 'voice') as regards what constitutes an adequate service. Affording service users increased scope for exit and voice effectively strengthens their property rights, that is, their right to receive adequate services or other forms of publicly financed support from service providers. If the public money follows the service user, service providers can be expected to pay much closer attention to satisfaction of the users of their services. If service users went to alternative providers, effectively taking public finance with them, the current provider's income would fall and the organisation would have to make workers redundant and, in the extreme case, would ultimately go bankrupt. In contrast, service providers catering more effectively for service providers would see their revenues rise, so financing additional levels of service output in line with users' preferences.

Of course, organisations cannot simply cater for the whims of their clients. They also have to pay attention to professional practice and the requirements of the provider of public finance commissioning the service or other output. Service users are not the only stakeholder group. Nevertheless, whilst recognising such constraints, allowing service users even moderate scope for exit and voice can be expected to result in improved service quality and so improved outcome-effectiveness. Increased scope for exit can be expected to improve the effectiveness of voice because, ultimately, if service providers do not respond to the expression of voice, service users can take the public money elsewhere as they exit the current provider. Put simply, voice is weak without the exit option.

In principle, therefore, public finance should be disbursed as far as possible on the basis of 'the money follows the service user', service clients being afforded adequate scope for choice from amongst alternative service providers. A 'money follows the user' policy effectively adopts vouchers, even though they may be implicit (see Chapter 9). Explicit vouchers could also be used to target subsidy on prioritised groups as they access their preferred service provider. In turn, this implies that those of higher income and lower need would have to pay charges for service use (see Chapter 5). This would result in differential subsidisation of service *user* as distinct from subsidisation of service *provider*, the degree of subsidy being based on assessment of both need and ability to pay. Use of vouchers (whether explicit or implicit) ensures that public money follows the service user and so allows preferences to be judged in much the same way as the exchange of private property rights in competitive markets reveals preferences.

In general, therefore, service providers can be expected to be more efficient and effective if they have to earn public finance. Likewise, service users can be expected to use public finance more effectively if they are required to be more proactive in deciding how or where to spend it. Outcome-effectiveness is therefore promoted.

ADDITIONALITY IN PUBLIC FINANCE

It was noted above that, inter alia, outcome-effectiveness requires public finance to provide truly additional benefits. Additionality can be defined as 'the extent to which public finance induces spending or activity that would otherwise not have occurred'.

Public finance could still be wasted even with full economy in inputs and processes, complete correspondence between outputs and outcomes, and fully utilised outputs. This would be the case when public finance does not secure additionality. Consistent with the above analysis, there are various concepts of additionality:

■ *input additionality* (securing more inputs with which to produce services)
■ *process additionality* (making more productive, in terms of delivery of

service objectives, the behaviour of practitioners and/or the recipients of public finance)

■ *output additionality* (securing additional outputs)
■ *outcome additionality* (improving the impact of services, this being the ultimate definition of additionality).

These four concepts of additionality can be operationalised by defining additionality in terms that can be measured:

■ *Financial additionality* – the inducement of spending that would not otherwise have occurred, leading to an increased volume of service inputs and/or level of provision or other such activity (input and output additionality respectively)
■ *Quality additionality* – the inducement of a higher level of service quality or activity quality that would not otherwise have occurred (a form of process or output additionality)
■ *Temporal additionality* – the earlier inducement of the same quantity and/or quality of service or activity that would otherwise have occurred at a later date (a form of process additionality)
■ *Geographical additionality* – the refocusing of a given level of spending or activity that would otherwise have been at a broader area (for example regional) scale within narrower spatial (for example urban) boundaries (another form of process additionality)
■ *Economic additionality* – refers to increased economic welfare resulting from the use of public finance to ameliorate market failure, the clarification of tradable property rights allowing resources to be properly valued and so used more efficiently (a form of outcome additionality)
■ *Social additionality* – in terms of using public finance to secure additional negative and/or positive rights for citizens (another form of outcome additionality). They may include improved equity in terms of equal access to services, equality of opportunity, absence of discrimination and so on.

Clearly, the concept of additionality relates to any use of public finance, not just for service provision; nor is it restricted to financial additionality. The concept has been used in the evaluation of policies relating to regional and local economic development initiatives and these will be used to illustrate the concept. EU funds such as the European Regional Development Fund (ERDF) have been used to attract inward investment to economically depressed regions by subsidising private companies' capital expenditures on plant and machinery in those areas. By such means it is hoped that public finance encourages job creation and so offsets a region's economic disadvantage. However, rather than creating additional jobs, those ERDF funds could have no impact whatsoever:

- ERDF funds may have been directly offset by a reduction in the recipient member states' own regional development spending, this practice being alleged during the 1980s and 90s. This is a particular case of 'fiscal substitution', one source of public finance replacing another source.
- ERDF funds may have subsidised investment that would have gone ahead anyway. For example, investments in North Sea oil production by the major multinational oil companies attracted EU and national subsidies at a time when they would almost certainly have explored for and produced oil anyway in response to escalating crude oil prices during the mid to late 1970s and early 1980s. Such unnecessary use of public finance is referred to as 'deadweight subsidy'. It occurs when public finance is used to subsidise an activity that would have occurred without that payment of public money.
- Even if state subsidies do attract new investment to a region, that investment may fail to create new jobs. This would be the case if the newly created jobs simply displaced jobs elsewhere in the region or locality. Such 'displacement' of employment would occur if the subsidised inward investors were able to outcompete other producers in the region, such that the latter lost profits and so reduced their levels of investment and employment. Displacement occurs when an activity taking place as a result of receipt of public finance would otherwise have occurred elsewhere.

In these three examples public finance does not result in additional jobs, the level of additionality being zero in terms of employment. There may, however, still be an element of quality additionality in the third example above if the displaced jobs were less skilled than the newly created jobs. Even if skills would eventually have been upgraded without such inward investment, there may still be an element of temporal additionality if that upgrading occurred earlier than it would otherwise have done. Even if skills were not upgraded, there may still be an element of geographical or social additionality if those who got the new jobs were from groups the government had prioritised for employment, for example inner-city residents, ethnic groups, low-income households, or other such disadvantaged groups.

Thus ERDF funds may have achieved any or all or none of financial, quality, temporal, geographical and social additionality in a given region during a given period of time. In order to assess whether public funds are being used effectively, it is clearly necessary to try to measure the degree of additionality.

IDENTIFYING AND MEASURING ADDITIONALITY

In order to assess the degree of additionality, it is necessary to establish the counterfactual, that is, what would have occurred without that intervention. Thus additionality is measured by comparing the output or other such activity resulting from the spending of public finance with what would have occurred in the absence of that finance. This comparison is, of course, very difficult to make if there was no activity before payment of the public finance, since it would sometimes be very difficult to determine whether any activity would have occurred in the counterfactual case.

For *financial additionality*, this problem is greater for one-off capital expenditures than for ongoing current expenditures. Assuming a pre-existing level of activity, for example in terms of provision of a service prior to the payment of that public finance, there are three ways of measuring the counterfactual:

■ *Build a financial model* of past spending on the service or activity and use that model to predict what future spending would have been in the absence of that new or additional public finance. The most common approach is to extrapolate past expenditure trends into the future. This may be reasonably accurate if the future time horizon is short but it may become increasingly inaccurate the longer the period into the future the extrapolation is made. This is because service conditions or the activity's environment may change over time. Thus, a more sophisticated econometric model may be required in order to take account of the multitude of factors determining spending on the service or activity.

■ *Survey policy-makers, practitioners and/or intended and actual beneficiaries* of the service or activity. Surveys use either questionnaires (postal or email) and/or elite interviews (whether face to face or over the phone). The survey seeks views about what would have happened in the absence of the payment of that public finance. However, responses may be biased towards claiming a greater degree of additionality than actually occurred. This is particularly likely if respondents anticipate payment of more public finance if there is evidence of a significant degree of additionality. Likewise those who feel disadvantaged by the policy (for example local employers facing competition from subsidised inward investment) may exaggerate possible adverse effects (for example loss of profits and jobs), leading to a lower estimate of additionality.

■ *Establish a 'control group'* not in receipt of public finance and compare it with the organisation(s) in receipt of that public money. If the spending or activity of the recipient group significantly exceeds that of the control group following the payment of public finance, this suggests a high degree of additionality. It is crucial, therefore, that the control group and recipient group are truly comparable, meaning that the only difference between them is the receipt of public finance by one but not the other group. This will generally be very difficult to achieve for small numbers of organisations or service providers. Large numbers are needed in each group in order for statistically significant differences to be recorded.

Whether using an econometric model, survey, control group or a combination of two or all three methods, the intention is to build a 'baseline', counterfactual case against which to compare actual spending or activity. Without such a baseline case there is no way of separating the effects of payment of public finance from other changes occurring as a result of other causes. Certainly, it is methodologically invalid to adopt a 'before and after' approach in measuring the degree of additionality achieved by the payment of public finance. The methodologically correct approach is to use the baseline case to construct a 'with and without' public finance comparison. In this way, the difference in spending, employment or other such activity between the 'with and without' scenarios is a measure of additionality.

Use of all three research methods with large numbers in the survey and in the control and recipient groups should yield much more reliable measures of additionality than dependence on only one method and/or small numbers of observations. The more sophisticated the research method the more costly it will be and so, presumably, the less attractive it will be to policy-makers. Moreover, financial models cannot accurately identify the additionality of public finance in the case of one-off small-area financing initiatives, such as the economic regeneration of multiply-deprived inner cities. In general, the results of models are probably more robust if informed by 'expert opinion' surveys. Likewise expert opinion surveys are more robust if also supported by the results of the control group research method. Use of all three research methods ('triangulation') is the most methodologically robust means of identifying and measuring additionality. Ultimately, however, whatever the method, the assessment of the degree of additionality is a more or less well-informed judgement because it is simply impossible to verify the counterfactual.

Bearing this caveat in mind, and assuming statistical validity in terms of sufficient numbers of cases, in principle, it is possible to construct fairly robust 'with and without' measures of spending, jobs or other quantifiable activity in order to measure additionality. It is probably also possible to estimate temporal, geographical and social additionality with a reasonable degree of accuracy, especially where there were strong financial constraints prior to the payment of public finance. However, it is extremely difficult to develop robust measures of quality additionality simply because of the difficulties in defining and quantifying quality. Where measures of quality have been developed, they have tended to concentrate on inputs (for example the professional qualifications of practitioners), processes (for example time taken to deliver the service after the first enquiry or application) and outputs (for example numbers of patients treated per period of time or jobs created). However, the ultimate measure of quality is in terms of outcome quality, this possibly being unaffected (or only modestly so) by improvements in inputs, processes and outputs.

The European Commission has previously emphasised the role of ERDF in fostering social cohesion, reduction in intra-community disparities and programme integration outcomes. These forms of social additionality are clearly very difficult to define and measure. They are much broader than narrower audit-based approaches to financial additionality. In general, the broadest outcomes are in terms of improved quality of life resulting from public finance for education, health, inner-city regeneration and so on.

Output quality has recently been developed for public health services by measuring the quality of additional life years (QALYs). This measure recognises that output and outcome differ by distinguishing between added life years (output) and the quality of those years (outcome) in terms of the patient's ability to resume a normal lifestyle free of illness or disability. The question remains, however, as to who assesses the quality of the additional years of life a patient is afforded after medical treatment? Measures of quality have to reflect the views of stakeholders, in this example patients, medical practitioners, professional bodies, relatives of patients, taxpayers funding health services, local, regional and/or national communities and so on. It may be difficult to identify all relevant stakeholders. Moreover, unless each stakeholder group's views carry the same weight as all other groups, these views have to be weighted in order to derive a composite measure. This is obviously problematic because some stakeholder groups are more politically powerful or articulate than others.

Ultimately, therefore, the measurement of outcome additionality is an extremely imprecise science, qualified by subjective judgements of an arbitrarily determined group of respondents. As for all forms of additionality, the various stakeholder groups may attempt to distort the measurement of additionality to further their own agendas, for example seeking more public finance for their own group at the expense of other groups (see Chapters 3 and 7).

MAXIMISING THE ADDITIONALITY OF PUBLIC FINANCE

Whilst useful for assessing the efficacy of existing arrangements for the disbursement of public finance, the research methods described above measure the degree of additionality actually achieved retrospectively and do not indicate how additionality can be maximised. Even if the payment of public finance were to be made conditional upon the additional service or activity actually taking place, there is no guarantee that additionality will be maximised. The foregoing analysis made clear that fiscal substitution, deadweight loss, displacement or any combination of these three effects may substantially reduce additionality.

Concern about the lack of financial additionality is a particular problem for substantial ongoing public expenditures. This has already been highlighted in respect of the ERDF. It is also the case in respect of central, federal or regional governments' payments of intergovernmental grants to local government (see Chapter 8). Such grants-in-aid are paid in order that municipalities may expand their provision of services. However, higher level governments (grantors) cannot be sure that local governments (grantees) actually use those grants to expand service delivery as intended by the grantor. This can be demonstrated by considering three forms of financial additionality:

1. *Direct net additionality.* This occurs when grants-in-aid induce additional spending on the service or activity to which that finance is allocated and which would not have occurred in the absence of that grant. This is the usual purpose of grants-in-aid tied to a specific service (that is, a 'specific grant').
2. *Indirect (deflected) net additionality.* This occurs when grants-in-aid allocated to one service induce more spending on another service or services. This occurs when the grant releases revenues that would otherwise have been spent on the grant-assisted service and which are then used to finance increased spending on other services. Such fiscal substitution deflects financial additionality from the grant-assisted service to other services. A minor degree of deflection may be acceptable to the higher level governments paying the grant. If, however, they wished to expand provision of most or all municipal services, it would be better to pay an unconditional grant-in-aid rather than a tied grant-in-aid.
3. *Displacement.* This occurs when grants-in-aid replace local governments' own revenues derived from local taxation. Such displacement (another form of fiscal substitution) enables reductions in current or future levels of local government taxation and so leads to additionality in private sector spending unless directly offset by an increase in central or federal taxes in each and every municipality. Additionality in private (rather than public) finance may be the main objective of unconditional grants-in-aid (that is, 'general grants') paid to support the generality of municipal services, for example when central governments wish to restrain local tax levels. This is perhaps more likely to be the case where local government is restricted to a narrow and regressive tax, for example a local poll tax or property tax.

A mixture of all three forms of financial additionality is possible at any one point in time. The difficulties in establishing the counterfactual noted above mean that it may not be possible to measure and judge whether the grant-in-aid allocated to a particular service finances additional spending on it or not. In order to estimate direct and indirect financial additionality and displacement, it would be necessary to develop quantitative models of expenditure for each municipal service and for local tax levels. Account would also have to be taken of other exogenous factors, such as any reforms of local government and changing expenditure constraints. Such quantitative imponderables mean that the qualitative approaches described above may be more appropriate in attempting to identify net financial additionality.

In general, however, it can be expected that intergovernmental grants will usually achieve a substantial degree of financial additionality as long as there are no constraints on the growth of municipal expenditures. This is because the grant effectively increases the incomes of local voter-citizens, providing there are no offsetting increases in central, federal or regional government taxes (a positive 'income effect'). Thus they can be expected to vote for higher levels of municipal service provision (or local politicians act on their behalf in increasing service provision between elections). In addition, the grant reduces the local tax cost of municipal services relative to the cost of private sector services and so voters and/or their political representatives can be expected to demand more of them, reducing their expenditures on private sector goods and services accordingly (a 'substitution effect'). If the grant is tied to a particular municipal service (a specific grant) rather than being an unconditional grant (a general grant), local voters can be expected to substitute both private sector goods and services and other municipal services for the grant-assisted municipal service.

For a given amount of grant, direct financial additionality will be maximised for an individual municipal service by using a 'matching specific grant', because the more the municipality spends on the service the more grant it attracts. The municipality cannot simply substitute the grant for its own money that it otherwise would have spent on that service (that is, indirect net additionality is limited). In contrast, direct financial additionality will be limited if the grant is paid as a lump sum because it does not prevent deflection of the grant. Moreover, a 'lump-sum grant' has only an income effect, whereas the matching specific grant has both an income effect and a substitution effect.

By such means the grantor can both maximise and control the level of additionality arising from the payment of grants to grantees. The same principle applies whether the grantee is a municipality, a charity or voluntary organisation, or a private sector company. 'Open-ended specific matching grants' (that is, those with no upper limit) are much more effective in securing direct financial additionality for a service or activity than lump-sum grants, whether specific or general.

At a more general level, governments can perhaps be more sure of direct financial additionality if they require matching finance from other public, private and/or voluntary sector organisations to whom public finance is being directed. Generally referred to as 'financial leverage', this requirement would make less likely the substitution of (additional) public finance from the grantor for spending that would otherwise have been incurred by the grantee. In effect, that conditional public finance acts as 'pump-priming' for other expenditures.

CONCLUSIONS ON ADDITIONALITY

Whilst policy-makers, practitioners and beneficiaries inevitably focus on the immediate impacts of public finance, political philosophers take a much broader view. They identify extreme cases where additionality could be less than zero (that is, negative) or greater than 100 per cent:

■ Negative additionality occurs if the other expenditures replaced by public finance are greater than the public finance made available. Negative additionality would require 'crowding out' to be substantial, for example in creating a dependency culture as claimed by Libertarians (see Chapter 1)
■ Additionality could exceed 100 per cent if public finance acted as a catalyst in 'crowding in' (that is, creating) sustainable long-term social and economic benefits, the whole being greater than the sum of the individual parts, as claimed by Collectivists
■ Whilst being less extreme in their views, Neo-Liberals question claims of substantial additionality of public finance. They argue that crowding out is often greater than crowding in, especially when governments replace market systems with planned systems. They believe that crowding in is greatest where public finance complements market systems. This is because even substantial financial additionality may not increase economic additionality, especially when individual preferences are ignored via public property rights (see Chapter 2).

The same caveats apply to the other forms of additionality, namely quality, temporal, geographical and social additionality. Additionality is clearly a multifaceted concept. Its value depends on the political philosophy used to define and interpret the concept. Hence, measurement of the degree of additionality achieved by public finance is highly problematic, involving not just quantitative and qualitative empirical research techniques but also a philosophical interpretation of results. Even for a given political philosophy, empirical research is complicated because it is difficult to construct a model showing the counterfactual scenario (that is, the 'with and without' comparison). This difficulty is enhanced in the case of multi-funded initiatives and programmes (for example where there are many local economic development agencies and initiatives). Nevertheless, it is better to have an admittedly imprecise measure of a precise concept of additionality than a completely incorrect measure based on conceptually and methodologically invalid 'before and after' comparisons.

COST CONTAINMENT

Outcome-effectiveness depends not only upon ensuring and maximising additionality: it also depends on the minimisation of costs in absolute or relative terms. Cost containment can be defined as 'the attempt by governments to limit the increase in public service costs from year to year, either in absolute (that is, cash) terms or in relative terms (that is, as a proportion of GDP)'.

Relative cost containment can take two forms:

- limiting the proportion of GDP accounted for by total public expenditure
- limiting public expenditure on a particular service (for example health care) as a proportion of GDP.

Cost containment is therefore an attempt to control or limit the relative size of the public sector. It is a prerequisite of financial additionality, since if costs are greater than necessary, public finance is replacing private finance through unnecessarily high taxes. Cost containment usually refers to both strategic and operational economy in requiring the minimisation of costs and the avoidance of unnecessary spare capacity. The provision of health care will be used to illustrate the interdependence of additionality and cost containment.

Health care is funded by both public and private finance in most countries, an example of the latter being private purchases of over-the-counter medicines. Although public and private finance often provide for different medical services, public finance may substitute for private finance, such that the additional level of health expenditures is lower than the additional public finance. The public finance costs of health care are not minimised in this case. For example, publicly financed prescription medicines may substitute for the private purchase of over-the-counter (that is, non-prescription) medicines, leading to an increase in public finance but an offsetting reduction in private finance. Likewise, the earlier provision of public medical treatment may substitute for private health care to which more affluent groups had resorted because of the previously long periods waiting for public care.

It is generally accepted that rising demands for health care are the result of:

- changing demographic structures (for example ageing of the demographic profile: elderly people generally having significantly greater need for medical care than those of working age)
- technological advance making available expensive medical equipment for the treatment of more medical conditions (although existing costs of treatment may also be reduced by new technology)
- new or more prevalent diseases which are more expensive to treat (for example Aids)
- increasing consumer expectations regarding the availability and quality of medical care.

These factors are probably more important in determining health spending than are the precise arrangements for the delivery of health services, in that they impinge upon decision-making, whether democratically determined or not. Moreover, there appears to be a ratchet effect in that, once a service is provided up to any level, it is very difficult to cut spending even though there may be less objective need for it. This is perhaps the inevitable result of collective financing versus individual use of service because service users have little incentive to agree to service reductions, since they bring no off-setting benefit in terms of reduced (tax) payments for the individual (see Chapter 7).

In principle, therefore, cost containment could be facilitated by switching from public (that is, collective) finance to private (that is, individualised) finance. Whilst this strategy could contain the public finance input for health care, it would not necessarily contain total spending on health. Moreover, the USA's experience is that both public and private sector health expenditures may increase. For example, according to OECD health data, total health spending accounts for almost twice the proportion of GDP in the USA than in the UK (12.9 and 6.8 per cent respectively in 1998). The USA depends largely upon private health insurance (typically paid by employers on behalf of employees), whereas the UK depends largely on public sector provision of health care services. Encouraging private finance by offering tax relief on private health care insurance may reduce public expenditure but will not necessarily control total health expenditures because insurance is simply another form of collective finance. Moreover, tax relief will reduce public sector revenues, that revenue loss perhaps escalating as health insurance costs rise. Hence, cost containment may have to include both the private and public sectors if governments wish to contain total expenditure on a service.

Containing costs for all health expenditures as a percentage of GDP may be deemed necessary because, in principle, there is a threshold above which the additional benefits are less than the additional costs of incremental health expenditures, irrespective of the sector in which it occurs. This is the theoretical justification for cost containment in respect of both public and private finance for an individual service, rather than simply allowing private choices to determine health care expenditures in total and the total amount of tax relief it is afforded. Put simply, spending more on health care does not necessarily mean a nation's health will be improved. International comparisons make clear the lack of a definitive relationship between the state of health (for example measured by longevity) and how much is spent on health care or how it is financed, whether from public and/or private finance.

Cost containment may be problematic because of difficulties:

■ *in defining what exactly constitutes expenditure on a service.* For example, does expenditure on health care include all over-the-counter medicines and so-called 'alternative' health care (for example Chinese remedies)? Does expenditure on education include expenditures on arts and culture, which could be regarded as educational?
■ *in assessing the success of cost containment.* If expressed as a percentage of GDP, expenditure can appear to increase if GDP declines. This would give the impression of the failure of cost containment even though service costs were held constant (or even fell more slowly than GDP). Likewise cost

containment would appear successful if GDP rises faster than health expenditures, even though the latter was a result of the failure of cost controls.

■ *learning from cost containment in other countries.* Besides definitional problems one country may apparently be more successful in containing costs but only at the cost of reduced health outcomes.

FORMS OF COST CONTAINMENT

There are three main means of controlling public expenditures, political, economic and administrative and each is discussed in turn.

Political controls

Political controls recognise that public expenditures are determined, at least in part, by democratic processes. However, these democratic processes require clarification because they depend crucially on the prevailing model of government in a given country (see Chapter 3), most notably:

■ *fiscal exchange model of government:* expenditures being determined by voters' willingness to pay the tax costs of additional services
■ *fiscal transfer model of government:* the majority redistributes the costs and benefits of public services in order to achieve social equity or some such goal
■ *despotic benevolent model of government:* the government determines health expenditures on behalf of its citizens and in their best interests. It has complete control of spending, irrespective of the willingness of voters to pay (or not to pay) additional taxes
■ *leviathan model of government:* practitioners and bureaucrats maximise their budgets in order to promote their own interests and careers. In this case government spending may be out of control because democratic processes are weak.

These models of government are rather simplistic and not necessarily mutually exclusive. They emphasise the need to see political controls in very broad terms. The main political controls are listed below. They are complementary of each other and can all be used together at any one point in time to:

■ *implement a rigorous and effective top-down process of priority-setting* in which global financial allocations and/or ceilings upon what can be raised locally are determined. In this way, central governments are able to exert considerable influence over global amounts of money allocated to public services.

■ *improve democratic processes where voters determine expenditure levels,* for example referenda on spending levels for health. In general this would require the transfer of responsibility for public services to local government. Whilst it may be thought that voters would vote for even higher levels of spending, the connection with local taxation and/or the trade-off with other services would be made more explicit. A transferred service's expenditures would become subject to (perhaps more) rigorous central controls over local government expenditures. The alternative is to earmark (that is, hypothecate) a national tax to the health service.

■ *improve the accountability of service providers by introducing performance measures.* This is a long-term measure and may be of limited effectiveness if bureaucrats attempt to frustrate performance review by manipulating performance indicators for their own purposes. More generally, performance measurement has been criticised for 'measuring the measurable' whilst ignoring intangible but fundamental service characteristics.

■ *undertake public opinion surveys in order to determine the public's preferences for expenditure levels, types of public spending, quality of service and so on.* Although the results of such surveys are not binding upon central government, such surveys can elicit much more information about preferences than referenda or elections. They will not necessarily facilitate cost containment but could do so, for example if it transpired that the public had stronger preferences for more low-cost, accessible community hospitals than for a lesser number of higher cost, larger hospitals.

Economic controls

Economic controls attempt to control both the level of demand and the cost of meeting that demand. They therefore work on both the demand side and the supply side. In particular, they attempt to change the incentives faced by both those who demand public services and those who supply them, by reorganising property rights according to market principles (see Chapter 2). The main controls are to:

■ *introduce (increasing levels of) payment at point of use.* Although user-charges may limit overuse of services, this demand-side measure is likely to create social problems relating to equity in their use (unless account is taken of ability to pay) and perhaps incorrect decisions (for example because of potential patients' imperfect knowledge regarding their medical conditions). In practice, public services such as health care may still be supply (rather than demand) driven, for example where family doctors act as 'gatekeepers' for hospital services. Moreover, payment of charges for medical consultations could lead to increased medical costs if people refrained from seeing their family doctors until their medical conditions became more serious and, hence, more expensive to treat.

- *create internal markets by means of a purchaser–provider split,* for example where health authorities purchase specific medical services provided by hospitals. Inefficient hospitals failing to win contracts would lose patients and, in the extreme case, would close down. This would occur where 'the money followed the patient' (explained above). Costs could increase, however, if such hospitals retain excess capacity whilst hospitals winning contracts expand theirs. Put simply, quasi-markets rarely operate in the same way as free markets. Moreover, the level of competition may be limited and if there are a few hospitals, they may adopt a 'market-sharing' strategy (where they agree to bid for different medical contracts rather than compete for the same ones) in order that each ensures its own survival. Cost savings are limited in such cases and so are more likely to be largely offset by the costs of administering contracts. In addition, any such cost savings do not necessarily result in reduced spending; they may simply be used to provide more services for a given level of expenditure. This outcome is likely, since spending (rather than service) levels are either determined by political (demand-side) processes or, on the supply side, by doctors and bureaucrats.
- *exercise the monopsony (sole or main purchaser) power of the state* in order to suppress the costs of inputs, for example pharmaceuticals or medical staff. This supply-side measure may be ineffective over the longer term, if pharmaceutical companies threaten to take their research laboratories to other countries, medical staff associations threaten strike action, or key medical staff can easily transfer to jobs in the private sector or in other countries (for example those within the EU's Single European Market).
- *provide tax relief on insurance premia for private health care in order to encourage people to opt out of the public sector.* This demand-side measure is only appropriate if cost containment relates to public health expenditures only. Whilst tax relief encourages voluntary exchange through private markets, it is a disguised cost, since (as already noted) it reduces income accruing to the public sector (see tax expenditures below). Moreover, cost per treatment episode and per patient could rise if health insurance companies refuse insurance cover for the more expensive medical conditions. In that case, the reduction in public sector health expenditures may be proportionately much less than the outflow of patients to the private sector.
- *introduce new grant mechanisms,* in particular replacing 'open-ended grants' (where central government effectively guarantees to meet all hospital costs, even those in excess of plans) with 'closed-ended grants' (which are fixed and so do not accommodate deficits). A series of specific closed-ended (that is, lump-sum) grants could also replace block (that is, general) lump-sum grants in order to control the composition, as well as

the total, of spending. These types of grants were explained above in respect of local government but they can also be used specifically for health services. Whilst lump-sum grants control spending in any one year, their effectiveness in terms of cost containment over a period of years is questionable. Their effectiveness will be reduced if governments increase them over time in line with an index of service costs, taking account, for example, of rising pharmaceutical prices. Similarly, governments may give in to pressures to increase lump-sum grants from one year to the next because, for example, hospitals would otherwise increase their 'hotel charges' for hospital accommodation to politically unacceptable levels.

Administrative controls

Administrative controls can influence both the level and composition of spending by controlling inputs and processes, rather than outputs and outcomes.
Controls on inputs include:

■ *limiting the number of users by rationing* (for example patients via gatekeeper family doctors). This is not feasible in the case of serious or emergency medical conditions such that the potential for cost savings may be relatively small. Again, medical costs could increase if treatment for emerging serious conditions is delayed.
■ *limiting the number of public sector workers* (for example hospital doctors and other staff). However, some countries are short of medical staff.
■ *recruiting ready-trained staff from abroad* to reduce training costs.
■ *limiting the adoption of new equipment and new technologies.* However, as already noted, some new equipment and new technology can reduce costs over the longer term. Moreover, if many hospitals purchase new equipment, mass production usually lowers its costs (via 'economies of scale'). Hence, short-term cost containment may be at the expense of longer term savings.
■ *limiting the number of prescribed medicines.* However, patients may then buy more non-prescribed, over-the-counter medicines from pharmacies such that total public and private spending on drugs is not effectively controlled.
■ *limiting medicines prescribed to cheaper, generic (non-brand) drugs.* This is only effective for drugs which have 'run out of patent', whereas demand may be heavily concentrated on newly patented drugs which are either more efficacious in treating existing medical conditions or treat newly emerging medical conditions.
■ *limiting the number and type of hospitals*, to gain any economies of scale, these being considerable for medical conditions requiring expensive

equipment and specialist staff but limited for more general ailments. In fact, larger hospitals may experience managerial 'diseconomies of scale'. Moreover, larger hospitals may be more politically powerful than smaller ones in demanding increasing expenditures on new equipment, new medical specialities and the extra accommodation necessary to house it.

■ *limiting the conditions eligible for treatment.* For example, elective treatments such as cosmetic surgery could be excluded. However, the scope for savings are limited because they are generally not the most expensive conditions to treat.

■ *controlling the salary costs of hospital staff.* Besides exercising monopsony power (an economic control noted above), hospitals could seek to rebalance their staffing profiles, requiring lower cost staff grades to undertake some of the duties currently carried out by higher cost grades. For example, highly paid specialists need not be undertaking unnecessary clerical or administrative tasks. The potential for cost containment is high, given the generally large proportions of salary costs within total costs.

■ *limiting additional billing of patients by private health care organisations.* This is only applicable in countries with private sector provision but could be significant where the private sector is large relative to the public sector. There would obviously be savings in total health expenditures. There would also be savings for public sector health costs if patients facing additional billing are eligible for means-tested assistance from the state.

■ *abolish automatic payments* to doctors and dentists based on the number of persons registered with them (as distinct from the number who actually visit). This can be implemented by setting limits on the length of time a person can be registered without attending the practitioner.

Controls on processes include:

■ *restricting the nature of medical procedures to lower cost treatments.* This assumes equal efficacy of treatment and so there may only be limited scope for such measures.

■ *discharging patients who require social care rather than medical treatment,* giving another (lower cost) sector the responsibility to provide the non-medical support (for example using residential establishments rather than geriatric wards for the personal and social care of elderly people). Given demographic trends towards an ageing population, this measure has potential for significant cost containment.

■ *establishing hospitals and family doctor practices as separate cost centres,* in order that providers of services become more aware of the costs of the services they provide and so can be expected to become more cost conscious in adopting new medical procedures and setting priorities.

■ *introducing service-level agreements* (where formal contracts are not used) so that expectations about the volume, quality and cost of services are made more explicit, even if not legally binding. In such cases, unexpectedly high costs would have to be justified or remedial measures adopted.

■ *limiting case drift*, that is, the classification of medical conditions as more serious than they are in order to secure work for medical specialists, for example excessive dental work.

■ *increasing waiting lists*, especially for elective treatments, comments being similar to those for rationing above.

■ *achieving higher patient turnover per bed-space per period.* This is only effective as long as it does not result in increasing levels of readmission to hospital because patients have been released from medical care too early.

■ *reducing bureaucracy*, for example the costs of administering a purchaser–provider split (that is, drawing up and monitoring contracts for the supply of health care services). This may require abandonment of the purchaser–provider split and its replacement by service-level agreements (see above).

■ *reducing emergency admissions* by having someone to look after elderly people living on their own when they become ill. In fact the potential for cost savings is possibly even greater because the factors leading to an increase in the number and proportion of single-person (or single-parent) households is not just due to ageing populations: it also reflects increasing rates of divorce and later marriages.

■ *improving labour productivity* (for example of doctors) by regulating working patterns and work loads more effectively. For example, more accurate hospital and family doctor records regarding the medical conditions of, and treatments required for, patients and the better communication of that data could avoid delays in treatment and unnecessary repeat visits (because relevant data were missing).

■ *undertaking health education campaigns*, for example against smoking. It has been estimated that smokers have a 25 times greater risk of developing lung cancer than non-smokers. They also have relatively higher incidences of other diseases and ailments and so impose costs on public sector health care.

■ *setting efficiency targets for hospitals* in order that they are given strong incentives to adopt the various administrative controls capable of containing costs.

Three points are worth noting in summarising this exposition of political, economic and administrative controls. First, there is a potentially very wide range of cost-containment controls at the disposal of governments. Second, they will not all be equally effective in any one country nor will any one measure be equally effective in different countries. Third, the distinction between categories, whilst useful for the purpose of analysis, is often arbitrary. For example, the purchaser–provider split is as much an administrative control of process as it is an economic control.

CONCLUSIONS ON COST CONTAINMENT

The strategic issue is to identify which mixture of political, economic and administrative controls is most effective in controlling costs. Political controls seem not very effective in controlling the growth of public expenditures because voter-citizens expect and demand improved health services, especially if they are tax financed (see Chapter 7). Economic controls are limited in their acceptability (for example user-charges for health care) and cost-effectiveness (for example the high costs of competitive contracting). Therefore the emphasis has increasingly been on administrative controls to control both inputs and processes. It has to be recognised, however, that administrative controls are of limited effectiveness on their own.

There are several lessons:

■ the financing and control of public service costs have to take account of the political, economic, demographic and social conditions in each country
■ the containment of costs is an ongoing long-term exercise that requires a multiplicity of controls, at both the aggregate level of spending and the specific components of spending
■ few if any countries have been able to control public expenditures as much as they would have liked to do.

TAX EXPENDITURES

During recent decades, direct state spending in many countries has increasingly been replaced by various forms of tax relief. Where free markets result in insufficient consumption of a service, due to lack of information about the benefits of service consumption, myopia or lack of appreciation of risk (see Chapter 2), tax relief can be used to offset market failure. It may also be used to stimulate other socially beneficial activities and as a form of cost containment (as noted above). Examples are:

■ relief against income taxes for spending on private health insurance and privately funded schooling
■ relief against taxes on capital gains (for example for increases in the value of owner-occupied housing)
■ relief against profits taxes for companies' investments in buildings, equipment, research and development, employee training and so on
■ relief against wealth taxes for donations and bequests of cultural artefacts to state museums and galleries and so on (see Chapter 5).

In substituting for public expenditure, such forms of tax relief are often referred to as 'tax expenditures'. Their monetary value is equal to the amount

of expenditure (or value of capital gain or donation/bequest) multiplied by
the taxpayer's tax rate on additional income, wealth or capital gains. Thus,
the greater both the qualifying expenditure and tax rate, the greater the value
of the tax relief to an individual or company. As long as tax rates are less than
100 per cent, the value of the tax relief will be less than the expenditure
incurred by the individual, household or company. Nevertheless, the greater
the expenditure (for example on health insurance), the greater the monetary
value of the tax relief, so providing the incentive for private finance to
replace public finance.

Tax relief therefore has the advantage of reducing the overall burden of
taxation on the economy, whilst potentially achieving the same objectives as
the direct public expenditures that would otherwise have taken place. By such
means the state can enable adequate levels of health, education, housing and
so on, whilst avoiding any of the adverse effects of high tax rates on economic
activity (see Chapter 6). Thus, in theory, the state can achieve its public policy
objectives by using tax relief to modify (rather than replace) the market. The
tax relief levers private finance, the degree of leverage depending on the sen-
sitivity of private expenditure to that tax relief. This result is the same as that
for an effort-related (that is, matching) grant to local governments because it
creates a substitution effect (see above).

Spending on the service or other activity increases in much the same way
as it would do as a result of direct public expenditure. Assuming that total
spending on the tax-assisted service is unaltered because private spending
directly replaces public spending, public expenditure will fall. This is the case
as long as the monetary value of that tax relief is not entered into the public
accounts as a tax expenditure. In terms of the definitions of public and private
finance developed in Chapter 1, it would be wrong to enter such data because
they reflect private spending, not public expenditure. More generally, just
because a government encourages certain forms of private expenditure does
not mean that they can be counted as public expenditure.

The *advantages* of tax expenditures are:

- they are consistent with Libertarian philosophy which requires government intervention only to secure negative rights and which regards taxation as confiscation (see Chapter 1)
- they can facilitate limited or full positive rights as required by the Neo-
  Liberal and Collectivist philosophical positions respectively (again, see
  Chapter 1)
- they work with (rather than against) market systems by allowing, maintaining, or strengthening private property rights and so valuing preferences via voluntary exchange (see Chapter 2)
- they therefore allow individuals to increase their welfare by matching
  their levels of consumption with personal preferences, rather than having
  their consumption determined by the state

■ they provide incentives to self-sufficiency rather than dependence on the state for access to education, health and other public services
■ they allow individuals and households to choose their preferred service provider
■ they stimulate a plurality of provision by state and non-state sectors by dissolving statutory monopolies in the public sector (for example by allowing operation of private schools)
■ they minimise any disincentive-to-work effects resulting from high levels of taxation (see Chapter 6).

The *disadvantages* of tax expenditures are the opposite of the claimed advantages:

■ in practice, it is very difficult to use tax relief to ensure negative rights (that is, freedom from coercion, interference and discrimination)
■ access to positive rights is restricted to those who pay tax, non-taxpayers being unable to claim tax relief on tax-allowable expenditures with the result that they are regressive
■ they may further distort private preferences (that is, where government intervention exacerbates market failure) and so give misleading impressions of the value of resources
■ choice of level of consumption is particularly problematic for health services because they are usually allocated by medical practitioners, as noted above
■ incentives to self-sufficiency are likely to be weak for the vast majority of the population, because their incomes are not high enough to generate sufficient tax relief to allow private finance to completely replace public finance
■ choice of preferred service provider is often more apparent than real, either because none is close to where one lives or it is oversubscribed and so not available to all who wish to use it
■ a plurality of provision may be transitory, as market restructuring leads to dominance of only a few providers who collude to share the market
■ disincentive-to-work effects of high levels of taxation are extremely difficult to prove and so effectively remain an assertion (see Chapter 6).

Whatever the balance of advantage or disadvantage, governments may feel unable to rely solely or largely on tax expenditures as a means of ensuring the provision and use of education, health and other services in line with its objectives. Some groups are almost certain to be disadvantaged by tax expenditures. These include the long-term unemployed, those not seeking employment (for example single parents and the disabled), and those who do not fully appreciate the value to themselves of adequate levels of education or health care. Whilst, say, adequate private health insurance and private education could be made compulsory (as well as being supported by relief against income tax), this hardly reduces state paternalism and the supposed dependency culture. It would also cause great vertical inequity, precisely because poor groups would be forced to spend higher proportions of their income on education and health than would high-income groups. Hence, public finance proper is inevitable if services are to be provided in line with the public policy objectives of most developed countries.

CONCLUSIONS

The analysis of OECD data in Chapter 3 made clear the relatively high scale of public finance within West European countries, especially EU and Scandinavian countries. The more detailed analysis of the main components of public expenditures in this chapter has made clear that those high levels of public finance are largely and increasingly accounted for by current expenditures, notwithstanding the importance of capital expenditures to continued economic growth. Moreover, the growth in the current expenditure/GDP ratio has been almost wholly accounted for by the growth of social security transfers, most notably in EU countries. Whilst public sector service provision has increased, it has generally only kept up with the growth of GDP, such that the OECD average for government final consumption has remained remarkably stable as a proportion of GDP over the last four decades of the twentieth century.

Chapter 1 made clear the differing views of the legitimacy of redistribution through social security transfers. Irrespective of one's political philosophy, crucial questions must be addressed, namely:

- how can those growing transfers and other expenditures be financed (considered in Chapter 5)?
- can economies continue to finance growing social security transfers without adverse effects on the growth of GDP (considered in Chapter 6)?
- are such trends in public finance sustainable over the long term (considered in Chapter 7)?

This chapter has made clear that spending public finance is not a simple task if value for money is to be achieved. Strategic decisions have to be made regarding:

1. achievement of the 4Es
2. the outcome objectives of public finance and the services needed to deliver those outcomes
3. to whom public finance should be paid
4. the degree of additionality sought from the use of public finance

5. the attention to be paid to cost containment
6. the balance between direct expenditure and tax relief.

The first two decisions inevitably reflect political philosophy and will be the subject of intense debate. The third decision may require radical changes in the disbursement of public finance in a particular country. The fourth decision (on additionality) is complicated by a general inability to establish the counterfactual with a reasonable degree of accuracy. The fifth and sixth decisions (on cost containment and the relative use of tax expenditures) are controversial because of the potentially unfair or regressive impacts they have on different groups in society.

Additionality is increased if deadweight loss and displacement are minimised and public funds have a high degree of leverage of private funds. Cost containment is facilitated if democratic processes are improved (so voters determine expenditure based on their willingness to pay taxes), a rigorous and effective top-down process of priority-setting is implemented and the accountability of service providers is increased by introducing performance indicators, service charters and so on. Economic cost controls include payment at point of use, competition in the supply of services, using the purchasing power of the state to control input costs, tax relief on private provision, and grant mechanisms for local governments and other public sector bodies that encourage control of costs. Administrative cost controls seek to control inputs and processes whilst avoiding any unwanted effects on outputs and outcomes.

Clearly, value for money is unlikely to be achieved in the spending of public finance if governments simply give public money to largely unaccountable monopoly service providers and where service users have little or no scope for exit or expression of voice. Spending public money on services to secure the public interest may seem simple but the devil is most definitely in the detail. Moreover, spending is only half the picture. The raising of public finance also has an important impact on the public interest. This is the subject of the following chapter.

FURTHER READING

Bailey, S. J. (1999) *Local Government Economics: Principles and Practice* (Basingstoke: Macmillan – now Palgrave Macmillan). [Chapters 3 and 4 on exit and voice; Chapter 9 on intergovernmental grants; Chapters 13 and 14 on quality of service].

Bailey. S. J. (2002) *Public Sector Economics: Theory, Policy and Practice* (second edition) (Basingstoke: Palgrave – now Palgrave Macmillan) [Chapter 15 on evidence that competition achieves substantial cost savings].

HM Treasury (1988) *Policy Evaluation: A Guide for Managers* (London: HMSO).

Pearce, G. and Martin, S. (1996) 'The Measurement of Additionality: Grasping the Slippery Eel' *Local Government Studies* vol. 22, no. 1, pp. 78–92.

Rose, R. (1984) *Do Parties Make a Difference?* (London: Macmillan – now Palgrave Macmillan).

Van Beers, C. and de Moor, A. (2001) *Public Subsidies and Policy Failures: How Subsidies Distort the Natural Environment, Equity and Trade and How to Reform Them* (Cheltenham: Edward Elgar).

Walsh, K., Deakin, N., Smith, P., Spurgeon, P. and Thomas, N. (1997) *Contracting for Change: Contracts in Health, Social Care and Other Local Government Services* (Oxford: Oxford University Press).

5 Raising Public Finance

INTRODUCTION

Whilst previous chapters considered strategic issues relating to the relative scale and spending of public finance, they provided only limited guidance as to which particular source of public finance should be utilised, reference being made only to taxes and user-charges. The property rights analysis of Chapter 2 made clear the theoretical justifications for both charges (in the form of market prices) and taxes, sole reliance on market prices being justified when property rights are clearly established and fully enforceable. Where they exist but are not fully enforceable, then taxes and prices can complement each other in modifying property rights, for example by taxing activities that create pollution or other environmental costs.

The tax and spend and spend and tax models of public finance (see Chapter 3) are deficient, in being preoccupied with taxation as the main (or even only) source of public finance. In fact there are many sources of public finance, some of which tend to be neglected by governments. Whilst politicians and bureaucrats are naturally concerned with whether there is sufficient money to finance state spending, a preoccupation with simply raising money may lead to the neglect of strategic issues that must be addressed when raising as well as spending public finance. Spending public finance (see Chapter 4) is only half the picture, since the potential benefits of public expenditure may be offset to a greater or lesser extent by the potentially large direct and indirect costs of raising public finance. For example, public spending intended to achieve greater equity will be frustrated if the raising of public finance itself creates considerable inequity.

This chapter therefore outlines a strategy for raising public finance from a multitude of sources. It considers a series of strategic questions relating to the possible alternative or complementary sources of public finance, the sources actually employed by European countries, the possible consequences of raising revenues from those sources and their optimal combination. These strategic issues relate to how the system of raising public finance affects equity, efficiency, economy and effectiveness ('the 4 Es' – defined in Chapter 1). It will be demonstrated that achievement of the 4Es whilst raising state revenues requires a judicious mix of the various alternative sources of public finance.

FROM WHAT SOURCES CAN PUBLIC FINANCE BE RAISED?

Public finance can be raised from the sources listed in Table 5.1. The current use of these various sources in any one country does not necessarily reflect a well-developed strategy for the raising of public finance. As is often the case for spending (see Chapter 4), there is a large degree of inheritance in the use (and therefore in the mix) of the various sources of public finance. Thus the balance between them may reflect historical patterns more than current strategic choices, explicitly in terms of the 4Es.

The property rights analysis of Chapter 2 demonstrated that taxation must be used to fully finance pure community-level services (the benefits of which are both non-rival and non-excludable) and that category of mixed goods with rival but non-excludable benefits, if they are to be provided. However, that chapter provided only limited guidance about what taxes can be used, alternative taxes being listed in Table 5.1. Chapter 2 also demonstrated that few public sector outputs fall within these two categories of services and so, in theory, user-charges should be used to finance services with private benefits. Hence, that chapter concluded that a combination of taxation and user-charges is usually most appropriate to strengthen property rights. There are, however, other sources of public finance that can also be considered, as made clear by Table 5.1. The rest of the chapter discusses each of these sources in more detail.

Table 5.1   Sources of public finance

Source	Examples
Taxes	*Personal income taxes:* on employment earnings, interest and dividends *Expenditure taxes:* on goods and services (for example VAT, excise duties) *Corporate income tax:* on companies' profits *Capital gains taxes:* on gains from sales of physical assets, shares and so on *Inherited wealth taxes:* on cash and physical assets transferred at death *Property taxes:* on domestic, commercial and industrial buildings *Land taxes:* on rising land values and/or value in its most profitable use *Payroll taxes:* levied on firms for each employee *Per capita taxes:* lump-sum poll taxes *Environmental taxes:* 'green' taxes on polluting activities *Other taxes:* for example stamp duty (on legal documents), licences (for vehicles)
Charges	User-charges, rents, processing/administration fees
Privatisation/sales	Land, buildings, enterprises, equipment, cultural artefacts, leases and so on
Borrowing	Domestic and foreign sources (banks, citizens, development agencies and so on)
State lotteries	Used at federal/central, regional and local levels
Donations/bequests	In the form of cash and/or physical assets
Payments in kind	In the form of physical assets instead of user-charges
Special assessments	Voluntary payment of extra taxes for specific improvements to property

Taxation

Being associated with a shift towards Neo-Liberalism (see Chapter 1), global-isation has arguably had a progressively profound impact on the use of taxa-tion to raise public finance. Globalisation seems increasingly to limit the ability of governments to increase their levels of taxation because of the potential adverse impacts on the economic competitiveness of their economies. Increasingly, nation states attempt to gain competitive advantage in international markets by cutting taxes on traded goods and services. This is complemented by the general movement towards free trade (that is, free of taxes and quotas on imports and free of subsidies on exports), already noted in Chapter 1. Although the impact on economic performance of those tax cuts is uncertain, it became generally accepted that a nation's prosperity depends cru-cially on the ability of its industrial and service sectors to trade profitably on world markets and, therefore, not being burdened by high levels of taxation.

Such 'tax competition' is complemented by moves towards 'tax harmoni-sation' within the major world trading blocs such as the EU, NAFTA (North American Free Trade Area), ASEAN (Association of South East Asian Nations) and so on. Both tax competition and tax harmonisation:

- limit the levels of taxation available to support welfare states, and/or
- change the composition of those tax funds away from taxes on traded activities (and the inputs of those activities, such as labour) and towards taxes on non-traded activities.

In particular, the fast growth in use of the Internet for economic transactions is thought to erode very substantially the tax base for many countries. This is because the Internet makes it much easier for people and firms to order goods and services from other countries and, inevitably, they will seek the lowest cost countries of supply. Substantial erosion of some countries' tax bases has already occurred as a result of the rapid growth of smuggling of goods from low-tax to high-tax countries. This particularly affects goods whose sales value is high relative to the costs of transport, for example cigarettes and spir-its. Smuggling is most well developed where border controls have been all but abolished, for example within the EU. It emphasises the need for tax harmon-isation to reduce the incentive to smuggle. These 'erosion-of-tax-base effects' have arguably been exacerbated by:

- increasingly skewed distributions of income in many countries, largely reflecting the economic changes associated with the growth of Neo-Liberalism and globalisation. An increased divergence between the high-est and lowest incomes has followed economic reforms in many countries, most notably the collapse of centrally planned economies and the privati-sation of state industries in both centrally planned and mixed economies.

Thus, incomes from employment increasingly reflect market forces as state control of both prices and incomes diminishes. Unless tax regimes are very highly progressive at the top of the income range, tax revenues may fall.

■ increasingly skewed demographic age profiles towards elderly populations in many developed countries. Thus, notwithstanding the potential impacts of pandemic diseases such as Aids, the 'dependency ratios' (of retired to economically active people) have risen in many countries, increasing the tax burden on workers to support retired groups' relatively high demands for public finance (that is, income support and health care). This is also associated with globalisation because, in general, rising economic prosperity is associated with falls in birth rates.

The explanation of falling birth rates is not self-evident. However, it is generally accepted that parents no longer need count on having so many children to support them in old age. Medical advances (again reflecting growing economic prosperity) have cut infant mortality rates in many countries, so that parents can be more sure that their offspring will survive to support them in old age if necessary. Combined with the increasing availability of reliable methods of contraception, the result is that families choose to have fewer children. This, together with the growth of opportunities for paid employment resulting from globalisation, enables increasingly high proportions of married women to take up paid employment rather than stay at home to have more children. In increasingly prosperous countries, citizens have come to believe that they can depend on the welfare state (instead of their families) to support them in old age. Thus, these profound and long-term events combine to enable people to limit family size, the incentive being that they can thus enjoy higher levels of material well-being as a result of having fewer children. Thus demands on welfare states increase as dependency rates rise, precisely at a time when the legitimacy of high levels of taxation has increasingly been brought into question within public debate. This is one of the causes of structural gaps in the public finances (see Chapter 7).

Besides the need to restrain taxation to maintain economic competitiveness, the questioning of high levels of taxation has also resulted in part because of the perceived unnecessarily high costs of public service provision and subsidies to the private sector (that is, additionality and cost containment are poor – see Chapter 4). In such a case taxation becomes increasingly stigmatised as offering poor value in terms of community benefits. Those benefits are seen as substantially (if not wholly) offset by what has to be given up in order to pay taxes. Negative terms are frequently used, most notably the 'burden of taxation'.

Whereas in the private sector the consumer sees a direct link between payment for a good or service and what is actually delivered, there is no such direct link between payment of taxes and receipt of public services. Voter-taxpayers cannot be sure that extra taxes will result in extra services. Extra tax payments do not necessarily result in more hospital beds, better protection against crime, better quality education and so on. Instead, extra taxes may simply be taken up by unnecessarily high costs and more wasteful use of public money (see Chapter 4). In short, voter-taxpayers may simply not trust governments to deliver better public services from their extra taxes. This can perhaps be remedied by a number of measures:

■ More information from government about the use of tax revenues
■ Likewise more information about how much tax is paid by each income group, taking account of household structure (that is, differentiated according to numbers of adults, dependent children, retired persons)
■ Specifying what any extra tax payments will actually be spent on (but see Chapter 4 on additionality)
■ Making clear how much of any extra tax each income group would be required to pay
■ Making clear that public finance is not being paid to the 'undeserving poor', namely those who will not accept personal responsibility for earning a living for themselves (see Chapter 6)
■ Devolution of taxes to lower tiers of government (see Chapter 8)
■ Greater use of user-charges (see below) and vouchers (see Chapter 9).

Libertarians argue that the burden of taxation is not simply financial (that is, the income and/or wealth that has to be given up in order to pay taxes). As noted in Chapter 1, in financing a burgeoning welfare state, the growth of public finance creates a dependency culture and moral hazard, the burden of which may be many times greater than the amount of tax revenues raised because of the resulting loss of economic growth and prosperity.

Even when public opinion surveys suggest a willingness to pay higher taxes for higher levels and quality of public sector services, such willingness may in large part reflect a belief amongst respondents that they themselves will not have to pay much more tax. Instead, they may believe that the extra tax revenues will be drawn largely from other taxpayers. This will especially be the case where the following conditions prevail:

■ the tax base is very narrow
■ the franchise is very wide
■ those who benefit from service provision have a significantly higher propensity to vote than those who pay higher taxes.

Under this scenario, non-voter taxpayers outnumber voter taxpayers so that the tax and spend and spend and tax models of public finance result in majority exploitation of the minority. This, of course, is an affront to Libertarians and implies that the tax base should be as broad as possible so that a majority of voters are liable to pay the extra taxes voted for. Only a poll tax (whether at national, regional or local government level) would require all voters to pay tax. Such a tax, however, reverses the 'no taxation without representation' constitutional maxim to one of 'no representation without taxation'. Collectivists' positive rights require all citizens to have the unconditional right to vote because only by voting can they secure those rights. A Libertarian public sector is restricted to purely collective goods conferring negative rights, such as defence and law and order (see Chapter 1). Libertarians argue that all citizens benefit from such protective services and so all should pay tax.

If raising the money necessary to finance the state sector were the only consideration, then complete reliance on taxation would be sufficient. In this case the simplest tax would be a flat-rate (that is, lump-sum) poll tax, raising 100 per cent of state revenues. Whilst acceptable to Libertarians, such a regressive tax would not be generally acceptable precisely because it would take no account of ability to pay the lump sum. Besides creating unacceptable levels of poverty amongst those with the lowest incomes (such as the involuntary unemployed, elderly retired, sick or disabled groups), it would almost certainly lead to a taxpayer revolt, especially if the poll tax was being used to finance a substantial welfare state. At the very least, voters could be expected to demand a fairer system of taxation, taking account of ability to pay in terms of income and wealth (that is, greater vertical equity). More generally, a strategically optimal tax system is one that as far as possible promotes the achievement of the 4Es:

■ *Equity* is usually thought of as being promoted if the post-tax distribution of income is more equal than the pre-tax distribution (that is, greater 'vertical equity') and if the tax system treats equally taxpayers in similar circumstances, for example married and unmarried couples with children (that is, 'horizontal equity'). However, equity is also concerned with reward for effort and personal responsibilities as well as with the right to keep most of one's own earned income – rather than have it taken (Libertarians would say 'confiscated') by the state. Strategically, therefore, governments must determine the optimal balance between a socially acceptable distribution of income that avoids the worst excesses of poverty and wealth, whilst avoiding creating the impression that the state is penalising those who seek to support themselves through hard work and enterprise. Put simply, greater vertical equity cannot be at the expense of social justice.

■ *Efficiency* means avoiding taxes which deter or significantly distort economic activity in ways that are economically and socially disadvantageous, for example by discouraging people from working and discouraging profitable investment by companies. This would cause GDP to be smaller than it would otherwise have been. In such cases, less tax revenues would be available to finance public services and welfare payments. In efficiency terms, it is better to tax 'bads' (for example making the polluter pay for the adverse environmental and health effects of burning fossil fuels) rather than 'goods' such as work (see Chapter 6). In general, therefore, efficiency requires that taxation should be concentrated on activities imposing costs on society so that the level of those activities is reduced if not eliminated. This is the Neo-Liberal solution in the case of unenforceable property rights (see Chapter 2).

■ *Economy* requires the costs of tax collection to be as low as possible relative to the tax revenues received. The minimisation of 'collection costs' will usually involve the computerisation of tax collection systems. However, any waste of money is not just in terms of unnecessarily high administrative costs incurred by the tax agency or bureau in collecting taxes. Waste also relates to unnecessarily high 'compliance costs' imposed on those who pay taxes. For example, retailers may face very high costs in complying with value added tax (VAT) regulations if not all goods and services are taxable and if, of those that are, many different rates of tax are imposed. Similarly, the administrative costs of taxes on incomes, capital gains and wealth will be exacerbated by highly progressive tax schedules, with many tax rates and allowances against tax made necessary to achieve both vertical and horizontal equity as well as using taxation to deter 'bads' whilst encouraging 'goods'. Whilst such high costs may be the acceptable result of tax systems designed to achieve equity and efficiency, they should be avoided if they are the result of arbitrary anomalies resulting from historical practice or piecemeal reforms to tax structures.

■ *Effectiveness* can be promoted by considering in strategic terms the precise mix of taxes referred to in Table 5.1. A highly progressive regime of income tax may cause severe disincentives to work and so reduce the level of economic activity below what it would otherwise have been. On the other hand, if taxes on goods and services are the primary sources of tax revenue, they may take higher proportions of the income of poor households than of affluent households because affluent households generally save higher proportions of their incomes than do low-income households. Again, this suggests that commodity taxes should focus on forms of consumption creating significant social costs (that is, 'bads'). Of course, if activities creating social costs are substantially reduced by the imposition of tax, then the public finances raised will be insufficient to fund public services. Thus, it will be necessary also to tax 'goods' such as income from employment. Nevertheless, some 'bads' could raise relatively large amounts of public finance, for example a carbon tax.

As already noted, in most countries the mix of the various different taxes on incomes, expenditures, wealth and beneficial use of property is shaped more by the historical development of their tax systems and structures than by a strategic review of the totality of taxes. Ultimately, a tax system has to be acceptable to the general public as well as to business. Taxes are usually only tolerated because they have been levied on generations of taxpayers: nobody likes paying new taxes.

The strategic issue is to consider how the structure of taxation can be slowly and progressively reformed to make more socially acceptable the distribution of income and wealth, to change behaviour in socially beneficial ways and, more generally, to influence the level of economic activity (see Chapter 1). Hence, taxes are not always burdensome because they can be used for socially and economically beneficial purposes. Hopefully, it has been made clear that even if all taxes are bad, some are much less bad than others.

Charges

Most countries make relatively little use of user-charges for public services (see below and Chapter 8), it being a generally accepted social principle that public services should be free at the point of consumption. In practice, there usually are charges for the outputs of trading services such as municipal power supplies and transport. There may also be charges for school meals, use of public leisure services and so on.

In the private sector companies generally charge as much as they can, the intention being to make as much profits as possible. Thus, they generally charge what consumers are willing to pay, that willingness reflecting the benefit consumers derive from the product and its availability from alternative lower cost suppliers. In contrast, charges levied for public sector services are generally based on costs of supply, rather than on benefits conferred by their consumption. There is a general reluctance in the public sector to be seen to be making a profit from the provision of goods and services. This is particularly the case when there is little or no competition from alternative suppliers, this usually being due to statutory monopolies (that is, where the law precludes provision by private sector companies). Making a profit would generally be regarded as exploitation of the consumer or service user. However, organisational slack (see Chapter 4) could be regarded as exploitation of the consumer in just the same way as prices incorporating an element of profit. Whether prices are high due to profits (in, say, the private sector) or due to unnecessarily high service costs (in, say, the public sector), the consumer could be regarded as 'exploited'. The same 'exploitation' occurs if taxes are higher than they need be due to lack of operational and strategic economy (see Chapter 1). Hence, user-charges are not necessarily more 'exploitative' than taxes, if such a value-laden term can be used.

In general, tax-financed subsidies are required because of the low proportions of cost recovery through user-charges, the degree of cost recovery varying substantially and often in a fairly arbitrary manner. As an extremely broad generalisation, however, the more technical the service and the greater the perceived individualised benefits arising from its consumption, the greater the proportion of service costs covered by charges. Conversely, the greater the perceived social benefits of the service, the greater the proportion of service costs financed by taxation. Perceptions of benefits are, however, extremely crude and ultimately arbitrary, there usually being no serious attempt to identify and measure them.

User-charges supplemented by state-financed subsidies could be an example of a complementary mix of alternative sources of public finance. In most cases, however, user-charges are seen by service providers almost entirely as a necessary and unavoidable source of additional revenue, without which the service budget would not balance (that is, income equal to expenditure). Whilst this view is highly pragmatic, the rationale for user-charges needs to be more broadly based in policy terms, in particular satisfying the 4Es:

■ *Equity* is generally thought to require the free provision of services. However, public services generally seem to benefit affluent socioeconomic groups as much as or more than poorer socioeconomic groups. In using services such as education and health, middle-income groups may benefit more than low-income groups. For example, higher proportions of teenagers from middle- and high-income households go to university than do those from low-income households. Such *middle-class capture* of subsidy also seems to extend to use of health services, recreational and cultural services, roads and so on. Nevertheless, modern welfare states have never been designed to be solely (or even largely) pro-poor even by Collectivists. Supporters of the welfare state usually argue that citizens have a moral right to free public services. Generally, they disagree with means-tested charges, arguing that the assessment of ability to pay is intrusive of privacy and demeaning, implying charity rather than a right to services as citizens. Proud people therefore are deterred from using the service and so both vertical and horizontal inequity ensue, even though means testing is intended specifically to prevent that outcome.

■ *Efficiency* in the use of public services is not likely to be secured if public services are completely free at the point of use. The fact is that very few public services are pure public goods (see Chapter 2) and money used to finance public services is money not spent on other goods and services. If this opportunity cost of free public services is greater than their benefits, then economic and social welfare is not being maximised. This is more likely to be the case if public services are not highly valued by their users and/or if wasteful use is made of them. These scenarios are typified, respectively, by underused services displaying considerable excess capacity and by service users taking more service outputs than they can really use. For example, only a minority of residents may use their municipal library and those who do use it may borrow many more books than they can possibly read during the borrowing period. The same waste may characterise other municipal services whose free use is at the discretion of citizens (for example water supply). Such waste is inconsistent with the efficient allocation of resources in an economy.

■ *Economy* in the provision of public services requires them to be provided at minimum cost. In practice, however, charges may be inconsistent with operational economy if they are too costly to levy relative to the revenue raised. This is particularly likely to be the case when efficiency and equity criteria justify subsidising consumption (for example because of wider social benefits and the need to avoid adverse impacts on low-income groups). In particular, the administrative costs of relating the levels of charges to the incomes of users may be excessive for some public services. Nonetheless, such practical constraints on charging rarely justify the completely free provision of public sector services to all users, this being inconsistent with strategic economy (see Chapter 1). Hence, to dismiss charges on the basis of operational economy may be misguided because of the much higher cost implications of contravening strategic economy.

■ *Effectiveness* requires the levels of user-charges broadly to reflect the level of personalised benefits of service consumption enjoyed by the individual service user, whilst state-financed subsidies reflect the broader social benefits and, as far as possible, each user's ability to pay. Categoric exemptions could be given (for example to the elderly, unemployed, students and disabled people) where means testing is uneconomical. In this way, equity, efficiency and economy can be achieved This complementary use of direct user-charges and tax-financed subsidies is consistent with property rights theory relating to mixed goods (see Chapter 2), whilst making economical use of public funds by maximising additionality (see Chapter 4). Likewise, the required subsidy could be minimised by using competitive bidding procedures to allocate public service contracts, so encouraging cost containment (again, see Chapter 4). An effective charging regime therefore minimises the need for the other sources of public finance and, at the same time, promotes efficiency and equity.

Thus, in principle, user-charges can make more effective the use of public finance:

■ by relating charges to the ability to pay and need for service
■ by using willingness to pay to estimate the social value of services
■ by avoiding the wasteful use of services.

This assumes that the administrative costs of testing for need for service and for income and/or wealth (that is, operational economy) do not exceed the benefits just described.

The strategic issue is to identify which particular socioeconomic groups use individual public services, what levels and frequency of use they enjoy, what costs they generate and what wider social benefits of service consumption are conferred on those who do not themselves use the service. Only with this information can the appropriate charging regime be determined.

Privatisation and private finance

Although such revenues are ultimately finite, they may be raised from the sale of municipal and other state assets. This is not necessarily 'asset stripping'. The sale of state assets can be justified as long as benefits from the use of the resulting revenues are greater than the value of those assets in their current use. For example, it may be a carefully considered use of municipal assets to improve services.

A more sustainable form of privatisation is public–private partnerships (or private finance initiatives). These exist when governments and companies agree contracts for the provision and financing of public sector services and their infrastructure. This is mutually beneficial where the public sector benefits from lower costs whilst the private sector derives profits.

Provision of the capital assets required for the provision of public sector services necessarily entails an element of risk in terms of their costs and benefits. Public sector construction costs have a history of being greater than budgeted for (referred to as 'cost overruns'). For example, construction of a bridge may take longer than expected because of unforeseen geological problems in respect of its foundations and there may be delays in delivery of equipment or components. Delays cost money, for example in terms of extra debt charges being incurred over the longer-than-expected period, say, between borrowing the money necessary to finance the construction project and revenues from bridge tolls (that is, user-charges) being used to repay the debt. Likewise, benefits may be less than expected, for example where traffic using the bridge is less than forecast because of unexpectedly slow economic growth in the region.

Although these outcomes are difficult to foresee for an individual project, analysis of the generality of public sector infrastructure projects allows fairly sophisticated risk assessments to be made. For example, the risk of delays in construction, cost overruns and revenue shortfalls can be assessed using past experience to assess likely degrees of error in forecasts for construction times and revenues generated from user-charges. Nevertheless, risk assessment is not wholly an objective exercise and assessments can be significantly influenced by the value judgements of the risk assessors.

Public sector workers often have vested interests in new construction projects going ahead because it benefits their job prospects. They therefore face incentives to understate the risk of higher costs and overstate the possible benefits (that is, 'optimism bias'). There may be no significant penalties (for example being sacked) for being overoptimistic. In contrast, the private sector incurs penalties for being overoptimistic in terms of the subsequent losses. Hence, in principle, risk can be more efficiently handled by utilising the private sector's expertise in dealing with commercial risk and transferring as much risk as possible to the private sector within public–private partnerships. More realistic risk assessments are thought likely to be the case because private sector companies have more experience of major construction projects and so can make more realistic risk assessments. However, they are likely to face incentives opposite to those of the public sector in overstating the risks of higher costs and lower revenue streams (or other such benefits). By such means they seek to maximise their profits from construction projects. These incentives can be countered by inviting competing companies to bid for construction projects, the greater the competition the less able are firms to overstate risk. Where, however, there are only a few companies they may collude with each other to avoid competition forcing down their assessments of risk and so efficiency would be compromised.

Alternatively, private companies may seek to transfer as much risk as possible back to the public sector or to users of the facility. For example, a private company may negotiate a monopoly position as part of its contract, taking control of any other river crossings as a condition of building a road bridge and being able to charge tolls on each crossing. In this way, construction companies substantially reduce the risk of revenues from bridge tolls being insufficient to cover construction and operating costs. Risk is effectively transferred to users of the bridge via tolls, or to the government if high tolls prove so politically unpopular that subsidies to bridge users are made necessary. In effect, the public sector guarantees that it will cover any deficit.

Whilst efficiency will be improved if the private sector is better able to handle risk than the public sector, it will be compromised if monopoly powers (in terms of market power or knowledge of costs) are conferred on private operators and used to levy excessive payments from users of the facility. This will be the case if the private company more than covers costs in maximising its profits. More generally, in terms of the 4Es:

- *Efficiency* will be promoted if the private sector is better than the public sector at assessing risk, controlling construction costs and managing the project once it is built and if public finance is only paid to the private operator in accordance with use.
- *Economy* may be reduced by the complexity of negotiations between governments and potential private sector contractors, especially regarding the transfer of risk. Moreover, private companies usually have to pay a higher rate of interest than the government on borrowed sums because there is a greater risk to the lender that a private company may default on its debt

repayment. Governments never go bankrupt because they can always raise taxes to repay debt. Hence, the savings from better risk management must be greater than the extra borrowing costs for economy to be improved.

■ *Equity* is improved where middle-class capture of subsidy occurs, for example where middle-income car owners use a bridge and where, in the absence of tolls, low-income groups unable to afford cars would have to contribute to its financing via taxes. On the other hand, in the tolled bridge example, current users finance the bridge typically over a period much shorter than its lifetime because the private sector company wishes to recover its costs as quickly as possible. Intergenerational inequity results.

■ *Effectiveness* will only be achieved where the value of savings resulting from better management of risk exceed the profits that must be paid to the private operator plus any higher borrowing costs of private companies. Given that public–private partnership projects are typically of long duration (up to, say, 25 years), it cannot be determined for certain whether cost savings will be achieved.

The further into the future that savings or additional costs are expected, the less certain those financial flows are, assuming that uncertainty is a positive function of time. Moreover, it is invalid to compare directly expected savings or additional costs because they occur at different periods of time. In order to compare, say, upfront savings in the public finances with higher future expenditures, those financial flows must be standardised by converting them into current values. This requires revenue and cost streams occurring at different periods of time to be discounted into present values. 'Discounting' results in the present value of a future sum being less than that sum. Specifically, the present value is that amount which would earn just enough money at the current rate of interest over the intervening years sufficient to make it equal to the future sum. In other words, discounting is the opposite of compound interest and so the longer the period of time and the greater the discount rate, the less the present value of a future sum. In practice, those periods of time and the appropriate discount rate are uncertain and so, therefore, are the present values of costs and savings.

Thus, whether public–private partnerships do actually save money compared with solely public sector provision of services over long periods of time cannot be known with any certainty. Any conclusion is ultimately a best guess and so it is extremely difficult to determine the effectiveness of such arrangements before they take place. Given these caveats, public–private partnerships are only likely to be effective in particular circumstances. The strategic issue, therefore, is to ensure that there should be such a substantial transfer of risk to the private sector that there is a large net gain for the public sector in achieving the 4Es.

Borrowing

As already noted in Chapter 3, public sector borrowing has implications for future tax rates, higher tax rates ultimately being required in order to repay the ensuing debt. The only exception to this rule is if charges or other non-tax revenues are used to repay debt, for example where borrowing is used to finance the building of roads, bridges and tunnels for whose use tolls are levied. In terms of the 4Es:

- *Equity* is compromised if governments borrow year after year, never repaying the mounting public debt. This is because future generations of taxpayers will ultimately have to repay public debt. It could be argued that future generations of taxpayers will be better off than the current generation, so that borrowing to finance current consumption (rather than investment) promotes intergenerational equity. However, the supposed greater affluence of future generations of taxpayers is by no means certain. Even if it were certain, such a redistribution of income between generations may be deemed unacceptable because future generations, by definition, are not afforded an opportunity to vote for or against such a redistribution. This could be regarded as unethical.
- *Efficiency* may also be compromised if governments borrow year after year. Whilst borrowing may be used for macroeconomic purposes during recessions, it is difficult to find any efficiency rationale that justifies continual and ever-increasing borrowing. Very high levels of public sector borrowing may make control of the economy more difficult, explaining the need for the Maastricht deficit and debt ratios (see Chapter 3). However, whilst they act as a constraint on public borrowing and debt, the Maastricht Treaty rules for the single European currency are essentially arbitrary. They are as much the outcome of political negotiation as a reflection of evidence of the adverse economic effects of public borrowing and debt in terms of higher interest rates, inflation and future taxes (see Chapter 6).
- *Economy* means avoiding borrowing at unnecessarily high rates of interest over excessively long periods of time. As just noted, high levels of public borrowing may drive up interest rates. This increases not just the cost of new borrowing but also the cost of servicing the stock of public debt (that is, paying interest on it). If the public debt/GDP ratio is large, even a small increase in interest rates could have a substantial impact on the proportion of public spending that must be devoted to paying interest. Likewise, borrowing over unnecessarily long periods of time means that more interest is being paid than absolutely necessary. In general, borrowing (and, hence, interest payments) should not extend beyond the life of the asset provided by borrowing, this rule being consistent with intergenerational equity.
- *Effectiveness* is difficult to judge because the economic lives of real assets may be much less than their physical lives. For example, population

movements out of cities into surrounding suburban and rural areas may result in redundant school buildings, even though their physical structures are still sound. In such cases, relating repayment periods to the expected economic (rather than physical) lives of real assets would result in their debt being repaid more quickly. In practice, the terms (that is, length) of loans are determined more by custom and practice than by realistic assessments of the economic life of assets. The apparent trend towards faster social and economic restructuring should be reflected in shorter debt repayment periods if efficiency, equity and economy are to be achieved.

The golden rule of public finance (see Chapter 3) would appear to safeguard intergenerational equity because it prevents the current generation borrowing to finance current consumption. Hence, borrowing to finance current expenditure should be short term, loans only covering the mismatch between incurring current expenditures and receiving current revenues, most being repaid within the current financial year. Otherwise, the current account should be in balance over the financial year as a whole if the golden rule is to be adhered to. However, intergenerational inequity can still result because the accounting definitions of current and capital spending are hazy at the margins. For example, future generations are disadvantaged if what is defined as capital expenditure is in fact current expenditure (for example repairs and maintenance of buildings, roads and bridges). Intergenerational inequity would be reversed if significant proportions of capital expenditures were to be defined as current expenditures, current taxpayers therefore having to finance capital expenditures on a 'pay as you go' basis.

State lotteries

State lotteries are operated in many countries to raise finance for public services. They are a form of gambling in offering a chance of a monetary prize following the purchase of a lottery ticket. The greater the potential prize the smaller the chances of winning it. A lottery is not a tax since the purchase of lottery tickets is voluntary. Nor is that purchase a user-charge since there is no direct provision of service following payment (unless the excitement of gambling could be so described). In avoiding the opprobrium of taxes and user-charges, lotteries may appear to be the ideal source of funds, there being no apparent limit to the extent to which they can be used to finance public services. Although prohibited in some countries for religious or ethical reasons, gambling has recently become more socially acceptable in many others. In terms of the 4Es:

■ *Equity* problems may arise if lottery revenues come disproportionately from low-income groups, the poor perhaps having a greater incentive to gamble because winning the jackpot would result in a significant improvement in their material standard of living. Such equity problems would be exacerbated if those revenues are used to finance public services that disproportionately benefit higher income groups.

■ *Efficiency* may be greater when additional public finances are raised by state lotteries rather than by taxation. This would be the case if lottery finance substituted for tax revenues and so avoided any severe disincentive-to-work or disincentive-to-enterprise effects caused by the higher rates of tax that would otherwise have to be levied on additional earned incomes, profits and expenditures (see Chapter 6).

■ *Economy* is more likely to be achieved where companies or organisations have to compete for the opportunity to run the state lottery and also share in the revenues raised. This is because they face incentives to minimise operating costs in order to win the contract. They also face profit incentives to maximise revenues through effective marketing campaigns. State-run lotteries do not face such incentives, their statutory monopoly shielding them from competitive pressures to minimise operating costs, and there being no profit incentive to maximise revenues and/or minimise costs.

■ *Effectiveness* therefore depends upon how state lotteries are operated, which social groups participate, how the revenues raised are spent and whether the money they raise is additional to or a replacement of other forms of public finance (see Chapter 4 on additionality).

More generally, some would question the ethics of gambling, both in generic terms and, more specifically, in tempting poor households to make unwise use of their limited money that would be better spent on feeding and otherwise sustaining themselves and their children. Put simply, in their desperation to improve their lot, the poorest groups effectively throw away their money, their chances of winning major sums being extremely small. Although rather patronising, according to this view state lotteries are therefore neither ethical nor equitable. The counter-argument is that the poor will gamble anyway since other opportunities are almost always available. Nevertheless, it seems that the introduction of state lotteries leads to a general increase in the incidence of gambling, especially if state regulation of the gaming industry is relaxed in line with the development of state lotteries.

Nonetheless, after their initial popularity, it seems that interest in lotteries tends to diminish as they lose their novelty value and as the public begins to appreciate that hopes of a major win are unrealistically optimistic. Therefore, state lotteries need to be innovative in developing new ideas so as to avoid diminishing interest and falling participation rates. Again, privately run state lotteries provide more incentives for innovation.

Thus, the case for the unlimited use of state lotteries instead of taxation or other sources of finance is not self-evident. In practice, there are limits on the extent to which state lotteries can be used to raise public finance, although these limits can be relaxed by a strategic approach that avoids or minimises any adverse effects. Certainly, their operation should be closely monitored to ensure that the 4Es are met.

Donations and bequests

Donations are contributions made during a person's lifetime, whereas bequests are gifts made after death in the deceased person's will. More generally known as 'benefactions', donations and bequests may take the form of money or property. Benefactions are usually made to charities and other voluntary organisations but they are also sometimes made to the public sector, this being consistent with the Libertarians' 'active citizen model'. They can be encouraged by offering tax relief on certain types of donation or bequest. Examples include major works of art or other cultural artefacts donated to public art galleries and museums and property of historic or architectural value given to the state in lieu of death duties and inheritance taxes. These donations in kind replace payment of taxes on incomes and/or wealth and so are known as 'tax expenditures' (see Chapter 4).

Clearly, a benefaction that does not attract tax relief represents a net gain in terms of public finance. Financial additionality is reduced, however, when the benefaction is used to reduce tax liability. It is difficult to calculate the extent of financial additionality in such a case (see Chapter 4 on additionality). In terms of the 4Es:

■ *Equity* will be improved by benefactions if they are predominantly made by high-income and wealthy groups. However, the situation is less clear-cut when the benefaction attracts tax relief. Equity would be compromised if both the tax offset and the use of services (for example the arts) disproportionately benefit high-income groups. This may particularly be the case in respect of museums, galleries and other forms of 'high culture'.
■ *Efficiency* would be reduced where donations and bequests pre-empt public finances which would otherwise have been used for other more socially productive services. This could be the case irrespective of whether the benefaction attracts tax relief. An example is where the operation of medical equipment donated to a hospital (for example by a medical charity) requires medical staff who would otherwise have been used for other treatments more highly prioritised by the health authority. The authority may be unwilling to 'look a gift horse in the mouth' (that is, find fault with a donation or bequest and so refuse it) because to do so may discourage future benefactions. Benefactions may therefore yield lower social and economic welfare by distorting the provision of public services. This inefficiency will be exacerbated if other services are forgone as a result of an associated tax

allowance. For example, a valuable painting donated in lieu of tax payment effectively boosts the arts and culture budget of the recipient authority and reduces the tax revenues available to other parts of the public sector. Of course, the government could reduce the recipient authority's budget by the annualised value of the artefact but such budgetary adjustments are seldom made. The benefaction could be recorded as an equivalent flow of income in the authority's financial accounts and whose current budget would then be reduced accordingly. Alternatively, the benefaction could be recorded as an increase in the authority's capital asset base and whose capital budget would then be reduced accordingly. If neither such financial adjustments are made, then the benefaction may, in effect, be replacing a new hospital that would otherwise have been built with the tax revenues foregone as a result of the benefaction.

■ *Economy* will generally be reduced if benefactions are associated with tax relief. This is because they tend to incur high administrative costs relative to the tax equivalent of their values and/or relative to the administrative costs of raising the same amount in taxes. In particular, administrative costs relating to cultural artefacts are usually much greater than the cost of raising the same amount of revenue through the tax system. This is because such benefactions have to be expertly valued and/or the resultant tax offset has to be negotiated item by item.

■ *Effectiveness* is therefore likely to be greater for unconditional donations and bequests and for those in cash instead of 'in kind' (that is, non-financial assets). However, there is little incentive for people and businesses to make unconditional benefactions to the state since they attract no tax relief or other such benefit. Effectiveness is likely to be reduced when there are explicit or implicit conditions attached to them. For this reason donations and bequests have strictly limited potential as sources of public finance despite the Libertarian preference for active citizenship, voluntary giving and charity instead of state intervention (see Chapter 1).

Payments in kind

As already noted, the term 'in kind' denotes physical form, not being in the form of cash. They will count as public finance as long as their capital values are entered into the public accounts (that is, recorded as an increase in public sector assets). Payments in kind may be made directly for services provided by the public sector or, alternatively, to facilitate their provision without being a direct payment per se. An example of the first is when a private sector developer donates land necessary for a new station on a state-run underground railway system serving a new commercial development. The value of the land is assumed to at least equal the cost of construction of the subway station. An example of the second is when private companies finance, or provide directly, public infrastructure that complements or otherwise expedites their own operations. Thus, construction companies may voluntarily build a road, school or other such facility and donate it to the relevant municipality in order to bring forward planning permission to build a new housing estate or business development. The facility does not necessarily have to be directly related to the new development. Instead, it can simply relieve a financial constraint experienced by the municipality. Hence, payments in kind are likely to be used more extensively in countries with highly formalised (critics would say bureaucratised) land-use planning systems. Examples are 'planning gain' and 'planning obligations' in the UK and 'impact fees', 'development fees' and 'exactions' in the USA and Canada. In terms of the 4Es:

- *Equity* depends upon who ultimately finances the payments in kind. For example, it was noted above that intergenerational equity is promoted if borrowing is used to finance infrastructure. In this way the current generation of taxpayers is not required to fully finance roads, bridges and buildings also benefiting future generations. Intergenerational inequity results, however, if developers recoup their payments in kind through higher house prices. This is because the buyers of those houses are not only paying for their use of existing infrastructure through property taxes, they are also fully funding new infrastructure through higher house prices.
- *Efficiency* will be improved if, in relieving a municipality's capital constraint, such payments in kind promote efficiency in the local economy by facilitating local economic development and therefore higher local and regional GDP. However, inefficiency (and inequity) may result if, for example, municipalities are bribed by developers into granting planning permissions that lead to excessive development or if municipalities extort such payments by abusing their statutory monopoly planning powers (assuming they have them). Excessive development could result in congestion and other social costs such as incompatible land use (for example toxic industrial processes taking place in residential areas). However, Libertarians would welcome a free market in land development because the buying and selling of planning permissions through voluntary exchange reveals the true market values of individual plots of land. In the Libertarian view the efficiency problem is created (rather than solved) by the nationalisation of land development rights.
- *Economy* is achieved if the costs of negotiating such payments are negligible relative to the benefits received by the municipality. In practice, the costs of such negotiations may be considerable, although they are difficult to determine since, being commercial in nature, such negotiations are confidential.
- *Effectiveness* of payments in kind in the land-use development case is judged in terms of achievement of an optimal level of development: neither underdeveloped (resulting in a relatively low per capita GDP) or

overdeveloped (leading to excessive congestion and soaring land and house prices). However, effectiveness is difficult to determine because of the uncertain impacts on house prices and municipal capital budgets and the confidential and secretive nature of such payments in kind. Hence, it is extremely difficult to determine whether intergenerational equity has been compromised, whether efficiency has been improved and whether economy has been secured. The Libertarian solution (namely, privatisation of the right to develop land) would dispense with the need to be concerned with the 4Es. Otherwise, the use of payments in cash (a form of 'development charge') is a more flexible form of public finance. Nevertheless, they may still experience the same equity, efficiency and economy problems as payments in kind.

Special assessments

Whereas payments in kind are used to finance *new* infrastructure, special assessments are used to finance improvements in *existing* infrastructure. Their use is very limited, being used by some municipalities in the USA to finance specific improvements (for example to the water and sewerage systems) serving a specific neighbourhood. They take the form of payment of additional property taxes and have to be approved by referenda. The extra tax to be paid is calculated using a crude rule of thumb, payment being in accordance with the acreage or front-footage of the property (these being measures of spatial scale). Tax deferment may be allowed, the tax payment being recouped upon sale of the property or death of the owner, whichever occurs first. In terms of the 4Es:

■ *Equity* problems are generally avoided by the need for referenda, the degree to which tax payments are related to income and/or wealth, and the option of tax deferment
■ *Efficiency* is facilitated by provision of additional service in accordance with willingness to pay, there presumably being no adverse impacts resulting from higher tax payments (see Chapter 6)
■ *Economy* is facilitated by use of the existing system for the collection of local property taxes
■ *Effectiveness* is achieved since there are few if any problems in respect of the other 3Es.

HOW IS PUBLIC FINANCE RAISED IN PRACTICE?

Chapter 3 made clear the steady rise in the average tax/GDP ratio in OECD countries, from a quarter of GDP in 1965 to a third in 1999. Given that public expenditure rose from just over a quarter to between a third and two-fifths, it is clear that taxation is the primary source of public finance. Therefore the other sources of finance discussed above are clearly relatively very small (see also Chapter 8). In terms of OECD averages, Figure 5.1 reveals that:

■ personal income tax rose from almost 7 per cent of GDP in 1965 to just over 10 per cent in 1989, that proportion falling back slightly to just under 10 per cent thereafter
■ social security contributions levied on both employees and employers almost doubled as a proportion of GDP between 1965 and 1990 (5.4 and 10.3 respectively), thereafter falling back slightly to an OECD average of 9.3 in 1999
■ taxes on goods and services remained very stable as a proportion of GDP at 7 per cent in all but three years, when the ratio rose to 8.1 in each of those years
■ property taxes remained just under 3 per cent of GDP in every year
■ taxes on corporate income remained around 3 per cent of GDP throughout the period.

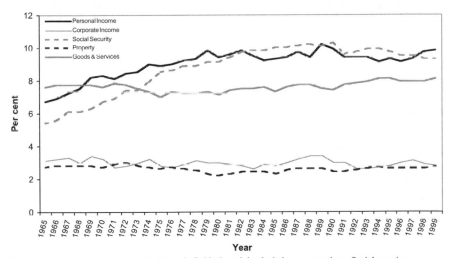

Notes: Income tax is split into that levied on individuals and that levied on corporations. Social security contributions includes all compulsory payments made by insured persons to governments providing welfare benefits. Property tax includes betterment levies and other special levies, tax on the transfer or inheritance of property, taxes based on the development of property and those based on a presumed rental value. Taxes on goods and services includes all taxes on the production, sale, transfer, leasing and delivery of goods and services, including VAT and excise duties

Figure 5.1 Taxes as a percentage of GDP: OECD averages

Sources: OECD (1981) Tables 10, 12, 14, 22 and 24; OECD (1987) Tables 10, 12, 14, 22 and 24; OECD (1992b) Tables 10, 12, 14, 22 and 24; OECD (1993) Table 19; OECD (1996) Tables 10, 12, 14, 22 and 24; OECD (1997) Tables 10, 12, 14, 22 and 24; OECD (2001d) Tables 10, 12, 14, 22 and 24

Thus, although taxation is the primary source of public finance, the
contribution of individual taxes in financing the growing public expendit-
ure/GDP ratio varies enormously. Moreover, the balance between the different
sources of tax revenues also varies very significantly between countries.
Whilst the following analysis is restricted to groups of countries for the sake
of brevity, it should be noted that there may also be substantial variation
within groups of countries.

Figures 5.2 and 5.3 reveal that only the Nordic and Scandinavian group of
countries consistently and significantly exceed the OECD average *personal
income tax/GDP ratio*. Indeed, the only country ever to exceed a ratio of 25
per cent was Denmark (in 1974, the late 1980s and all years of the 1990s).
Only two other countries exceeded a ratio of 20 per cent, namely New
Zealand (four years in the early to mid-1980s) and Sweden (14 years, but all
before 1991). In the 1990s, Korea had the lowest personal income tax/GDP
ratios (4 per cent or less).

Figures 5.4 and 5.5 make clear that European countries as a group and the
EU in particular consistently exceed the OECD average *social security/GDP
ratio*. Interestingly, the Nordic and Scandinavian group fall below the OECD
average prior to the 1990s, the change of position being due to a sharp rise in
the ratio for Finland in 1991. Denmark's ratio has been lowest or second
lowest throughout the period, being below 2 per cent until 1999 (2.1). Clearly,
this reflects the relatively high levels of personal income tax/GDP ratios in the

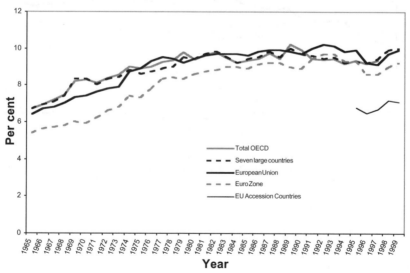

Note: Groups are as defined in Figure 3.1

Figure 5.2   Personal income tax as a percentage of GDP:
OECD versus EU and large economies

Sources: OECD (1981); OECD (1987); OECD (1993) Table 19; OECD (1996);
OECD (1997); OECD (2001d) Table 10 unless otherwise specified

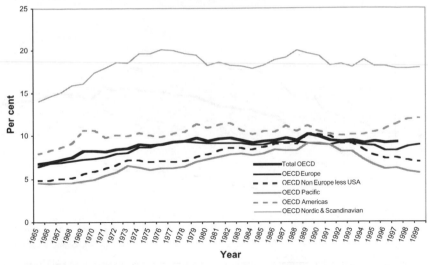

Note: Personal income tax includes only tax levied on individual's income and not corporate income. Groups are as defined in Figure 3.2

Figure 5.3 Personal income tax as a percentage of GDP:
OECD versus Europe and non-European nations

Sources: OECD (1981); OECD (1987); OECD (1992b); OECD (1993) Table 19;
OECD (1996); OECD (1997); OECD (2001d) Table 10 unless otherwise specified

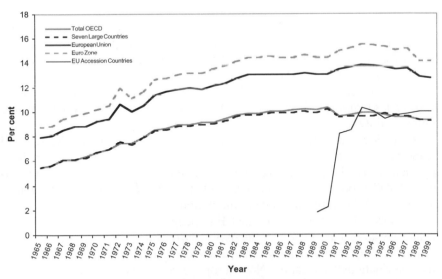

Notes: Groups arc as defined in Figure 3.1. Social security contributions includes all compulsory payments made by insured persons/employers to governments providing social welfare benefits

Figure 5.4 Social security contributions as a percentage of GDP:
OECD versus EU and large economies

Sources: OECD (1981); OECD (1987); OECD (1992b); OECD (1996);
OECD (1997); OECD (2001d) Table 14 in each publication

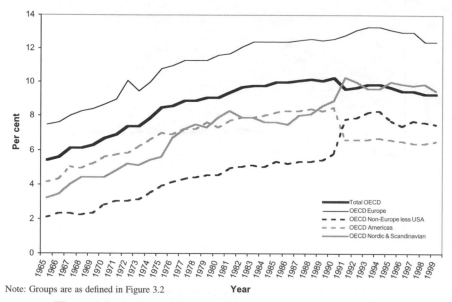

Note: Groups are as defined in Figure 3.2   **Year**

Figure 5.5   Social security contributions as a percentage of GDP:
OECD versus Europe and non-European nations
Sources: As Figure 5.4

Nordic and Scandinavian group in general and Denmark's position as high outlier for the personal income tax/GDP ratio in particular.

Figures 5.6 and 5.7 show that European countries and the Nordic and Scandinavian group in particular levy higher *taxes on goods and services/ GDP ratios* than the OECD average, Denmark being consistently amongst the highest ratios.

Figures 5.8 and 5.9 reveal that European and in particular Nordic and Scandinavian countries raise relatively low *property tax/GDP ratios*, reflecting their relatively high personal income tax/GDP or social security contributions/GDP ratios. Canada, the UK and the USA have levied the highest property tax/GDP ratios throughout the period.

Figures 5.10 and 5.11 show that European and in particular Nordic and Scandinavian countries raise relatively low *corporate income tax/GDP ratios*, again reflecting their relatively high personal income tax/GDP or social security contributions/GDP ratios. Non-European countries (excluding the USA) have tended to levy relatively high corporate income tax/GDP ratios throughout the period, most notably Japan. Amongst European countries, Luxembourg is notable for raising a substantially higher corporate income tax/GDP ratio than the OECD average. The USA is notable for having progressively transformed itself from a high ratio country during the 1960s and 70s to a low corporate income tax/GDP ratio country during the 1980s and 90s.

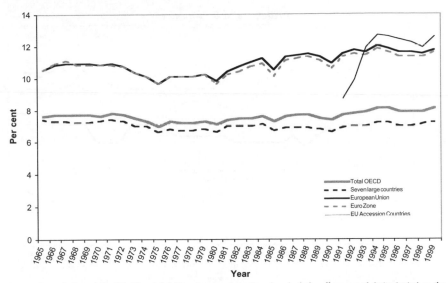

Notes: Groups are as defined in Figure 3.1. Taxes on goods and services includes all taxes and duties levied on the production, sale, transfer, leasing and delivery of goods and services. Includes VAT, sales taxes, import/export taxes and excises

Figure 5.6   Tax on goods and services as a percentage of GDP: OECD versus EU and large economies

Sources: OECD (1981); OECD (1987); OECD (1992b); OECD (1996); OECD (1997); OECD (2001d) Table 24 in each publication

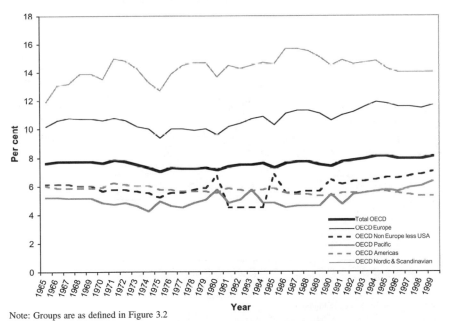

Note: Groups are as defined in Figure 3.2

Figure 5.7   Tax on goods and services as a percentage of GDP: OECD versus Europe and non-European nations

Sources: As Figure 5.6

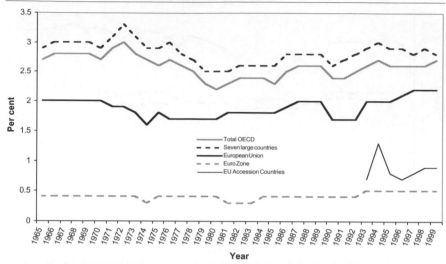

Notes: Groups are as defined in Figure 3.1. Property tax includes tax on the transfer or inheritance of property, betterment and other levies, taxes on the improvement of property through development, taxes based on a presumed rental value, and taxes on net wealth which includes immovable property

Figure 5.8   Property tax as a percentage of GDP:
OECD versus EU and large economies

Sources: OECD (1981); OECD (1987); OECD (1992b); OECD (1996);
OECD (1997); OECD (2001d) Table 22 in each publication

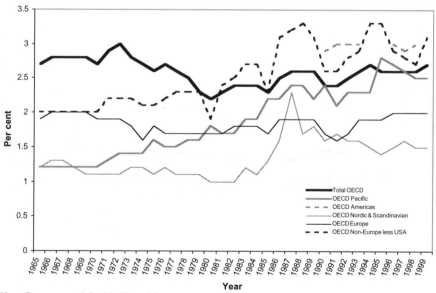

Note: Groups are as defined in Figure 3.2

Figure 5.9   Property tax as a percentage of GDP:
OECD versus Europe and non-European nations

Sources: As Figure 5.8

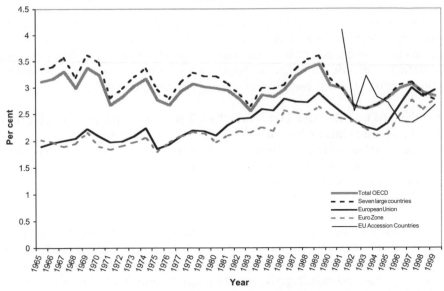

Notes: Groups are as defined in Figure 3.1. Corporate income tax includes taxes levied on profits and capital gains

Figure 5.10 Tax on corporate income as a percentage of GDP:
OECD versus EU and large economies

Sources: OECD (1981); OECD (1987); OECD (1992b); OECD (1996);
OECD (1997); OECD (2001d) Table 12 in each publication

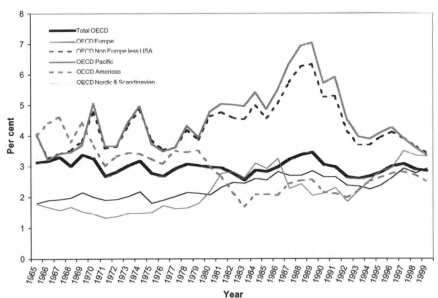

Note: Groups are as defined in Figure 3.2

Figure 5.11 Tax on corporate income as a percentage of GDP:
OECD versus Europe and non-European nations

Source: As Figure 5.10

It was noted above that taxes are not just used to raise revenue and some taxes are much less bad than others in terms of the 4Es. In that sense, there seems to be an undue emphasis on taxes on 'goods' (that is, employment) and insufficient attention to taxes on 'bads' (that is, polluting activities related to consumption of goods and services). Between 1965 and 1999:

■ the total tax/GDP OECD ratio rose by 6.7 percentage points (see Table 3.2)
■ the personal income tax/GDP ratio rose by 2.7 percentage points
■ the social security contributions/GDP ratio rose by 3.9 percentage points
■ the taxes on goods and services/GDP ratio rose by 0.5 percentage points
■ the property tax/GDP ratio neither rose nor fell
■ the corporate income tax/GDP ratio likewise neither rose nor fell.

Whilst attention has to be paid to economy of collection and vertical equity, there does seem to have been a neglect of efficiency considerations by increasing taxes on both earned incomes and payrolls much more than taxes on other economic activities. This conclusion is all the more telling given that:

■ both personal income tax and social security contributions had already fallen by 1999 from their earlier non-recession peaks relative to GDP of 11.9 and 10.2 respectively in 1988
■ total taxes were still relatively high in EU and especially Nordic/Scandinavian countries in 1999 and had consistently been so since 1965.

Put simply, it seems that European (and especially EU and Nordic/Scandinavian countries in particular) have been too ready to raise taxes on employment incomes. This may simply have been because they are the easiest ways of raising further tax revenues and the easiest to justify politically and socially in terms of increased vertical equity. Nevertheless, this may have been at the expense of economic growth (see Chapter 6). Neo-Liberals would favour a shift in the balance of taxation away from 'goods' to 'bads' in order to help markets function more efficiently. Collectivists would accept somewhat slower economic growth as the price to be paid for greater equality in the distribution of positive rights (see Chapter 1).

WHAT IS THE OPTIMUM COMBINATION OF THE DIFFERENT SOURCES OF PUBLIC FINANCE?

In principle, the optimum combination of the various sources of public finance is that which minimises the direct and indirect resource costs of raising a given amount of finance:

■ *Direct resource costs* are those of collecting revenues and servicing loans and debt. Some taxes are more expensive to collect than others, wealth and capital gains taxes generally being more expensive to collect than personal and corporate income taxes. This is because incomes are easier to identify and measure than are capital gains and wealth. As already noted, besides the direct costs to the public sector in actually collecting revenues, there may also be substantial compliance costs imposed on companies in calculating their liability to pay taxes such as VAT. This diverts potentially productive resources away from producing goods and services and towards calculation of tax liabilities.

■ *Indirect resource costs* take the form of reduced revenue yields. Indirect costs are likely to be much greater than direct costs, especially if high rates of income and profits taxes cause significant disincentive-to-work and disincentive-to-invest effects (see Chapter 6). The consequently reduced level of economic activity leads to a reduced tax base in terms of the incomes and profits on which personal and corporate taxes are levied.

To dismiss increased use of user-charges because of high collection costs relative to tax collection costs is to ignore the potentially significant indirect resource costs of taxation. Combined with the advantages of user-charges in terms of promoting strategic economy, it is clear that greater use of user-charges (related to costs and ability to pay rather than to benefits) can be justified in terms of the 4Es.

In practice, it is extremely difficult to identify the optimal combination of sources of public finance because indirect resource costs are not known with any degree of accuracy, for example the size and pervasiveness of any disincentive-to-work effects. Moreover, direct and indirect resource costs are not exogenous, both capable of being reduced by simplified tax structures (for example less progressive tax schedules) and adoption of computerised information systems. However, as a general rule, an optimum combination of the different sources of public finance is one that avoids being overreliant upon one or two sources employing punitively high rates of tax or levels of user-charges. The above analysis suggests an overuse of taxes on incomes and employment.

CONCLUSIONS

The foregoing analysis has made clear that raising public finance is not simply about making sure that there is enough money to pay for an agreed level of public services. Nor is raising finance simply a matter of levying taxes. The ways in which public finance is levied is a strategic issue, not a purely financial or administrative one. Raising public finance has profound public policy implications in terms of equity, efficiency, economy and effectiveness. Each possible source of public finance has different implications for achieving the 4Es. Close attention has to be paid to:

■ the precise structure of each individual source of public finance (for example the progressiveness of tax schedules and the exemptions and concessions applied to user-charges) if beneficial effects are to be maximised and adverse effects avoided
■ the precise mix of those alternative sources, it being advisable to avoid overdependence upon only one or two sources of public finance.

The a priori analysis of disincentive effects (in Chapter 6) makes clear that the tax structure is more important than the tax/GDP ratio, since that structure (of tax rates and allowances) determines the magnitude of any disincentive effects. Nevertheless, the above analysis of OECD data suggests that many European countries have relied too heavily on taxation as the main source of finance and been too ready to raise taxes on employment rather than on socially and economically undesirable polluting activities.

Clearly, many countries could make more use of user-charges than they currently do and also seek to generate income by other means. Certainly, they should consider making use of a greater plurality of sources of public finance, the simple tax and spend and spend and tax models of public finance being increasingly open to question. Although controversial in terms of whether they do actually result in financial savings in the long term, public–private partnerships offer considerable potential in reducing the need for public finance by levering private finance.

In questioning the need for public provision and public finance, Libertarians favour the use wherever possible of user-charges, lotteries and voluntary donations and bequests (encouraged, if necessary, by tax reliefs). This is because, unlike taxes, the payment of these other sources of finance is voluntary and so is consistent with freedom of the individual citizen from state oppression. For Libertarians, taxation is only required to ensure negative rights. Neo-liberals and Collectivists have a greater preference for compulsory levies to ensure, respectively, limited and full positive rights. Using the property rights categorisation, Chapter 2 demonstrated that public services are capable of being fully financed by user-charges when property rights are enforceable.

The property rights categorisation makes clear that taxation has to be used fully to finance pure community-level services (that is, pure public goods) and rival but non-excludable mixed goods unless use of complementary services can be charged for. This is because payment of user-charges cannot be enforced and the altruism of voluntary donations and bequests cannot be relied on to finance these two categories of services. User-charges should be used for all other services. The property rights analysis therefore makes clear that user-charges should be the primary source of public finance.

However, conclusions based on the theory of property rights ignore equity issues. A comprehensive system of means testing would be needed to address equity issues if the Libertarian argument that equity is not a relevant issue is dismissed. In such a case it seems more effective to replace user-charges by taxation. However, pursuit of greater equity may be at the cost of lost national output. If so, equity is achieved at the cost of making the average citizen poorer than they would otherwise have been. Whether this is the case is the subject of the next chapter.

FURTHER READING

Bailey, S. J. (1999) *Local Government Economics: Principles and Practice* (Basingstoke: Macmillan – now Palgrave Macmillan) [Chapter 7 on user-charges].

Bailey, S. J. (2002) *Public Sector Economics: Theory, Policy and Practice* (second edition) (Basingstoke: Palgrave – now Palgrave Macmillan) [Chapter 6 on user charges, Chapter 10 on taxation, Chapter 11 on borrowing].

Bailey, S. J. and Bruce, A. (1994) 'Funding the National Health Service: the Continuing Search for Alternatives' *Journal of Social Policy* vol. 23, no. 4, pp. 489–516.

Ball, R., Heafey, M. and King, D. (2001) 'Private Finance Initiative – A Good Deal for the Public Purse or a Drain on Future Generations?' *Policy and Politics* vol. 29, no. 1, pp. 95–108.

Berg, S. V., Pollitt, M. G. and Tsuji, M. (2002) *Private Initiatives in Infrastructure: Priorities, Incentives and Performance* (Cheltenham: Edward Elgar).

Brannlund, R. and Gren, I-M. (1999) *Green Taxes: Economic Theory and Empirical Evidence from Scandinavia* (Cheltenham: Edward Elgar).

Commission on Taxation and Citizenship (2000) *Paying for Progress: A New Politics of Tax for Public Spending* (London: Fabian Society).

DTLGR (2001) *Working Together: Effective Partnering Between Local Government and Business for Service Delivery* (London: Department for Transport, Local Government and the Regions).

Gladstone, D. (1997) (editor) *How to Pay for Health Care: Public and Private Alternatives* IEA Health and Welfare Unit Choice in Welfare No. 37 (London: Institute of Economic Affairs).

Heald, D. and Geaughan, N. (1999) The Private Financing of Public Infrastructure. In G. Stoker (editor) *The New Management of British Local Governance* (Basingstoke: Macmillan – now Palgrave Macmillan).

Hughes, P., Poole, F. and Seely, A. (1997) *Green Taxes* House of Commons Research Paper 97/46 (London: House of Commons Library).

LGA (1999) *Environmental Taxation: A Discussion Paper* (London: Local Government Association).

Meade, J. E. (1978) *The Structure and Reform of Direct Taxation: Report of a Committee chaired by Professor J. E. Meade* (London: Institute of Fiscal Studies).

Messere, K. (1998) (editor) *The Tax System in Industrialised Countries* (Oxford: Oxford University Press).

Musgrave, P. B. (2002) *Tax Policy in the Global Economy: Selected Essays of Peggy B. Musgrave* (Cheltenham: Edward Elgar).

OECD (1995) *Environmental Taxes and Green Tax Reform* (Paris: Organization for Economic Co-operation and Development).

OECD (1997) *Environmental Taxes in OECD Countries* (Paris: Organization for Economic Co-operation and Development).

Sevigny, M. (1998) *Taxing Automobiles for Pollution Control* New Horizons in Environmental Economics (Cheltenham: Edward Elgar).

Smith, S. (1995) *'Green' Taxes and Charges: Policy and Practice in Britain and Germany* (London: Institute of Fiscal Studies).

6 Beneficial and Adverse Effects of Public Finance

INTRODUCTION

Most people would agree that, used sparingly and judiciously, public finance yields many social and economic benefits. It has the potential to improve considerably the population's standard of living, both by fostering national prosperity and sharing it out in a more efficacious manner. However, it cannot be assumed that raising and spending public finance is always solely beneficial. At the very least, private spending has to be given up in order to finance public spending (for example via payment of taxes). In other words, there is a direct opportunity cost associated with public expenditure, namely the private spending that could otherwise have taken place were it not for payment of taxes. If, however, public finance fosters national prosperity (for example through investment in physical and human capital), then this essentially short-term opportunity cost will eventually be offset by greater private sector income (including profits) and wealth in the future.

National prosperity will not be fostered by much or even at all if public finance has outcomes that are substantially harmful to economic prosperity. Libertarians ague that most public spending and revenue raising is harmful to economy and society in creating a dependency culture (see Chapter 1). Neo-Liberals take a more qualified view according to whether or not public finance helps the efficient functioning of markets by strengthening property rights (see Chapter 2). Whether public finance does actually foster national prosperity is the subject of this chapter. It will be demonstrated that the possibility of harmful outcomes is of much greater concern than simply the direct opportunity costs of public expenditures (measured by their tax costs). Harmful outcomes could partially or wholly offset the perceived benefits of services securing negative and positive rights. In other words, it may simply be too costly to ensure those rights when both its short-term direct and long-term indirect costs are considered.

Hence, the fact that a service yields benefits in terms of negative or positive rights is not a sufficient justification for its provision to be supported by public finance. Even restricting public finance to only supporting services securing negative rights (as advocated by Libertarians) could conceivably lead to costs exceeding benefits. For example, very high levels of protection against crime may cost more than the value of the ensuing individual and social benefits, costs here possibly also including infringement of civil liberties by a police state.

Thus, being based on a priori justifications for public finance, the application of the philosophies and theories developed in Chapters 1 and 2 to the public finances may have to be qualified by pragmatic considerations in respect of any deleterious effects arising from the raising and spending of public finance. Therefore, this chapter pays particular attention to the possible adverse effects of public finance. It will be made clear that the concern about adverse effects is greater the greater the relative scale of public finance (see Chapter 3).

ASSESSING THE IMPACT OF PUBLIC FINANCE ON THE ECONOMY

Chapter 4 considered the additionality of public finance. It noted how difficult it is to determine whether or not public expenditure creates truly additional spending on individual services because it is not possible to determine precisely how much would have been spent on a service in the absence of public finance. It is even more difficult to determine the net additional impact of changes in public finance on the efficiency of the economy as a whole. Again, methodological imponderables relate to establishing the counterfactual, namely what would have happened to economic growth in the absence of the changes in the public finances. One cannot simply compare economic activity before and after, say, a change in tax in assessing the impact of that change. As noted in Chapter 4, the proper comparison is the rate of economic growth 'with and without' rather than 'before and after' any change in public finance, the latter comparison being methodologically flawed.

Establishing the counterfactual, however, is essentially guesswork, even though it may be based on a projection into the future of past trends in economic growth. It is not self-evident that those trends would have continued, either at the same rate of change or even in the same direction of change. For example, changes in world trading conditions may affect the employment prospects of particular groups of workers (for example the unskilled) and so have impacts on the distribution of income. If, at the same time, the government had altered taxes and state benefits to bring about a more equal distribution of income, the effectiveness of that reform of public finance can only be determined by allowing for the (complementary or offsetting) effects arising from changes in world trading conditions.

Although very difficult in practice, such an approach is nonetheless methodologically correct. Put simply, it is probably impossible to prove categorically either that public finance in aggregate has net harmful or net beneficial effects or that particular changes in public finance (for example more or less public expenditure) have such effects. Nevertheless, the competing theories about the possible economic effects of public finance are well developed, namely:

■ *Crowding in*, public and private expenditures being mutually complementary
■ *Crowding out*, public and private expenditures being mutually exclusive.

Public and private expenditures may be complementary in stimulating economic growth and national prosperity. In this case, public finance is crowding in private finance, the state enabling the population as a whole to improve its standard of living. For example, public finance is used to provide the infrastructure necessary for market systems to work efficiently (see Chapter 3), namely:

■ provision of the legal infrastructure for market systems based on contracts
■ provision of the physical infrastructure (for example roads) to facilitate the movement of workers and goods
■ provision of the social (for example public services) and economic (for example vocational training) infrastructure to help workers become more productive.

By such means the 4Es of economy (both operational and strategic), efficiency, equity (for example in terms of equality of opportunity for employment) and effectiveness may be promoted (see Chapter 1).

However, profligate and injudicious use of the public finances can have the opposite effect. Instead of crowding in, growth of the public sector may lead to crowding out of the private sector. Crowding out may be caused by a number of factors:

■ High tax rates on people and businesses
■ Generous out-of-work social security benefits
■ High interest rates or inflation reflecting high public sector borrowing.

All these outcomes of public finance may deter economic activity by making work and enterprise less worthwhile. In this case public finance is at the expense of private sector output, not just because it directly replaces private expenditures through taxation but also because it deters economic activity within the private sector.

Crowding out means that the supposed beneficial effects of public finance are either (possibly significantly) diminished or simply illusory. In the extreme case, public finance could actually make populations worse off in the longer term than they otherwise would have been without that public finance. This possibility is the focus of public policy debate in developed countries, being expressed in terms of questioning whether the relative scale of the public sector is too big or too small. Only in extreme cases, however, would GDP actually fall. What is more likely to happen is that GDP grows more slowly than it would otherwise have done as a result of crowding out.

Taxes on people and businesses

The possibility of taxation causing disincentive-to-work effects in particular
and disincentive-to-enterprise effects in general has been frequently referred
to in earlier chapters. However, the magnitude of disincentive effects to productive effort is not known with any certainty because many factors affect
people's decisions to work and companies' decisions to invest. Whilst high
rates of income tax may deter work effort, work also confers social status and
helps to sustain social networks and so may be as much a cultural phenomenon as an activity dependent upon the financial returns it yields. People may
take pride in supporting themselves and their families and wish to avoid the
social stigma of 'living off others' (that is, state handouts or charity).

However, some workers may choose to work abroad because of high
taxes on earned incomes in their home country. Generally, this option is only
readily available to highly educated and/or highly skilled workers whose
response is not constrained by family ties. Nevertheless, it could result in a
country losing a significant proportion of its workers with key skills, leading
to negative impacts upon the growth of the more innovative business sectors.

Workers who have no option but to remain in their relatively high-taxed
home country face a reduced financial incentive to work harder when the
rates of income tax are increased. Nevertheless, a worker may need a minimum level of 'disposable income' (that is, income from whatever source
after deduction of income taxes) simply to meet the financial needs of his or
her household. In particular, children have to be clothed and fed, housing
costs (mortgages or rents) met, domestic utility (for example energy) bills
paid and so on. Therefore, there is also an incentive to work harder or longer
when disposable income falls in order to restore household income to the
level it was prior to the increase in the rate of income tax. The net effect on
work effort of an increase in the rates of income tax therefore depends on
which is greater:

- the financial incentive to do less work as the financial return from work
  falls or
- the opposite incentive to do more work to restore the household's disposable income to its former level.

Hence, it is not necessarily the case that high rates of income tax create a disincentive to work: they may in fact have the opposite effect for households
with fixed financial commitments that must be met irrespective of the rates of
tax. Moreover, some occupations have fixed working hours whilst others do
not pay employees for working overtime. Therefore the ability to work fewer
or more hours is heavily constrained by institutional factors. This limits the
choice to whether to work at all or, perhaps, whether to work full time or part
time. Such choices may only be possible where generous state welfare pay-

ments are available (see below). The same broad analysis and conditional conclusions apply to taxes on expenditures and wealth which, in combination with all other taxes (that is, on incomes, capital gains and so on), reduce 'post-tax income' (that is, income from all sources after payment of all taxes).

It may be expected that disincentive effects are stronger for business than for households because companies and firms are only in business to earn profits for their owners. Ultimately, companies cannot expand unless they earn profits after payment of taxes. If business taxes in one country rise above those in other countries, then mobile economic activity has an incentive to move to the low-tax country or, more realistically given the high costs of moving, direct new investment to those other countries rather than to their current location. This will especially be the case if firms cannot raise their sales prices to recover profits, for example where the home market is open to competing foreign supplies of goods and services. In such cases firms remaining in the high-tax country will generally have less post-tax profits to reinvest and so their business will tend to grow more slowly. They may be able to reduce the dividends they pay to their shareholders but this may make it more difficult to raise investment finance on stock markets in future years because of poor returns on shareholdings. Businesses may also seek to recoup the tax by negotiating lower input prices (for example the wages and salaries of their workers and the rents they pay for their premises) than they otherwise would have done. Again, this may be difficult in practice and, even where possible, it may take several years to renegotiate contracts. Ignoring the use to which the resulting revenues are put, relatively high business taxes can therefore be expected to deter private enterprise.

Again, the evidence is indeterminate and this line of reasoning assumes that firms are only in business to maximise their profits. To do so they would have to achieve the lowest possible level of costs. In this case a profits, payroll or other such tax would be likely to have a more substantial effect than if there was a considerable degree of organisational slack (that is, unnecessarily high production costs) that could be reduced to offset the impact of the tax. Put simply, many companies do not pare their costs to the bone and so may be able to accommodate the larger part of increases in business taxes. For example, a payroll tax encourages firms to make effective use of labour by using capital-intensive methods of production (that is, substituting plant and machinery and new technology for labour). Companies may blame high taxes for low profits (or even losses) and lack of investment when, in fact, the cause is their general lack of competitiveness. Thus the size of any disincentive-to-enterprise effects may be much less than first thought.

Hence, it would be easy to exaggerate any such disincentive effects of taxes on people and businesses. Moreover, they are likely to differ between:

■ different occupational groups (for example professional versus unskilled workers)

- different industrial and commercial sectors (for example manufacturing versus services)
- different regions within a given country (for example depressed versus prosperous regions)
- from one country to another (for example with stronger or weaker work ethics).

Whilst easy to exaggerate and difficult to generalise, to the extent that disincentive effects occur, they are likely to be exacerbated if 'tax thresholds' (above which higher rates of tax are payable) are not increased each year in line with inflation. In such a case the real value of tax thresholds is reduced so that the real average tax rate increases even though both the tax rate and tax base remain unaltered in nominal terms. For example, most countries have income tax schedules that incorporate an initial amount of earnings and other forms of income free of tax, income above the tax-free threshold usually being subjected to tiered rates of tax. Thus, successively higher rates of tax are raised on those parts of income rising above successive tax thresholds, this being the structure of a progressive tax schedule. If those thresholds remain unaltered, inflation of wages and other forms of income results in taxpayers paying higher proportions of their income in taxation as their incomes increasingly fall within the successively higher tax brackets. Hence, inflation results in more people and their incomes being dragged into the fiscal (in this case, income tax) net, a process known as 'fiscal drag'.

Generous out-of-work social security benefits

Generous out-of-work social security benefits may strengthen any weak disincentive-to-work effects arising from personal income tax by substantially increasing the effective incremental tax rate faced by unskilled heads of large households. There are two cases:

- *The unemployment trap.* This occurs when disposable income for someone out of work is almost as great or even greater than that in work. It typically applies to unskilled manual workers who are *unemployed* heads of households with three or more children. In most developed countries such persons receive substantial income-related social security benefits in respect of themselves, their partners and their children. Typically, they also pay little income tax. They would lose some or all of those income-related benefits if they took up even low-paid employment because their incomes rise. They would also pay more income tax and social security taxes/contributions. In addition, they may incur travel-to-work costs and other work-related expenses (for example meals, work clothing, tools and so on). Hence, the extra household income from a week's work may be little more than the income received when not working. Heads of such large households may effectively be trapped in unemployment and so in being dependent on the state.

■ *The poverty trap.* This occurs when an individual in paid employment works longer and harder in an attempt to increase his or her take-home pay but, in fact, the household gains little extra disposable income. In developed countries, this occurs typically for unskilled, low-paid *employed* heads of households with several children, who are therefore in receipt of in-work, income-related benefits. The household gains little extra income because additional earned income is again directly offset by loss of income-related benefits and payment of additional tax. The household is therefore trapped in poverty and so remains dependent on state support. Like the unemployment trap, the poverty trap creates a disincentive-to-work effect, although this time by discouraging the head of household to work harder and longer as distinct from not working at all.

Thus, disincentive-to-work effects and welfare dependency are generally thought to be potentially significant only for particular socioeconomic groups within particular types of household. Disincentive-to-work effects may also be stronger for part-time workers, especially where the money so earned is a secondary income for the household, again because of the consequential loss of income-related welfare payments. Thus, evidence of disincentive-to-work effects for one group of workers (for example low-paid) or one type of household (for example single-parent families) cannot be generalised to all groups of workers because of the differential influences of domestic, social, institutional and other factors on decisions whether to work or not. This caveat applies even more strongly to evidence from one particular country being generalised to other countries.

High interest rates or inflation reflecting high public sector borrowing

Similar disincentives to productive effort may be created for companies by high levels of government borrowing and debt. High levels of public sector borrowing may lead to higher interest rates, especially if governments have to compete with the private sector for lenders' funds. Governments can always out-compete private sector borrowers by offering higher interest rates on borrowed funds, secure in the knowledge that they can raise future taxes to repay debt. Either the private sector is thus starved of funds for investments, or the increased cost of borrowing simply makes some investments unprofitable.

Alternatively, as monopoly providers of national currencies, central and federal governments can always 'print' more money (although it usually takes the form of credit being provided to governments by the central bank). By such means they can always finance their expenditures (the EU countries adopting the euro being an obvious exception). However, this may give rise to an inflationary economy if the money supply rises faster than national economic output. In that case prices are bid upwards, either as intending buyers compete with each other or as firms realise that their stocks of goods are rapidly diminishing. Market prices rise in either case. Inflation reduces the purchasing power of money and so crowds out purchases by the private sector.

The net impact on GDP in the short to medium term will depend on whether the resultant fall in private sector spending (if any) is greater or less than the increase in public sector current and/or capital spending. The long-term impact on efficiency, and hence on the growth of GDP, will depend on whether current and/or capital spending by the public sector is more economically productive than any by the private sector it replaces. In practice, it may complement private sector investment. Nevertheless, it cannot be taken for granted that public spending is necessarily more productive than, or complementary with, private expenditure.

If neither is the case, GDP is smaller than it would otherwise have been. Crowding out will occur if people work less and firms invest less as a result of any or all of higher taxes, higher interest rates and higher inflation. This is the opposite of the crowding in which occurs if the public sector undertakes highly productive investments in physical and human capital. Clearly, therefore, a sharply rising long-term trend in the public finance/GDP ratios is a cause for concern because the greater and faster the rise in those ratios, the greater the suspicion that crowding out is occurring because it suggests that the growth of GDP is increasingly constrained.

Thus, as a general rule tax revenues and public borrowing should be used to finance investments in economically productive infrastructure, such as the roads and vocational training examples noted above. If those funds are used instead to finance increased payments of unconditional social security benefits, then there is no resulting increase in GDP, the government simply redistributing incomes and wealth rather than increasing them. Thus, another general rule is that social security benefits should as far as possible be made conditional upon recipients undertaking training for employment.

EVIDENCE OF CROWDING OUT

Difficulties in establishing the counterfactual have already been discussed above, making econometric studies highly problematic. Alternatively people and firms could simply be asked if they think they pay too much tax and, if so, if it has adverse effects on work effort and enterprise. Such loaded questions are highly likely to lead to biased responses in the affirmative. Most people and businesses believe they pay too much in tax, generally ignoring (if not being completely unaware of) the public services financed by the payment of taxes. If they believe their responses may lead to a cut in taxes, then they have an incentive to exaggerate disincentive effects. If, instead, they were simply asked what determines work effort and profits, they would be likely to state many influences other than taxation, for example family expenditure commitments and general trading conditions respectively.

It could reasonably be expected that any crowding out effects are likely to become increasingly significant if tax rates are particularly high. For example, whilst households may wish to restore their disposable incomes to the levels prior to a rise income tax rates, the higher those rates the less able they are so to do and so the greater the net disincentive to work. If this is the case, then increases in taxes will raise fairly substantial amounts of revenue as they increase from a low base but not as they increase from a high base. Thus it can be expected that as tax rates rise steadily, disincentive effects start to become significant. If that is the case then:

- tax revenues rise fairly rapidly at first as tax rates are increased but then progressively more slowly as rates rise further
- the increase in tax revenues reaches a plateau at which tax revenues are maximised
- tax revenues fall as tax rates are increased thereafter because disincentive effects become very strong.

Such trends in tax rates and revenues were apparent in the USA and the UK during the 1980s. Those who advocated lower taxes claimed the results proved that the degree of crowding out grows disproportionately fast as tax rates rise. However, there were many other changes during that decade that could be expected to lead to rises in tax revenues. In the UK, for example, the transition from a recession to an economic boom led to a rise in tax revenues quite independently of cuts in the higher rates of tax on personal and corporate incomes. Clearly, a statistical correlation between two events does not prove that one necessarily causes the other.

A fall in tax revenues may occur as tax rates rise, not just because of disincentive effects but also because they create incentives for people and companies to seek to avoid paying tax on their incomes and wealth. People may be able to avoid taxes by converting what would otherwise be highly taxed incomes into, say, capital gains, subject to lower rates of tax when they are realised by the sale of assets such as equities. Such 'tax avoidance' is the reduction or minimisation of tax liability by lawful methods and so is perfectly legal. However, it may result in a large part of company investment being determined by any allowances against profits tax instead of by what is truly profitable pre-tax. If so then there is still an adverse effect on economic growth.

Higher tax rates also create incentives to evade (as distinct from avoid) tax by not declaring to the tax authorities all taxable income or wealth. 'Tax evasion' is therefore illegal because it contravenes tax law. It occurs in the so-called 'black economy' where people (for example illegal immigrants and those committing tax and social security fraud) work for cash, so avoiding the need to register their earnings with the authorities. Ironically, tax evasion may have little or no impact on the rate of economic growth because workers are still being employed (albeit illegally) to produce economic outputs. If this is increasingly significant, then GDP figures become increasingly unreliable and so cannot be used to assess accurately the relative scale of public finance.

ASSESSING THE IMPACT OF PUBLIC FINANCE ON SOCIETY

Clearly, both the theory and evidence regarding disincentive effects are indeterminate. Moreover, it is not self-evident that rising amounts of public finance necessarily make societies more equal or improve social welfare. This is because equity and welfare are highly normative concepts, incorporating value judgements, for example about the acceptable degrees of horizontal and vertical equity and the rights of people and companies to retain greater or lesser proportions of their own incomes. Thus, what one person sees as an improvement in welfare another person may see as deterioration (see Chapter 1). If those changes in welfare could be precisely measured and compared with each other, it would be possible to say whether the gains outweigh the losses. However, even if all such gains and losses could be identified (a potentially very costly exercise in practice), changes in welfare cannot be measured in cardinal terms (that is, numerically quantified). Instead, welfare changes can only be measured in ordinal terms. For example, one can say whether one is made better off (or worse off) by consuming one item more (or less) than before, but not precisely how much better (or worse) off. Hence, it is not possible directly to compare winners and losers following a change in the distribution of post-tax income and so not possible to say whether total social welfare has improved or deteriorated as a result of the change in tax or public expenditure.

One possible way out of this apparent impasse is to determine whether the gainers could fully compensate the losers and still be better off. However, as already noted in Chapter 2, it may not be possible in practice to determine willingness to pay and willingness to accept compensation with an acceptable degree of accuracy. Moreover, there are ethical questions about:

- whether the valuations of high-income groups (who can afford to pay more than low-income groups) should be prioritised
- whether some groups should be so disadvantaged that compensation is thought necessary
- whether those who prosper should be obliged to compensate those who do not.

Another argument against a high level of public finance noted in Chapter 1 is that it may create moral hazard and so foster a dependency culture. Generous state benefits for retired, ill and disabled people may discourage citizens from making their own financial arrangements against such future contingencies. For example, during their working lives people may not save sufficient amounts for their old age, believing that they are guaranteed a sufficient level of state retirement pension on which they can live reasonably comfortably. Likewise, they may take out no insurance to cover the medical and other costs (for example lost earnings) of ill health and disability, secure in the knowledge that they can rely on the public health service and state benefits if misfortune strikes. People may even increase their risk of ill health by taking less care of themselves in terms of not taking regular exercise, eating an unhealthy diet (for example high in fat and sugar), smoking cigarettes and overindulging in alcohol.

Whereas private insurance premiums are generally higher for high-risk groups, no such distinction is made by state systems based on a philosophy of treatment according to medical need irrespective of how that need arose. In such cases, by creating moral hazard, government intervention creates the very circumstances it is intended to pre-empt. In this case the dependency culture is self-reinforcing and extends far beyond the relatively small number of citizens in the unemployment and poverty traps. Put simply, an overgenerous welfare state may encourage irresponsible behaviour.

Consistent with the growing dependency culture thesis, Chapter 4 made clear that the growth of public expenditure relative to GDP has been driven much more by the growth of social security transfers than by expenditures on public sector services. Moreover, social security transfers have rarely been fully financed by social security contributions, as demonstrated by Table 6.1. It could be expected that transfers would exceed contributions during the recessions of the early 1980s and 90s because of higher expenditure on unemployment benefits and lower revenues from incomes and profits. Nevertheless, the preponderance of negative figures even during periods of economic recovery and boom confirm the ratchet effect noted in Chapter 4.

The fact that the social security budgets of virtually all countries are in persistent (and often rising) deficit strengthens the growing dependency culture thesis. The implication is that further increases in personal income tax (as well as other non-social security taxes) will not be used fully to improve public services. In that case citizens are deprived of high-quality public services, perhaps creating or exacerbating the private affluence–public squalor syndrome (see Chapter 7).

Thus, in addition to a growing and increasingly profound dependency culture, higher levels of public finance may lead to citizens increasingly distrusting their governments. This is especially the case if governments are largely unresponsive to citizens' wishes expressed through the ballot box. In such a

Table 6.1 *Social security contributions less social security transfers*

	1971	1972	1973	1974	1975	1976	1977	1978	1979	1980	1981	1982	1983	1984	1985
Australia	-5.7	-6.3	-6.4	-7.4	-8.8	-9.3	-9.6	-9.3	-8.9	-8.8	-9.1	-10.1	0.0	-9.8	-9.5
Austria	-6.2	-10.0	-5.6	-5.5	-6.2	-6.9	-6.5	-6.6	-6.6	-6.3	-6.3	-6.7	-7.0	-6.7	-6.9
Belgium	-3.0	-3.4	-3.6	-3.9	-5.7	-6.2	-6.8	-7.2	-7.7	-7.7	-9.1	-9.1	-9.1	-10.6	-9.5
Canada	-5.8	-6.5	-6.2	-6.2	-6.9	-6.4	-6.8	-7.0	-6.4	-6.8	-6.1	-7.9	-8.1	-7.8	-7.8
CzechRepublic															
Denmark	-9.6	-9.7	-10.3	-11.4	-13.3	-13.0	-13.5	-14.3	-14.7	-15.8	-16.8	-16.7	-16.0	-15.1	-14.4
Finland	-4.5	-4.7	-3.9	-4.3	-4.4	-4.6	-5.6	-6.3	-5.9	-5.6	-5.8	-6.6	-7.2	-7.1	-7.4
France	-4.0	-4.1	-4.3	-4.3	-5.1	-4.9	-4.9	-5.6	-5.1	-4.9	-6.3	-6.8	-6.5	-2.0	-2.2
Germany	-2.6	1.3	-2.0	-2.9	-5.3	-4.6	-4.4	-4.0	-3.8	-3.4	-3.9	-4.1	-3.8	-2.9	-2.4
Greece	-1.4	-0.8	-0.5	-0.7	-0.7	-0.2	-0.4	-0.7	-0.4	0.4	-0.9	-2.5	-1.8	-1.9	-2.6
Hungary															
Iceland	-9.5	-10.2	-11.3	-10.3	-10.5	-10.0	-9.9	-10.6	-10.9	-11.1				-4.4	-4.7
Ireland	-6.7	-6.5	-7.2	-7.7	-8.2	-7.9	-6.9	-6.8	-6.6	-7.8	-8.8	5.5	5.8	-10.3	-10.7
Italy	-2.1	-2.8	-3.0	-2.0	-2.3	-2.9	-3.1	-4.4	-4.6	-4.4	-6.3	-6.2	-7.1	-4.6	-5.1
Japan	-0.1	-0.5	-0.3	-0.5	-1.6	-2.0	-2.0	-2.3	-2.8	-2.8	-2.9	-3.1	-3.3	-2.9	-2.4
Korea															
Luxembourg	-5.3	-5.8	-5.2	-4.1	-6.8	-6.7	-7.7	-8.1	-8.5	-10.8	11.9	11.4	11.1	-11.2	-11.1
Mexico															
Netherlands	-3.8	-4.8	-4.2	-4.5	-6.4	-7.1	-6.5	-7.0	-7.2	-8.4	-8.8	-9.6	21.0	-7.4	-6.4
NewZealand				0.5										-13.7	-13.7
Norway	-5.6	-5.4	-5.0	-5.3	-5.3	-5.6	-5.8	-6.6	-7.6	-4.5	-4.3	-4.7	-5.3	-5.3	-4.9
Poland															
Portugal	2.4	1.7	1.3	0.9	-0.8	-3.6	-2.9	-2.3	-2.6	-2.1	-2.6	8.8	8.6	-2.6	-2.7
SlovakRepublic															
Spain	-2.4	-1.7	-1.6	-1.4	-1.0	-2.2	-1.0	-2.0	-2.8	-3.3	-4.1	-4.3	12.5	-4.0	-4.0
Sweden	-5.7	-5.8	-5.6	-5.9	-5.6	-3.8	-3.8	-3.8	-4.0	-3.6	-3.4	-4.7	13.6	-4.4	-5.7
Switzerland	-2.6	-2.7	-2.9	-2.8	-3.9	-4.1	-3.9	-3.6	-3.3	-3.2	-2.9	-3.6	-3.5	-3.8	-3.4
Turkey	0.2	-0.1	1.6	1.6	1.9	1.5	1.5	1.3	1.3	1.1	0.9	1.0	1.0	0.8	0.8
UK	-3.5	-4.0	-3.5	-3.5	-3.6	-3.8	-4.3	-5.1	-5.3	-5.6	-7.0	-7.2	-6.9	-7.1	-7.2
United States	-2.6	-2.5	-2.3	-2.8	-4.0	-4.0	-3.2	-2.6	-2.4	-3.5	-3.3	-3.8	-3.9	-2.7	-2.4
Weighted average	**-2.6**	**-2.4**	**-2.5**	**-2.8**	**-3.8**	**-3.9**	**-3.6**	**-3.6**	**-3.6**	**-4.0**	**-4.3**	**-4.6**	**-3.3**	**-3.8**	**-3.6**
Standarddeviation	*2.9*	*3.4*	*3.2*	*3.3*	*3.5*	*3.3*	*3.4*	*3.5*	*3.6*	*3.9*	*5.2*	*6.2*	*8.9*	*4.1*	*4.0*

continued

scenario the relationship between the state and the citizen is fundamentally altered to the detriment of society. For example:

- the belief that high taxes are tantamount to theft because they are often spent on the 'undeserving poor' encourages tax evasion (including smuggling)
- high levels of state income-related benefits and subsidies to industry and agriculture arguably encourage substantial fraud.

Tax evasion may become pervasive, almost becoming socially acceptable, albeit illegal. Certainly, tax avoidance is much more socially acceptable, rich groups and businesses often employing accountants to reorder their assets so as to minimise their tax liabilities. Such activities are unproductive in eco-

-ther than financial) terms.

ther than raising living standards over time by strengthening a cul-
ter self-sufficiency through work and enterprise, the expansion of
nances may have the opposite effect in weakening that culture. The

Table 6.1   *continued*

	1986	1987	1988	1989	1990	1991	1992	1993	1994	1995	1996	1997	1998	1999
Australia	-9.4	-9.2	-8.6	-8.7		-8.3	-8.5	-8.8	-8.6	-8.6	-8.6	-8.2	-8.0	
Austria	-6.8	-7.4	-6.7	-6.3	-6.2	-4.1	-3.8	-4.7	-4.6	-4.1	-4.4	-3.7	-3.5	-3.5
Belgium	-8.9	-8.8	-7.6	-7.7	-7.1	-1.0	-0.9	-1.0	-1.3	-1.2	-1.9	-1.7	-1.5	-1.2
Canada	-7.8	-7.4	-7.2	-7.1	-7.3	-7.5	-8.4	-8.7	-7.7	-7.0	-7.8	-7.5	-7.3	5.2
CzechRepublic							-12.9	6.5	7.2	6.7	4.8	4.4	16.8	17.6
Denmark	-13.6	-14.7	-15.4	-16.8	-16.9	-16.9	-17.4	-18.2	-19.6	-18.8	-18.2	-17.3	-16.7	-15.6
Finland	-7.6	-7.4	-6.3	-6.0	-7.2	-7.3	-11.6	-12.0	-11.7	-9.4	-9.3	-8.3	-6.8	-6.1
France	-2.6	-2.8	-2.4	-2.0	-2.1	1.9	1.7	1.1	0.7	0.8	0.2	-0.4	-2.1	-1.8
Germany	-2.0	-2.2	-1.9	-1.8	-1.4	-1.0	-1.3	-2.2	-2.3	-2.7	-4.3	-4.1	-3.9	-4.1
Greece	-2.4	-3.6	-4.1	-5.4	-5.6	-2.2	-1.8	-0.9	-0.1	-1.2	-5.7	-4.7	-4.4	-4.3
Hungary						13.5	14.7	14.9	14.1	-3.8	0.1	1.0	0.3	13.2
Iceland	-3.9	-4.1	-4.6	-4.8	-4.4	-4.0	-4.2	-4.5	-4.3	-4.5	-3.8	2.8	2.8	2.9
Ireland	-11.4	-11.0	-10.6	-8.7	5.5	-6.6	-6.9	-6.6	-6.7	-6.4	-6.6	-6.3	-5.8	-5.4
Italy	-5.3	-4.9	-5.0	-5.1	-5.1	-5.2	-6.0	-5.7	-6.5	-5.9	-2.3	-2.5	-4.5	-5.1
Japan	-2.8	-3.1	-2.9	-2.4	-2.3	-1.5	-1.9	-2.1	-2.7	-3.0	-3.3	-3.4	-4.7	9.7
Korea						-2.2	-2.3	-2.3	-2.3	-0.3	-0.6	0.6	0.6	4.1
Luxembourg	-9.2	12.4	14.0	13.4	13.9	-3.3	-3.0	-3.8	-4.0	-4.7	-5.3	-5.0	-4.8	-4.2
Mexico						2.8	3.1	2.3	2.4	1.5	1.3	1.4	1.5	3.0
Netherlands	-6.0	-6.9	-5.2	-6.5	-9.4	-8.4	-8.2	-8.4	-6.1	3.1	1.7	3.3	3.2	4.2
NewZealand	-13.7	-13.6	-13.4	-13.3	-15.4									
Norway	-6.1	-5.3	-6.8	-6.5	12.1	-5.5	-6.1	-6.8	-6.5	-6.0	-5.7	-5.2	-5.4	-5.3
Poland						-6.2	-8.7	-7.5	-6.0	-5.1	-5.7	-5.2	-5.2	9.9
Portugal	-3.4	-3.5	-3.6	-2.9	9.6	-3.3	-4.0	-5.5	-5.2	-2.6	-3.5	-3.2	-3.1	-3.1
SlovakRepublic													15.2	14.2
Spain	-3.7	-3.6	-3.5	12.0	12.2	-4.4	-4.3	-5.2	-4.1	-4.9	-5.5	11.8	12.0	12.2
Sweden	-5.9	-5.4	-6.0	-4.9	-4.0	-5.5	-8.4	-9.6	-8.9	-6.8	-5.4	-4.6	-4.5	-5.7
Switzerland	-3.3	-3.4	-3.5	-3.0	-3.0	1.7	1.0	1.2	1.3	1.5	0.8	0.0	0.5	12.2
Turkey	2.8	3.1	3.8	4.5	5.5	4.1	4.6	4.5	3.5	2.7	4.0	4.0	4.1	5.8
UK	-7.4	-6.5	-5.6	-5.4	-5.8	-7.8	-9.3	-10.0	-9.6	-9.1	-8.8	-8.3	-7.2	-7.3
United States	-2.4	-2.2	-1.9	-2.2	8.8	-5.2	-5.9	-6.1	-6.0	-6.0	-6.0	-5.8	6.8	6.9
Weighted average	-3.6	-3.5	-3.2	-2.7	1.9	-3.6	-4.2	-4.4	-4.3	-4.3	-4.4	-3.7	0.6	3.7
Standard deviation	3.9	5.4	5.6	6.6	8.4	5.4	6.2	6.4	6.3	4.9	4.7	5.5	7.1	8.1

Notes: For definition of social security contributions see Figure 5.4. For definition of social security transfers see Table 4.2

Sources: OECD (1981) Table 14; OECD (1985) Table 6.3; OECD (1987) Table 14; OECD (1992b) Table 14; OECD (1997) Table 14; OECD (2000) Table 6.3; OECD (2001d) Table 14

state of public finance is crucially dependent on a strong private sector based on a culture of work and enterprise, since this generates the public revenues necessary for the welfare state. Thus, if public finance weakens the private sector's creation of income and wealth, the growth of the state creates a fiscal crisis in the public finances (see Chapter 7). This leads to the state increasingly having to infringe personal liberty by appropriating (confiscating) ever-higher proportions of income and wealth through taxation and becoming ever more the 'nanny state' in making decisions on behalf of citizens.

Whilst these Libertarian arguments are, of course, highly controversial, they illustrate the potentially profound nature and consequences of crowding out. It is not simply a matter of whether high tax rates reduce work effort and enterprise. Instead, it is a matter of a potentially deleterious effect on cultural, moral and ethical values. In sharp contrast, supporters of the welfare state emphasise the complementary nature of much public and private spending, so creating greater social and economic prosperity through higher levels of investment and employment. Collectivists argue that moral hazard, infringement of individual liberty, crowding out, disincentive-to-work/invest effects and dependency cultures are all exaggerated by those hostile to government intervention. They argue that profound social benefits arise from a more caring and sharing society.

IS CONCERN ABOUT EXCESSIVE PUBLIC FINANCE JUSTIFIED?

On the basis of the above analysis (in both this and previous chapters), cause for concern about a long-term rising trend in the public finance/GDP ratios is perhaps more likely to be justified if all or a substantial number of the following occur:

■ public expenditure, taxation, public borrowing and debt account for ever-increasing proportions of GDP and begin to substantially exceed those ratios in other countries
■ the growth of public expenditure is predominantly on the current account instead of the capital account
■ the growth in current expenditure is primarily due to rising social security expenditures
■ the growth in taxation is primarily centred on work and enterprise
■ rising tax rates are associated with progressively diminishing additional tax revenues
■ the increasing demands on the public finances seem to bear little relationship to the state of the economy (that is, a ratchet effect exists for social security expenditures)
■ governments 'print money' or increase interest rates in order to offset a growing structural imbalance in the public finances
■ the public sector hires increasing proportions of the nation's productive resources, most notably skilled labour
■ the public sector becomes subject to increasing levels of organisational slack, demonstrated by unnecessarily high costs of service provision
■ particular social groups, industries, regions and localities become increasingly dependent on the state for adequate standards of living
■ public services become increasingly characterised as providing poor value for money and belief in the efficacy of government intervention begins to diminish.

Chapters 3, 4 and 5 made clear that there have, indeed, been long-term increases in public finance/GDP ratios, especially in terms of growth of taxes on personal incomes, growth of current expenditure and, within that, of social security expenditures. Those chapters also made clear that increases in these ratios were much greater than the OECD averages for a number of countries, especially in Europe. Although evidence may be less systematic in relation to the other causes for concern, there is certainly a clear rationale for being prudent with the public finances. A prudent strategy is outlined in Chapter 10.

CONCLUSIONS

This chapter has demonstrated that, notwithstanding the demonstrable wider social benefits of many services, to support them with ever more public finance may not, after all, be beneficial in net terms because of overriding, long-term, potentially adverse impacts on economy and society.

It is essential to recognise the limits of this apparently rather sweeping (although tentative) conclusion that public finance may do more harm than good. What it relates to in practice is the optimal level of public finance, both in aggregate and by activity (that is, service or programme). It has been made clear in this chapter that, ultimately, the direct and indirect costs of increasing levels of public finance rise faster than the direct and indirect benefits it delivers. Thus, one is talking about the relative scale of public finance and, in particular, whether it is too high a proportion of GDP.

As regards individual services, the relevant policy question is: At what level of spending does additional public finance for the service result in incremental costs beginning to exceed incremental benefits? Put concisely, the optimum level of public finance used to support a service is that at which the additional social benefits just equal the additional social costs. Higher or lower levels of public finance are socially suboptimal. This is the conventional social efficiency argument used by economists. It is, however, partial in approach and may still lead to excessive levels of public finance. This will be the case if the combined effect of the aggregate of public finance is to create a profound dependency culture. In that case the optimum level of public finance will be less than that calculated on a service-by-service basis. Put simply, public finance must be considered in its totality as well as in terms of its constituent parts. This is the subject of the following chapter.

FURTHER READING

Agell, J., Lindh, T. and Ohlsson, H. (1997) 'Growth and the Public Sector: A Critical Review Essay' *European Journal of Political Economy* vol. 13, pp. 33–52.

Atkinson, A. B. and Mogensen, G. V. (1993) *Welfare and Work Incentives: A North European Perspective* (Oxford: Clarendon Press).

Bailey, S. J. (2002) *Public Sector Economics: Theory, Policy and Practice* (second edition) (Basingstoke: Palgrave Macmillan) [Chapters 4 and 5 on disincentive effects and crowding out].

Bhatta, S. D. (2001) 'Are Inequality and Poverty Harmful for Economic Growth? Evidence from the Metropolitan Areas of the United States' *Journal of Urban Affairs* vol. 23, no. 3–4, pp. 335–59.

Bougrine, H. (2000) (editor) *The Economics of Public Spending: Debts, Deficits and Economic Performance* (Cheltenham: Edward Elgar).

Buti, M., Franco, D. and Pench, L. R. (1999) *The Welfare State in Europe: Challenges and Reforms* (Cheltenham: Edward Elgar).

Creedy, J. (2001) *Taxation and Economic Behaviour: Introductory Surveys in Economics,* vol. 1 (Cheltenham: Edward Elgar).

Daly, M. (1997) 'Welfare States Under Pressure: Cash Benefits in European Welfare States Over the Last Ten Years' *Journal of European Social Policy* vol. 7, no. 2, pp.129–46.

Gough, I. (1997) 'Social Assistance in OECD Countries' *Journal of European Social Policy* vol. 7, no. 1, pp.17–43.

Green, D. G. (1998) *Benefit Dependency: How Welfare Undermines Independence* (London: Institute of Economic Affairs).

Grimshaw, D. and Rubery, J. (1997) 'Workforce Heterogeneity and Unemployment Benefits: The Need for Policy Reassessment in the European Union' *Journal of European Social Policy* vol. 7, no. 4, pp. 291–318.

Newbery, D. M. G. (1995) (editor) *Tax and Benefit Reform in Central and Eastern Europe* (London: Centre for Economic Policy Research).

Rowley, C. K., Shughart, W. F. and Tollison, R. D. (2002) (editors) *The Economics of Budget Deficits* (Cheltenham: Edward Elgar).

Sturm, J. E. (1998) *Public Capital Expenditure in OECD Countries: The Causes and Impact of the Decline in Public Capital Spending* (Cheltenham: Edward Elgar).

Sturm, R. (1999) *Public Deficits: A Comparative Study of their Economic and Political Consequences in Britain, Canada, Germany and the United States* (Harlow: Pearson Education).

Sykes, R. and Alcock, P. (1998) (editors) *Developments in European Social Policy: Convergence and Diversity* (Bristol: Policy Press).

7 Structural Gaps in Public Finance

INTRODUCTION

A 'structural gap' in public finance refers to a scenario whereby public expenditure grows faster than revenues over the long term. In such a case, public finance becomes increasingly unsustainable. A structural gap does not necessarily mean that public expenditure is too high or that tax revenues are too low. All a gap indicates is that expenditure is greater than can be sustained by income over an extended period of time. The term 'structural gap' is therefore value-free and does not reflect a particular political philosophy, whether Libertarian, Neo-Liberal or Collectivist. Instead, it reflects the state of the public finances in objective accounting terms.

In comparison, 'fiscal crisis' of the state implies revenues are insufficient to finance much-needed expenditures, this being a highly emotive description of the state of public finances. Hence, 'structural gap' is used instead of 'fiscal crisis' since it has no normative connotations. It is not the purpose of this chapter to determine whether the public finances in any one country are excessive, insufficient or optimal. Instead, the focus is to determine:

- why structural gaps in the public finances are a cause for concern
- evidence of structural gaps
- the causes of structural gaps
- how to eliminate and avoid structural gaps.

WHY STRUCTURAL GAPS IN THE PUBLIC FINANCES ARE A CAUSE FOR CONCERN

Structural gaps are a cause for concern because they may lead to:

- rising levels of borrowing and debt that must ultimately be repaid by future generations of taxpayers, possibly leading to intergenerational inequity (see Chapter 5)
- financial markets becoming progressively less willing to continue lending to governments increasingly regarded as borrowing beyond their capacity to repay debt and thus risking default

179

- reduced economic prosperity, assuming that higher interest rates and/or inflation are associated with excessive levels of debt and that they crowd out the private sector (see Chapter 6)
- a negative feedback spiral, whereby crowding out erodes the tax base of the economy and so its ability to pay taxes to liquidate debt, thus requiring ever-higher levels of borrowing and debt and so exacerbating crowding out
- increasingly unsustainable public expenditure levels, with adverse implications for public services and their users.

Whether redeemed or refinanced, the debt legacy left by previous generations living beyond their means can lead to reduced levels of economic growth which, in turn, reduces the incomes and wealth of future generations. The consequent lower standards of living (lower relative to what they would otherwise have been) are unlikely to be evenly distributed over that future generation because ongoing socioeconomic restructuring seems to benefit affluent groups more than poorer sections of the community. Therefore, those who bear the burden of the 'live now pay later' culture of past generations may be those least able to pay in future generations. In that sense, an overhang of public debt exacerbates the potentially severe problems of socioeconomic restructuring.

It is arguable, therefore, that structural gaps are unsustainable in terms of both intergenerational equity and economic growth. Ultimately, corrective action will be required. This may involve radical cuts in public expenditures as well as sharp increases in taxation.

EVIDENCE OF STRUCTURAL GAPS: FINANCIAL INDICATORS

As will be made clear, it is difficult to prove categorically whether a structural gap exists at any one point in time. This is because there is no single unambiguous indicator of a structural gap and data may not be available over a sufficiently long period of time. Nevertheless, there are a number of financial indicators of a structural gap in the public finances, notably:

- the balance between tax revenues and expenditure over the long term
- long-term trends in the national debt/GDP ratio.

The balance between tax revenues and government expenditure over the long-term

Figure 3.5 has already noted the (at times growing) imbalance between tax revenues and government expenditure for the OECD as a whole. Table 7.1 now provides data for individual countries in respect of *total* government expenditure and tax revenues over the period 1965–99. It reveals:

Table 7.1 *Total government expenditure minus*
total taxation (percentages of GDP)

	1965	1966	1967	1968	1969	1970	1971	1972	1973	1974	1975	1976	1977
Australia	1.8	1.7	1.6	0.6	-0.2	0.0	0.3	1.3	0.1	-1.9	3.2	3.1	4.4
Austria	3.3	2.9	5.2	5.3	4.5	3.5	3.3	2.7	3.7	3.5	7.6	8.4	7.4
Belgium	1.1	0.2	0.5	1.5	1.1	0.5	1.8	2.4	1.7	1.1	3.4	3.6	3.8
Canada	3.2	2.6	3.3	3.4	1.5	3.7	5.5	5.4	4.7	3.5	7.9	6.9	8.5
CzechRepublic													
Denmark	-0.2	-1.0	1.2	0.1	0.6	0.0	-0.4	-0.1	0.1	1.9	7.2	6.9	7.6
Finland	1.2	1.1	1.1	0.8	0.8	-0.8	-1.5	-1.3	-3.3	-1.5	-1.9	-2.6	-0.9
France	3.5	4.2	3.9	4.9	3.3	3.3	3.2	3.0	2.8	3.4	6.1	8.6	4.7
Germany	5.1	4.7	6.6	7.1	4.9	5.9	6.9	6.1	5.2	8.3	12.2	11.3	10.1
Greece	0.0	-0.7	0.3	-0.8	-1.9	-1.9	-1.6	-2.6	-2.1	1.0	2.1	0.1	1.4
Hungary													
Iceland													
Ireland	7.1	5.5	5.9	6.1	6.8	8.4	8.1	7.7	7.6	10.9	14.1	10.3	9.2
Italy	7.1	7.3	5.7	5.9	6.0	6.3	7.9	10.1	11.5	9.6	14.2	11.9	11.6
Japan	2.0	2.7	1.3	1.6	1.1	-0.3	0.8	1.1	-0.4	1.5	6.2	6.3	6.4
Korea													
Luxembourg	2.5	4.3	6.6	7.5	3.9	1.2	2.3	2.1	0.5	-0.3	5.3	5.4	3.7
Mexico													
Netherlands	3.2	3.7	4.5	5.1	5.3	6.9	6.4	6.1	5.6	7.1	10.8	11.2	8.4
NewZealand													
Norway	1.0	0.3	-0.1	0.3	0.9	1.8	0.6	-0.2	-0.6	-0.1	1.8	0.3	2.9
Poland													
Portugal	1.5	1.2	1.0	1.0	0.2	-1.6	-1.6	0.1	-0.8	2.1	5.5	6.1	7.7
SlovakRepublic													
Spain	4.9	5.9	4.0	4.9	4.8	5.0	6.2	4.8	4.0	4.9	9.1	10.4	6.0
Sweden	0.5	1.9	2.5	3.0	2.3	2.8	4.3	3.6	2.9	5.3	5.1	3.8	7.2
Switzerland	-1.0	-1.4	-1.2	-1.9	-1.9	-2.5	-1.6	-2.0	-2.1	-1.8	-0.9	-1.0	-1.2
Turkey	5.7	5.5	4.9	6.0	5.9	4.3	2.7	3.4					
UK	5.6	3.7	5.4	4.9	4.9	1.8	2.8	5.8	8.8	9.5	10.3	9.9	8.3
United States	1.4	2.4	3.1	3.0	0.0	2.2	3.6	2.1	1.6	2.7	5.4	5.2	3.1
Weighted average	**2.8**	**3.2**	**3.4**	**3.9**	**2.2**	**2.5**	**3.6**	**3.3**	**2.9**	**3.9**	**7.2**	**7.0**	**5.7**
Standard deviation	*2.3*	*2.4*	*2.4*	*2.7*	*2.6*	*3.0*	*3.2*	*3.2*	*3.8*	*3.9*	*4.4*	*4.3*	*3.4*

continued

- a surplus of tax revenues over total government expenditure (indicated by a negative figure) have been more the exception than the rule for most countries
- there have been more years of (typically small) surpluses before the mid-1970s than has been the case since
- excesses of tax revenues over total government expenditures have generally been much less than the excesses of spending over taxation
- the weighted averages indicate an upward trend in deficits (that is, expenditure has been greater than tax revenues) over the 35-year period, deficits peaking in the mid-1970s, early 1980s and early 1990s as recessions took hold
- the trend for the OECD *weighted* average is common to virtually all countries
- measures of standard deviation display an upward trend, with the greatest

Table 7.1   continued

	1978	1979	1980	1981	1982	1983	1984	1985	1986	1987	1988	1989	1990
Australia	4.5	7.1	5.8	6.1	8.1		9.5	8.9	7.7	6.4	3.8	3.0	3.8
Austria	7.9	7.5	9.1	9.3	10.6		9.6	8.4	9.4	10.2	9.3	8.9	8.4
Belgium	3.9	4.7	8.7	13.2	12.0	11.9	17.3	11.3	10.8	8.3	7.7	7.7	7.3
Canada	9.2	8.3	8.4	7.5	12.1	12.9	13.1	11.6	10.3	7.5	7.5	7.1	9.1
CzechRepublic													
Denmark	7.7	9.1	12.3	16.3	18.1		14.2	11.9	6.4	7.3	3.8	5.0	6.5
Finland	1.8	2.4	1.0	0.0	2.9	3.5	5.0	2.3	1.7	4.2	0.4	-1.6	-0.3
France	5.6	4.3	5.8	8.2	8.9	8.9	8.4	8.1	7.8	6.4	6.8	6.0	6.5
Germany	10.1	10.3	15.3	16.5	16.8	16.2	15.6	12.7	12.3	12.4	12.2	10.2	11.2
Greece	2.0	2.0	6.3	12.5	10.1	10.4	11.6	15.2	12.9	12.6	13.8	16.4	18.1
Hungary													
Iceland			5.5				4.3	7.2	9.2	5.7	7.8	9.4	8.0
Ireland	11.0	13.9	20.5	22.1			17.9	15.7	14.8	12.1	8.2	5.3	6.4
Italy	14.9	14.5	15.7	19.8	21.1	21.6	12.2	15.3	13.7	13.3	12.8	12.5	14.0
Japan	6.8	6.8	6.7	8.3	7.9	7.8	5.7	1.9	1.4	0.5	-0.5	-1.3	-0.2
Korea								0.7	0.4	-0.9	-0.8	-0.7	-0.8
Luxembourg	1.5	6.6	14.5				8.6	7.3	8.3				0.8
Mexico													
Netherlands	8.9	10.6	16.1	18.4	20.5		18.4	9.5	8.9	7.7	5.6	5.8	6.6
NewZealand										17.9	11.0	12.6	8.4	10.1
Norway	4.0	4.8	6.2	4.1	5.1	6.4	4.6	-1.8	-0.1	4.0	6.4	7.8	7.9
Poland													
Portugal	9.9	10.0	0.8	16.6			16.9	13.0	11.9	12.1	8.9	7.5	10.2
SlovakRepublic													
Spain	6.6	7.2	9.5	10.0	12.3		12.0	12.1	11.3	8.4	7.6	7.6	8.6
Sweden	8.3	10.7	14.6	16.2	18.9		15.4	11.9	7.8	1.3	2.4	1.8	2.3
Switzerland	-1.4	-1.2	0.4	-0.1	0.4	0.4	0.8	0.8	-0.8	-1.0	-0.9	-0.6	0.3
Turkey													
UK	9.3	9.1	9.9	11.1	8.2	9.7	12.1	13.7	13.1	3.5	1.1	0.9	3.2
United States	2.6	1.7	8.0	7.8	10.5	12.5	10.0	7.7	8.3	6.8	6.1	5.8	6.9
Weighted average	**6.0**	**5.6**	**9.0**	**10.1**	**11.3**	**11.8**	**10.4**	**8.3**	**8.1**	**6.4**	**5.6**	**5.1**	**6.2**
Standard deviation	*3.9*	*4.0*	*5.3*	*6.2*	*5.9*	*5.6*	*4.9*	*5.1*	*5.0*	*4.3*	*4.5*	*4.6*	*4.7*

continued

divergence from the *unweighted* mean occurring in the early 1980s, although the late 1990s also saw a sharp rise, attributable to the inclusion of data for Mexico

■ the major cause of increasing standard deviations is the occurrence of particularly large budget deficits rather than surpluses.

About half the listed countries had not a single year in which tax revenues exceeded total expenditure, this being made clear by Table 7.2 which provides a summary of Table 7.1, taking account of the number of years for which data is available for each country. Table 7.2 also makes clear that only Korea and Switzerland have more years for which tax revenues exceeded total expenditure than the reverse case, these two countries being notable for their relatively small public expenditure/GDP ratios (see Chapter 3). However, even Switzerland seems to have reversed its fiscal position during the 1990s (see Table 7.1). Finland and Greece had a preponderance of such sur-

Table 7.1 continued

	1991	1992	1993	1994	1995	1996	1997	1998	1999
Australia	7.0	9.2	9.1	6.9	6.3	4.7	3.8	3.5	2.3
Austria	9.0	8.1	10.6	10.0	10.9	8.5	5.5	5.9	5.6
Belgium	8.3	8.2	9.1	5.7	5.4	5.1	3.0	2.1	1.7
Canada	11.6	12.9	12.1	9.7	8.4	5.9	2.5	1.9	0.5
CzechRepublic			1.0	3.5	3.8	3.9	4.0	3.4	3.5
Denmark	7.6	8.2	9.3	8.1	7.2	6.4	4.6	3.9	1.4
Finland	6.6	11.8	14.5	10.9	9.4	6.7	5.2	2.2	0.9
France	6.8	8.6	10.6	10.1	9.5	8.8	7.6	7.0	6.0
Germany	7.4	7.3	8.3	7.8	8.1	9.9	9.5	9.0	8.5
Greece	14.4	15.5	17.2	14.8	22.9	20.6	17.4	15.0	15.0
Hungary			13.3	19.4	13.8	12.5	13.2	14.3	10.8
Iceland	8.9	8.5	9.2	9.3	8.0	6.2	5.0	3.6	2.8
Ireland	7.2	7.3	6.9	5.6	5.2	3.5	2.0	0.5	-0.4
Italy	14.7	11.5	11.2	11.3	9.9	8.6	4.3	4.8	3.4
Japan	0.4	2.8	4.7	6.2	6.5	7.1	5.9	8.0	9.7
Korea	0.7	1.2	0.2	-0.7	-1.2	-0.7	-1.2	1.2	-0.3
Luxembourg	3.8	4.8	2.7	0.5	1.6	0.2	-0.6	-1.1	-1.7
Mexico							2.5	2.3	29.0
Netherlands	4.2	5.1	4.7	4.6	5.8	4.1	2.5	2.5	1.2
NewZealand	8.7	7.8	4.5	2.0	0.6	1.5	2.0	4.0	3.4
Norway	8.8	11.0	10.9	8.6	6.1	3.9	1.4	2.9	4.2
Poland			11.9	9.0	7.4	6.7	6.8	6.2	8.2
Portugal	11.4	9.9	13.2	10.9	8.8	9.4	7.2	6.7	6.3
SlovakRepublic								19.2	
Spain	9.4	9.6	13.7	11.6	11.2	10.2	7.6	6.5	4.5
Sweden	7.0	14.8	19.1	16.1	14.3	10.1	6.8	3.9	2.9
Switzerland	2.2	4.1	4.8	1.0	0.4	0.3			
Turkey									
UK	5.9	8.3	9.9	8.7	7.1	5.7	3.7	0.6	0.8
United States	7.4	8.2	7.2	5.8	5.3	4.5	3.1	1.7	1.3
Weighted average	**6.7**	**7.6**	**8.0**	**7.2**	**6.7**	**6.2**	**4.6**	**4.2**	**4.7**
Standard deviation	*3.6*	*3.4*	*4.6*	*4.7*	*4.8*	*4.3*	*3.9*	*4.6*	*6.2*

Notes. A negative sign denotes tax revenues are greater than expenditure. Total expenditure equals current plus capital expenditures for all levels of government

Sources: Tables 3.1 and 3.2

pluses during the first decade or so, but those surpluses all but disappeared completely after the mid-1970s.

Table 7.3 shows that, almost without exception, the average deficit of tax revenues against total government expenditure rose (usually very substantially – often into double figures) from the 1960s, through the 1970s and 80s (for countries where comparable data is available). It then fell in a majority of countries during the 1990s, the exceptions being Finland, France, Greece, Japan and Norway, whose average deficits continued to rise as a proportion of GDP. Despite falls in a majority of countries, the average deficit in the 1990s remains higher than in the 1960s for all countries except Ireland, Luxembourg and Netherlands. Moreover, countries earning surpluses have not been able to increase substantially the average surplus. Average surpluses remained very small (usually less than one per cent of GDP in each of the four sub-periods).

The data of Tables 7.1 to 7.3 relate to *total* government expenditure, without distinguishing between capital and current expenditures and so may give an exaggerated picture of structural gaps. This is because capital expenditures could account for use of a significant proportion of tax revenues. Hence, Tables 7.4 to 7.6 provide the same comparisons as the previous three tables except that they relate only to *current* expenditure.

Not surprisingly, Table 7.4 shows that Switzerland and Korea again achieved surpluses in most and all years respectively, but now the Czech Republic, Finland, Japan and Luxembourg also have a majority of years in which these surpluses were achieved, this being made clear by Table 7.5. Iceland had as many years of surplus as deficit. Italy and Spain had not a single year in which tax revenues exceeded current government spending during the 35 and 29 years respectively for which data is available (and, likewise, Poland but for only eight years of data). Canada, Ireland, the Netherlands, the UK and the USA are also notable for having very few years in which these surpluses were recorded, those years being within the first decade except for Ireland. Table 7.6 paints a picture similar to Table 7.3, in that average surpluses have not increased substantially from decade to decade whereas deficits have (again, where comparable data is available). The main difference in respect of the 'total expenditure versus tax' picture is that for 'current expenditure versus tax' there have been more increases than decreases in the average deficit comparing the 1980s and 90s. For all countries, average deficits remain higher in the 1990s than in the 1960s or 70s (for those countries with deficits in the 1960s), there being no exceptions this time.

Comparing Table 7.4 with 7.1 reveals that:

■ many more countries had a surplus of tax revenues over current government expenditure than over total government expenditure
■ a majority of countries achieved these surpluses during the period 1965–74
■ only a minority achieved these surpluses in most years after 1974
■ although fluctuating throughout the period, there was a tendency for deficits (for both total and current expenditure versus taxation) to grow increasingly large as a proportion of GDP over the period as a whole
■ there was a particularly marked tendency for deficits (for both total and current expenditure versus taxation) to grow increasingly large as a proportion of GDP during the mid-1970s, early 1980s and early 1990s, these being periods of downturn in economic growth and employment in most OECD countries
■ the rise in the weighted average over the full period was much greater for current expenditure minus tax than for total expenditure minus tax, indic-

Table 7.2 *Total government expenditure minus total taxation revenue (summary)*

	No of years for which data available	No. of years in which tax > expenditure	Percentage of years in which tax > expenditure
Australia	34	2	6
Austria	34	0	0
Belgium	35	0	0
Canada	35	0	0
Czech Republic	7	0	0
Denmark	34	4	12
Finland	35	10	29
France	35	0	0
Germany	35	0	0
Greece	35	7	20
Hungary	7	0	0
Iceland	17	0	0
Ireland	33	1	3
Italy	35	0	0
Japan	35	5	14
Korea	15	9	60
Luxembourg	29	4	14
Mexico	3	0	0
Netherlands	34	0	0
New Zealand	14	0	0
Norway	35	6	17
Poland	7	0	0
Portugal	33	3	9
Slovak Republic	1	0	0
Spain	34	0	0
Sweden	34	0	0
Switzerland	32	20	63
Turkey	8	0	0
UK	35	0	0
United States	35	0	0

Note: > means 'greater than'
Source: Table 7.1

ating that borrowing was increasingly being used to finance current expenditure

■ the standard deviations for current expenditure minus tax are less than those for total expenditure minus tax every year in the period 1965–83 but greater for every year in the period 1984–97, indicating that the outliers became more extreme for current than for total expenditure minus tax.

Table 7.3 *Comparison of surpluses and deficits*
(total government expenditure minus tax) (percentage of GDP)

	1965–69		1970–79		1980–89		1990–99	
	Deficit	Surplus	Deficit	Surplus	Deficit	Surplus	Deficit	Surplus
Australia	1.4	−0.2	2.7	−1.9	6.6		5.7	
Austria	4.3		5.6		9.4		8.3	
Belgium	0.9		2.7		10.9		5.6	
Canada	2.8		6.3		9.8		7.5	
Czech Republic							3.3	
Denmark	0.6	−0.6	5.1	−0.2	10.9		6.3	
Finland	1.0		2.1	−1.7	2.3	−0.3	7.6	−0.3
France	4.0		4.5		7.5		8.2	
Germany	5.7		8.6		14.0		8.7	
Greece	0.2	−0.8	1.4	−2.0	12.2		17.1	
Hungary							13.9	
Iceland					7.0		7.0	
Ireland	6.3		10.1		14.6		5.0	−0.4
Italy	6.4		11.3		15.8		9.4	
Japan	1.7		4.5	−0.3	5.0	−0.2	5.7	−0.2
Korea					0.6	−0.8	0.8	−0.8
Luxembourg	5.0		2.8	−0.3	9.7		2.1	−1.1
Mexico							11.3	
Netherlands	4.4		8.2		12.3		4.1	
New Zealand					12.5		4.5	
Norway	0.6	−0.1	2.3	−0.3	5.6	−0.9	6.6	
Poland							8.0	
Portugal	1.0		5.9	−1.3	11.0		9.4	
Slovak Republic							19.2	
Spain	4.9		6.4		10.1		9.3	
Sweden	2.1		5.4		10.0		9.7	
Switzerland		−1.5		−1.6	0.6	−0.7	1.9	
Turkey	5.6		3.5					
UK	4.9		7.6		8.3		5.4	
United States	2.3		3.0		8.4		5.1	

Note: These figures are averages per year of surplus or deficit
Source: Table 7.1

Table 7.4 *Total government current expenditure minus*
total taxation revenue (percentage of GDP)

	1965	1966	1967	1968	1969	1970	1971	1972	1973	1974	1975	1976	1977
Australia	-2.5	-2.3	-2.5	-3.2	-3.8	-3.7	-3.5	-2.3	-3.5	-3.1	-1.6	-1.0	0.5
Austria	-3.2	-3.5	-2.0	-1.5	-1.7	-2.6	-3.1	-4.2	-4.3	-3.8	0.1	1.6	1.0
Belgium	-1.4	-2.7	-2.6	-1.9	-2.1	-3.0	-2.2	-1.5	-1.6	-1.9	0.1	0.2	0.6
Canada	-0.9	-1.8	-1.0	-0.5	-2.2	0.2	1.6	1.7	1.1	-0.3	3.9	3.4	5.1
CzechRepublic													
Denmark	-4.4	-5.4	-3.7	-4.9	-4.6	-5.6	-6.0	-5.1	-4.2	-2.8	2.5	2.3	3.4
Finland	-4.3	-4.2	-4.2	-4.2	-3.7	-4.8	-5.5	-5.6	-7.5	-5.4	-6.8	-6.6	-5.1
France	-1.3	-1.2	-1.2	0.0	-1.2	-0.9	-0.8	-1.1	-0.9	-0.4	1.8	4.3	1.3
Germany	-0.8	-0.9	1.5	2.1	-0.6	-0.2	0.6	0.4	-0.2	2.5	6.6	5.9	4.8
Greece	0.0	-0.7	0.3	-0.8	-1.9	-1.9	-1.6	-2.6	-2.1	1.0	2.1	0.1	1.4
Hungary													
Iceland													
Ireland	1.6	0.4	0.2	0.4	0.5	3.0	2.4	2.9	2.7	5.1	8.8	5.6	4.7
Italy	3.4	3.7	2.0	2.2	2.4	2.3	4.4	6.5	8.1	6.1	9.3	7.7	7.6
Japan	-3.9	-3.4	-4.2	-3.9	-4.6	-5.7	-5.2	-5.2	-6.8	-4.9	-0.2	0.0	-0.1
Korea													
Luxembourg	-1.2	0.4	2.7	3.0	0.1	-3.3	-3.2	-3.5	-5.6	-6.4	-2.3	-1.8	-2.8
Mexico													
Netherlands	-2.0	-1.7	-1.2	-1.0	-0.5	1.1	0.6	0.8	0.6	2.4	5.2	6.1	4.1
NewZealand													
Norway	-2.9	-3.7	-4.5	-4.0	-3.8	-2.7	-4.1	-5.2	-5.3	-4.7	-3.0	-4.4	-1.9
Poland													
Portugal	-0.9	-1.3	-1.3	-1.3	-2.5	-3.7	-3.8	-2.7	-2.6	0.1	2.4	1.9	3.3
Spain	1.1	2.1	0.0	1.4	1.1	1.6	2.3	1.3	0.7	1.6	5.6	7.2	2.2
Sweden	-5.4	-4.4	-4.1	-3.9	-4.2	-3.7	-1.8	-2.2	-2.0	0.0	0.0	0.6	2.3
Switzerland	-1.0	-1.4	-1.2	-1.9	-1.9	-2.5	-1.6	-2.0	-2.1	-1.8	-0.9	-1.0	-1.2
Turkey													
UK	0.1	-0.6	0.2	-1.1	-3.6	-4.3	-2.6	0.4	2.3	3.4	4.5	4.8	4.0
United States	-1.1	-0.3	0.42	1.4	-1.4	0.2	1.4	0.7	0.0	1.0	3.4	3.8	1.8
Weighted average	**-1.2**	**-0.9**	**-0.6**	**0.0**	**-1.8**	**-1.2**	**-0.3**	**-0.3**	**-0.7**	**0.3**	**3.3**	**3.5**	**2.3**
Standarddeviation	*2.1*	*2.2*	*2.1*	*2.3*	*1.9*	*2.6*	*2.9*	*3.1*	*3.6*	*3.5*	*3.9*	*3.8*	*3.0*

continued

Table 7.4 continued

	1978	1979	1980	1981	1982	1983	1984	1985	1986	1987	1988	1989	1990
Australia	0.8	3.6	2.6	2.8	4.5		6.1	6.3	5.2	3.7	2.6	2.7	
Austria	1.5	1.5	3.0	3.0	5.3	6.1	3.9	4.1	4.8	5.9	4.5	4.8	4.5
Belgium	0.8	1.5	5.2	9.8	8.8	9.1	13.7	13.4	13.5	11.6	10.6	10.7	10.0
Canada	5.9	5.3	5.3	4.5	8.5	9.1	9.6	10.0	8.9	6.6	6.6	6.0	7.4
CzechRepublic													
Denmark	3.5	4.8	8.3	11.9	14.3	13.4	11.6	9.0	4.1	5.0	6.5	7.7	9.4
Finland	-2.1	-1.3	-2.9	-3.8	-1.2	-0.7	-2.2	-2.1	-3.1	-1.2	-6.5	-7.7	-7.2
France	2.4	1.1	2.4	4.9	5.4	5.6	5.1	5.0	4.7	3.8	3.6	2.9	3.2
Germany	5.0	5.0	9.7	11.6	12.2	12.0	11.6	11.0	10.6	10.8	10.8	8.7	10.0
Greece	2.0	2.0	6.3	12.5	10.1	10.4	11.6	15.1	12.9	14.3	17.6	19.7	21.6
Hungary													
Iceland			-1.3				-3.1	-0.3	-0.6	-1.1	-0.7	-0.5	0.5
Ireland	6.2	8.6	14.6	15.8			13.5	15.5	14.5	13.6	10.4	7.6	
Italy	10.5	10.0	11.1	14.8	15.5	15.7	10.0	10.9	10.0	9.4	9.1	9.2	9.2
Japan	-1.0	-0.6	-0.3	0.3	0.7	1.1	-0.2	-0.9	-1.3	-2.6	-3.7	-4.7	-4.5
Korea													
Luxembourg	-5.2	-0.8	5.9				2.0	1.0	2.3				
Mexico													
Netherlands	4.8	6.1	10.7	12.8	15.2		13.1	12.4	11.3	9.8	8.0	8.6	8.9
NewZealand													
Norway	-1.2	0.5	2.1	0.6	1.9	3.4	1.7	-0.3	1.2	4.2	6.7	9.6	
Poland													
Portugal	5.3	5.2	9.3	11.5			11.0	12.5	12.0	12.3	10.4	8.4	
Spain	3.5	4.4	6.3	6.2	7.5		7.3	9.0	6.9	4.6	4.1		
Sweden	3.1	5.1	9.8	11.2	13.8		11.5	12.4	8.8	4.6	4.3	3.9	5.5
Switzerland	-1.4	-1.2	0.4	-0.1	0.4	0.4	0.8	0.8	-0.8	-1.0	-0.9	-0.6	0.1
Turkey													
UK	5.5	5.7	6.6	7.3	5.3	6.8	6.4	5.8	4.4	3.9	1.6	1.3	2.2
United States	1.1	0.2	6.5	6.6	9.3	11.3	9.2	9.2	9.9	8.2	7.9	7.6	
Weighted average	**2.4**	**2.1**	**5.6**	**6.5**	**7.9**	**8.8**	**7.5**	**7.4**	**7.2**	**6.0**	**5.4**	**4.9**	**2.1**
Standard deviation	*3.5*	*3.2*	*4.4*	*5.6*	*5.3*	*5.1*	*5.3*	*5.6*	*5.3*	*5.0*	*5.6*	*6.0*	*6.9*

continued

Table 7.4 *continued*

	1991	1992	1993	1994	1995	1996	1997	1998	1999
Australia	6.7	7.5	7.7	6.0	5.1	3.4	2.5	2.1	
Austria	6.2	5.3	7.6	7.1	8.1	5.9	3.3	3.3	3.4
Belgium	9.3	9.0	9.5	6.1	6.1	5.9	3.6	2.6	2.3
Canada	12.1	13.7	13.2	10.8	9.5	7.3	4.5	4.2	
CzechRepublic			-3.6	-2.0	-3.5	-2.5	-1.2		
Denmark	8.7	8.9	10	8.8	7.9	6.9	5.3	4.7	2.5
Finland	4.6	10.2	13.8	9.8	8.8	5.7	4.6	1.7	0.2
France	2.8	4.2	6.5	5.6	5.2	5.0	4.6	3.5	2.7
Germany	4.8	5.0	6.2	6.1	6.7	8.8	8.5	7.8	7.1
Greece	10.7	11.2	13.1	13.2	19.7	18.5	15.0	12.5	11.2
Hungary									
Iceland	2.5	2.8	3.7	3.8	3.9	1.6			
Ireland	6.6	6.7	6.2	4.0	4.0	2.3	1.4	-0.6	-3.2
Italy	10.3	10.1	8.9	9.7	8.1	6.5	3.2	3.2	1.7
Japan	-4.9	-2.7	-1.7	0.0	0.6	0.5	0.8	3.2	
Korea	-4.4	-4.5	-5.0	-5.9	-6.2	-6.6	-7.6	-5.8	
Luxembourg	-0.4	0.3	-1.6	-2.8	-1.9	-2.9	-2.8	-3.0	-3.8
Mexico			-1.0	0.2	2.1	1.1	0.1	0.5	
Netherlands	9.5	10.5	10.4	10.0	5.5	4.4	2.8	2.8	1.1
NewZealand									
Norway	6.3	8.5	8.9	6.6	4.1	2.2	-0.6	0.9	2.3
Poland	12.1	14.0	9.1	5.3	4.6	2.8	2.6	2.0	
Portugal	9.1	7.2	10.3	8.8	7.1	7.2	5.4	4.3	4.3
Spain	5.5	6.4	10.1	8.9	8.7	8.5			
Sweden	8.3	14.8	15.7	14.1	13.0	9.8	6.3	4.7	2.8
Switzerland	0.3	1.8	1.8	1.1	0.5	0.4	1.2	-0.4	
Turkey									
UK	4.0	7.3	9.0	8.0	6.4	5.8	4.0	1.1	1.4
United States	9.2	9.3	8.3	6.9	6.6	5.7	4.4		
Weighted average	**5.6**	**6.4**	**6.2**	**5.6**	**5.3**	**4.8**	**3.5**	**3.1**	**3.5**
Standard deviation	*4.7*	*4.9*	*5.6*	*4.9*	*5.1*	*4.8*	*4.2*	*3.6*	*3.6*

Note: A negative sign denotes tax revenue greater than expenditure
Sources: OECD (1985) Table 6.4; OECD (1992b) Table 6.4; OECD (2001d) Table 3

Strategic Public Finance

Table 7.5 *Total current expenditure minus total taxation revenue (summary)*

	No. of years where data available	No. of years where tax > expenditure	Percentage of years in which tax > expenditure
Australia	32	12	38
Austria	35	10	29
Belgium	35	10	29
Canada	34	6	18
Czech Republic	5	5	100
Denmark	35	10	29
Finland	35	26	74
France	35	9	26
Germany	35	5	14
Greece	35	7	20
Hungary	0	0	
Iceland	14	7	50
Ireland	32	2	6
Italy	35	0	0
Japan	34	25	74
Korea	8	8	100
Luxembourg	28	19	68
Mexico	6	1	17
Netherlands	34	5	15
New Zealand	0	0	
Norway	34	16	47
Poland	8	0	0
Portugal	32	9	28
Spain	29	0	0
Sweden	34	10	29
Switzerland	34	20	59
Turkey	0	0	
UK	35	5	14
United States	32	3	9

Note: > means 'greater than'
Source: Table 7.4

Table 7.6 *Comparison of surpluses and deficits
(current expenditure minus tax) (percentage of GDP)*

	1965–69		1970–79		1980–89		1990–99	
	Deficit	Surplus	Deficit	Surplus	Deficit	Surplus	Deficit	Surplus
Australia		−2.9	1.6	−2.7	3.7		4.1	
Austria		−2.4	1.1	−3.6	4.5		5.5	
Belgium		−2.2	0.6	−2.0	10.6		6.4	
Canada		−1.3	3.1	−0.3	7.5		8.3	
Czech Republic								−2.6
Denmark		−4.6	3.3	−4.7	9.2		7.3	
Finland		−4.1		−5.1		−3.1	6.6	−7.2
France		−1.2	2.2	−0.8	4.3		4.3	
Germany	1.8	−0.8	3.8	−0.2	10.9		7.1	
Greece	0.3	−0.8	1.4	−2.0	13.1		14.7	
Hungary								
Iceland						−1.1	2.7	
Ireland	0.6		5.0		13.2	`	3.9	−1.9
Italy	2.7		7.3		11.6		7.1	
Japan		−4.0		−3.3	0.7	−2.0	1.3	−3.5
Korea								−5.8
Luxembourg	1.6	−1.2		−3.5	2.8		0.3	−2.4
Mexico							0.7	−1.0
Netherlands		−1.3	3.2		11.3		6.6	
New Zealand								
Norway		−3.8	0.5	−3.6	3.5	−0.3	5.0	−0.6
Poland							6.6	
Portugal		−1.5	3.0	−3.2	9.7		7.1	
Spain	1.4		3.0		6.5		8.0	
Sweden		−4.4	2.4	−2.0	8.9		9.5	
Switzerland		−1.5		−1.6	0.6	−0.7	0.9	−0.4
Turkey								
UK	0.1	−1.7	3.8	−3.4	4.9		5.0	
United States	0.9	−0.9	1.4		8.6		7.2	
Unweighted average	1.2	−2.3	2.7	−2.6	7.3	−1.4	5.7	−2.8

Note: These figures are averages for years of deficit or surplus
Source: Table 7.4

Perhaps the most telling conclusions to be drawn from the six tables are that, irrespective of whether *total* expenditure or *current* expenditure is being compared with tax revenues:

- surpluses of tax revenues over government expenditures are predominantly confined to the period before the mid-1970s
- very few countries maintained surpluses of tax revenues into the 1980s and even fewer into the 1990s
- even countries with a strong track record of surpluses in the early part of the period found it increasingly difficult to maintain those surpluses throughout the period as a whole
- the increasing degree of variability in the balance between tax revenues and expenditures is predominantly due to increases in deficits rather than increases in surpluses
- although the rise in deficits during the early 1980s and early 1990s was reversed during the periods of rapid economic growth during the late 1980s and late 1990s, there was no return to the levels of the late 1960s and early 1970s
- despite the caveat noted above, comparing total expenditure with tax revenues understates the evidence of growing structural gaps, those gaps being initially disguised by cuts in capital expenditure/GDP ratios after the early 1970s (see Table 4.4)
- this 'step change' in public finance is not confined to a particular constitutional type of country (that is, federal versus unitary states) or group of countries (for example EU versus non-EU).

These conclusions are qualified because they do not take account of sources of income other than taxation, most notably income from user-charges and asset sales (see Chapter 5). Notwithstanding the fact that these other sources of revenue are relatively small and/or of only limited duration, they should be taken into account because they reduce deficits and so avoid the need for borrowing and debt. Ultimately, therefore, the prime indicator of sustainability of public finance is the trend in the national debt/GDP ratio. A rise in that ratio suggests that deficits have been used for wasteful (that is, unproductive) infrastructural investments and/or to finance current expenditure. Public finance becomes increasingly unsustainable in such cases.

The long-term trend in the national debt/GDP ratio

A structural gap would be reflected in a long-term and inexorable rise in that ratio (see Chapter 3 for a general discussion of the ratio). Unfortunately, OECD data only relates to central government debt, these figures excluding debt created by sub-national governments, and is only available since 1990. Hence, only very tentative conclusions can be drawn.

Table 7.7   Central government debt (percentage of GDP)

	1990	1991	1992	1993	1994	1995	1996	1997	1998	1999
Australia	6.5	7.4	10.2	14.0	16.9	19.7	20.3	19.5	16.4	14.5
Austria	46.9	47.6	47.5	51.3	54.0	57.0	57.8	59.5	60.2	62.3
Belgium	109.5	112.2	113.9	122.1	119.8	117.2	115.3	112.4	107.4	105.6
Canada	43.7	47.0	49.5	51.4	52.5	54.9	55.3	54.2	51.5	46.8
Czech Republic				15.6	13.3	11.2	9.9	10.0	10.6	12.1
Denmark	63.6	64.5	69.3	80.7	77.4	75.6	73.4	69.7	63.7	60.0
Finland	10.3	16.9	34.0	51.9	58.9	63.3	67.1	65.2	60.1	56.0
France			28.6	32.8	37.3	40.2	42.4	43.6	44.8	48.4
Germany	20.0	20.1	19.8	21.7	21.5	21.6	23.4	24.8	26.5	34.7
Greece				109.4	115.6	117.4	121.1	117.8	115.3	114.7
Hungary	60.7	73.4	77.6	87.9	85.1	84.3	71.5	62.9	61.1	60.4
Iceland	32.3	34.5	40.5	48.2	50.5	52.7	50.1	46.4	41.4	35.8
Ireland	86.6	84.6	82.3	83.4	79.0	71.9	65.0	57.9	48.4	44.8
Italy	95.4	98.0	105.1	112.9	116.8	116.0	116.1	113.4	110.5	107.8
Japan	50.7	48.8	49.8	55.0	59.4	66.1	69.8	73.4	84.2	95.4
Korea	7.7	7.9	8.1	7.5	6.8	6.2	6.1	6.3	10.5	13.6
Luxembourg	2.1	1.5	1.8	2.2	2.2	3.0	3.9	3.9	4.2	3.8
Mexico	45.0	37.6	27.9	25.3	35.2	40.8	31.1	25.7	27.8	25.6
Netherlands	58.3	59.3	60.5	60.9	57.5	59.5	58.5	55.3	53.3	50.7
New Zealand			65.1	63.7	56.0	49.9	43.0	37.2	39.3	37.2
Norway	22.8	23.3	27.6	36.0	33.4	31.3	28.0	25.2	22.9	21.8
Poland			86.6	88.5	68.0	54.3	47.8	47.0	42.9	43.0
Portugal	36.6	37.7	55.3	61.5	63.5	65.2	64.2	61.0	58.2	58.9
Spain	37.0	36.7	38.4	48.7	50.2	52.4	56.1	54.9	53.2	52.3
Sweden	43.9	46.2	59.0	75.6	80.8	82.0	82.3	80.3	77.8	70.5
Switzerland	12.8	13.6	16.2	19.8	21.8	22.6	24.7	26.2	28.8	26.3
Turkey	14.5	15.5	17.8	18.0	20.7	17.5	21.3	21.8	22.2	29.6
UK	25.8	27.3	32.2	42.7	45.6	51.4	52.0	53.1	53.8	48.9
United States	41.8	46.1	48.5	49.6	49.4	49.1	48.4	45.9	42.8	39.5
Weighted average	**42.3**	**44.0**	**45.6**	**49.2**	**50.5**	**51.9**	**52.2**	**51.4**	**51.7**	**52.3**
Standard deviation	*28.5*	*29.0*	*29.0*	*32.2*	*31.4*	*31.0*	*30.8*	*29.9*	*28.9*	*28.6*

Note: Data not available for years prior to 1990
Source: OECD (2001a) Table 1b

Table 7.7 shows central government debt/GDP ratios during the 1990s. Although central government debt has typically been greater than GDP in Belgium, Greece and Italy, this is not necessarily evidence of structural gaps in those three countries. It may be, at least in part, because municipal expenditure is a relatively small proportion of general government expenditure in those countries (see Table 8.4). Hence, it would appear that central government in those three countries is borrowing to finance local and/or regional

Table 7.8 *Changes in the central government debt/GDP ratio*

	1991	1992	1993	1994	1995	1996	1997	1998	1999
Australia	0.9	2.8	3.8	2.9	2.8	0.6	−0.8	−3.1	−1.9
Austria	0.7	−0.1	3.8	2.7	3.0	0.8	1.7	0.7	2.1
Belgium	2.7	1.7	8.2	−2.3	−2.6	−1.9	−2.9	−5.0	−1.8
Canada	3.3	2.5	1.9	1.1	2.4	0.4	−1.1	−2.7	−4.7
Czech Republic				−2.3	−2.1	−1.3	0.1	0.6	1.5
Denmark	0.9	4.8	11.4	−3.3	−1.8	−2.2	−3.7	−6.0	−3.7
Finland	6.6	17.1	17.9	7.0	4.4	3.8	−1.9	−5.1	−4.1
France			4.2	4.5	2.9	2.2	1.2	1.2	3.6
Germany	0.1	−0.3	1.9	−0.2	0.1	1.8	1.4	1.7	8.2
Greece				6.2	1.8	3.7	−3.3	−2.5	−0.6
Hungary	12.7	4.2	10.3	−2.8	−0.8	−12.8	−8.6	−1.8	−0.7
Iceland	2.2	6.0	7.7	2.3	2.2	−2.6	−3.7	−5.0	−5.6
Ireland	−2.0	−2.3	1.1	−4.4	−7.1	−6.9	−7.1	−9.5	−3.6
Italy	2.6	7.1	7.8	3.9	−0.8	0.1	−2.7	−2.9	−2.7
Japan	−1.9	1.0	5.2	4.4	6.7	3.7	3.6	10.8	11.2
Korea	0.2	0.2	−6.0	−0.7	−0.6	−0.1	0.2	4.2	3.1
Luxembourg	−0.6	0.3	0.4	0.0	0.8	0.9	0.0	0.3	−0.4
Mexico	−7.4	−9.7	−2.6	9.9	5.6	−9.7	−5.4	2.1	−2.2
Netherlands	1.0	1.2	0.4	−3.4	2.0	−1.0	−3.2	−2.0	−2.6
New Zealand			−1.4	−7.7	−6.1	−6.9	−5.8	2.1	−2.1
Norway	0.5	4.3	8.4	−2.6	−2.1	−3.3	−2.8	−2.3	−1.1
Poland			1.9	−20.5	−13.7	−6.5	−0.8	−4.1	0.1
Portugal	1.1	−2.4	6.2	2.0	1.7	−1.0	−3.2	−2.8	0.7
Spain	−0.3	1.7	10.3	1.5	2.2	3.7	−1.2	−1.7	−0.9
Sweden	2.3	12.8	16.6	5.2	1.2	0.3	−2.0	−2.5	−7.3
Switzerland	0.8	2.6	3.6	2.0	0.8	2.1	1.5	2.6	−2.5
Turkey	1.0	2.3	0.2	2.7	−3.2	3.8	0.5	0.4	7.4
UK	1.5	4.9	10.5	2.9	5.8	0.6	1.1	0.7	−4.9
United States	4.3	2.4	1.1	−0.2	−0.3	−0.7	−2.5	−3.1	−3.3
Weighted average	**1.7**	**1.6**	**3.6**	**1.3**	**1.4**	**0.3**	**−0.8**	**0.3**	**0.6**
Standard deviation	*3.5*	*5.1*	*5.6*	*5.5*	*4.2*	*4.2*	*2.8*	*3.8*	*4.2*

Note: Data are calculated by subtracting the debt figure for one year from the following year in Table 7.7
Source: Table 7.7

government expenditures that in other countries enters the accounts of sub-national governments instead of central government and so is not included in Table 7.7. Whilst the average debt/GDP ratio rose fairly steadily, Table 7.8 reveals that not a single country experienced a rise in the debt/GDP ratio in all years during the 1990s (data for France not being available for the first two years). Particularly sharp rises in ratios over the period as a whole occurred for ten countries, particularly sharp falls for five, the rest being characterised by rises more or less offset by subsequent falls.

Table 7.9 *Changes in capital expenditure/GDP ratio*

	1991	1992	1993	1994	1995	1996	1997	1998	1999
Australia	2.2	0.6	0.5	1.3	−9.0	0.3	0.8	0.3	0.0
Austria	−0.1	−0.5	−0.5	0.3	−0.2	0.0	0.2	0.0	0.2
Belgium	1.2	−0.2	−0.8	−0.5	0.2	0.0	0.4	0.3	0.4
Canada	−2.0	−0.9	−0.8	0.7	−1.1	0.2	1.9	0.2	0.2
Czech Republic		3.8	0.5	0.3	3.3	−0.2	−1.0	−2.5	−1.9
Denmark	1.4	−1.2	−0.8	0.2	1.3	0.0	0.8	0.8	−0.5
Finland	−1.9	−4.5	−3.5	−0.9	0.8	0.7	1.0	0.7	0.1
France	0.8	−1.1	−1.5	−0.3	−0.3	−0.3	−0.5	0.3	0.7
Germany	2.6	0.2	−1.0	0.1	−0.7	−0.6	−0.4	−0.1	0.0
Greece	2.9	−1.3	−1.0	−1.7	0.0	0.9	0.5	1.6	0.9
Hungary		−1.1	−1.0	1.3	−1.2	1.4	0.8	1.4	0.2
Iceland	1.6	−1.8	−1.8	−0.4	−0.3	3.5	0.7	3.7	−1.8
Ireland	−2.0	−0.2	−0.1	1.0	0.7	1.6	1.5	1.6	1.5
Italy	0.8	−0.5	−2.1	0.0	0.3	0.0	−0.2	0.3	0.5
Japan	−0.8	−0.9	−1.0	−0.9	−0.1	1.0	−0.9	−1.8	−0.7
Korea		−2.0	−0.8	−0.2	0.7	0.1	−1.7	−5.3	−1.8
Luxembourg	0.1	−2.7	1.5	−3.5	1.0	−1.4	−0.2	−0.9	3.2
Mexico		0.9	−1.0	0.8	−3.2	1.7	1.6	1.4	0.1
Netherlands	0.3	−0.4	−0.9	−0.5	0.3	0.8	0.3	0.3	0.6
New Zealand	−3.8	0.5	1.8	2.0	0.7	0.3	−1.1	−1.0	0.3
Norway	1.7	−0.7	0.5	0.3	0.0	0.6	1.7	2.0	2.3
Poland		−2.7	−0.9	2.0	0.7	2.1	2.8	1.6	1.1
Portugal	−2.1	−1.1	−1.6	0.1	0.2	0.5	1.5	0.8	0.2
Spain	0.6	−2.1	−2.1	0.0	1.0	−0.4	0.3	1.0	1.3
Sweden	0.1	−2.5	−3.0	−0.2	0.4	0.2	−0.5	0.8	0.8
Switzerland	−1.6	−2.5	−1.4	0.4	−0.6	−1.2	−0.6	0.4	−0.1
Turkey	1.1	−0.2	2.9	−1.9	−0.8	1.3	1.3	−1.8	−2.8
UK	−1.3	1.4	0.7	0.0	0.5	0.3	0.1	0.7	0.4
United States	0.1	0.0	0.5	0.6	0.4	0.5	0.4	0.6	0.7
Weighted average	**−0.7**	**−0.4**	**−0.5**	**0.1**	**0.5**	**0.4**	**0.1**	**−0.1**	**0.2**
Standard deviation	*1.7*	*1.5*	*1.3*	*1.1*	*2.0*	*1.0*	*1.0*	*1.6*	*1.2*

Note: Data are calculated by subtracting the expenditure figure for one year from the following year (starting 1990) in Table 4.4
Source: Table 4.4

As already noted, a structural gap is more likely to be created by use of debt for unproductive infrastructural investments and/or current expenditure. It is not possible to determine from the data whether capital expenditures have been productive or not. Hence, it will now be assumed that all capital expenditure is productive in economic terms and so effectively repays debt over the longer term. On this basis, occurrence of an emerging structural gap would be suggested when debt rises faster than capital expenditure because it implies debt is being incurred to finance current consumption.

A simple comparison of percentage increases in debt and capital expenditures would be misleading, given the fact that such increases would be calculated on bases of radically different sizes. Hence, it is more valid to compare increases in terms of the increase in the ratios of debt and capital expenditure against GDP. Comparison of Tables 7.7 and 4.4 make clear that capital expenditure was much more stable than central government debt during the 1990s. Whereas there was a fairly steady rise in the weighted average for the debt/GDP ratio (increasing by ten percentage points over those ten years), the capital expenditure/GDP ratio actually fell marginally. Comparison of Tables 7.8 and 7.9 show that falls in capital expenditure as a proportion of GDP occurred mainly in the early 1990s, precisely when debt was increasing particularly rapidly as a share of GDP. Thereafter, debt tended to increase faster than capital expenditure. Thus it is clear that increases in debt were not being used solely for capital expenditure. Indeed, Table 7.10 reveals that:

- the increase in debt ratio was greater than the increase in the capital expenditure ratio in 4 countries
- in 14 countries an increase in the debt ratio occurred when the capital expenditure ratio fell
- in 10 countries the capital expenditure ratio increased whilst the debt ratio fell
- in one country both the debt and capital expenditure ratios fell
- on average, the debt ratio increased whilst the capital expenditure ratio fell.

Thus, there is some evidence that debt was being used to finance current expenditures over the decade as a whole. Considering that the comparison between total capital expenditure and central government debt excludes debt held by sub-national governments, the five bullet points above probably underestimate structural gaps. At the very least, they corroborate the qualified evidence of structural gaps resulting from a comparison of tax revenues with total and current government expenditures.

This conclusion is further strengthened when account is taken of the fact that structural gaps seem to have been disguised in the short to medium term by fairly rapid inflation that served to reduce the real level of debt in many countries in the past. Table 7.11 shows that inflation rose fairly steadily during the 1960s and early 1970s (from an average of just over 2 per cent to 5 per cent). Inflation then rose sharply during the mid-1970s into double digits (peaking at an average of 14.3 per cent in 1974) and, although it fell back slightly, it rose back into double digits in the late 1970s and early 1980s. Inflation did not fall back to the previously low levels of the 1960s until the late 1990s. Inflation causes the value of debt to fall, not just in real monetary terms but also as a share of GDP (GDP being increased by inflation).

Table 7.10   *Percentage point changes in the capital expenditure/GDP ratio and the central government debt/GDP ratio, 1990 versus 1999*

	Debt	Capital expenditure
Australia	8.0	0.7
Austria	15.4	−0.6
Belgium	−3.9	1.0
Canada	3.1	−1.6
Czech Republic	−3.5	2.3
Denmark	−3.6	2.0
Finland	45.7	−7.5
France	19.8	−2.2
Germany	14.7	0.1
Greece	5.3	2.8
Hungary	−0.3	1.8
Iceland	3.5	3.4
Ireland	−41.8	4.3
Italy	12.4	−1.3
Japan	44.7	−6.1
Korea	5.9	−11.0
Luxembourg	1.7	−2.9
Mexico	−19.4	2.3
Netherlands	−7.6	0.8
New Zealand	−27.9	−0.3
Norway	−1.0	3.3
Poland	−43.6	6.7
Portugal	2.3	−1.5
Spain	15.3	−0.4
Sweden	26.6	−3.9
Switzerland	13.5	−7.2
Turkey	15.1	−0.9
UK	23.1	−1.4
United States	−2.3	3.8
Weighted average	**10.0**	**−0.4**

Note: Changes are calculated as the differences in the GDP ratios for 1990 and 1999 (a negative sign indicating a fall) except 1993 debt data used for the Czech Republic and Greece, 1992 debt data used for France, New Zealand and Poland, and 1991 capital expenditure data used for the Czech Republic, Hungary, Korea, Mexico and Poland

Sources: Tables 4.4 and 7.7

Table 7.11 *Consumer price index (percentage change from previous year)*

	1960	1961	1962	1963	1964	1965	1966	1967	1968	1969	1970	1971	1972	1973	1974
Australia	3.8	2.5	-0.3	0.6	2.3	4.0	2.9	3.2	2.7	2.9	3.9	6.1	5.8	9.5	15.1
Austria	1.9	3.6	4.4	2.7	3.8	5.0	2.2	4.0	2.8	3.1	4.4	4.7	6.3	7.6	9.5
Belgium	0.3	1.0	1.4	2.1	4.2	4.1	4.2	2.9	2.7	3.8	3.9	4.3	5.5	7.0	12.7
Canada	1.0	0.6	1.2	1.7	1.8	2.4	3.7	3.6	4.0	4.5	3.4	2.8	4.8	7.6	10.9
CzechRepublic															
Denmark	1.2	4.2	7.5	5.3	3.6	6.5	6.7	6.9	8.6	4.2	5.8	5.8	6.6	9.3	15.3
Finland	2.9	1.9	4.5	5.2	9.9	5.3	3.6	5.5	9.2	2.2	2.8	6.5	7.1	10.7	16.9
France	3.6	3.3	4.8	4.8	3.4	2.5	2.7	2.7	4.5	6.4	5.2	5.5	6.2	7.3	13.7
Germany	1.4	2.3	3.0	3.0	2.3	3.4	3.5	1.4	2.9	1.9	3.4	5.3	5.5	6.9	7.0
Greece	1.6	1.8	-0.3	3	0.8	3.0	5.0	1.7	0.3	2.4	3.2	3.0	4.3	15.5	26.9
Hungary															
Iceland	1.9	4.8	11.0	12.9	19.5	7.2	10.7	3.4	15.3	21.9	13.6	6.6	9.7	20.6	42.9
Ireland	0.4	2.7	4.2	2.5	6.7	5.0	3.0	3.2	4.7	7.4	8.2	8.9	8.7	11.4	17.0
Italy	2.3	2.1	4.7	7.5	5.9	4.6	2.3	3.7	1.4	2.6	5.0	4.8	5.7	10.8	19.1
Japan	3.6	5.3	6.8	8.5	3.9	6.6	5.1	4.0	5.3	5.2	7.7	6.1	4.5	11.7	24.5
Korea															
Luxembourg	0.5	0.5	0.9	2.9	3.1	3.3	3.3	2.2	2.6	2.3	4.6	4.7	5.2	6.1	9.5
Mexico															
Netherlands	3.8	1.8	1.9	3.8	5.5	4.0	5.8	3.5	3.7	7.5	3.6	7.5	7.8	8.0	9.6
NewZealand	0.7	1.8	2.6	2.1	4.1	2.8	2.8	6.0	4.3	4.9	6.5	10.4	6.9	8.2	11.1
Norway	0.3	2.6	5.2	2.6	5.7	4.3	33.0	4.4	3.5	3.1	10.6	6.2	7.2	7.5	9.4
Poland															
Portugal	3.1	-8.0	2.5	2.0	4.3	3.4	5.7	3.8	4.6	7.0	6.3	8.3	8.9	11.5	29.2
SlovakRepublic															
Spain	1.5	0.9	5.7	8.8	7.0	13.2	6.2	6.4	4.9	2.2	5.7	8.3	8.3	11.4	15.7
Sweden	4.1	2.2	4.8	2.9	3.4	5.0	6.4	4.3	1.9	2.7	7.0	7.4	6.0	6.7	9.9
Switzerland	1.4	1.9	4.3	3.4	3.1	3.4	4.7	4.0	2.4	2.5	3.6	6.6	6.7	8.7	9.8
Turkey	6.0	3.1	3.8	6.5	0.8	4.6	8.7	14.0	5.3	4.8	7.9	19.0	15.4	14.0	23.9
UK	1.0	3.4	4.3	2.0	3.3	4.8	3.9	2.5	4.7	5.4	6.4	9.4	7.1	9.2	16.0
United States	1.6	1.1	1.2	1.2	1.3	1.7	2.9	2.8	4.2	5.4	5.9	4.3	3.3	6.2	11.0
Weighted average	**2.2**	**2.2**	**3.2**	**3.6**	**2.8**	**3.7**	**3.9**	**3.3**	**4.1**	**4.7**	**5.7**	**5.6**	**5.0**	**8.3**	**14.3**
Standard deviation	*1.5*	*2.5*	*2.6*	*2.9*	*3.8*	*2.3*	*6.2*	*2.5*	*3.0*	*4.0*	*2.5*	*3.2*	*2.4*	*3.4*	*8.3*

continued

Table 7.11 *continued*

	1975	1976	1977	1978	1979	1980	1981	1982	1983	1984	1985	1986	1987	1988
Australia	15.1	13.5	12.3	7.9	9.1	10.2	9.7							
Austria	8.4	7.3	5.5	3.6	3.7	6.4	6.8	5.4	3.3	5.7	3.2	1.7	1.5	1.9
Belgium	12.8	9.2	7.1	4.5	4.5	6.6	7.6	8.7	7.7	6.3	4.9	1.3	1.6	1.2
Canada	10.8	7.5	8.0	8.9	9.2	10.2	12.5	10.8	5.9	4.3	4.0	4.2	4.3	4.0
CzechRepublic														
Denmark	9.6	9.0	11.1	10.0	9.6	12.3	11.7	10.1	6.9	6.3	4.7	3.7	4.0	4.5
Finland	17.9	14.4	12.2	7.8	7.5	11.6	12.0	9.6	8.4	7.1	5.2	2.9	4.1	5.1
France	11.8	9.6	9.4	9.1	10.8	13.6	13.4	12.0	9.5	7.7	5.8	2.5	3.3	2.7
Germany	6.0	4.5	3.7	2.7	4.1	5.5	5.9	5.2	3.3	2.4	2.1	-0.1	0.2	1.3
Greece	13.4	13.3	12.1	12.6	19.0	24.9	24.5	21.0	20.2	18.5	19.3	23.0	16.4	13.5
Hungary														
Iceland	49.1	33.0	29.9	44.9	44.1	57.5	51.6	50.2	84.0	30.9	32.0	22.1	18.3	25.7
Ireland	20.9	18.0	13.6	7.6	13.3	18.2	20.4	17.1	10.5	8.6	5.5	3.8	3.1	2.1
Italy	17.0	16.8	18.4	12.1	14.8	21.2	19.5	16.5	14.6	10.8	9.2	5.8	4.7	5.1
Japan	11.8	9.3	8.1	3.8	3.6	8.0	4.9	2.7	1.9	2.3	2.0	0.6	0.1	0.7
Korea														
Luxembourg	10.7	9.8	6.7	3.1	4.5	6.3	8.1	9.4	8.7	6.4	4.1	0.3	-0.1	1.4
Mexico								59.0	102.3	65.3	57.8	86.2	131.8	114.2
Netherlands	10.2	8.8	6.4	4.1	4.2	6.5	6.7	5.9	2.7	3.3	2.3	0.1	-0.7	0.7
NewZealand	14.7	16.9	14.3	12.0	13.8	17.1	15.4	16.2	7.3	6.2	15.4	13.2	15.7	6.4
Norway	11.7	9.1	9.1	8.1	4.8	10.9	13.6	11.3	8.4	6.3	5.7	7.2	8.7	6.7
Poland														
Portugal	20.4	19.3	27.2	22.5	23.9	16.6	20	22.7	25.1	28.9	19.6	11.8	9.4	9.7
SlovakRepublic														
Spain	16.9	17.7	24.5	19.8	15.7	15.5	14.6	14.4	12.2	11.3	8.8	8.8	5.2	4.8
Sweden	9.8	10.3	11.4	10.0	7.2	13.7	12.1	8.6	8.9	8.0	7.4	4.2	4.2	6.1
Switzerland	6.7	1.7	1.3	1.1	3.6	4.0	6.5	5.7	2.9	2.9	3.4	0.8	1.4	1.9
Turkey	21.2	17.4	26.0	61.9	63.5	94.3	37.6	29.1	31.4	48.4	45.0	34.6	38.9	68.8
UK	24.2	16.5	15.8	8.3	13.4	18.0	11.9	8.6	4.6	5.0	6.1	3.4	4.1	4.9
United States	9.1	5.8	6.5	7.7	11.3	13.5	10.4	6.1	3.2	4.3	3.5	1.9	3.7	4.1
Weighted average	**11.6**	**8.9**	**9.3**	**8.4**	**10.5**	**13.8**	**10.8**	**9.5**	**8.7**	**7.8**	**6.7**	**5.7**	**7.7**	**8.0**
Standard deviation	*8.7*	*6.5*	*7.7*	*13.8*	*13.9*	*19.5*	*10.6*	*13.7*	*24.9*	*15.6*	*14.3*	*18.3*	*27.0*	*25.8*

continued

Table 7.11 *continued*

	1989	1990	1991	1992	1993	1994	1995	1996	1997	1998	1999	2000
Australia												
Austria	2.6	3.3	3.3	4.0	3.6	3.0	2.2	1.5	1.3	0.9	0.6	2.4
Belgium	3.1	3.4	3.2	2.4	2.8	2.4	1.5	2.1	1.6	1.0	1.1	2.5
Canada	5.0	4.8	5.6	1.5	1.9	0.2	2.2	1.6	1.6	1.0	1.7	2.7
CzechRepublic						10.0	9.1	8.8	8.5	10.7	2.1	3.9
Denmark	4.8	2.6	2.4	2.1	1.3	2.0	2.1	2.1	2.2	1.8	2.5	2.9
Finland	6.6	6.1	4.3	2.9	2.2	1.1	0.8	0.6	1.2	1.4	1.2	3.4
France	3.5	3.6	3.2	2.4	2.1	1.7	1.8	2.0	1.2	0.8	0.5	1.7
Germany	2.8	2.7	3.6	5.1	4.4	2.8	1.7	1.4	1.9	0.9	0.6	1.9
Greece	13.7	20.4	19.5	15.9	14.4	10.9	8.9	8.2	5.5	4.8	2.6	3.2
Hungary						18.9	28.3	23.5	18.3	14.2	10.0	9.8
Iceland	20.8	15.5	6.8	4.0	4.1	1.6	1.7	2.3	1.8	1.7	3.2	5.1
Ireland	4.1	3.3	3.2	3.1	1.4	2.3	2.5	1.7	1.4	2.4	1.6	5.6
Italy	6.3	6.5	6.3	5.3	4.6	4.1	5.2	4.0	2.0	2.0	1.6	2.6
Japan	2.3	3.1	3.2	1.7	1.3	0.7	-0.1	0.1	1.7	0.7	-0.3	-0.7
Korea		8.6	9.3	6.2	4.8	6.3	4.5	4.9	4.4	7.5	0.8	2.3
Luxembourg	3.4	3.3	3.1	3.2	3.6	2.2	1.9	1.3	1.4	1.0	1.0	3.2
Mexico	20.0	26.7	22.7	15.5	9.8	7.0	35.0	34.4	20.6	15.9	16.6	9.5
Netherlands	1.1	2.5	3.2	3.2	2.6	2.8	1.9	2.0	2.2	2.0	2.2	2.5
NewZealand	5.7	6.1	2.6	1.0	1.3	1.7	3.8	2.3	1.2	1.3	-0.1	2.6
Norway	4.5	4.1	3.4	2.3	2.3	1.4	2.4	1.2	2.6	2.3	2.3	3.1
Poland						32.2	27.8	19.9	14.9	11.6	7.3	10.1
Portugal	12.6	13.4	10.5	9.4	6.7	5.4	4.2	3.1	2.3	2.8	2.3	2.9
SlovakRepublic						13.4	9.9	5.8	6.1	6.7	10.6	12.0
Spain	6.8	6.7	5.9	5.9	4.6	4.7	4.7	3.6	2.0	1.8	2.3	3.4
Sweden	6.6	10.4	9.7	2.6	4.7	2.4	2.9	0.8	0.9	0.4	0.3	1.3
Switzerland	3.2	5.4	5.9	4.0	3.3	0.9	1.8	0.8	0.5	0.0	0.8	1.6
Turkey	63.3	60.3	66.0	70.1	66.1	105.2	89.1	80.4	85.7	84.6	64.9	54.9
UK	7.8	9.5	5.9	3.7	1.6	2.5	3.4	2.4	3.1	3.4	1.6	2.9
United States	4.8	5.4	4.2	3.0	3.0	2.6	2.8	2.9	2.3	1.6	2.2	3.4
Weighted average	**6.0**	**6.8**	**6.2**	**4.9**	**4.3**	**4.9**	**5.4**	**4.9**	**4.4**	**3.7**	**3.0**	**3.6**
Standard deviation	*12.7*	*12.2*	*13.0*	*13.6*	*12.8*	*19.7*	*17.7*	*16.0*	*16.0*	*15.6*	*12.1*	*9.9*

Sources: OECD (1979) p. 149; OECD (1983a) Table R11; OECD (2001b) Table 16

Inflation was consistently very high relative to the OECD average in Turkey throughout the period, and likewise Iceland until the 1990s. The governments of these two countries benefited substantially from the effect of inflation in eroding the real values of their debt. Relatively high inflation occurred in the mid-1970s in Finland, Greece, Ireland, Italy, Japan, New Zealand, Portugal, Spain and the UK. Inflation remained relatively high in Greece (1980s and 1990s) and Portugal (1980s), with newly available data showing relatively rapid inflation in Mexico (since 1982) and Poland (since 1994).

The majority of countries (20 out of 30) had double-digit inflation for at least one year during the mid-1970s. However, very high levels of inflation

Table 7.12 Real long-term interest rates

	1967	1968	1969	1970	1971	1972	1973	1974	1975	1976	1977	1978	1979
Australia				2.5			-4.1	-7.4	-5.3	-2.9	1.2	1.5	0.1
Austria				2.9	1.4	-0.2	0.2	0.2	3.0	3.0	3.3	2.8	3.7
Belgium	3.5	3.7	3.1	3.0	1.6	0.8	0.2	-3.4	-3.2	1.4	1.2	4.0	4.9
Canada	2.0	3.4	3.1	3.1	3.7	2.1	-1.5	-5.7	-1.6	-0.5	1.1	2.4	-0.1
CzechRepublic													
Denmark	2.9	1.4	2.7	2.8	2.8	1.8	1.9	2.7	-0.1	5.4	7.0	7.2	9.1
Finland						-0.4	-5.1	-11.2	-5.0	-2.2	0.5	1.9	1.2
France	3.5	2.8	1.6	3.0	2.6	1.8	1.0	-0.1	-2.6	0.5	1.8	1.1	0.1
Germany	5.6	4.3	2.5	0.7	0.2	2.4	2.6	3.4	2.3	4.3	2.4	1.4	3.3
Greece													
Hungary													
Iceland													
Ireland					-1.2	-3.9	-4.0	8.0	-6.8	-4.7		2.1	1.6
Italy	2.7	3.8	1.7	0.8	-0.1	0.3	-4.3	-7.9	-6.3	-4.6	-3.7	-0.6	-2.4
Japan	1.1	1.8	2.2	-0.1	2.0	1.4	-4.2	-9.4	1.3	2.2	1.6	1.4	4.9
Korea													
Luxembourg													
Mexico													
Netherlands	1.7	1.9	0.6	2.3	-0.8	-1.9	-0.4	0.5	-2.2	0.1	1.7	2.2	4.7
NewZealand	1.1	0.6	2.7	-5.7			-1.9	2.9	-8.8	-7.7	-5.8	-3.7	-7.2
Norway	2.0	0.5	1.0	-5.8	-0.3	1.2	-2.7	-2.9	-2.5	-0.2	-0.9	1.9	1.9
Poland													
Portugal													
SlovakRepublic													
Spain													
Sweden	1.0	3.8	3.4	1.3	0.1	0.3	0.3	1.5	-5.0	-2.3	-0.7	0.5	2.3
Switzerland	0.1	1.3	2.3	1.0	-3.6	-4.4	-2.4	0.2	-0.7	2.2	3.8	-0.3	1.4
Turkey													
UK	3.7	3.3	3.3	1.8	-0.4	0.9	3.5	0.2	-9.9	-0.6	-1.5	0.8	-2.8
United States	1.9	0.3	1.0	1.2	0.4	1.2	0.7	-1.9	-2.0	0.9	1.2	0.4	0.2

continued

(over 20 per cent p.a.) for more than one year are restricted to Greece, Hungary, Iceland, Mexico, Poland, Portugal, and Turkey. Triple-digit inflation occurred in Mexico and Turkey. Hence, the governments of most countries benefited from the impact of inflation in the mid-1970s reducing the real value of the stock of debt they owed to lenders.

Lenders seem to have been doubly disadvantaged because inflation also reduced the real interest rates paid on that debt. Indeed, Table 7.12 shows that real interest rates were negative on average during the mid-1970s, interest rates being less than inflation. Negative interest rates mean that lenders are effectively paying borrowers (in this case, governments) to borrow their money.

Table 7.12   continued

	1980	1981	1982	1983	1984	1985	1986	1987	1988	1989	1990	1991	1992
Australia	0.2	4.6	3.4	5.1	7.5	6.6	5.7	5.3	3.0	7.5	9.4	8.6	8.0
Austria	4.0	4.0	3.1	4.3	3.0	4.6	2.9	4.4	5.0		5.2	4.6	4.4
Belgium	8.0	8.1	5.9	5.5	6.7	4.6	2.9	5.7	6.1	3.5	6.9	6.4	4.8
Canada	1.0	4.2	3.5	6.2	9.3	8.3	7.0	5.0	5.3	4.9	7.3	6.7	7.3
CzechRepublic													
Denmark	10.1	8.4	8.2	5.8	7.8	6.6	5.3	6.3	6.0	4.3	6.7	6.3	5.9
Finland	1.1	-0.4	1.7	1.5	2.1	5.1	4.2	3.1	0.2	5.6	7.4	9.9	11.1
France	1.6	3.8	3.7	4.4	5.7	5.7	3.6	7.0	6.0	5.9	7.3	6.4	6.9
Germany	3.9	5.9	4.1	4.6	5.8	4.9	2.9	4.3	4.9		5.1	3.6	2.7
Greece					2.1	5.1	4.2	3.1	0.2				
Hungary													
Iceland													
Ireland	1.1	0.1	1.6	3.0	7.7	7.1	5.0	8.9	6.2	3.5	11.1	7.4	6.3
Italy	-4.4	0.8	2.0	2.8	3.6	4.4	3.3	4.3	3.6				8.3
Japan	6.2	5.8	6.2	6.7	4.8	4.7	3.2	4.4	4.3	3.1	4.4	3.3	3.6
Korea												5.1	6.9
Luxembourg													
Mexico					-5.9	4.4	8.7	-15.4	-17.8	15.1	4.3	-1.6	1.3
Netherlands	4.3	5.7	3.8	6.6	6.2	5.4	6.2	6.9	5.1	6.0	6.5	5.7	5.6
NewZealand	-0.4	-2.4	1.8	9.1	4.4	2.7	-0.9	3.2	4.5	7.2	9.9	8.9	6.2
Norway	-3.8	-1.4	3.0	5.4	5.4	7.2	14.9	5.7	8.1	4.8	6.6	7.4	10.1
Poland													
Portugal													
SlovakRepublic													
Spain					4.4	5.3	0.3	6.5	5.8	6.2	6.9	5.0	5.0
Sweden		3.7	4.0	2.6	4.4	6.0	3.2	6.6	4.6	2.9	4.0	3.2	8.9
Switzerland	2.0	-1.3	-2.3	1.2	1.7	1.6	0.4	1.4	1.6	2.1	2.1	0.2	3.6
Turkey													
UK	-6.5	1.2	4.4	4.9	6.0	4.4	6.5	4.3	3.1	2.5	4.0	3.2	4.9
United States	1.1	3.7	4.9	6.1	7.7	7.0	5.5	5.4	4.9	4.5	4.7	4.3	5.0

continued

Negative interest rates occurred in the mid-1970s for a majority of countries (16 out of 30) and were negative for most of that decade in Italy, New Zealand and the UK. After falling during the mid-1970s, real interest rates generally rose during the 1980s before falling throughout the 1990s to close to the (positive) levels of the late 1960s. Only a few cases of negative interest rates occurred during the 1980s and even fewer during the 1990s, as inflation was brought increasingly under control in most countries, the exception being Mexico.

The conclusions to be drawn from the financial indicators of structural gaps are:

Table 7.12 *continued*

	1993	1994	1995	1996	1997	1998	1999	2000
Australia	6.3	7.6	6.6	6.4	5.4	5.4	4.0	1.7
Austria	3.7	4.2	4.5	4.9	4.8	4.1	3.9	4.3
Belgium	3.3	5.8	5.5	5.1	4.2	3.1	3.4	4.2
Canada	6.3	7.3	5.9	5.8	5.3	5.9	4.3	2.1
CzechRepublic								
Denmark	5.8	6.0	6.4	4.6	4.0	4.0	2.2	1.9
Finland	6.3	6.9	4.5	7.3	3.8	1.7	4.9	2.3
France	4.6	5.7	5.9	5.0	4.3	3.8	4.5	4.9
Germany	2.7	4.3	4.7	5.1	4.9	3.4	4.0	5.7
Greece								
Hungary								
Iceland		5.0	6.7	7.1	5.0	2.6	4.7	8.0
Ireland	2.3	6.2	5.0	4.9	2.0	-1.1	0.6	1.2
Italy	7.0	6.8	6.8	3.9	4.4	2.1	3.1	3.3
Japan	3.7	4.3	3.8	4.0	2.0	1.6	3.2	3.8
Korea	4.7	4.3	4.9	6.8	8.3	7.4	11.0	10.2
Luxembourg		2.3	7.0	4.4	2.7	2.0	2.1	1.8
Mexico	5.0							
Netherlands	4.4	4.4	4.8	4.9	3.5	2.9	2.9	1.6
NewZealand	5.1	5.8	5.7	6.3	6.2	5.1	6.4	3.7
Norway	4.6	7.6	4.2	2.3	2.8	6.1	-0.7	-8.6
Poland								
Portugal		3.0	7.8	5.3	2.5	1.0	1.4	2.5
SlovakRepublic								
Spain	5.6	5.5	5.9	4.5	3.4	2.1	1.4	1.9
Sweden	5.7	7.0	6.5	6.5	4.8	4.1	4.3	4.3
Switzerland	1.8	3.3	3.4	3.6	3.6	3.1	2.4	2.8
Turkey								
UK	4.7	6.7	5.5	4.4	4.1	2.5	2.4	3.5
United States	4.0	5.3	4.6	4.8	4.6	4.3	4.7	3.7

Sources: OECD (1983b) Table 10.10; OECD (1985) Table 10.10; OECD
(1995) Table 10.10; OECD (2001c) Table 9.10

■ comparison of both expenditures with tax revenues and debt with capital
    expenditures suggests increasing structural gaps after the mid-1970s
■ those emergent structural gaps occurred despite high inflation during the
    mid-1970s which:
   ■ significantly reduced the real value of government debt
   ■ resulted in negative real interest rates
   ■ caused fiscal drag in many countries as inflation eroded the real values
       of tax thresholds on incomes, profits and wealth and so increased real
       tax revenues (see Chapter 6)

■   these structural gaps also emerged despite an increasing tendency of gov-
    ernments to raise substantial (but finite, short-term) revenues from the
    privatisation of state-owned enterprises and other assets during the 1980s
    and 90s
■   structural gaps emerged because debt was increasingly being used to
    finance current (rather than capital) expenditures, contrary to the golden
    rule of public finance (see Chapter 3)
■   lenders financed a large part of structural gaps in the public finances
    during the inflationary period of the mid-1970s
■   unless rapid inflation re-emerges, taxes will ultimately have to rise above
    what they otherwise would have been and/or public expenditures be less
    than they otherwise would have been if debt is to be repaid
■   the former course of action would result in future generations of taxpayers
    financing those structural gaps
■   the latter course of action would result in future generations of users of
    public services effectively bearing the burden through lower levels of
    consumption of public services
■   these effects will be exacerbated if continual borrowing and increases in
    national debt cause crowding out (see Chapter 6).

Thus, although the financial data analysed above cannot categorically prove
that structural gaps exist, the data corroborate the hypothesis of an increasing
tendency towards increasingly large structural gaps in the public finances of
developed countries. Put simply, public finance appears to be becoming
increasingly unsustainable.

EVIDENCE OF STRUCTURAL GAPS: NON-FINANCIAL
INDICATORS

The most obvious non-financial indicator of a structural gap in the public
finances is the 'private affluence–public squalor syndrome'. This syndrome
occurs when high levels of personal and corporate income and wealth are used
by individuals and companies to finance:

■   relatively high levels of consumption of relatively high-quality services in
    the private sector
■   relatively low levels of consumption of relatively poor-quality services in
    the public sector.

The syndrome was first remarked upon in the USA in the late 1950s, where
the sharp contrast between the availability and quality of public sector and private sector services was noted and which subsequently seemed to become
even more marked as urbanisation proceeded apace. It is regarded as paradox-

ical that affluent populations are willing to spend so heavily on private sector goods and services but much less willing to agree higher taxes to finance better public services. The syndrome is demonstrated in any one local government jurisdiction, for example, by social despoliation existing alongside ostentatious private sector consumption.

Social despoliation includes any or all of the following:

- relatively poor-quality state schools, hospitals and municipal housing
- neglected public parks and civic spaces
- underfunded public transport systems
- inadequate public water and sewerage systems
- poor-quality road networks, inadequately maintained
- public libraries characterised by poor book stocks, lack of take-up of new information technology and so on
- deterioration of the environment caused by insufficient recycling of waste collected from households and businesses
- insufficient policing to protect citizens and businesses against crime.

Private sector ostentation (that is, conspicuous consumption) includes relatively high levels of expenditure on:

- cars, households increasingly being characterised by multiple car ownership, those vehicles being built to extremely high technical specifications but typically being used only for very short journeys within urban areas
- household appliances such as kitchen equipment (dishwashers and so on), multichannel televisions and home computers, again increasingly technologically sophisticated
- personal equipment and services, such as mobile phones and access to Internet services, often used for seemingly trivial purposes
- leisure equipment built to professional standards (for example for golf, skiing, sailing) and associated club memberships
- restaurant meals and convenience foods, many families now depending on these for their main meals
- foreign holidays, often several each year and to increasingly exotic and far-flung places
- health and beauty treatments, cosmetic operations, alternative medicines and therapies and other, essentially peripheral, treatments
- alcohol, speciality beverages and bottled mineral waters.

Public squalor existing alongside private affluence seems paradoxical because a high standard of living is directly dependent upon consumption of both public and private sector goods and services, these often being complementary (for example roads and cars respectively). Moreover, the manifestation of the private affluence–public squalor syndrome seems to be increasingly asymmetrical in that private affluence and public squalor seem to be becoming increasingly polarised. As already noted in Chapter 6, income and wealth seem to be increasingly unequally distributed amongst the population and public squalor is increasingly experienced by the poorer (some would say socially excluded) sections of the community most heavily dependent upon the welfare state, for example workless families with children. Both the syndrome and its increasing asymmetry will now be explained in theoretical terms.

THE CAUSES OF STRUCTURAL GAPS: PRAGMATIC EXPLANATIONS

Practitioners and politicians tend to explain structural gaps by arguing that revenues are insufficient to finance essential public services: tax revenues are too small rather than expenditures too large. Thus for example, local governments typically argue that they suffer from inherent fiscal stress (see Chapter 8). This, they argue, is the inevitable result of financing a broad range of increasingly expensive local public services (for example education, care of the elderly, law and order) from a narrow tax base (for example a property tax). Demand for those services rises from year to year, as local populations become more affluent and/or experience higher needs as the numbers of children or elderly people increase (see Chapter 3). However, revenues from the local taxes grow relatively slowly because:

- the base for the property tax (that is, property values) is revalued only infrequently and so tax revenues are inflexible (that is, too stable)
- increasingly affluent populations move out of cities, preferring to live in more pleasant environments, leaving behind the elderly and poor families most in need of local public services but least able to pay for them via taxes and user-charges
- economic activity moves out of cities because land is too expensive, potential building sites of the required size are too fragmented (in terms of ownership), roads are heavily congested and skilled workers can be hired more easily elsewhere
- other local revenue sources are unstable, for example where revenues from a local sales tax fluctuate markedly reflecting equally sharp fluctuations in retail spending as the local economy moves from, say, a consumer boom to a recession.

Hence, the gap between expenditure and income tends to increase over time, with periodic fiscal crises during recessions. Economic recession may cause fiscal stress at the national and regional levels as well as at the local levels of government. However, this is only a short-term explanation since subsequent economic recovery should bring public finances back into balance.

Regional public finance may also be adversely affected over the medium term by economic restructuring (as distinct from recession), for example by the decline of traditional heavy industries (for example coal and steel-making). Once again, however, these pragmatic explanations cannot explain structural gaps persisting over the long term. Hence, recourse has to be made to more comprehensive theoretical explanations of structural gaps. Any theory has to be able to explain a persistent mismatch between public expenditures and public revenues, the former being greater than the latter.

THE CAUSES OF STRUCTURAL GAPS: DISCIPLINE-SPECIFIC EXPLANATIONS

Political theories of structural gaps take their most radical form in the 'crisis of capitalism'. This theory asserts that private sector profit-making companies are unwilling to pay the amounts of tax sufficient to finance the public services they depend upon to deliver highly productive workers, education and health care, for example. Thus the profits of economy activity are accumulated by the private sector whilst the costs of engendering that growth fall on the public sector. In addition, the public sector has to cover the social costs created by capitalism, most notably pollution and the associated medical, environmental and social problems. Testing this theory requires public finance time-series data to be examined to see if public finance is significantly more likely to 'go critical' in broadly capitalist states than in centrally planned states. This would be a very large research project, the interpretation of the outcome of which would be highly problematical. Suffice it to say for the purposes of this book that it appears communism is more prone to collapse than capitalism as globalisation of economic activity proceeds apace (see Chapter 1). It is arguable that the revenues for public services are enhanced by economic growth, in that it creates a wider tax base from which public finance can be raised. In addition, economic growth reduces demands upon public expenditure in so far as it reduces the need for income maintenance payments by the state. Whilst both these propositions are qualified below, public finances may be more likely to 'go critical' as a result of economic stagnation, irrespective of whether economies are capitalistic, centrally planned or mixed.

Sociological theories are based on the premise that some groups of people are more able to capture the benefits of public services whilst being more able to avoid paying for them than are other groups. It is argued that affluent middle-class groups disproportionately benefit from public services because they are more able than lower income (working-class) groups to access services. This middle-class capture has been referred to in previous chapters. Thus, for example, in many countries the children of parents in professional and managerial occupations are more likely to go to university than the offspring of parents in unskilled low-paid occupations. Middle-class groups also tend to make disproportionately high use of public sector cultural and leisure services (a reflection of lifestyle factors). They also make disproportionately high use of roads (because of their higher rates of car ownership), rail subsidies (because of their higher rates of commuting to work), public sector health services (because they are more articulate and more demanding of doctors and surgeons) and so on. Thus, sociological theories rely on social segmentation and the transmission of privilege and discrimination to create social exclusion both within and across successive generations. They can help to explain social exclusion within localities such as deprived inner cities. However, it is not self-evident why middle-class capture would create a structural gap in the public finances as distinct from inequity in the distribution of the costs and benefits of public services.

Economic theories of the growth of public expenditure were briefly outlined in Chapter 3. The intention of that chapter was to explain the rising public finance/GDP ratios, not explain a structural gap. Demand-side theories of the growth of public expenditure within a fiscal exchange model of government (see Chapter 3) do not suggest a structural gap. If public expenditures were the outcome of voters' demand for public services and a given degree of income redistribution, they would be matched by a willingness of the totality of voters to pay taxes and charges yielding revenues sufficient to cover expenditure. Use of borrowing would be tempered by the fact that voter's know that they and/or their sons and daughters ultimately have to pay back borrowed sums, even if over several decades. For example, high future tax liabilities within a local government jurisdiction could be expected to reduce the value of properties (under a local property tax) and so an increase in current consumption is at the expense of a reduction in current wealth. Similarly, a fear that high taxes could drive business out of a locality would also serve to limit tax levels raised by a despotic benevolent government (see Chapter 3) because of adverse consequences for employment prospects and so standards of living. These factors can be expected to serve as disincentives to 'live now, pay later'.

Likewise, supply-side theories of public expenditure growth within a leviathan model of government (see Chapter 3) are themselves incapable of explaining structural gaps. Whilst the preferences of politicians and bureaucrats may influence the level and composition of expenditures, ultimately they cannot explain structural gaps because they imply sufficient tax revenues will be raised over the long term. For example, whilst the 'fiscal illusion' theory of the growth of public expenditure posits that people do not realise just how much they pay in taxation, it implies sufficient revenues can always be raised to cover expenditure. Similarly, the 'productivity differential model' simply provides a reason why public services may become more expensive relative to private sector outputs, not why revenues would necessarily be insufficient.

Thus, a more comprehensive theory is required to explain structural gaps in the public finances. It must provide a theoretical reason why public expenditure can be expected to grow faster than public revenues. In order to do this, a theoretical model must predict that a growing demand for and/or supply of services is not matched by a greater willingness and/or ability to pay for them. Thus, even though policies for public finance are the outcome of rational decision-making processes, those processes are asymmetrical in respect of the balance between public spending and revenues. Irrational decision-making processes would not explain why expenditure exceeds income over the long term, the opposite outcome being just as likely.

A COMPREHENSIVE THEORY OF STRUCTURAL GAPS: THE LOGIC OF COLLECTIVE ACTION

For a mismatch between demand/supply and willingness/ability to pay to occur there has to be both:

- an incentive for voter-taxpayers to demand more public expenditure simultaneously with an unwillingness/inability to pay more tax or user-charges
- an incentive for politicians and practitioners to supply more whilst raising insufficient revenues from taxes and user charges, whether by design or by default.

Two factors underpin the *logic of collective action*:

- insuperable informational problems
- political self-interest working with the economic incentives created by the democratic polity.

In the absence of market prices, central planning systems are incapable of judging willingness to pay for public sector services and other outputs and so incapable of measuring the benefits they confer on their users (see Chapter 2). Thus collective choices are 'blind' in being made in the absence of the information required for them to be optimal in terms of maximising the public interest. This is the basic tenet of the 'Austrian/Hayekian school of public choice' (see Chapter 1) which holds that governments simply do not know what the public interest is and so may provide too much or too little in terms of service provision. Such shortages or excess would not persist for long in a competitive market system since prices would adjust, upwards in the case of shortages and downwards in the case of excess. Such price adjustments remove excesses and shortages by bringing supply and demand into balance. Thus a rise in prices creates profits incentives to increase supply, those higher prices simultaneously reducing demand. A fall in prices likewise provides incentives to reduce supply (because profits fall), those lower prices simultaneously increasing demand. Thus, demand and supply are brought back into balance automatically by the free operation of competitive market forces. Shortages and surpluses cannot persist in a competitive market system free of government controls. This is simply a recasting of the property rights theory in Chapter 2.

Whereas the shortage of information can result in too much or too little service provision, that indeterminacy is made determinant by the incentives to excess provision faced by those who work in the public sector, namely politicians and bureaucrats. Those incentives are stronger the weaker the systems of political and administrative accountability existing (respectively) within democratic processes and governance structures. This is because a lack of accountability affords more scope for some groups systematically to gain at the expense of other groups. The assumption is that self-serving behaviour is endemic within political systems as well as within economic (that is, market) systems. This is the basic tenet of the 'Virginia school of public choice'.

In addition to assuming imperfect information and that political actors pursue their own self-interests, 'public choice theory' also assumes that large groups are characterised by a lack of 'political mobilisation'. Individuals in large groups have an incentive to free ride (or freeload – see Chapter 2), that is, assume that others will act on their behalf in the political process. This is because the upfront costs of participating (in terms of time and effort) in the political process are usually greater than the uncertain benefits that, even if they do transpire, are spread widely over the collective as a whole.

In sharp contrast, the special interests of pressure groups are more focused on their members and so the individual's benefit/cost ratio is higher than for the much wider collective, thus creating a greater incentive to incur the personal costs of political participation. Moreover, smaller special interest groups make free riding more difficult because it is more readily noticed by other members and the group may be able to impose a sanction for non-participation, for example expulsion from membership of that group. The result is that pressure (special interest) groups have a much greater degree of political mobilisation than the general public.

In other words, special interest groups are more able than the wider electorate to overcome problems inherent in collective action and so more able to exercise political power because they have stronger incentives to participate in collective action. They derive both material (for example service consumption) and non-material (for example the group approval of socialising and co-operating with like-minded people) benefits from membership of their special interest group.

Thus smaller special interest groups are able to increase the benefit/cost ratio of participation in the political process. Indeed, political entrepreneurs may foster the belief amongst group members that political participation within such concentrated lobby groups is a benefit rather than a cost, again increasing the incentives to political action. For example, defence of (perhaps excessively) high budgets for the arts through political lobbying becomes a worthy exercise in its own terms, bringing with it high levels of social approval within arts and culture pressure groups. Even though the general population of taxpayers may prefer to spend less on arts and culture, the high level of political mobilisation within arts and culture networks results in more being spent. This is because, in achieving a higher level of political mobilisation than the general population, those special interest groups have a disproportionately high influence on public choices.

Similar outcomes result for other public services where there are high levels of political mobilisation amongst pressure groups. In many developed countries there are particularly strong lobby groups in the construction industry, agriculture, defence contracting, the professions and so on. These groups are thus able to secure high levels of state protection, through land-use planning systems, agricultural subsidies, highly regulated professional practices and so on. In contrast, the general body of citizens, consumers and taxpayers is grossly underrepresented because, being very large collective groups, they face much weaker incentives to mobilise and so lack effective political voice. Attempting to give them more avenues for political representation, for example through additional consultative mechanisms, is doomed to failure because it does not change the 'logic of collective action', namely the much weaker incentives for political engagement amongst large groups. Essentially, the logic of collective action concentrates the benefits of government intervention on organised lobbies but spreads the tax costs much more widely.

It can be expected that those who are not members of special interest groups would object to this asymmetry between the benefits and costs of public services. However, as already noted, individuals in the general populace of voters have an incentive not to take the time and incur the personal effort to vote because the benefits they derive from voting are so small relative to the costs of participation in the electoral ballot. An individual's vote is unlikely to yield significant benefits in terms of affecting service provision. Hence, the incentive is not to vote or, at least, not to become fully informed when voting. 'Rational ignorance' would appear to be the best strategy for the general body of voters.

The resulting chronic rational ignorance results in a poor-quality public debate about what constitutes the public interest. This allows the political agenda to be set by pressure groups, politicians and bureaucrats. Thus, even in cases where the losses (that is, tax costs) are greater than the benefits (that is, from greater service provision) public spending increases. Politicians meet the demands of special interest groups in order to 'buy' votes and so increase their chances of re-election.

Furthermore, bureaucrats are generally happy to respond to politicians' decisions for more services to be provided because it promotes their own self-interest in leading to bigger budgets, yielding greater job security and perquisites of office and also higher status. Indeed, bureaucrats themselves face incentives to support special interest groups demanding higher levels of spending on services that the bureaucrat is employed to provide. For example, they may exaggerate the benefit/cost ratio relating to those services, in particular by selectively feeding information to special interest groups and policy-makers which emphasises benefits and understates costs. Bureaucrats are able to do this because they often have a monopoly over the supply of information about the services that they provide.

Rather than simply attempting to maximise the output of their services, bureaucrats may focus on maximising their 'discretionary budget'. This is the difference between the minimum cost of producing a given level of service output and the maximum amount of financial resources that can be obtained from the political authority for production of a given level of service. Both oversupply and excessive costs lead to larger budgets upon which bureaucrats' careers depend. Thus, besides having an incentive to *oversupply services* for which they are responsible, bureaucrats face incentives to produce those services at unnecessarily *high costs*.

To summarise, the interaction of incentive structures (on both the demand side and supply side of public services) and the lack of accurate information results in asymmetries of political power and, consequently, decision-making. These asymmetries cause public expenditures to rise faster than the income needed to finance them, so creating structural gaps in the public finances. Decision-making relating to service provision and so to the public finances becomes characterised by short-termism. As a consequence, the possibility of a structural gap in the public finances is not seriously considered.

Even allowing for both rational ignorance and fiscal illusion (that is, that taxpayers underestimate the tax costs of services), it can be expected that, ultimately, the general populace of taxpayers would revolt against excessive taxes. In theory, electoral competition amongst opposing political parties should allow voters to choose to vote for a party promising to cut taxes. Whilst electoral competition and public opinion can, indeed, influence policy-making, the logic of collective action outlined above suggests that electoral processes cannot exercise effective control over politicians, bureaucrats and special interest groups. Whilst politicians have to pay attention to the unwillingness of the collective body of taxpayers to pay ever-higher taxes, they also have incentives to increase public spending. This is the scenario of the unstoppable force running into the immovable object. This quandary can easily be resolved, however, by borrowing to bridge the gap between expenditures and revenues. By such means, the current electorate is largely relieved of paying the resultant higher taxes.

Public spending will therefore have an inherent tendency to grow faster than public revenues, self-serving incentives and the associated political lobbying resulting in both demand-side (via lobbies) and supply-side pressures on public finance. These pressures from distributional coalitions (that is, all politically mobilised groups) lead to perennial budget deficits, borrowing and rising levels of national debt and so to a structural gap in the public finances. Therefore the government does not secure the public interest, the meaning of which becomes distorted due to the poor political debate resulting from rational ignorance.

Hence, structural gaps in the public finances are the outcome of the logic of collective action. Public finance therefore becomes structurally unsustainable.

The logic of collective action also explains why some public services seem to correspond more to the private affluence–public squalor syndrome than others. Given that the explanatory variable is political mobilisation, the most neglected public services (in terms of lack of investment) are those for which political mobilisation is most difficult. Thus, in theory, public parks will tend to be more run down than state schools because parents and teachers at any one school have more incentive and find it easier to mobilise themselves politically than does the much larger population served by a public park. This is because the benefit/cost ratio is higher in the school case than in the park case. Thus, the logic of collective action helps to explain, in theoretical terms, why school budgets tend to be more heavily protected than budgets for other municipal services.

EXACERBATION OF STRUCTURAL GAPS

The above analysis focused on the logic of collective action to demonstrate why structural gaps in public finance are an inevitable outcome of public choice. However, it is arguable that structural gaps in the public finances are being increasingly exacerbated by the economic, social and demographic restructuring associated with globalisation. In theoretical terms, such restructuring affects the distribution of property rights, as will be demonstrated below. It will then be argued that this restructuring of property rights impinges upon the logic of collective action, exacerbating structural gaps.

The factors leading to increasingly severe structural gaps over the medium to long term include:

- globalisation requiring lower taxes
- economic restructuring
- demographic restructuring
- household restructuring
- lifestyle restructuring.

These factors are clearly not independent of each other. For example, economic and household restructuring are interdependent, rising prosperity in developed countries allowing more people to live independently of family, thus resulting in a trend to smaller household size. Nor is the causation one way, from globalisation to socioeconomic and demographic restructuring. For example, whilst globalisation facilitates larger industrial units gaining economies of scale, such economic restructuring facilitates greater international specialisation of production leading to further globalisation in a feedback loop of causality. These factors are now dealt with in turn.

Globalisation of economic activity tends to lead to downward pressures on taxes, in order for countries' industries to remain competitive on world markets, as noted in Chapters 1 and 5. It also increases the scope for tax avoidance and tax evasion as people and companies find it increasingly easy to move their incomes, profits, savings and wealth 'offshore' to countries with lower tax rates (those with the lowest rates often being referred to as 'tax havens'). This leads to erosion of the national tax base in much the same way as the out-migration of population and industry erodes the tax base of local and regional governments.

Whilst such concerns are not new, it is arguable that international borders are becoming increasingly less relevant to the location of economic activity and therefore its associated tax bases. The increasingly rapid growth of internationally mobile, multinational company investment means that countries with relatively high tax rates fail to attract investment. Likewise, they may see their own domestic companies move to lower taxed states. In addition, they may lose their internationally mobile top executives and professional groups of workers. The growth of electronic commerce exacerbates such effects, since it makes it much harder for tax authorities to trace transactions and so makes it increasingly difficult for them to levy the appropriate sales taxes. Such Internet-based transactions can easily be 'relocated' in tax havens. Thus, globalisation leads to a constant bidding down of tax rates and/or erosion of their associated bases and so it becomes increasingly difficult to match tax revenues with public spending. Whilst this growing structural imbalance in the public finances can be slowed down by tax harmonisation amongst countries trading with each other in any one trading bloc, trading blocs still have to compete on world markets.

Moreover, this growing structural imbalance is exacerbated by the growing inequity in the distribution of the tax burden. As companies, their shareholders, and high-income earners pay less tax (in real and/or proportionate terms), the tax burden falls increasingly on the less mobile, less affluent groups, including those who cannot afford tax accountants to 'shelter' their incomes and wealth from tax. Widespread tax avoidance and tax evasion reinforces the view that the tax burden is unfairly distributed. Perceptions of lower taxes and/or better services in other countries may lead to taxpayers' demands for lower taxes.

Admittedly, there is a danger of the exaggeration of these effects on tax revenues, both in terms of their proportionate impact and speed of occurrence. This is because tax differentials are not the only (or, perhaps, even major) influence on the location of business investment and jobs. Political stability, closeness to market and availability of skilled labour with a tradition of stable industrial relations are also major influences on business location decisions. Nevertheless, globalisation and the growth of e-commerce ultimately require lower taxes to minimise the erosion of tax bases, leading inevitably to growing structural gaps in the public finances.

Economic restructuring interacts with globalisation in terms of greater economies of scale and specialisation of production, as noted above. Some industries locate new investment in countries with relatively low labour costs (that is, low wages and payroll taxes), typically developing countries and Far Eastern economies. This puts downward pressure on wages in the same industries in developed economies in order for them to be able to compete in world markets. This results in more low-pay households in receipt of higher income-related welfare payments (creating the poverty trap – see Chapter 6) as well as lower income tax revenues, putting strain on the public finances. However, specialisation of production also results in developed countries concentrating increasingly on high-tech industries (such as telecommunications, information technology and pharmaceuticals) and internationally tradable services (such as financial services). Nonetheless, the development of high-tech industries and services also seems to put increasing strains on public finance, in that it seems to lead to more 'dual-income households' and more 'no-income households'.

No-income households are those where nobody is in paid employment. This is particularly the case for those whose heads lack the increasingly advanced educational qualifications and vocational skills required by companies seeking to compete in increasingly global markets. People tend to marry or find partners from within their own social group. Thus, if the head of a household lacks educational qualifications, his (or her) partner typically also lacks qualifications. They are therefore more likely to be in low-paid unskilled jobs. Therefore, if one partner becomes unemployed, it is generally not financially worthwhile for the other partner to be in low-paid employment because of the loss of income-related benefits. Put simply, the unemployment trap (see Chapter 6) is more pronounced for households lacking skills and educational qualifications because if one partner becomes unemployed the other is also likely to cease paid employment.

Similarly, highly qualified/skilled people (for example university graduates) tend to marry or partner other qualified/skilled people, both spouses or partners thus having jobs, creating dual-income households. At least one of those jobs will be full time and well paid, the other possibly being part time. Ironically, it is more worthwhile for the qualified/skilled household whose head is in full-time, well-paid employment to have a partner or spouse in part-time, low-paid employment than it is for the unskilled/unqualified unemployed household. This is because the former household does not qualify for income-related benefits (because the other partner is in well-paid, full-time employment) and so is not affected by the unemployment trap. Even though advanced educational qualifications may not be necessary for the jobs they offer, employers may also prefer to employ well-educated people in part-time jobs because they come from (what are perceived to be) stable, middle-class families and neighbourhoods.

Growth of dual-income and no-income households increases the demands on social security budgets faster than the tax revenues necessary to meet those demands. Tax revenues grow more slowly because the spouse/partner in the educated/skilled household who is working part time pays little or no income tax, since most countries' tax schedules contain a tax-free personal allowance. Of course, little or no income tax would have been paid if that part-time job had been held instead by a member of the unskilled/uneducated household. Nonetheless, the need for income-related social security payments would have been reduced. The growth of low-pay households has similar effects. Those effects are exacerbated if low-pay and no-pay households tend to have more children than high-income households because of the consequent impact on income-related benefits in respect of children. Hence, industrial, labour market and household restructuring seems to exacerbate structural gaps in the public finances.

Demographic restructuring also causes social security payments to rise as more and more people become eligible for them. Demography is linked to globalisation, in that growing economic prosperity increases life expectancy, more as a result of higher standards of living (for example better housing conditions and safer and more plentiful supplies of water) than increased public expenditures on health care. Developing countries have typically experienced sharp reductions in child mortality, whereas developed countries have typically experienced sharply rising numbers of elderly age groups. Rising proportions of children and/or elderly people in the population increase the dependency ratio and hence require more taxes to be paid by non-dependent (that is, working) groups. For example, rising numbers of people of retirement age relative to those of working age lead to increased payments of state retirement pensions and income-related benefits. Thus, such demographic restructuring exacerbates structural gaps in the public finances.

Lifestyle restructuring seems to be leading to higher service costs as younger age groups seem to be becoming increasingly less fit and healthy, as an indirect result of the growing economic prosperity associated with globalisation. The rising incidence of car ownership and growth of physically passive forms of work (that is, sedentary jobs) and leisure (television, computer games and so on) means that people take less and less exercise as part of their daily routines. Simultaneously, the growth of convenience (oven-ready) foods, typically with high fat, salt and sugar content results in people eating insufficient fruit and vegetables. This increasingly unbalanced diet is exacerbated by the growing consumption of snack foods and soft drinks in between main meals. These changes in diet interact with lack of exercise, leading to increasing prevalence of obesity and associated health problems. Obesity leads to higher rates of heart attacks, strokes, diabetes and other health problems. Mortality amongst the obese is typically twice as high as amongst the non-obese, and a quarter greater for those categorised as overweight but not obese.

Growing obesity therefore puts more demands on public sector health expenditures and, simultaneously, results in a loss of income tax revenues due to being off work ill. For example, whilst obesity was estimated to cost the

NHS in England £500 million in 2001/02, it was estimated to have cost £2 billion in terms of lost economic output. Thus the cost in terms of lost economic output is likely to be many times greater than the cost of health care. This lost output results in lost tax revenues at the very time when demands on public expenditures (including income maintenance whilst ill) are increasing.

Obesity seems to be on the increase in most developed countries. It is also prevalent in some developing countries, for example in parts of the South Pacific such as Samoa and Nauru. It also seems to be affecting all sections of society, affluent and poor, young and old and so on. The growth of welfare states has broken the historical link between poverty and starvation and obesity now seems to be on the increase amongst children. The International Obesity Task Force estimates that one billion people worldwide are either pre-obese or obese and that the global incidence of obesity is increasing over time. To the extent that obesity reflects permanent changes in lifestyle, it augurs badly for the sustainability of public finance in many countries. The spread of subtropical diseases and illnesses to temperate regions as global warming proceeds apace will exacerbate rising medical costs.

To summarise, the economic, demographic, household and lifestyle restructuring associated with globalisation exacerbate emergent structural gaps resulting from the logic of collective action. Restructuring increases the needs and demands for public services and income maintenance programmes, without providing commensurate increases in the revenues necessary to finance them. Nevertheless, access to services and state support remains largely unrestricted. In effect, the reconfiguration of property rights onto an increasingly collective basis occurs as governments intervene more and more to deal with the adverse impacts of economic progress through globalisation. This weakens private property rights, resulting in the tragedy of the commons (see Chapter 2), typified in the private affluence–public squalor syndrome. This process reinforces the logic of collective action that was argued above to lead the growth of public expenditure to outstrip the growth of public revenues.

HOW TO ELIMINATE AND AVOID STRUCTURAL GAPS

Unfortunately for policy-making, being a long-term phenomenon, structural gaps only become evident with hindsight and pressure groups make it very difficult to cut public expenditure. This is because no group of self-interested people could be expected to agree readily to a cut in the provision of services they receive, when there would be little or no corresponding reduction in their liability to pay taxes that, by definition, are unrequited payments. This would be the case whether the resultant financial savings were used to finance tax cuts (which benefit all taxpayers, not just those losing the service benefit) or to expand service provision directed to other groups. The result is institutional sclerosis, making it politically very difficult to restructure public services in response to

changing needs, new needs having to be met by raising more public finance
instead of redirecting it from other less socially valuable lines of expenditure.

Politically, the 'cure' may seem worse than the 'disease' of a structural gap,
such that, by the time it is accepted that such a gap exists, the combination of
tax increases and public expenditure cuts necessary to bridge the gap are seen
as simply too draconian to implement. This helps to explain the ratchet effect
whereby public expenditures go up but never come down (see Chapter 4).

Once a structural gap exists, the most politically acceptable policy
response is likely to be:

■ to cut sharply levels of capital expenditures, on the grounds that voters
   will not miss what they never had in the first place
■ where borrowing is used mainly for current expenditures, cut the borrow-
   ing/GDP ratio only slowly because, otherwise, public sector employment
   would have to be cut, leading public sector trades unions to take industrial
   action and the users of public services to complain about falling standards
   of service
■ seek to limit increases in public sector pay and staffing
■ hope for rapid economic growth.

Politicians seem to find it more politically palatable to hope for unrealistically
high rates of growth of GDP than to seriously address the financial problem.
They believe that rapid growth of GDP would mean that the problem solves
itself, as tax revenues rise and the need for income maintenance, social security payments fall. However, the logic of collective action and the impact of
globalisation on the economy and society suggest that such hopes are unreal-
istic. The problem simply will not go away of its own accord over the long
term. Politically unpalatable though they may be, proactive remedial measures
are required to remove a structural gap.

So how can structural gaps be avoided in the first place? Put simply, structural gaps arise because there is no symmetry between decisions to spend and
decisions to raise public revenues. The only solution to this problem is to
secure such symmetry by making people bear directly more of the costs of
their actions so that costs match benefits. In other words, the only solution is
to change the incentive structure underlying the provision and use of public
sector outputs by changing the structure of property rights. This requires a
combination of measures to be implemented:

■ restricting the public sector to core functions by privatising assets (for
   example land and buildings) and the provision of services wherever possible, the public sector only providing those services which the private
   sector is incapable of providing (that is, truly collective services such as
   defence, although even parts of those can be privatised – see Chapter 2)
■ otherwise, levy user-charges for public services to make sure that those

who benefit most from services bear most of the costs through directly requited payments rather than through broad-based taxes (see Chapter 5)

- where user-charges cannot be levied, devolve public choices to the lowest possible levels of government, local governments more accurately matching the tax costs and benefits of services (see Chapter 8)
- adopt the golden rule of public finance, namely that borrowing only be used to finance capital expenditures, not current expenditure (see Chapter 3).

Without these measures, public expenditure can be expected to grow faster than revenues. They will constrain (but not eliminate completely) the growth of structural gaps in the public finances. Likewise, so will measures intended to reduce tax avoidance and tax evasion, including tax harmonisation. Nevertheless, the most radical way of avoiding structural gaps is to move from a Collectivist or Neo-Liberal philosophy to a Libertarian state. This would involve the wholehearted adoption of the enterprise culture of capitalism, people's life chances and achievements being determined within a meritocracy with little compassion (Libertarians would say condescension) for 'losers' (that is, those lacking ability and personal ambition). The welfare state would be restricted to providing a universal minimal safety net, not being concerned with promoting social mobility through greater equality of opportunity (see Chapter 1). That safety net would ensure that everyone had enough to eat and could get medical care when needed but would avoid the rising social security bills associated with economic and household restructuring noted above. According to Libertarians, this could largely be paid for by reducing the enormous bureaucracies that have arisen throughout the Western world, bureaucracies that increasingly attempt to monitor and control how welfare recipients use their benefits, how local and regional governments spend their money and so on. Without such draconian reforms, structural gaps are inevitable.

The EU's fiscal rules for Economic and Monetary Union (EMU) require national governments to maintain a sound and sustainable fiscal stance. Those rules require the overall budget to be balanced in the medium term and the Maastricht deficit and debt ratios to be observed (see Chapter 3). The Stability and Growth Pact requires each country to aim for a budgetary position close to balance or in surplus. This effectively means that capital expenditure has to be financed on a 'pay as you go' basis out of current revenues, so that current taxpayers pay for physical infrastructure benefiting future generations. This effectively vetoes the golden rule and reverses the intergenerational inequity created by borrowing to finance current consumption. The severe constraint on member states' ability to finance capital expenditures helps to explain the trends noted in Tables 4.4 and 7.9, at least for those countries.

The EMU rules clearly do not specifically relate to those specified in the above four bullet points and so do not address the theoretical inevitability of structural gaps arising out of the logic of collective action. Moreover, EMU fiscal rules are binding only on national-level governments. Regional and local governments could act in breach of those rules and yet face no financial penalty for non-compliance. Thus, it remains to be seen whether the EMU fiscal rules will remove and/or avoid structural gaps in the long term.

CONCLUSIONS

There seems to have been a step change in the public finances of most OECD countries since the mid-1970s, towards an increasingly unsustainable approach to paying for public services. Structural gaps seem increasingly prevalent and increasingly large in the public finances of developed countries, particularly within Europe and North America. This step change was disguised initially by high inflation and subsequently by revenues raised from privatisation. Nevertheless, structural gaps emerged despite the impact of inflation reducing the real value of public sector debt and the real interest rates paid on that debt, at least prior to the 1990s. Those gaps seem to have been financed by lenders (particularly in the mid-1970s), otherwise by future generations of taxpayers and/or service users.

Ultimately, the step change reflects an increasing tendency of current generations to live at the expense of future generations. Structural gaps arise because there is no symmetry between decisions to spend and decisions to raise public revenues from sustainable sources. The theoretical explanation of this phenomenon is provided by the logic of collective action resulting in chronic government failure. Politicians and bureaucrats do not maximise social welfare. Instead, they pursue their own self-interest by serving the special interests of lobbies and pressure groups. Therefore, electoral processes are unable to exert effective control over public finance. This results in politicians and bureaucrats having considerable discretion to implement policies that do not accord with the preferences of the general body of voter-taxpayers. Taxpayer resistance to higher levels of taxation is side-stepped by borrowing year after year and accumulating public sector debt.

The ultimate explanation of structural gaps is therefore theoretical, not pragmatic. The model outlined above combines theories relating to collective action and property rights. It is able to explain not just why structural gaps exist but also why those gaps are growing over time. In effect, structural gaps in the public finances are the financial symptom of the tragedy of the commons, whilst the private affluence–public squalor syndrome is the modern-day equivalent of that tragedy.

Structural gaps occur irrespective of whether the overall political philosophy of any one country is Libertarian, Neo-Liberal or Collectivist. They can exist irrespective of the levels of public spending and revenues in relation to GDP, there being no threshold of spending above which structural gaps emerge. Nonetheless, the absolute and relative size of any structural gap is likely to be much greater under Collectivist than Libertarian regimes. This is not just because the former requires a much greater and more rapidly increasing level of public finance to secure positive rights. It is also because a Collectivist regime has a much greater impact on property rights, this serving to exacerbate the logic of collective action in leading to a structural gap.

From a Libertarian perspective, structural gaps are the inevitable consequence of any level of state intervention above the minimalist state, which only serves to create dependency cultures and so is self-defeating. From a theoretical perspective, however, this is because the incentives for political mobilisation are enhanced, there being more public expenditure and its associated benefits to be 'captured' by pressure groups, special interest groups, distributional coalitions or whatever the term for self-serving elites.

Given the fairly draconian measures needed to remove a structural gap, prevention is better than cure. If structural gaps are to be avoided, a long-term strategy must be adopted. This requires a strategic long-term approach to public finance, including rolling back the frontiers of the state to core functions, levying charges for public services, political devolution, adoption of the golden rule of public finance and, ultimately, an increasingly Libertarian state.

FURTHER READING

Artis, M. J. and Buti, M. (2000) 'Close to Balance or in Surplus – A Policy Maker's Guide to the Implementation of the Stability and Growth Pact' *Journal of Common Market Studies* vol. 38, no. 4, pp. 563–91.

Balassone, F. and Franco, D. (2000) 'Public Investment, the Stability Pact and the Golden Rule' *Fiscal Studies* vol. 21, no. 2, pp. 207–29.

Borcherding, T. E. (editor) (1977) *Budgets and Bureaucrats: The Sources of Government Growth* (Durham, North Carolina: Duke University Press).

Breton, A. and Wintrobe, R. (1975) 'The Equilibrium Size of a Budget Maximising Bureau: A Note on Niskanen's Theory of Bureaucracy' *Journal of Political Economy* no. 83, pp 195–207.

Brunila, A., Buti, M. and Franco, D. (editors) (2001) *The Stability and Growth Pact – The Architecture of Fiscal Policy in EMU* (Basingstoke: Palgrave – now Palgrave Macmillan).

Downs, A. (1957) *An Economic Theory of Democracy* (New York: Harper & Row).

Downs, A. (1967) *Inside Bureacracy* (Boston: Little, Brown).

Dunleavy, P. (1991) *Democracy, Bureaucracy and Public Choice: Economic Explanations in Political Science* (London: Harvester Wheatsheaf).

Galbraith, J. K. (1967) *The New Industrial State* (Boston: Houghton Mifflin).

Mishra, R. (1999) *Globalization and the Welfare State* (Cheltenham: Edward Elgar).

Mueller, D. C. (2003) *Public Choice III* (third edition) (Cambridge: Cambridge University Press).

Musgrave, P. B. (2002) *Tax Policy in the Global Economy: Selected Essays of Peggy B. Musgrave* (Cheltenham: Edward Elgar).

Niskanen, W. A. (1971) *Bureaucracy and Representative Government* (Chicago: Aldine Atherton).

Niskanen, W. A. (1975) 'Bureaucrats and Politicians' *Journal of Law and Economics* vol. 18, no. 4. pp. 617–43.

Niskanen, W. A. (1991) 'Introduction' in Blais, A. and Dion, S. (editors) *The Budget Maximising Bureaucrat: Appraisals and Evidence* (Pittsburgh: University of Pittsburgh Press).

Niskanen, W. A. (1994) *Bureaucracy and Public Economics* (Cheltenham: Edward Elgar).

Olson, M. (1965) *The Logic of Collective Action* (Cambridge, MA: Harvard University Press).

Olson, M. (1982) *The Rise and Decline of Nations* (New Haven, CT: Yale University Press).

Pennington, M. (2000) *Planning and the Political Market: Public Choice and the Politics of Government Failure* (London: The Athlone Press).

Perotti, R., Strauch, R. and von Hagen, J. (1998) *Sustainability of Public Finances* (London: Centre for Economic Policy Research).

Tullock, G. (1989) *The Economics of Special Privilege and Rent Seeking* (London: Kluwer Academic Press).

Tullock, G. (1993) *Rent Seeking* (Cheltenham: Edward Elgar).

Tullock, G., Seldon, A. and Brady, G. L. (2000) *Government: Whose Obedient Servant? A Primer in Public Choice* (London: Institute of Economic Affairs).

8 Strategic Issues for Local Public Finance

INTRODUCTION

Whilst the foregoing chapters concentrated on an analysis of the totality of public finance, occasional reference was made to local government. In particular, devolution of political decision-making from national to local government was recommended in Chapters 6 and 7 in order to more closely match willingness to pay taxes with decisions about service provision. This accords with the conventional approach to the financing of local governments, which is to consider how financial arrangements can be made consistent with service responsibilities. However, the conventional approach is pragmatic rather than strategic, in simply being concerned with the need to ensure that local governments have sufficient revenues with which to finance their services. In contrast, Chapter 7 recommended a closer matching of public service expenditures with their financing as a way of constraining the emergence of structural gaps arising from the logic of collective action.

Put simply, a strategic approach to the financing of local government seeks, as far as possible, to achieve symmetry between decisions relating to expenditures and revenues. Symmetry is more closely achieved by direct charges for service use than by local taxation. Thus, unlike the pragmatic approach, the strategic approach does not assume that local taxes should be the primary form of public finance for local government. Indeed, the logic of collective action predicts that there will be an inherent tendency for structural gaps to emerge as long as collective financing exists. Whilst practitioners believe that such fiscal stress can be remedied by more taxation, the logic of collective action makes clear that such expectations will ultimately be dashed as structural gaps re-emerge.

More specifically, the conventional approach to the financing of local government fails to recognise the profound multidirectional interdependencies between *structure*, *functions* and *finance*. In other words, the interdependence is not one way from structure and functions to finance. Service responsibilities interact with local government structure and both affect and are affected by financial arrangements. A strategic approach to municipal finance would be to consider simultaneously structure, functions and finance, in order to minimise the requirement for public finance whilst ensuring that local governments can meet their civil, social and economic responsibilities. Adoption of the prag-

223

matic approach seems to result in a general tendency for central and regional governments to finance increasingly greater proportions of local government income, as local governments' service responsibilities increase over time whilst their financial arrangements remain largely unchanged.

True local government only exists when democratically elected bodies have well-defined *discretionary* powers to provide services to their citizens and finance them with the proceeds of one or more exclusive local taxes of which they can determine the base and/or the rate of tax. This means that municipalities can make their own decisions free of control by higher levels of government. Nonetheless, some central and/or regional government finance will almost always be necessary to even out differences in per capita expenditure needs and per capita taxable resources. Moreover, central, federal or regional governments have usually sought to influence the nature and extent of municipal service provision through the payment to local governments of intergovernmental transfers. Nevertheless, the need for such intergovernmental 'subventions' (that is, grants) can be minimised by strategic consideration simultaneously of structure, functions and finance. That is the purpose of this chapter.

STRATEGIC ISSUES FOR LOCAL GOVERNMENT SERVICE RESPONSIBILITIES

Citizens' welfare would not be maximised if everybody received the same nationally determined quantities and qualities of public services, which took no account of variations in preferences between local jurisdictions and the willingness to pay the tax costs of services. The result would be that:

- some people would be forced to pay taxes for services that they either did not want at all or did not want at such high quantities or qualities
- some people would be denied some services completely or be denied higher quantities or qualities of services for which they would be willing to pay additional taxes.

This would lead to the wasteful use of productive resources of local governments in the first group, contrary to strategic economy (see Chapter 1) and inadequate levels of resources in the second group. Hence, efficiency in the allocation of resources ('allocative efficiency') used to provide public services requires local rather than central decisions regarding the provision of public services such as education, health care, leisure and recreation. It also requires local rather than central decisions regarding paying the associated tax costs. Clearly, this has implications for how public services should be financed (that is, whether by central or local taxes).

This allocative efficiency argument underpins the decentralisation principle adopted by the Council of Europe's European Charter of Local Self-Government (Article 4), namely that public responsibilities shall generally be exercised, in preference, by those authorities which are closest to the citizen. In advocating decentralisation of decision-making to the lowest possible level of government, the Council of Europe is referring to the benefits to be gained from expression of voice at the local level (see Chapter 4). Centralised decision-making ignores local voice and therefore can lead to substantial inefficiency in the allocation of resources such as labour and capital.

However, whilst these service responsibilities should be allocated to local rather than central government, this argument does not necessarily require local governments themselves to make direct provision of such services. Instead, they can enable them to be provided by allowing private sector companies to compete for government contracts to provide refuse collection and disposal, municipal rental housing, school education and so on (see Chapter 2). Used wisely, competitive contracting can yield significant cost savings and so reduce the need for local public finance (see Chapter 4).

Local public finance may also be used more effectively by allowing service users greater choice of service provider, as long as that choice determines the allocation of public finance to service providers. This is generally referred to as 'the money follows the user'. This happens automatically when individuals and households decide where to live, in effect choosing between alternative local government jurisdictions. They take with them their tax potential and any capitation-based intergovernmental transfers (that is, central and regional government grants to municipalities). This 'voting with one's feet' is referred to as 'exit' (see Chapter 4). Hence, both expression of voice through democratic processes and the ability to exit local governments facilitate the matching of service provision with citizens' preferences.

Scope for 'voting with one's feet' and individualised choices could also be extended *within* local government by abolishing statutory monopolies. Such liberalisation measures can create competition in the supply of local government services, enabling citizens to choose between alternative suppliers of, for example, education or leisure and recreation facilities. Creating a plurality of providers strengthens the scope for exit and thereby strengthens voice, as long as the public money follows the service user. As noted in Chapter 4, service providers threatened with loss of their budgets can be expected to pay more attention to expression of voice, for example complaints about inadequate service availability and quality.

Liberalisation can be used to create competition only amongst public sector service providers ('internal markets') or to create competition with private sector and voluntary sector providers ('external markets'). For example, voucher schemes can be used to liberalise markets by stimulating exit and voice (see Chapter 9). Local governments can fulfil their service objectives whilst simultaneously creating competition in the provision of services so as to increase citizens' choices. By such means, the budgets of service providers would no longer be guaranteed by the municipality and, in particular, there would be no automatic 'bailing out' of any deficits arising from any inefficiencies of service providers. This financial arrangement would enable local governments to deal with organisational slack (see Chapter 4).

The strategic approach to service responsibilities therefore is that:

■ local (rather than central) government should be made responsible for the provision of services, preferences for which vary substantially amongst local communities, as does willingness to pay the associated tax costs
■ services should therefore be financed predominantly by local (rather than central) governments
■ where preferences do not vary substantially between local jurisdictions, there is no reason why such services should remain a local government responsibility and powerful allocative efficiency and equity arguments why they should not.

An example of the last bullet point is health care when citizens want the same access to hospital services irrespective of where they live. This may be demonstrated by opinion surveys and/or by complaints about there being a 'postcode lottery' as regards availability of medical treatment for specific illnesses, services in some areas not being available at all or only after much longer waiting times than in other areas. In such a case there is no rationale for those particular health care services being a municipal responsibility because willingness to pay (in terms of local taxation) does not vary between local government jurisdictions. Instead, allocative efficiency requires the service to be a national (or perhaps regional) government service. There may, however, be local variations in preferences for other medical services such as convalescent homes.

Clearly, preferences for specific service components must be measured and the degree of any inter-jurisdictional variations considered. However, measurement of preferences using willingness to pay is problematic (see Chapter 2). Thus there may be little objective evidence that preferences for major local government services such as school education do vary significantly between one jurisdiction and another. Indeed, central governments have increasingly seen school (like university) education as a crucial national supply-side policy instrument in improving the skills of the labour force, equalising opportunity for self-improvement and thus promoting social justice. This begs the question as to whether school (secondary, but not necessarily primary or nursery) education should remain a local government responsibility or be taken under the direct control of central (or regional) government. The European Charter clearly adopts decentralisation of decision-making as a matter of democratic principle, emphasising the right of local authorities to act in the interests of their local populations. In some cases, however, democratic principle may have to be qualified by these allocative efficiency considerations.

In summary, local governments' service responsibilities relate to consumption and availability of services, rather than to their production. Hence, they should:

- restrict their service responsibilities to core functions, namely political decision-making
- only take on responsibility for those services that unregulated private sector markets would fail to provide to allocatively efficient or socially acceptable levels
- enable services to be provided by the private sector, for example through public service contracts and voucher schemes.

STRATEGIC ISSUES FOR LOCAL GOVERNMENT SIZE AND STRUCTURE

Decentralisation of decision-making clearly requires local governments to be as small as possible, consistent with avoiding unnecessarily high costs of service provision, that is, where average service costs could be substantially reduced by larger local governments providing higher levels of output. Such economies of scale require larger local governments, whereas decentralisation of decision-making requires smaller ones. Economies of scale are evident in the municipal provision of electricity, gas, water and sewerage services, particularly in their distribution and transmission networks. Average costs can be substantially reduced by spreading the high fixed costs of transmission systems over higher rates of output. The common solution is to establish inter-municipal enterprises for such services.

More generally, it is difficult to measure the trade-off between the potential welfare gains from increased decentralisation and the potential cost advantages arising from economies of scale achievable by larger local governments:

- it is extremely difficult to measure in financial terms the benefits arising from greater decentralisation of decision-making in respect of school education and so on
- the costs of service provision are also often difficult to identify and measure precisely.

There are practical problems in the assignment of overhead costs between services, in the use of esoteric accountancy practices (such as costing the depreciation of assets) and in the valuation of assets such as land and buildings in their most profitable uses (rather than in terms of their present uses). A further difficulty is that most studies of economies of scale are misconstrued because they compare service costs with the population sizes of local authorities, population not being the service output. For example, the output of a school is not numbers of pupils nor even educational attainment in terms of examination results. Instead, that output is 'human capital', broadly defined to mean the acquisition of skills, aptitude, knowledge and analytical abilities necessary to function in the modern economy.

The optimal size of local governments is therefore a trade-off between the benefits of greater decentralisation to allow for diverse local preferences and the possible loss of economies of scale for at least some services. Despite difficulties in assessing the severity of that trade-off, it appears that concern with economies of scale has been predominant, there having been dramatic reductions in the numbers of local authorities in many European countries (see Table 8.1). It would appear that the uncertain benefits of decentralisation of decision-making compared with the clarity of apparently higher costs leads to a general trend towards larger local governments. This in turn has implications for the required levels of public finances. Less public finance will be required to the extent that service costs are reduced through economies of scale.

Despite the sharp reductions in their numbers, local governments remain very small in most countries (see Table 8.2). There may therefore still be considerable scope for further cost reductions through economies of scale. However, the geographic size of municipalities needs to match the areas benefiting from service provision in order that those who benefit from a service bear the local tax costs of financing it. This would ensure the necessary symmetry between decisions relating to expenditures and revenues, referred to in the introduction to this chapter. If *benefit* areas do not match *financing* areas, then either the tax costs of some services may be borne by non-residents (that is, tax costs are 'exported' – by a local sales tax for example) or benefits would 'spill over' municipal boundaries into adjacent areas:

- *Tax exporting* would result in excessive service provision in the benefiting jurisdictions because service costs would effectively be subsidised by non-residents
- *Spillovers* would lead to underprovision of services because those who bear the local tax costs may not wish to finance services benefiting non-residents.

An optimal local jurisdiction is therefore one that matches the geographical spread of benefits with liability to pay local taxes. In general, it would only be possible to match benefit areas with liability to pay if there was a separate local authority for each service. However, European local governments typically provide a broad range of services. Hence, the benefits of some services will inevitably spill over boundaries and benefit citizens in other local authorities, for example metropolitan services such as transport infrastructure and culture. Such spillovers may be accommodated by assigning some service functions to regional or national government, higher education for example. In comparison with higher education, benefit areas for refuse

Table 8.1   Total number of local authorities 1950 and 1992

Country	1950	1992	Change Number	Per cent
Austria	3,999	2,301	–1,698	–42
Belgium	2,699	589ᵃ	–2,080	–78
Bulgaria	2,178ᵇ	255ᵃ	–1,932	–88
Czech Rep.	11,051	6,196ᵃ	–4,855	–44
Denmark	1,387	275	–1,112	–80
Finland	547	460	-87	–16
France	38,814ᶜ	36,763ᵈ	–2,051	–5
Germany¹	24,272	8,077	–16,195	–67
Greece	5,959	5,922	–37	–0.6
Hungary	n.a.	3,109	n.a.	n.a.
Iceland	229	197	–32	–14
Italy	7,781	8,100	+319	+4
Luxembourg	127	118	–9	–7
Malta	n.a.	67	n.a.	n.a.
Netherlands	1,015	647	–368	–36
Norway	744	439	–305	–41
Poland	n.a.	2,459	n.a.	n.a.
Portugal	303	305	+2	+0.7
Slovakia	n.a.	2,467	n.a.	n.a.
Spain	9,214	8,082	–1,132	–12
Sweden	2,281	286	–1,995	–87
Switzerland	3,097	3,021	–76	–2
Turkey	n.a.	2,378	n.a.	n.a.
UK	2,028	484	–1,544	–76

Notes: Reproduced with permission of the Council of Europe
n.a. denotes not available
1: West Germany only: 1950 data for the ex-Soviet East Germany is not available
a: data relate to 1991   c: data relate to 1945
b: data relate to 1949   d: data relate to 1990
Source: Council of Europe (1995)

collection and disposal, municipal housing, leisure, recreation and personal social services will typically be relatively small. Hence, these services should remain local government responsibilities, although their provision could be contracted out to the private and voluntary sectors. In general, the greater the range of municipal services, the more difficult it will be to attain optimal size of local jurisdictions.

In summary, the size and structure of local governments has profound implications for the amount of public finance required to enable services to be provided. This is because size and structure substantially influence the costs of service provision and also the amount of public expenditure necessary to deal

Table 8.2 *Population size of local authorities 1990*

Country	Average population per local authority	Percentage of municipalities by size of population				
		Less than 1,000	1,001– 5,000	5,001– 10,000	10,001– 100,000	Over 100,000
Austria	3,340	25.8	65.7	5.6	2.7	0.2
Belgium	16,960	0.2	17.1	29.0	52.3	1.4
Bulgaria	35,000	0	8.2	21.9	63.6	6.3
Czech Rep.[1]	13,730	79.8	15.9	2.1	2.1	0.1
Denmark	18,760	0	7.0	44.0	47.6	1.4
Finland	10,870	4.9	44.6	26.3	22.9	1.3
France	1,580	77.1	18.1	2.5	2.2	0.1
Germany[2]	4,925	53.6	30.4	7.1	8.4	0.5
Greece	1,700	79.4	17.3	1.3	1.9	0.1
Hungary	3,340	54.3	37.1	4.2	4.1	0.3
Iceland	1,330	83.3	13.2	1.5	1.5	0.5
Italy	7,130	23.9	49.0	14.2	12.2	0.7
Luxembourg	3,210	51.0	41.0	5.0	3.0	0
Malta	5,425	11.0	45.0	28.0	16.0	0
Netherlands	23,200	0.2	11.0	27.6	58.4	2.8
Norway	9,000	3.9	52.4	21.4	21.6	0.7
Poland	15,560	0	27.7	47.3	23.3	1.7
Portugal	32,300	0.3	8.2	25.0	59.0	7.5
Slovakia	1,850	67.7	27.9	1.8	2.5	0.1
Spain	4,930	60.6	25.6	6.4	6.7	0.7
Sweden	30,040	0	3.1	19.2	73.8	3.9
Switzerland	2,210	59.5	31.5	5.3	3.5	0.2
Turkey[3]	23,340	0.1		79.3	17.2	3.4
UK[4]	118,440	n.a.	n.a.	n.a.	n.a.	n.a.

Notes: Reproduced with permission of the Council of Europe

n.a. denotes not available

1. Data for 1/1/91
2. Data relate to all of Germany
3. Data for Turkey cannot be split between 1,001–5,000 and 5,001–10,000
4. All local authorities in the UK have more than 10,000 inhabitants. The average population of local authorities in 1990 was 127,000 in England, 91,620 in Scotland and 75,370 in Wales (Council of Europe 1992). The overall average of 118,440 in 1990 rose to 139,300 in 1995 (Chandler 1996)

Source: Council of Europe (1995)

with problems of allocative efficiency and equity. Whilst smaller local governments can more closely match service provision with local preferences:

- allocative efficiency problems are created by spillovers and tax exporting
- horizontal equity problems are created by substantial differences in the abilities of affluent and poor municipalities to provide socially adequate levels of public services.

Thus, there is also a rationale for larger (rather than smaller) local governments because they:

- achieve economies of scale
- minimise both spillovers and tax exporting
- reduce the need for public finance by bringing together within a single jurisdiction both poor and affluent areas and so reduce the need for public expenditure on financial equalisation (see below).

STRATEGIC ISSUES FOR THE FINANCING OF LOCAL GOVERNMENTS

It is a general economic prescription for efficiency in the allocation of resources that the most efficient means of financing the provision of goods and services is to charge individual consumers and users directly at the point of consumption. In this way, willingness to pay can be matched directly with the provision and use of goods and services whether by organisations in the public or private sectors. There are four resulting benefits:

- the wasteful use of free services is avoided
- individual service users are not deprived of levels of service for which they wish to pay – they can consume as much as they want
- in replacing compulsory tax payments, user-charges would result in the 'money following the user' and so would encourage service providers to respond more to citizens' preferences
- symmetry is achieved in decisions relating to expenditures and revenues and so the problems arising from the logic of collective action are avoided.

In effect, user-charges give citizens the choice not just of whether to use the service or not but also whether to pay for it. Typically, however, governments are worried that many citizens would not have enough income to be able to pay for municipal services such as school education. In principle, ability-to-pay problems can be resolved either by providing cash benefits to the poor through national or regional government social security systems or by local governments directly relating the levels of service charges to the incomes of service users (see Chapter 5). This could be implemented by giving citizens service vouchers, the monetary values of which would be means tested and/or based upon need for service (see Chapter 9). As already noted, wider social benefits leading to market failure can be addressed by the payment of subsidies designed to bring levels of service use up to the economic and social optimum. Such 'allocative efficiency subsidies' can be financed by both local and national taxpayers. Locally financed subsidies are necessary when the

Table 8.3   *Sources of municipal funding (percentages)*

Country	Exclusive local taxes	Fees and charges	Intergovernmental transfers[1]	Borrowing	Other
Albania	3	3	94	0	1
Austria	15	19	35	8	23
Belgium	32	5	40	13	10
Bulgaria	1	10	78	2	9
Cyprus	25	33	30	12	0
Czech Rep.	16	12	45	11	16
Denmark	51	22	24	2	1
Estonia[2]	0	1	91	2	6
Finland	34	11	31	3	21
France	36	2	26	10	26
Germany	19	16	45	9	11
Greece	2	22	58	6	12
Hungary	4	8	66	4	18
Iceland	12	16	53	5	14
Ireland	18	10	57	2	13
Italy	18	11	38	9	24
Latvia	6	1	68	0	25
Luxembourg	31	29	37	3	0
Malta	0	0	98	0	2
Netherlands	5	13	60	19	3
Norway	42	16	33	7	2
Poland	21	7	60	0	12
Portugal	20	19	38	6	17
Romania	5	16	79	0	0
San Marino	0	0	31	69	0
Slovakia	10	9	39	5	37
Slovenia	5	9	67	1	18
Spain	31	16	37	10	6
Sweden	61	8	19	1	11
Switzerland	46	24	18	3	9
Turkey	7	1	56	0	36
United Kingdom	11	6	77	0	6

Notes: Reproduced with permission of the Council of Europe
1. Intergovernmental transfers include shared taxes and grants (see Table 8.5)
2. Estonian municipalities raised 0.1 per cent of their funding from exclusive local taxes
   Funding sources may not total to 100 due to rounding

Source: Council of Europe (1997)

local community benefits as well as the individual service user. Nationally/ regionally financed subsidies are necessary when the benefits of service provision extend beyond a local government's boundaries (that is, when spillovers occur).

Hence, there are both efficiency and equity rationales for the subsidisation of service provision. Nevertheless, the matching of payment for and benefit from services means that charges should be the primary means of financing the provision of local government services. This is in direct contradiction of the conventional view that charges are a last resort when local taxes and intergovernmental grants are insufficient to cover a municipality's expenditures. Ultimately, achievement of efficiency in the allocation of resources is predicated upon consumer sovereignty ensuring that the provision of service outputs and the benefits derived from them match willingness to pay, ability to pay being ensured through concessions/exemptions, service vouchers or national social security systems.

Acceptance of the principle of consumer sovereignty means that only where absolutely necessary should ability-to-pay subsidies and allocative efficiency subsidies be used to allow willingness to pay to be expressed. In practice, however, charges are almost invariably the smallest source of local finance, as shown by Table 8.3. In general, fees and charges account for a relatively low proportion of funding, no more than a tenth in 16 of the 32 countries listed.

Allocative efficiency subsidies should be financed mainly by *local* taxation for those services whose wider social benefits are focused primarily on the local community, for example refuse collection and disposal, water and sewerage, local transport and care of elderly citizens. However, local taxes should only finance a relatively small share of the costs of local services when benefits to the individual service user are greater than the benefits to the local community. This may be the case in respect of use of sports facilities, for example. National/regional taxes should only be used to support services providing significant national/regional benefits spilling over local governments' boundaries, school and vocational education for example. In general, the degree of financial support for service use should be directly proportional to the wider social benefits generated.

In fact, the more efficient arrangement for sub-regional spillovers is for the adjacent municipalities (rather than central/regional government) to pay subsidies to central cities in support of the services generating spillovers from which they benefit. However, such municipalities are usually under no compulsion to pay such subsidies and so rarely do so. Such disparities between expenditure needs and local taxable resources may lead central governments to introduce financial equalisation measures (see below).

Notwithstanding any need for financial equalisation, the means of financing an allocatively efficient level of local government services in order of priority is charges, local taxes and national taxes. In general, however, transfers from central to local government (that is, shared taxes and intergovernmental grants) were the largest component of municipal funding in Europe in the mid-1990s (Table 8.3). Transfers accounted for two-thirds or more of municipal funding in nine European countries and between half and two-thirds in a further six. These proportions are probably greatly in excess of those which could be justified in terms of spillovers and/or by equalisation payments to local governments with relatively high expenditure needs per capita and relatively low taxable resources per capita.

Exclusive local taxes (that is, those controlled solely by local governments) accounted for over half of municipal funding in only two countries, compared with less than 20 per cent in 20 countries (Table 8.3). The two most common taxes are property taxes, levied on both residential and business properties (used by three-quarters of the countries listed in Table 8.3) and personal income taxes (used by two-fifths of those countries). Local sales taxes and local taxes on business incomes are sometimes used but are really only feasible at regional government level. If there are substantial variations in the levels of such taxes raised locally, people and businesses may migrate from high-tax to low-tax authorities, or choose not to locate in the former in the first place (see Chapter 6).

This is also the reason why local governments should not undertake highly redistributive policies because poorer socioeconomic groups would tend to move in simultaneously with the out-migration of affluent groups. The local per capita tax base would be seriously eroded as both businesses and affluent groups out-migrated and a structural gap would open up in the local public finances. Local governments losing affluent populations and businesses would become increasingly unable to raise sufficient finance from their local taxes to provide services for which demand was increasing as a result of an increasingly service-dependent population. Ultimately, central and/or regional governments would have to pay increasing amounts of public finance to such local governments.

In general, therefore, local governments should tax bases that:

- have low mobility
- are not heavily redistributive
- are evenly distributed across the country
- rise in line with service costs so tax revenues rise without having to raise the tax rate.

This would facilitate stability in the local public finances and so minimise the need for financial assistance from central or regional government.

STRATEGIC ISSUES FOR THE CONTROL OF LOCAL GOVERNMENT SPENDING

If the above strategic arrangements for local government structure, functions and finance are put into practice, the need for central government control of local government spending is substantially reduced. Local government *capital expenditures* are almost always controlled for macroeconomic purposes because of the potential impacts of borrowing (used to finance those expenditures). In particular, high levels of government borrowing and debt may lead to higher interest rates and/or inflation with potentially undesirable consequences for the national economy (see Chapter 6). The need for central control can therefore be minimised as long as borrowing is used only to finance capital (rather than current) expenditures. This is the golden rule of public finance (see Chapter 3).

In addition, however, central governments may wish to control total local government expenditure for macroeconomic purposes. Macroeconomic control requires only control of *aggregate* local expenditures. There should be no need for central or regional governments to directly control the spending of *individual* local authorities. Individual local authorities only have to be centrally controlled if there is a serious 'democratic deficit' in terms of a lack of local accountability and/or a serious 'efficiency deficit' in terms of a lack of any incentive to control costs. A democratic deficit is particularly likely to be the case if individual local authorities are dominated by the same political party over very long periods, especially if it is the result of low voter turnout under first-past-the-post electoral systems. In such cases, a minority of citizens effectively determines the levels of local government expenditures and taxes. An efficiency deficit is particularly likely to be the case if local governments are monopoly providers of services to their citizens.

However, the solution to these problems is to introduce measures to increase local accountability and efficiency rather than impose central control, the latter clearly being contrary to decentralisation of decision-making. Thus:

- local governments should be given buoyant exclusive local taxes which, combined with user-charges, make local governments predominantly self-financing
- central and regional governments should limit their use of intergovernmental transfers to the minimum amount necessary for dealing with spillovers and financial equalisation
- the need for such transfers can be minimised by adjusting the size, structure and functions of local governments (as well as by giving them buoyant autonomous local taxes).

In general, however, central governments find it easier to pay greater intergovernmental transfers and impose greater central control than to strategically strengthen local public finances.

STRATEGIC ISSUES FOR CENTRAL FINANCING OF LOCAL GOVERNMENTS

It was argued above that some central finance may be required to encourage local government provision of services generating substantial spillovers. Central finance will also be required for financial equalisation purposes. 'Financial (fiscal) equalisation' refers to intergovernmental grants designed to compensate local governments for relatively high per capita expenditure needs, relatively low per capita taxable resources, or relatively high unavoidable costs of service provision. Not all countries have financial equalisation schemes and, of those that do, not all seek equalisation of all three characteristics. Equalisation of differing per capita taxable resources is the most common form of fiscal equalisation.

Variations in the abilities of local governments to raise local tax revenues per head of population largely reflect the uneven distribution of economic activity, some municipalities having relatively large business sectors. Central governments may therefore pay 'resource-equalising grants' to local governments with relatively low per capita tax bases. Differences in the need to spend per head of population reflect differences between local governments in their demographic, socioeconomic, geographic and other structures. For example, even if all municipalities incurred the same school expenditure per pupil, those with relatively high proportions of children of school age in their populations would spend more per head of total population than municipalities with relatively low proportions of that age group. Such differences in per capita expenditure needs can be compensated by payment of central government grants. Amongst the member states of the Council of Europe, the most commonly used objective criteria to assess payment of 'needs-equalising grants' are total resident population, its age structure (children, elderly and so on), its client structure (school pupils, ethnic groups, the unemployed and so on) and structural features (geographic size, length of road network and so on).

Without financial equalisation, inequalities in the abilities of local governments to raise revenues and inequalities in their need to spend, each per head of population, may result in severe fiscal stress. This occurs when high per capita expenditure needs combine with low local taxable resources per capita, resulting in high tax rates simultaneously with inadequate quantities and/or qualities of services. This outcome may be unacceptable to central governments for five reasons:

1. It creates horizontal inequity in that people in similar circumstances living in *different* local governments will have to pay differing amounts of local tax for the same standard of service
2. The horizontal and vertical incquities of the local government tax *within* a given jurisdiction will be exacerbated by very high tax levels, especially for taxes not directly related to ability to pay (for example a property tax)
3. High local tax levels could restrain local expenditures so much that spillover effects from services also benefiting other local authorities are lost
4. The local welfare state could collapse in municipalities experiencing severe fiscal stress

5. Central governments may be trying to restore the local economies of cities with adverse industrial structures, on the grounds of both equity and efficiency. High levels of local taxation may lead to cumulative decline (fiscal stress syndrome) as selective out-migration of population and out-migration of business activity occurs, leaving behind an increasingly multiply-deprived population unable to finance adequate services.

There are two alternative systems of financial equalisation:

1. the *Robin Hood system*, whereby more affluent authorities (with low expenditure needs and high taxable resources per capita) finance horizontal transfers to poorer authorities (with high expenditure needs and low taxable resources per capita) to equalise service provision across municipalities and so promote horizontal equity
2. the *levelling-up system*, whereby national (or regional) governments pay grants to bring poorer authorities up to either the national (or regional) average municipal fiscal position or to the level of the richest/lowest expenditure need per capita municipality.

In unitary states, levelling up to the national average is more common than levelling up to the most prosperous authority, simply because the latter is much more expensive in terms of public finance. The Robin Hood system of financial equalisation requires the least additional public finance because it creates 'losers' (that is, municipalities giving finance to other authorities) whereas the levelling-up system creates only 'gainers' (that is, municipalities receiving grants from central government). The latter therefore requires more public finance for a given level of equalisation. Nevertheless, the Robin Hood system is much less common than levelling up, precisely because it creates 'losers' and so is generally not politically acceptable.

In fact, the nature and extent of financial equalisation is crucially dependent upon the constitutional position of local government, the relative role of local government in society and economy, the ways in which it is financed, and the legacy of history. For example, Tables 8.1 and 8.2 demonstrate that, in the longer term, a probably substantial degree of (implicit) equalisation has already been achieved simply by creating fewer larger local authorities, especially in Belgium, Bulgaria, Denmark, Sweden and the UK. As a general rule, greater geographic coverage of local authority boundaries can be expected to have combined areas of differing per capita taxable capacities and expenditure needs, especially in urbanised areas. Explicit equalisation measures will generally be more feasible the smaller the disparities between a lesser number of local authorities because any required grant payments will be minimised. Ultimately, therefore, there may be a trade-off between a greater degree of decentralised decision-making and the feasibility of measures to promote greater horizontal equity between local governments.

Table 8.4 makes clear that Sweden differs markedly from other countries in terms of the relatively large proportion of municipal spending in the national economy and that local government spending also accounts for a relatively high proportion within the totality of government spending. Equalisation of per capita spending needs and taxable resources in Sweden therefore has a more profound effect on living standards than in countries such as

Table 8.4 *Municipal expenditure relative to GDP and GGE*

Country	Year	Percentage of GDP	Percentage of GGE
Albania	1995	7.7	25.4
Austria	1993	12.7	20.2
Belgium	1993	4.9	10.9
Bulgaria	1994	9.0	20.0
Cyprus	1993	1.4	4.1
Czech Rep.	1994	9.3	20.9
Denmark	1994	19.9	31.3
Estonia	1994	7.1	17.6
Finland	1993	18.0	29.5
France	1992	5.5	27.2
Germany	1993	8.1	28.7
Greece	1989	3.3	5.6
Hungary	1994	17.0	53.0
Iceland	1994	9.1	22.3
Ireland	1994	4.9	13.8
Italy	1993	7.0	13.0
Latvia	1994	12.5	24.0
Lithuania	1993	13.1	58.8
Luxembourg	1993	9.9	32.3
Malta	1995	0.3	0.6
Netherlands	1994	13.3	23.1
Norway	1994	18.9	60.0
Poland	1994	7.0	21.6
Portugal	1993	4.6	9.7
Romania	1993	3.5	16.9
San Marino	1993	0.1	0.2
Slovakia	1994	4.8	11.8
Slovenia	1995	4.4	10.1
Spain	1994	4.9	12.2
Sweden	1994	27.5	38.0
Switzerland	1993	10.8	27.9
Turkey	1992	2.4	12.3
United Kingdom	1994	11.0	27.0

Notes: Reproduced with permission of the Council of Europe
GDP denotes gross domestic product; GGE denotes general government expenditure
Source: Council of Europe (1997)

Table 8.5 *Intergovernmental transfers[1] (percentages of total municipal resources)*

Country	Shared taxes	General grants	Earmarked grants[2]	Other
Albania	1	59	29	5
Austria	26	1	0	8
Belgium	0	25	5	10
Bulgaria	34	37	7	0
Cyprus	0	7	22	1
Czech Rep.	23	8	10	4
Denmark	2	12	0	11
Estonia	60	27	4	0
Finland	1	28	1	0
France	0	24	0	2
Germany	17	15	13	0
Greece	25	25	0	8
Hungary	7	52	5	2
Iceland	43	7	1	2
Ireland	0	11	46	0
Italy	2	8	24	5
Latvia	23	35	6	3
Luxembourg	24	2	0	11
Malta	0	91	0	7
Netherlands	0	20	38	3
Norway	0	17	14	2
Poland	23	15	22	0
Portugal	1	31	4	2
Romania	33	25	21	0
San Marino	0	31	0	0
Slovakia	30	1	8	0
Spain	0	8	29	0
Sweden	0	11	8	0
Switzerland	1	3	14	0
Turkey	3	0	3	51
United Kingdom	17	32	27	0

Notes: Reproduced with permission of the Council of Europe
1. For the relative importance of all transfers in municipal funding see Table 8.3
2. Also known as specific grants
Source: Council of Europe (1997)

France, Germany, Italy and the UK, local government accounting for much lower proportions of GDP.

Despite the relatively high proportion of local government spending in Sweden, intergovernmental grants form a relatively low proportion of municipal funding (Table 8.3). In contrast, local authorities in the UK are heavily dependent upon intergovernmental transfers – much more so than Germany

and France, for example, even though municipal expenditures are similar proportions of general government expenditure (Table 8.4). This reflects the very
low proportion of municipal funding derived from exclusive local taxation in
the UK. In effect, most explicit equalisation in the UK is achieved by the central government taxes used to finance central grants that finance over three-
quarters of municipal expenditure (Table 8.3).

However, equalisation of local per capita taxes in the UK is necessarily
much less effective for its property tax than for Sweden's local income tax
when considered in terms of broader socioeconomic factors – rather than in
terms of the much narrower objectives of financial equalisation regimes.
Local governments in France, Germany and Italy have a much broader tax
base that, besides property, also includes taxes on goods and services, incomes
and profits. In turn, however, the broader tax base in these three countries
makes equalisation much more problematic. Equalisation is clearly more
straightforward in Sweden and the UK given their single local taxes.

The general conclusion drawn from the above analysis is that the more
restricted the local tax base and the greater the dependence upon local taxes
not related to incomes, the greater therefore the dependence upon intergovernmental transfers. Table 8.3 shows that the UK has a relatively low share of
exclusive local taxes within municipal funding and Sweden the highest. The
UK, like Sweden, has a very small number of very large local authorities
(Tables 8.1 and 8.2), such that the most severe inequalities in per capita taxable resources and expenditure needs have probably been overcome by
boundary adjustments. Therefore the clear message is that intergovernmental
grants in the UK are compensating for an inadequate local tax base more than
they are compensating for horizontal inequities amongst local authorities.

Table 8.5 provides a breakdown of the data in Table 8.3 relating to intergovernmental transfers and demonstrates that in most countries they are probably much greater than strictly necessary for equalisation purposes and
subsidising spillovers. This is because of the high proportions of shared taxes
and earmarked grants within total transfers, neither being suitable for equalisation purposes. In combination, shared taxes and earmarked grants are
greater than general grants in 18 of the 31 countries. However, general grants
are the most effective means of implementing equalisation because they are
not tied to specific services and so can be distributed to offset differences in
per capita local taxable resources and expenditure needs. Nevertheless, this
does not mean that a country with a high proportion of general grants within
municipal funding necessarily achieves a high degree of equalisation. For
example, general grants account for almost a third of municipal resources in
the UK (Table 8.5) but the largest proportion of the UK general grants is paid
as a lump sum per head of population. Similarly, whilst general grants are a
greater proportion of municipal resources in France than in Sweden, the
Swedish system of intergovernmental transfers achieves a much greater
degree of financial equalisation. This is because Sweden uses a Robin Hood

system whereas France's main state grant to municipalities is almost wholly a flat rate of grant per head of population. This indicates that a high proportion of general grants within total municipal resources is a necessary but not sufficient condition for a high degree of equalisation.

In summary, the need for public finance for financial equalisation can be minimised by:

■ reforms to local government size and structure designed, as far as possible, to minimise fiscal disparities in taxable resources and expenditure needs per capita by combining rich and poor suburbs into single-city municipalities
■ eliminate any remaining fiscal disparities by means of a Robin Hood system of financial equalisation.

These strategic reforms minimise the public expenditure costs of the desired degree of equalisation. However, care should be taken not compromise the decentralisation principle of the European Charter.

CONCLUSIONS

Putting these strategic principles into practice does not necessarily require that all countries adopt the exactly the same local government structures, functions and financing arrangements. This is because economic, technological, social, cultural, democratic and other relevant factors vary from country to country – and even amongst regions within any one country. These factors affect the scope for both the articulation of demand for, and the organisation of supply of, individual local government services. In particular, the scope for exit and voice differ in reflection of differing constitutional, cultural and other contexts amongst and within countries. Likewise, the diversity of potential supply arrangements reflects the capacities of both the public and private sectors within particular countries (or regions within any one country) and so restrict or facilitate the securing of economies of scale.

Nonetheless, a set of public finance prescriptions can be derived from consideration of these strategic issues:

■ local governments in any one country should seek (as a group) to reduce their dependence on central finances by making the case for their own exclusive local taxes in place of shared taxes and intergovernmental grants
■ they must demonstrate convincingly that they have democratic legitimacy by continually seeking to secure a high level of citizen participation in democratic procedures
■ they must be able to demonstrate that their services are provided efficiently so that value for money is achieved and unnecessarily high costs avoided

- they should 'steer rather than row', enabling services to be provided by a plurality of competitive providers instead of relying on direct provision
- local governments should consider how to introduce greater scope for exit and voice, where feasible creating internal or external markets for service contracts and/or promoting efficiency and choice through voucher schemes (see Chapter 9) and so on
- whilst recognising the equity and efficiency cases for subsidy and taking account of any legal constraints, local governments should make much greater use of user-charges, regarding them as the primary (rather than the residual) source of their finance
- they should argue that central and regional government grants should only be paid to finance services providing substantial spillover benefits and to compensate municipalities for relatively low locally taxable resources per capita and/or relatively high expenditure needs per capita
- ideally, they should argue the case for their own Robin Hood systems of equalisation and appropriate reforms to local government size and structure in order to reduce dependence upon central grants.

FURTHER READING

Bahl, R. (2003) (editor) *Restructuring Local Government Finance in Developing Countries: Lessons from South Africa* (Cheltenham: Edward Elgar).

Bailey, S. J. (1999) *Local Government Economics: Principles and Practice* (Basingstoke: Macmillan – now Palgrave Macmillan).

Bailey, S. J. (2003) 'More Tinkering with Local Government Finance' *Local Government Studies* vol. 29, no. 1, pp. 17–32.

Dafflon, B. (2002) (editor) *Local Public Finance in Europe: Balancing the Budget and Controlling Debt* (Cheltenham: Edward Elgar).

Gidlund, J. and Jerneck, M. (2000) (editors) *Local and Regional Governance in Europe: Evidence from Nordic Countries* (Cheltenham: Edward Elgar).

REFERENCES

Chandler, J. A. (1996) *Local Government Today* (2nd edition) (Manchester: Manchester University Press).

Council of Europe (1992) *Decentralisation and the Strengthening of Local Self-Government*, Local and Regional Authorities in Europe, no. 48 (Strasbourg: Council of Europe).

Council of Europe (1995) *The Size of Municipalities, Efficiency and Citizen Participation*, Local and Regional Authorities in Europe, no. 56 (Strasbourg: Council of Europe).

Council of Europe (1997) *Local Finance in Europe*, Local and Regional Authorities in Europe, no. 61 (Strasbourg: Council of Europe).

Sjoquist, D. L. (2003) (editor) *State and Local Finances under Pressure* (Cheltenham: Edward Elgar).

9 Vouchers as an Alternative Public Service Funding System

INTRODUCTION

Reference to vouchers has been made in earlier chapters. Chapter 4 noted that vouchers can be used to distribute public finance amongst alternative service providers in direct proportion to users of their service outputs, facilitating exit and voice on the part of service users and providing incentives to reduce organisational slack on the part of service providers. This chapter provides a comprehensive overview of the literature on vouchers, bringing together many of the key concepts developed in earlier chapters. Within the literature (referenced in text) the term 'voucher' is subject to some indeterminacy and so it is necessary to consider alternative definitions.

A voucher has been defined as 'a token that may be exchanged for goods or services' (Lamming and Bessant 1988, page 218; OECD 1998, page 3); as 'paper given instead of money' (Collin, Weiland and Dohn 1990, page 295); as 'a document that controls and/or separates expenditures by authorizing and/or recording them separately' (Nisberg 1988, page 296); and as 'a state benefit tied to a specific defined purchase, the financing of which comes from a source other than where the actual purchase takes place' (Glennerster 1992, page 9).

These definitions emphasise the the holder's purchasing power and ability to consume and acquire service(s). The subsequent analysis demonstrates their narrowness and is used to derive a better understanding of the voucher concept. It attempts to develop a new, fully comprehensive, generic definition of vouchers from which a definition of public service vouchers can be derived. In so doing, this chapter attempts to clarify the diversity of voucher schemes, such a 'clarification of concept' being necessary before attempting to assess the success of individual voucher schemes. Such assessment is not the subject of this chapter.

Whilst their introduction usually requires legislative reform or some other act of approval by the state, the potential use of vouchers to allocate public services is enormous. Savas (1987, pages 93–4) argues that vouchers can be used to distribute all goods and services except those which are purely collective. Non-collective or private goods (and services) are excludable and rival in use (for example a municipal tennis court). Collective or pure public goods (and services) are non-excludable and non-rival in use, the service benefits everyone simultaneously and no one can be prevented from benefiting (for example municipal environmental health services). The financing of collective goods (pure public goods) can be based only on tax income, because nobody can be excluded from using them and so payment (by money and/or voucher) cannot be enforced (see Chapter 2). Hence, private goods are the most suitable goods for distribution through vouchers because payment can be enforced at the point of use of service.

Only a small number of local government services are pure public goods. Such services as schooling, personal social services and culture and leisure services are private goods, because a person can be prevented from consuming them and rivalness in use is present. They may have significant and positive social effects, but they are still private goods – which is why they can also be distributed through vouchers. The examples of vouchers in this chapter are all private goods because they are excludable and rival in use.

AN EMPIRICAL TYPOLOGY OF VOUCHERS

Vouchers are not restricted to public services: they are also used in the private sector (see Figure 9.1). In the private sector, 'cash vouchers' are sometimes given to the purchaser of a product or service of certain value. They can be exchanged for cash when purchasing another product within a limited period of time. 'Gift vouchers' can, in turn, be exchanged for goods or services supplied by a particular store. 'Luncheon vouchers' are provided by some employers to their employees and can be used to purchase meals at participating food outlets.

Public sector vouchers can be divided into three different categories:

1. *Privatisation vouchers:* given to the public free of charge or for a registration fee (in some East European countries). With these vouchers, citizens have been able to buy stocks in the privatised companies. Alternatively, they have been able to entrust their vouchers to unit trusts (Uvalic and Vaughan-Whitehead 1997, pages 2–4).

2. *Employment vouchers:* help get people into work by subsidising work or training.
   - *Job vouchers.* When a job seeker qualifying for a voucher finds a job, the state pays the employer financial support that covers part of the salary costs (say for a maximum of one year). Objectives are to familiarise those entering the labour market with working life, to help the unemployed maintain their professional skills and their ability to work, and to make households more independent of state income support by subsidising the salary of the previously unemployed head of household. The payment for work consists of two elements: the work voucher paid to the employee by the state and the so-called 'excess share' for which the employers are themselves responsible (Rönkkö 1999, pages 24–5).

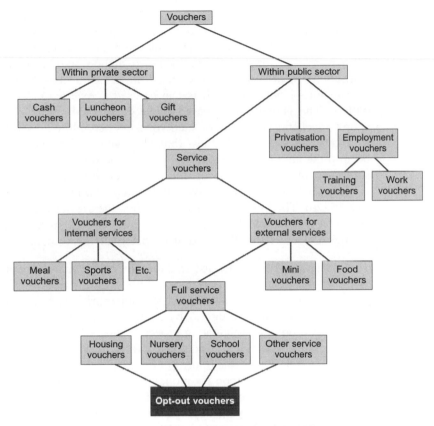

Figure 9.1 Vouchers in the private and public sectors

■ *Training vouchers.* These vouchers are used to cover all or a share of the fixed and variable costs of training. For example, they could be used to enable university and college students look for a trainee position in private sector companies, either as part of their studies or after graduating (Becker and Becker 1997, page 84). Likewise they can finance training of the unemployed to improve their chances of finding jobs.

3. ***Service vouchers:*** used to support consumption of specific internal and external services.

   (a) *Internal service vouchers* – given to employees by their employer for use of in-house facilities:
      ■ *Sports vouchers.* Some municipalities give sports vouchers to their staff to help them maintain their physical well-being. The human resource management (HRM) rationale is that this increases employees' productivity, reducing absenteeism and sick leave. The

vouchers may be valid only in specified sports facilities or for particular activities or times of use. If the service is more expensive than the value of the voucher, the employee pays the remainder.

■ *Meal vouchers.* Some municipalities also support staff meals by distributing meal vouchers, to be used in staff canteens (the private sector's luncheon vouchers can be used at external catering outlets). This is presumably based on the same HRM rationale for sports vouchers. The value of such vouchers may ultimately lead to wages and salaries being less than they would otherwise have been in the absence of vouchers, either by the full cash value or some part of it. In such cases, the net effective additionality of vouchers is less than their gross additionality, and in the extreme case is zero. The lower the net additionality, the greater the influence of the (municipal) state on how its employees spend their salaries – whether for HRM and/or for paternalistic reasons.

(b) *External service vouchers* – for use in either the public and/or private sectors:

■ *Food vouchers* are given to poor and underprivileged people (sometimes including refugees) by social welfare workers. The holder buys food in participating grocery shops. Change may not necessarily be given if the purchased food items do not fully exhaust the monetary value of the voucher. After the purchase, the shop exchanges the coupon for money through the social welfare office. These food vouchers differ from meals vouchers in that they are meant for buying unprepared food rather than catering services (Savas 1987, pages 113–14).

■ *Mini-vouchers* afford holders additional levels of service. For example, all pupils could be offered the basic level of schooling but for further studies, such as supplementary courses and ancillary educational services, pupils could, with their mini-vouchers, select courses from the private or public sectors according to their individual preferences (Levin 1997, pages 38–9).

(c) *Full service vouchers* differ from mini-vouchers in that they entitle the holder to the full public service. They include:

■ *Housing vouchers* – used in the USA in particular, the policy goal being to support those facing the worst housing conditions and the greatest rent burden (OECD 1993, page 50).

■ *Nursery vouchers* – used to stimulate the supply of daycare for preschool children. They have recently been experimented with in the UK (but subsequently abandoned) and in Finland, where they were subsequently introduced permanently in most municipalities that participated in the 1995–97 experiment (Heikkilä et al. 1997, page 121).

■ *Home help and nursing vouchers* – used in old people's home-help services and in home nursing. Elderly people can usually choose between private and public services. The old person is usually him/herself the voucher, because there are no actual coupons but the municipality pays the care costs. Elderly people can usually buy additional services at their own expense.

■ *Taxi vouchers.* Handicapped and elderly people who fulfil the required criteria could be given transport support in the form of taxi vouchers. A person using a taxi voucher would pay a standard fixed cost (equivalent, say, to the cost of local public transport), after which the remaining part can be paid with a voucher. After the trip, the taxi driver invoices the municipality for the value of the voucher. The taxi voucher is not valid for other means of transport.

■ *Health service vouchers.* Voucher-like support systems can be used for rehabilitation services and to provide medical aid equipment. Municipalities could require producers of rehabilitation services and medical aid equipment to compete with each other. They then select the least expensive service producers to participate in the scheme. The municipality pays the cost of services for the people who need them, each individual service user choosing the most appropriate eligible service producer for his or her needs. In this two-stage quasi-market, the municipality makes service producers compete for the right to produce the service but the service user determines the competitive outcome. This arrangement allows municipalities to regulate the market in terms of maximum cost and minimum (medically assessed/objec tive) quality criteria, whilst still allowing each service user a degree of choice in terms of personal/subjective quality when making his/her final choice. Hence, vouchers can combine both professional and layperson's judgement in attributing value-added to services.

■ *Arts vouchers* are sometimes given to low-income groups to stimulate their attendance at museums and galleries. This assumes that they are easily deterred by an admission charge.

■ *School vouchers* exist in implicit form where parents have free choice of school for their children and schools receive state support in proportion to the number of pupils they educate. With these vouchers, parents 'purchase' education for their children in any approved institution run either by profit-making or non-profit bodies. Education vouchers were proposed several centuries ago by Adam Smith in *The Wealth of Nations* (1776), Thomas Paine in *The Rights of Man* (1791) and, more recently, Friedman 1962, Maynard 1975, Blaug 1984, Ahonen 1994 and Cohn 1997.

Any or all of the full service vouchers listed above may allow (or indeed require) holders to use their own financial resources to supplement (top up) the value of the voucher in order to purchase services (Suomen 1994, page 4; Heikkilä et al. 1997, page 40). This is particularly the case for:

- *Opt-out vouchers* which allow service users to choose private services instead of public services (for example for home helps, nursing or medical services). Private health care services are generally more expensive, but the queues are usually shorter. If a patient does not want to be on a long waiting list, he/she could ask the municipality for a voucher, the value of which would be equal to the expense of treatment in public health care. The patient could then supplement the voucher's value with his/her own money in order to get faster treatment in the private sector. Such an arrangement allows service users greater choice in terms of speed of service, and their top-up payments could be used to increase health service capacity in the private sector – but not in the public sector (which must still pay its 'share' of costs). The possibility of 'queue jumping' by those with greater ability to pay (as distinct from greater medical need) arises because the top-up payments pre-empt public funds. Here, people of equal or greater medical need but unable to pay a top-up charge are made to wait longer for the public service (possibly leading to a deterioration in their medical condition) than those with higher incomes. This may be regarded as unethical. Moreover, the greater the use of the opt-out facility, the more individualised choice overrides central planning of health services.

A CONCEPTUAL TYPOLOGY OF VOUCHERS

A conceptual typology of vouchers can be drawn from the above empirical typology (see Figure 9.2). It encompasses both the definitions of vouchers in the introduction and the more comprehensive definition developed below.

The nature of vouchers

There are three basic forms:

1. *Birthright vouchers*. Such vouchers are distributed to those who are registered citizens but not to temporary residents or immigrants (at least those not yet granted nationality), for example privatisation vouchers.
2. *Compensation vouchers*. These vouchers are distributed to those judged to be in need of a public service (for example hospital treatment) but to whom access to that service is denied because of a shortage of supply or other such capacity constraint. Such vouchers can be used to access comparable (for example medical) services in the private and/or voluntary sector and

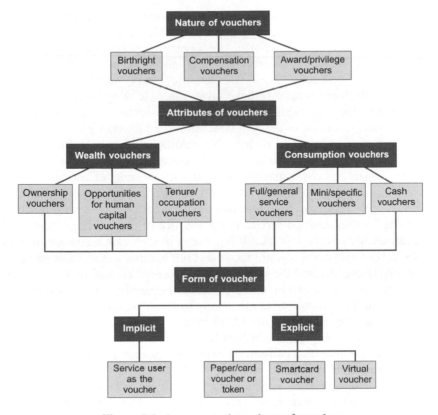

Figure 9.2 A conceptual typology of vouchers

so compensate the holder for lack (or poor quality) of public supply. Opt-out vouchers may effectively act as compensation vouchers. Internal service vouchers, luncheon and meals vouchers may be intended (at least in part) to compensate employees for relatively low wages and salaries.

3. *Award/privilege vouchers.* This category of voucher is allocated neither as compensation nor as a birthright. Instead, such vouchers confer privileges on their holders, examples being higher education vouchers (perhaps means tested) and employment vouchers (perhaps based on length of unemployment or lack of skills). Private sector gift vouchers fall into this category.

Attributes of vouchers

There are two distinct categories:

1. *Consumption vouchers.* This type of voucher increases the recipient's consumption possibilities either generally (that is, cash vouchers) or specifi-

cally in respect of a particular good (for example gift and luncheon/food vouchers) or service (that is, service vouchers). However, consumption vouchers do not necessarily achieve 100 per cent net additionality (that is, where the increase in consumption equals the value of the voucher – see Chapter 4). For example, cash vouchers may simply substitute for expenditure that would otherwise have taken place, leading to an increase in savings by their recipients. Net additionality is zero if the increase in savings equals the value of the cash voucher. Net additionality is 100 per cent if there is no increase in savings. Net additionality is between zero and 100 per cent if the increase in savings is less than the value of the voucher. Even service vouchers may not achieve 100 per cent net additionality of service consumption. They may divert to other public and private sector goods and services expenditure that would otherwise have been incurred on the voucher-assisted service in the absence of that voucher. Whilst net additionality will be less than 100 per cent in such cases, consumption of the service will normally still increase, both because the voucher makes it relatively cheaper and the increase in real income created by the voucher can be expected to lead to increased demand generally. Most consumption voucher schemes' objectives are merely to stimulate consumption without referring to the concept of net additionality.

2. *Wealth vouchers.* Wealth vouchers lead to direct or indirect increases in the wealth (rather than consumption) of the recipient. Privatisation vouchers increase the recipient's wealth directly in terms of giving the holder ownership of a share of the value of a capital asset or business (that is, full property rights). Vouchers may also give holders rights of tenure, occupation or other such use of capital assets without conferring ownership. Examples are vouchers for use of land or property conferring usufruct (see Chapter 2). In this case they confer only limited (not full) property rights. Employment and training vouchers increase the recipient's wealth indirectly by allowing the holder to accumulate human capital in terms of acquired skills and work experience.

Form of vouchers

■ *Explicit vouchers.* These have physical form, traditionally resembling banknotes, coupons or cards on which marks are made, or from which parts are detached, as the voucher's value is used. More recently, plastic cards have been used as vouchers, carrying information on a magnetic strip about the holder and his or her eligibility for subsidy. The electronic chip in modern 'smartcards' can carry much more information, allowing information to be inputted and processed, for example about the frequency, location and type of use of services. Ultimately, physical cards may be replaced by virtual vouchers using personal identification numbers (PINs) and information networks to distribute service rights.

■ *Implicit vouchers.* In this case the beneficiary is effectively the voucher. This is the case for consumption vouchers conferring right of access to public services (for example school education or health care) where 'the money follows the user' without an explicit paper or card voucher being used. Wealth vouchers are likewise implicit where trainees are sent on training schemes by a public sector agency without using physical vouchers.

These conceptual categories are not necessarily mutually exclusive. For example, training vouchers increase the lifetime earnings potential of their recipients leading to both increased consumption and wealth possibilities. If their net additionality is less than 100 per cent because voucher holders' savings increase, then service vouchers can create an increase in wealth as well as an increase in consumption. Similarly, voucher schemes may have both explicit and implicit characteristics. For example, a specified (or maximum) number of children may be able to use a service even without a voucher if they are accompanied by an adult who does possess a voucher. Such vouchers are used for access to museums and public transport services. It is clear that many vouchers are, in effect, multi-attribute vouchers.

A GENERAL MODEL OF VOUCHERS

The two basic features of vouchers are:

1. the user of the service is given a voucher worth a certain cash value
2. a voucher can only be used by the holder and only to purchase a specified commodity (good or service) for him or herself. If the good or service is not defined, the voucher is no longer a voucher but, instead, an income transfer, such as a child benefit.

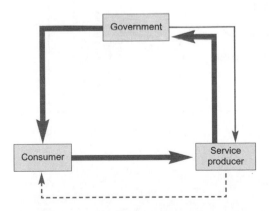

Figure 9.3 A simplified voucher model

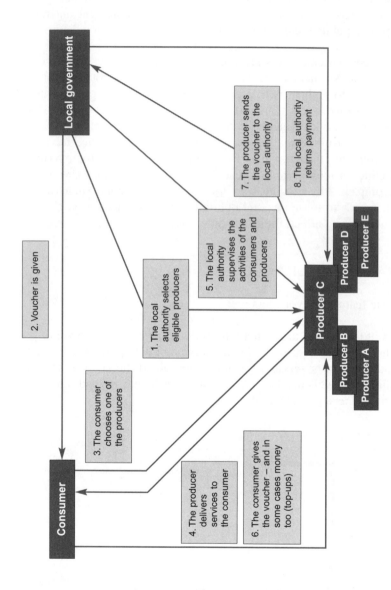

Figure 9.4 A local government voucher model

The first feature means the state is not necessarily committing itself to cover all the expenses involved in the use of a particular service. The second feature excludes the possibility of the voucher being transferred to another person (Ahonen 1994; Lacasse 1992).

Figure 9.3 illustrates a voucher model based on Savas (1987, page 78). The solid lines denote financial flows (thick lines vouchers, thin line money) whilst the dashed line denotes non-financial flows (that is, service provision). The arrows indicate the direction of flow.

The government supports the service user's (consumer's) purchasing power by giving him/her a voucher (thick line), allowing the consumer to select the service producer. The service producer can be a private firm, a non-profit organisation or a public sector service unit. The service producer delivers the service to the consumer (dashed line) and the consumer 'pays' the producer using the voucher (thick line). The service producer hands the voucher to the government, exchanging the voucher for money (thin line). A more detailed model of vouchers within local government is outlined in Figure 9.4 (cf. Heikkilä et al. 1997, page 61).

The rather restricted basic voucher model can be relaxed as follows:

- The voucher can be either a fixed monetary value or income-related (that is, means tested)
- The voucher can be given to a representative of the service user, instead of to the user him/herself
- Vouchers can be defined in service rather than in cash terms (for example entitling the holder to one hour of domestic help or a specified amount of dental treatment)
- The voucher may directly benefit both the holder and someone else (for example school education vouchers held by parents benefit both them and their children).

PERSPECTIVES FOR ANALYSING ARGUMENTS FOR AND AGAINST VOUCHERS

Table 9.1 sets down ideological, theoretical, populist and pragmatic perspectives within which arguments for and against vouchers will be summarised and analysed below. Right-wing think tanks advocate 'rolling back the frontiers of the state' to enhance individual liberty and so are ideologically predisposed in favour of vouchers as one means of achieving their objectives. Left-wing groups are typically ideologically predisposed against vouchers, instead preferring a greater direct role for the state in society and economy. However, Walsh (1995, page 90), claimed that vouchers gained support among leftist parties because they are a means of limiting the power of technocrats. Free-market economists are theoretically predisposed in favour of vouchers as a means of strengthening market mechanisms via competition, leading to improved effic-

Table 9.1 *Perspectives for analysing vouchers*

Perspective	Objective	Rationale	Response
Ideological	To promote individual liberty, freedom of choice, privatisation and markets.	People know their own needs best and can fulfil them using vouchers to choose the supplier, location and time of service use.	Service professionals are the best judges of need for service and market forces are not suitable for public services because clients are vulnerable.
	To defend public services, public employees and democracy and to increase participation and collective control.	Vouchers threaten public sector service providers and it is for political decision-makers to bear responsibility for democratic decisions.	The rationale for local government is not to protect in-house service providers; vouchers deny neither democratic decision-making nor collective control of subsidy; they increase participation in service use.
Theoretical	To abolish public monopolies by introducing competition which, in turn, stimulates internal and external entrepreneurship and cost control.	Vouchers promote pluralism in service supply and so encourage customer orientation through competition for clients. This renews patterns of resource allocation, improves availability and use of information and avoids wasteful public spending.	Vouchers would not be successful because of excessive transaction costs and significant barriers to entry against potential new suppliers. More suppliers of a given output would result in lost economies of scale and so higher costs. In theory, the market optimum is unobtainable.
Populist	To support the interests of ordinary people by making living easier.	Vouchers decrease dependence on bureaucratised decision-making and so living becomes more carefree.	Having to handle vouchers would increase the amount of work for service users and actually increase bureaucracy in allocating vouchers.
Pragmatic	To improve the supply of publicly and privately financed and produced services and to make more effective use of resources.	Vouchers encourage rational behaviour which, in turn, improves the allocation and utilisation of resources through better targeting of subsidy and careful use of vouchers by their holders.	For vouchers to be functional alternative competing producers are required. They usually do not exist; nor would they develop quickly enough. Hence vouchers would not bring any significant gains and the risk of failure is too great in practice.

iency in both production and consumption of services. However, institutional economists argue that these beneficial effects will not be achieved because the free-market theoretical case fails to take account of institutional, behavioural and cultural barriers to competition. Populists are not concerned with ideology or theory, instead focusing on the experiences of those using vouchers, in particular whether voucher schemes provide a better standard of service for users. Pragmatists are concerned with whether voucher schemes actually work, not just in terms of acceptability to service users but also in reducing costs, increasing choice and meeting other objectives such as targeting subsidy more accurately and improving service quality.

Ultimately, any voucher scheme will only be viable if it is consistent with the dominant ideology of the policy-making body or organisation, attracts the support of those who finance and those who use the scheme, and is both theoretically and empirically validated in terms of the expected and actual outcomes satisfying the scheme's objectives. More specifically, an effective voucher system must satisfy the following conditions (Savas 1987, page 113):

- there have to be widespread differences in people's preferences for the service, and these differences are recognised and accepted as legitimate
- individuals must have incentives to shop aggressively for the service (that is, to find the best supplier)
- individuals have to be well informed about market conditions
- an optimal market situation needs many competing service suppliers, or else start-up costs need to be so low that the market is fully contestable – even if there are only very few producers
- service users can easily assess and determine the quality of the service
- the service has to be relatively inexpensive and purchased frequently, so the users learn by experience.

Put concisely, heterogeneous preferences and low 'transaction costs' (see below) have to exist simultaneously if a voucher system is to work effectively, namely to enable public policy-making and yet maximise consumer choice (Kogan 1988, page 151). These strict conditions limit the feasibility of voucher schemes where:

- some preferences are not legitimised by the policy-making body (for example opting out of public sector health care services into the private sector)
- individuals either have limited ability to shop aggressively for the service or are unwilling to do so
- there is a lack of information about alternative suppliers or an inability to comprehend information that may be highly complex and/or subject to frequent change and revision
- the private sector either lacks the organisational capacity to provide the service or newly established providers simply could not cover their costs

- individuals are unable to distinguish between good and poor quality of service, for example health services or personal social services
- the service is used infrequently, for example one-off medical treatments such as hip-joint replacement.

However, these constraints may be relaxed by carefully designed voucher schemes, the operation of which is monitored and modified as necessary after an initial pilot scheme or over time for full-blown schemes. The particular dimensions, characteristics, rights and responsibilities of voucher schemes are considered in detail below but, clearly, opt-out vouchers would not be used where the issuing authority wants to prevent voucher holders using private sector providers. Individuals can be expected to become more discriminating between alternative service providers as information and experience is accumulated over time – aided by public disclosure of information regarding the success rates of hospitals in treating medical conditions, the examination performances of schools and so on. Private sector capacity usually takes time to grow, as was made evident by the UK's former compulsory competitive tendering regime for certain local government and hospital services (for example catering, cleaning, managing leisure facilities and so on). Almost certainly, a transitional period will be required if voucher schemes are to be adopted as a long-term approach towards improving delivery of service.

Ideological arguments for and against vouchers

One of the most frequently stated arguments in favour of vouchers is that 'vouchers enhance the service users' freedom of choice' (Savas 1987, page 114; Heikkilä et al. 1997, page 28; Appleton 1997, page 28; Blaug 1984, pages 166–7; Seldon 1986, pages 33–4). Freedom of choice is valued for its own sake and because it encourages diversity. Choice is maximised by using an unlimited (that is, opt-out) voucher, recipients deciding whether to select a private or public service producer. Moreover, freedom of choice brings about a need and demand for greater information. The public has little incentive to search for information when they do not have the opportunity to choose between different suppliers, especially when there is no provision for them to express their wants or if it is ineffective. Having freedom of choice may make them more interested in the relative performance of alternative service providers. Furthermore, Culpitt (1992, page 153) argues that vouchers maximise the participation and decision-making power of service users when they define their own needs.

The counter-argument by opponents of vouchers is that in many situations freedom of choice is dangerous if only because voucher holders do not possess enough information about the different options or about well-grounded selection criteria. Not all people know what a good service unit is and so vouchers do not enhance freedom of choice. The shortage of information is said to be especially acute within mentally or physically challenged client groups (Rosen 1995, page 85; Cohn 1997, page 7; Blaug 1984, page 167). Indeed, service producers and voucher providers (that is, political decision-makers) may themselves experience insufficient information. The producers are not familiar with the needs of their clients and neither are the political elite necessarily aware of the needs of the public (Blaug 1984, page 167; Heikkilä et al. 1997, page 39).

Moreover, even if fully comprehensive information were made available, freedom of choice is also dangerous because voucher holders are often not competent enough to make rational decisions. People simply are not competent enough to choose a doctor, a hospital or a health care service, for example. Public services are so complicated and users so incompetent that the right to choose should not be left in the hands of individuals. As regards schooling, however, whilst parents may not be able adequately to assess schools' relative performance, vouchers may result in the emergence of new actors who evaluate the information given by service units and make the necessary further inquiries on behalf of consumers (Blaug 1984, page 167; Appleton 1997, page 29). Competent and rational choices are more likely if the municipality or other such policy-making body obliges service producers to provide relevant information about their activities and to publish benchmarking information. As regards medical services, people do not have to buy the service itself in all cases but only an insurance (sold to them by competing companies) that covers different cases of illness and which specifies eligible service providers (Savas 1987, page 113). Whilst ideologues argue about *who* should take the decision (politicians, officials or consumers), proponents of vouchers argue that service users have stronger incentives to make careful choices because they have to live with any unwanted consequences of those decisions.

Other ideological arguments relate to the interests of the *service provider* (as distinct from the *service user*). Both advocates and opponents of vouchers argue that voucher systems are likely to change employment practices. For proponents this is a necessary and beneficial outcome of increased competition which often leads to structural changes (Seldon 1986, page 25). Some service producers would have to hire new personnel while others will have to make employees redundant. It would be necessary, for example, to let popular schools expand and to close the least popular ones. Hence, teachers' trade unions have been strongly against vouchers, fearing redundancies and also that they might adversely affect teachers' rights, salaries and other benefits (Cohn 1997, page 7). Nevertheless, if vouchers are to be successful in terms of allowing choices, the public sector must allow popular schools to invest in expansion and draw up a bankruptcy plan for the unpopular ones. Some voucher experiments have not succeeded, because functioning mechanisms for the expansion and reduction of schools have not been created (Appleton 1997, page 27; Glennerster 1992, page 220).

Theoretical arguments for and against vouchers

Free-market groups argue that vouchers create competition and so increase the efficiency of service producers (Seldon 1986, pages 33–4; Kogan 1988, page 151; Savas 1987, page 272; Pommerehne and Frey 1997, page 82; Heikkilä et al. 1997, page 28). Lack of competition causes inefficiency and wasteful use of public funds and there is some evidence that the quality of private services is better and that their costs are considerably lower than those of the municipal services (Seldon 1986, page 21; Heikkilä et al. 1997, pages 28 and 118–19). Competitive pressures can be introduced into the public sector through quasi-markets utilising vouchers.

Efficiency is improved where vouchers increase productivity, enhance technical development and improve the responsiveness of service producers (Blaug 1984; Heikkilä et al. 1997). Service producers have to clarify their objectives and assess whether they have been successful. This forces them to change internal patterns of allocation, make innovations in the processing and content of services and to give up unnecessary activities (Seldon 1986, pages 33–4; Culpitt 1992, page 153; Ahonen 1994, page 9). Nevertheless, it cannot be concluded that all private sector services are more cost-effective than their public sector equivalents, or that efficiency will necessarily be improved if services are transferred from the public to the private sector. As noted above, it is the threat or degree of competition, rather than the number of alternative suppliers, that brings improved efficiency – markets must be truly contestable for efficiency savings to be achieved. Competitive pressures will be great even if there are only a few alternative suppliers as long as other potential producers can easily set up production (that is, the costs of entering the market are low).

The theoretical counter-argument is that high transaction costs may inhibit competition. High transaction costs occur when three service characteristics occur *simultaneously*. The first characteristic is 'bounded rationality' which occurs due to imperfect information and limited abilities to process information. An example is the extent to which a sick person needs medical treatment and the relative competencies of alternative suppliers of that treatment. This issue has already been addressed above under ideological arguments. Theoretical arguments avoid ideology by simply noting that competition is predicated on full information and calculative rationality (that is, perfect knowledge). The second characteristic is 'asset specificity' which occurs when service infrastructure cannot easily be redeployed, for example specialist medical facilities such as kidney-dialysis units. This limits competition because service providers find it difficult to exit the service, thus creating a disincentive for potential new providers to invest in it. Asset specificity therefore tends to make buyers and sellers of a service mutually dependent upon each (for example a health authority and a privately run specialist hospital). The third characteristic is 'scope for opportunism'. This occurs when the service contract between principal and agent (or between agent and user) is ambiguous, for example in specifying and monitoring the efficacy of medical treatment. Such ambiguity allows the service provider or agent (for example a hospital) to exploit the service principal (for example health authority) and/or the service user (for example patient) in providing a lower quality of service than intended by the principal when drawing up the contract. Significant exploitation is only possible where bounded rationality and asset specificity also occur at the same time as scope for opportunism.

The extent and size of transaction costs is an empirical question (see Bailey 1999 in respect of local government services). If they are high then it is more efficient to provide the service internally than to buy it from the open market, there being little or no scope for competition. If they are low then the competitive market is the most efficient source of supply. However, even if transaction costs are low, increasing the number of competing service providers may ultimately result in lost economies of scale otherwise achievable by one or a few large providers. Again, the scope for economies of scale is an empirical question and it cannot be assumed that they will necessarily result in lower service costs because the resulting few providers may collude rather than compete with each other so that service cost savings are not achieved.

Populist and pragmatic arguments for and against vouchers

Populist advocates of vouchers argue that vouchers bring about psychological benefits, the consumer being encouraged to become an active decision-maker, less dependent on the services produced by society (Harisalo 1993, page 7; Culpitt 1992, page 153). Being proactive, consumers become more self-confident and learn to trust their own judgement. Ahonen (1994, page 9) also emphasises indirect benefits of voucher systems but notes that those benefits take quite a long time to be effected.

The counter-argument by opponents of vouchers is that there is simply no private production of public services in many municipalities. Hence, the ability of the market mechanism to meet the clients' needs quickly and responsively enough has been questioned (Culpitt 1992, page 153). However, Seldon (1986) argues that such criticism based on the hypothesis of inflexible supply is a presupposition that lacks evidence. Any lack of alternative supply is often the result of the 'direct provision' policies pursued by municipalities. For example, when nursery vouchers were tried in Finland from 1995 to 1997, the voucher system brought new entrepreneurs into the field, and many of the new entrepreneurs cited the voucher experiment as being the main reason for their setting up the service (Heikkilä et al. 1997, pages 118–19).

Even so, another populist counter-argument is that vouchers may cause social discord or social problems by leading to two-tier services. Service units charging higher prices and attracting wealthier clients could hire more qualified staff, acquire better equipment and provide a higher standard of service.

Less affluent consumers would purchase services that are more affordable and, as a consequence, service units would be classified into those for the poor and those for the wealthy. Hence, vouchers might exacerbate current trends towards social polarisation. This outcome can be avoided either by giving clients vouchers that cannot be supplemented (topped-up) by the holder or by issuing income-related vouchers so that all income groups have the same ability to pay top-ups (Blaug 1984, page 168).

Nevertheless, 'cream skimming' could occur if vouchers are of equal value for all clients. In such cases service producers are likely to act rationally and only select clients that are easy (and therefore less costly) to treat. The result would be that nobody serves the needs of the clients with more difficult (and therefore more expensive) problems (Heikkilä et al. 1997, pages 39–40). Cream skimming can be eliminated by relating the values of vouchers to needs and costs and/or by requiring service producers to give all those in need equal access to service. Nonetheless, vouchers could exacerbate racial and social discrimination (Cohn 1997, page 7). Again, however, this can be avoided by making vouchers equally available to all groups (in relation to both need and income/wealth) and by making service producers responsible for treating all population groups equally.

More generally, populist advocates of vouchers argue that vouchers can lead to greater equity in relation to need and ability to pay. Many public services are produced in the form of services for the public as a whole, and everyone has the right to use them freely. In comparison, vouchers are directed at specific individuals and families. In a means-tested voucher system, people with higher incomes and/or wealth receive vouchers of a lower value than those with lower incomes/wealth. Hence, more affluent individuals have to pay a greater amount, this being the difference between service costs and the value of the voucher. For example, it is arguable that the state effectively subsidises the affluent 'art elite' if admission to arts venues is free or if everyone pays a standard admission charge. If demand amongst low-income groups is highly sensitive to price, use of arts vouchers to attract low-income groups previously making relatively little use of arts venues will lead to a radical redistribution of public subsidy. Moreover, these newly participating groups may inspire cultural productions by minorities and other groups who previously have not been able to participate because of the lack of state subsidy (West 1986, page 10).

Opponents of vouchers argue that they may in fact increase inequity, notwithstanding means testing. Not all municipalities would introduce vouchers and those that did would have different schemes in terms of means testing, top-ups and so on (see Figure 9.5 below). Vertical equity within a given local authority could be improved but probably at the expense of greater horizontal inequity between municipalities.

A pragmatic argument in favour of vouchers is that vouchers enable public funds to be used more effectively by more accurately targeting subsidy on need. Nevertheless, whilst better targeting may reduce wasteful spending, means testing can be expensive to administer. More generally, however, vouchers may save public money by radically changing the funding structure of public services. Supporting the *service producer* is the focus of a system based on state-funded 'production subsidies'. An example is the municipal finance system, in which the central state grants subsidies to municipalities, thus subsidising local government service producers directly. In contrast, voucher systems support the *service user* directly by means of 'consumption subsidies'. Production subsidies support the service user indirectly by reducing or eliminating direct payment for service at the point of consumption. Consumption subsidies support the service user directly by enhancing his/her ability to make direct payment for service (Seldon 1991, page 62). Replacement of intergovernmental grants by vouchers as the main means of funding local services would clearly constitute a radical change in the financing and philosophy of the welfare state. Service producers within voucher schemes can only charge the municipality for the services that they have actually delivered to voucher holders (Harisalo 1993, page 7; Culpitt 1992, page 153). Hence, vouchers could also lead to public expenditure savings by encouraging service providers to eliminate excess capacity.

Pragmatic counter-arguments are that vouchers lead to increased expenditures if their holders choose to use privately produced services. If this switch happens almost immediately vouchers are introduced, the municipality will not be able to reduce its personnel quickly enough and it must still pay the fixed costs of past investments in service production. Hence, underutilisation of capacity occurs in both the short run and long run (Suomen 1994, pages 31–2). Nevertheless, fixed costs are 'embedded costs' and must be ignored in cost comparisons – bygones are bygones. Additionally, however, public expenditures could rise in countries where some parents have traditionally put their children into private schools because all parents would now share funds distributed by the state as vouchers. Hence, public funds financing vouchers would replace private expenditures, leading to a rise in public expenditure. Moreover, any additional taxes and any increase in the allocation of funds for education may get more support than before because parents whose children have attended private schools paid their taxes but did not get their share from common tax funds (Blaug 1984, pages 165–6). Some would regard this as positively advantageous. The same outcomes could occur for health care vouchers when affluent groups' payments for private health expenditures had not previously been offset against taxes used to finance public sector health services.

Public expenditures would also rise if vouchers increase administrative costs. According to West (1986, pages 9–10), this is the most common criticism of vouchers aired by public administrators. This is especially the case for means-tested vouchers and where holders of vouchers change their choices constantly, causing management and logistics problems in municipal service units, at least in the short run (Seldon 1986, page 24). Public expenditure costs could also be higher than expected because there is little experience of vouchers. They present an enormous challenge to the political system because they are an uncommonly flexible instrument. According to Blaug (1984, page 168), almost any goal of the public sector can be reached with a voucher. However, this is also its weakness. When a proposal is put forward for a voucher system, there begins an endless debate about what exactly the system should be like. As a consequence, it is extremely difficult to develop and implement vouchers.

Additionally, vouchers may make budgeting much more complicated, again leading to higher public expenditures. Service providers' budgets depend upon receipt of vouchers, the number of which is uncertain. Moreover, a voucher system's ability to control public expenditure is questionable because hurried decisions concerning the distribution of vouchers would pre-empt proper financial calculations (Savas 1987, page 114). Budgeting is made even more complicated where vouchers frustrate the coordination of services. Some needs are accompanied by such complex problems, that solutions can only be found when different fields of activity are coordinated: housing, social work and education for example. Service coordination could be a much bigger problem if services were separated, individualised and financed and consumed through vouchers.

Nevertheless, as already noted above, there is some evidence that vouchers can improve cost-effectiveness in terms of lower production costs and improved quality of service. Likewise as already noted, vouchers can achieve public expenditure savings more generally by only financing services actually used – as distinct from financing unused spare capacity. In particular, state grants finance services *before* consumption (assuming consumption will actually occur) whereas vouchers finance services *after* consumption and so automatically distinguish between used and unused service capacity.

Clearly, the arguments presented in the literature (whether in favour of or against vouchers) are mostly unsubstantiated, being based mainly on conventional wisdom and presuppositions instead of on research data or practical experiences. The arguments are predominantly a priori and anecdotal. The preponderance of pragmatic arguments against vouchers simply emphasises the need for pilot-testing of voucher schemes to see which are substantiated and which refuted by empirical evidence. Those empirical outcomes will, in turn, be crucially dependent upon the dimensions and characteristics of vouchers and on the rights and responsibilities they entail.

DIMENSIONS AND CHARACTERISTICS OF VOUCHERS

There is no single voucher type or voucher system, Figure 9.5 illustrates the decisions that must be made when designing a voucher scheme. However, voucher schemes have three generic dimensions into which any scheme's

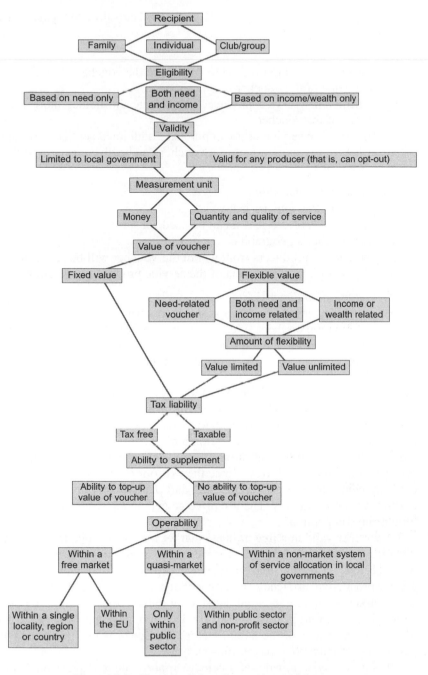

Figure 9.5 Characteristics of a service voucher

criteria can be grouped (Ahonen 1994, page 16; Harisalo 1993, page 4; Levin 1997, pages 31–3):

1. *The finance dimension:*
   - the measurement unit used to determine the voucher's value
   - the value of the voucher
   - whether the service producer can charge the holder more than the value of the voucher
   - whether the service user can purchase additional services (top-ups)
   - whether any unused part of a voucher can be given as cash to the service user.

2. *The regulation dimension:*
   - to whom the voucher is given
   - what goods or services it can be used for
   - the voucher's geographic area of validity
   - the service producers from whom the voucher will be redeemed
   - the conditions and criteria of the service producers' operations.

3. *The information dimension:*
   - eligibility criteria for receipt of the voucher
   - information on the service available to the holder of the voucher
   - from which suppliers the consumer can obtain services
   - what to do in the event of unsatisfactory service provision.

The last two bullet points refer to exit and voice respectively. Exit means the consumer is able to choose from alternative service producers. As noted above, this is the most common argument for vouchers. If one is dissatisfied with the supply, one may use the exit option and choose another producer. Procedures such as general liberalisation, competitive tendering, quasi-markets and privatisation can be used to reinforce the exit option. Voice is used to express one's opinion, for example complaining and participating in a pressure group to improve service quality. The use of voice is potentially useful when there is little or no competition.

A voucher valid in a free or quasi-market increases scope for exit because a choice can be made between service units in the public, private and non-profit sectors. In theory, this stimulates competition that, in turn, stimulates greater productive efficiency and cost savings. This is especially the case for a free market extending beyond local boundaries (that is, at the regional, national or even European Union level). The savings potential depends on the relative effectiveness of the public sector's service providers (Appleton 1997, pages 31–2; Blaug 1984, pages 162–3).

It is generally assumed that it is more appropriate to express one's preferences about services provided by local governments by using voice rather than exit, the latter being considered more appropriate within the private sector. Customers are considered selfish, whereas municipal residents are regarded as people who consider the community, even though customers and residents are often the same individuals. However, if voice is not reinforced by the exit option, local governments and service producers may not have adequate incentives to meet residents' requirements. Vouchers reinforce voice because their use directly affects a service provider's finances when exit is possible (Bailey 1999, pages 40–55, 70). Likewise, the ability to supplement or top up a voucher's value reinforces the use of voice. Voice is also enhanced if the measurement unit is in terms of the quantity and quality (that is, level) of service, defined after consulting service users.

RIGHTS AND RESPONSIBILITIES OF VOUCHERS

A voucher is not just an allocation instrument: it is also a control instrument, transferring both rights and responsibilities to the recipient and the service producer (see Figure 9.6).

A voucher gives *rights* to its recipient:

■ *Consumption rights:* rights to access a service, receive appropriate treatment from the service producer and make complaints. Consumption rights therefore reinforce use of voice
■ *Property rights:* exclusive rights to use the voucher. No other person has rights to use the voucher, so reinforcing the voice of the holder. However, ownership of the voucher usually remains with the issuing organisation. This ensures that the voucher can only be used for the purposes for which it is intended
■ *Transfer rights:* determine whether the recipient can give (as a gift, bequest or pledge) or sell the voucher to a third party. Transferability increases the voucher holder's exit options. However, transfer could lead to vouchers being used by people not satisfying eligibility criteria, contradicting the aims and objectives of the voucher scheme. Hence, their consumption rights are normally non-transferable. Likewise, because the aim of voucher schemes is to facilitate consumption of a particular service, any unused value or surplus (that is, where the monetary value of services received is less than the value of a voucher) cannot normally be given to the voucher holder. Any such surplus is usually retained by the supplier. This provides incentives for the holder to use the full monetary value of the voucher (for example purchasing food with a food voucher) and for the service supplier to improve efficiency (since any cost savings are retained).

A voucher also bestows *responsibilities* on its recipient:

■ *Consumption responsibilities:* a person receiving a voucher is obliged to consume (a specified level of) the service. Consumption responsibilities

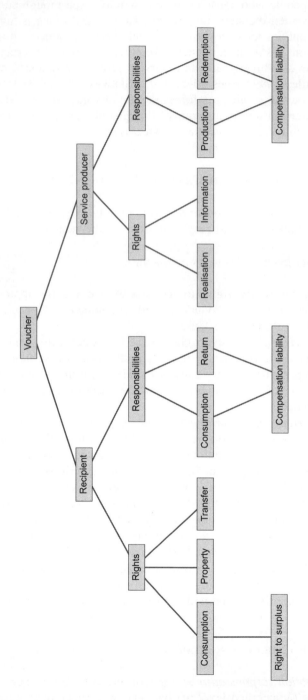

Figure 9.6 Rights and responsibilities of vouchers

may oblige the recipient to acquire offers from several service producers and use the least expensive producer

■ *Responsibility to return the voucher:* if the recipient has given the issuer false information regarding his or her eligibility or is no longer eligible, or if it is not used within a given period of time. This means that the voucher cannot be stored and added to other vouchers received later

■ *Compensation liability:* recipients can be made liable to pay compensation for any misuse of vouchers, including fraud or a similar offence.

The service producer also has *rights*:

■ *realisation rights:* the service producer is entitled to exchange vouchers for money paid by the issuer of the voucher

■ *information rights:* a competitive supply scenario requires that potential/alternative service producers receive information about voucher schemes.

The service producer also has *responsibilities*:

■ *production responsibilities:* the service producer must have suitable premises in which to provide the service(s); the staff hired by the service producer must meet certain formal requirements regarding skills, expertise or experience; and the services must meet the required quality. Furthermore, the service producer must not discriminate against the customers on grounds of their ethnic background, sex, age and so on. A monitoring system may be necessary to ensure that these responsibilities are fulfilled. This may require the authorities to make regular or random supervisory visits

■ *redemption responsibilities:* oblige the service producer to have the voucher redeemed within a certain time limit, after which it will be invalidated

■ *compensation liability:* as for recipients, service producers can also be made liable to pay compensation for any misuse of vouchers.

THE NEW DEFINITION OF VOUCHERS

A new generic definition of vouchers follows the above analysis. That analysis made clear that vouchers entail a distinction between principal, holder and agent. The principal is the organisation that finances and issues the voucher. The holder is the person receiving the voucher and, thereby, the service, commodity or other such benefit. The agent provides the service, commodity or other such benefit in exchange for the redeemable voucher. Hence, the new 'generic' definition of a voucher is that it is 'an instrument issued by a principal that can be redeemed by the holder for a service, commodity or other such benefit provided by an agent'.

The new generic definition of vouchers is not built solely or primarily on the concept of 'purchasing power', but instead on the power of 'choice, benefit and payment'. The concept of purchasing power is strongly associated with money. On the market, money is the medium of exchange and provides consumers with purchasing power. But a voucher cannot function as an equivalent medium of exchange because it does not hold the same transfer rights. Only income transfers can provide money-based purchasing power with the same transfer capabilities. Making a purchase with a voucher simply is not comparable to making a purchase with money.

A new definition of a 'public service' voucher can be derived from the new generic definition. It is simultaneously 'publicly directed consumption with individualised choice of production and payment'. A public service voucher is publicly directed consumption because it is given to those in need of a service, is limited in its purpose and manner of use, enables the use of public and/or private services, and transfers both rights and responsibilities to its holder and to the service producer. It is individualised choice of production because, within a competitive system of plural provision, vouchers enable choice of eligible service producer in any or all of the public sector, the non-profit sector and the private sector. It is individualised choice of payment because choice of service producer determines which supplier receives payment and payment can be withdrawn via exit. Therefore, consumption is publicly directed because the voucher leads to increased consumption of a particular service of regulated quantity and quality, whilst holders of vouchers are allowed to choose their preferred production outlet and make payment via the voucher.

Referring back to Figure 9.1, the new generic definition encompasses all types of vouchers, including employment and privatisation vouchers because they provide a particular benefit to their holder. The new definition of public service vouchers only applies to the 'service vouchers' subset within the public sector. Moreover, it only applies to internal or external services if there is a choice of service outlet (that is, there is no monopoly).

VOUCHERS AND THE NEW PUBLIC MANAGEMENT

Vouchers are consistent with the new public management in that properly designed voucher systems can be used to improve the cost-effectiveness of services by promoting a plurality of service providers within both internal and external markets. They are therefore consistent with the development of enabling government, with 'steering rather than rowing', and constitute a further development of the purchaser–provider split. These developments are intended to allow governments (national, regional and local) to pay more attention to strategic policy-making by avoiding becoming embroiled in the details of service delivery. Vouchers can help local governments to achieve best value for money in being an alternative to, or further development of, the competitive contracting of local public services. In particular, they can help promote quality initiatives by giving service users greater opportunities for exit and voice, the threat of lost customers or clients giving service providers greater incentives to respond to the views (voice) of service users.

Such reforms are commonplace in developed countries within central, regional and local governments. Those reforms typically seek to introduce constrained (rather than free-market) consumerism. The conditions set within voucher schemes can be designed to help secure this objective. In particular, the concepts and criteria contained within Figures 9.1 to 9.6 and within the analysis of arguments for and against charges structured by Table 9.1 can help practitioners to design viable voucher systems. It must be emphasised, however, that any schemes should first be piloted and subsequently monitored and evaluated in order to identify and deal with unexpected outcomes.

CONCLUSIONS

Vouchers could be used much more extensively than at present as an alternative public service delivery system, especially for local government services. They could be used to promote greater economic and social equality by basing both their allocation and their value on the ability to pay and on medical and/or social need. However, the use of public service vouchers in aggregate is limited by the generally perceived constraints on the degree of state intervention. They are a means to an end, not an end in themselves.

Moreover, the end in mind will not necessarily be achieved by an ill-prepared voucher scheme. The example of opt-out vouchers for health services demonstrated just how easily the use of vouchers to pursue multiple objectives could be counterproductive. Vouchers designed to give greater freedom of choice may conflict with more equal access to services by all social groups. Freedom of choice of service level through willingness to pay additional amounts (on top of the voucher's value) may deny services for those equally in need of service yet unable to pay top-ups because of low incomes. Hence, the details of individual voucher schemes have to be carefully constructed if objectives are to be met and unethical or otherwise undesirable outcomes avoided.

Given its wide service responsibilities, experimentation with and introduction of public service vouchers has usually depended on local government initiatives. National voucher systems typically relate to employment and training. Vouchers do not necessarily offer a way to cut public expenditure even though, according to some studies, they have brought about clear cost savings. Changes brought about by vouchers are primarily linked to the change in the role and status of the recipient as customer.

Earlier definitions of vouchers were incomplete because they did not incorporate exit and voice. The strengthening of exit and voice through voucher systems is potentially their greatest value in public policy terms because they guide the financing of services. These two key attributes of vouchers are encompassed within the new definition of public service vouchers developed within this chapter, namely 'publicly directed consumption with individualised choice of production and payment'.

Public service vouchers are much more than simply income transfers because they can more effectively match provision of service with user preferences *and* encourage greater efficiency in the production of services. Hence, vouchers are proactive instruments of public policy that can promote equity and efficiency in both production and consumption. However, these potential savings will be at least partially offset by the potentially relatively large administrative costs of voucher systems. Voucher systems must be carefully designed and regularly evaluated against objectives if increased potential for exit and voice is to benefit prioritised groups. Nevertheless, their role within the new public management is grossly underdeveloped. Vouchers have enormous potential as an alternative system by which to deliver and finance efficient, effective and equitable public sector services.

Whether that potential can be achieved in practice is open to question. Individual voucher schemes differ radically in terms of type of voucher, their characteristics, the rights and responsibilities of holders and service producers, the feasibility of monitoring and influencing their use, the potential for use of exit and voice and so on. Hence, it would be methodologically invalid to judge all public service voucher schemes on the basis of a few (possibly idiosyncratic) schemes. Learning from the success or failure of individual voucher schemes has to pay attention to the schema outlined in Figures 9.1 to 9.6 above.

REFERENCES

Ahonen, E. (1994) *Koulutussetelit korkeakoulussa*. Opiskelijan asema korkeakoulujen rahoituksessa. Opetusministeriö. (Koulutus- ja tiedepolitiikan linjan julkaisusarja, 17. Helsinki).

Appleton, S. (1997) *User Fees, Expenditure Restructuring and Voucher Systems in Education*. The United Nations University. World Institute for Development Economics Research (WIDER). Working Papers No. 134. May.

Bailey, S. J. (1999) *Local Government Economics: Principles and Practice*. (Basingstoke: Macmillan – now Palgrave Macmillan).

Becker, G. S. and Becker, G. N. (1997) *The Economics of Life. From Baseball to Affirmative Action in Immigration, How Real World Issues Affect Our Everyday Life*. (London: McGraw-Hill).

Blaug, M. (1984) 'Education Vouchers – It All Depends on What You Mean'. In *Privatisation and the Welfare State*. Edited by Julian Le Grand and Ray Robinson. (London: Allen & Unwin).

Cohn, E. (1997) 'Public and Private School Choices: Theoretical Considerations and Empirical Evidence'. In Elchanan Cohn (ed.) *Market Approaches to Education. Vouchers and School Choice*. (Oxford: Elsevier Science).

Collin, P. H., Weiland, C. and Dohn, D. S. (1990) *American Business Dictionary* (Middlesex: Peter Collin Publishing).

Culpitt, I. (1992) *Welfare and Citizenship: Beyond the Crisis of the Welfare State?* (London: Sage).

Friedman, M. (1962) *Capitalism and Freedom*. (Chicago: The University of Chicago Press).

Glennerster, H. (1992) *Paying for Welfare in the 1990s*. (Brighton: Harvester Wheatsheaf).

Harisalo, R. (1993) *Julkisten palveluiden tukijärjestelmä kunnallishallinnossa.* Kokeiluja, kokemuksia ja ideoita (Helsinki: Suomen Kunnallisliitto).

Heikkilä M., Sinikka, T. and Kati, M. (1997) *Palveluseteli lasten päivähoidossa.* Raportti valtakunnallisesta kokeilusta. Sosiaali- ja terveysalan tutkimus- ja kehittämiskeskus. Sosiaali- ja terveysministeriö. Raportteja 216. Jyväskylä.

Kogan, M. (1988) 'Normative Models of Accountability'. In Glatter, R., Preedy, M., Riches, C. and Masterton, M. (eds) *Understanding School Management* (Milton Keynes: Open University Press).

Lacasse, F. (1992) *Vouchers: Issues and Experiences.* OECD/PUMA, Market-Type Mechanisms Series No 4, (Paris: Organisation for Economic Co-operation and Development).

Lamming, R. and Bessant, J. (1988) *Macmillan Dictionary of Business and Management.* (Basingstoke: Macmillan – now Palgrave Macmillan).

Levin, H. M. (1997) 'The Economics of Educational Choice'. In Elchanan Cohn (editor) *Market Approaches to Education. Vouchers and School Choice.* (Oxford: Elsevier Science).

Maynard, A. (1975) *Experiment with Choice in Education.* (London: Institute of Economic Affairs).

Nisberg, J. N. (1988) *Handbook of Business Terms.* (New York: Random House).

OECD (1993) *Managing with Market-Type Mechanisms.* Puma Public Management Studies. (Paris: Organisation for Economic Co-operation and Development).

OECD (1998) *Voucher Programmes and their Role in Distributing Services.* Puma Public Management Committee. (Paris: Organisation for Economic Co-operation and Development).

Paine, T. (1791) *The Rights of Man.* Published by Penguin Classics 1984 (Harmondsworth: Penguin).

Pommerehne, W. W. and Frey, B. S. (1997) 'Public Promotion of the Arts: A Survey of Means'. In *Cultural Economics: The Arts, the Heritage and the Media Industries. Volume II.* Edited by Ruth Towse. (Cheltenham: Edward Elgar). [Also published in *Journal of Cultural Economics* 1990, 14 (2), December, 73–95.]

Rosen, H. S. (1995) *Public Finance.* 4th edition. (Chicago: Irwin).

Rönkkö, P. (1999) 'Kotitaloustyön tukimuotojen arviointi ja kehittäminen'. In Oulasvirta Lasse, Rönkkö Pentti and Yli-Olli Päivi (eds), *Pitkäaikaistyöttömyyden rakenne ja siihen haetut ratkaisumallit Tampereella.* Tampereen seudun kumppanuusprojekti yhteistyössä Tampereen yliopiston kanssa. 2/99. Tampereen Seudun Kumppanuusprojekti.

Savas, E. S. (1987) *Privatization. The Key to Better Government.* (London: Chatham House).

Seldon, A. (1986) *The Riddle of the Voucher. An Inquiry into the Obstacles to Introducing Choice and Competition in State Schools.* Hobart Paperback No. 21. (London: Institute of Economic Affairs).

Seldon, M. (1991) 'Vouchers for Schooling'. In *Empowering the Parents: How to Break the Schools Monopoly.* David G. Green (ed.) 55–63. Choice in Welfare No. 9. IEA Health and Welfare Unit. (London: Institute of Economic Affairs).

Smith, A. (1776) An Inquiry into the Nature and Causes of the Wealth of Nations. Edited by Campbell, R. H. and Skinner, A. S. (1982) (Indianapolis: Liberty Fund).

Suomen, K. (1994) *Palveluseteli ja peruspalvelut.* (Helsinki).

Uvalic, M. and Vaughan-Whitehead, D. (eds) (1997) *Privatization Surprises in Transition Economies. Employee-Ownership in Central and Eastern Europe.* (Cheltenham: Edward Elgar).

Walsh, K. (1995) *Public Services and Market Mechanisms: Competition, Contracting and the New Public Management.* (Basingstoke: Macmillan – now Palgrave Macmillan).

West, E. G. (1997) 'Arts Vouchers to Replace Grants'. In *Cultural Economics: The Arts, the Heritage and the Media Industries.* Vol. II. Edited by Ruth Towse. (Cheltenham: Edward Elgar). [Also published in *Economic Affairs* vol. 6, no. 3, 1986, pp. 9–11, 16.]

10 Conclusions – A Strategy for Public Finance

INTRODUCTION

This concluding chapter attempts to pull together the main strategic issues relating to public finance discussed in the previous chapters. Most people approach public finance from a particular perspective, whether as a service-specific policy-maker or practitioner, discipline-specific student or academic, financial auditor and so on. Being busy with the detail of the aspects of public finance for which they are responsible or with which they are concerned, they often cannot find sufficient time to stand back and think strategically about public finance. Hopefully, having worked through the previous chapters, the reader will now appreciate the extremely broad nature of public finance and the strategic issues underpinning it. It should, by now, be clear that public finance is not just a narrow budgeting issue. Nor, clearly, is it confined within the boundaries of any one discipline. Instead, public finance can only be studied and appreciated within a broad multidisciplinary perspective, besides economics and accountancy, also including philosophy, political science, sociology, public management, constitutional theory and so on. Given the limitations of the author's own expertise, not all these areas have been considered in equal or sufficient depth.

Nevertheless, it has been demonstrated that the 4Es analytical framework of economy, equity, efficiency and effectiveness used in this text is capable of encompassing the many perspectives used in the study of public finance, ranging from the deeply philosophical to the profoundly practical. Thus, it is clearly invalid to claim that public finance is purely an ideological issue, that the main constraint on service expansion is the 'dead hand of finance', or that economics is irrelevant. These and other such outlandish claims display a profound ignorance of the nature and scope of strategic issues underpinning public finance. These strategic issues will now be revisited in an integrative summary.

WHAT LESSONS ARE TO BE LEARNT FROM THIS STUDY OF PUBLIC FINANCE?

The first and most obvious lesson is that public finance is not simply concerned with raising and spending money. Those financial flows ultimately reflect the relationship between the citizen and the state that, in turn, reflects a dominant Libertarian, Neo-Liberal or Collectivist political philosophy, as made clear by Chapter 1. Not all citizens, politicians, state employees, taxpayers and service users adhere to whichever political philosophy is dominant at any one time in any one country. Thus, there is an ongoing debate about not just the levels of public revenues and expenditures but also about from what sources public finance is raised and on what it is spent. This often vibrant debate reflects perceptions about the appropriate balance between negative and positive rights, those perceptions changing over time as social, economic, global and other factors evolve. These changing contexts determine the extent to which principle may have to be balanced by pragmatism, that balance changing over time.

Hence, public finance can variously be concerned with:

■ allowing autonomous citizens to exercise full individual responsibility for their own standard of living whilst remaining totally free of state control (Libertarian role)
■ enabling responsible citizens to have the potential to secure an adequate standard of living by affording equality of opportunity in the marketplace (Neo-Liberal role)
■ guaranteeing protected citizens adequate standards of living through direct state control of their everyday lives in terms of access to and outcomes from state-provided services (Collectivist role).

These various political philosophies have radically different implications for the relative scale of public finance. Clearly, therefore, the role of public finance is not simply to enable the provision of services, redistribute incomes and wealth or overcome the perceived failings of private sector markets. Instead, the role of public finance is first and foremost a constitutional role – service provision – redistribution and adjustment of market outcomes having only subservient status. Ultimately, public finance gives effect to the constitutional relationship between state and citizen in securing the positive and/or negative rights of citizens. Precisely how and to what extent those rights can be secured is inevitably constrained by what is effective in a changing world.

Adopting an analytical framework based on the 4Es helps understand the broad implications for public finance of the various political philosophies. Each political philosophy has its own definition of each of equity, efficiency, economy and effectiveness. The different philosophical interpretations of the 4Es were outlined in Chapter 1. They are most effectively studied within a multidisciplinary perspective. However, even a multidisciplinary study of public finance such as that provided by this text will not be able to state definitively whether public expenditure, taxation and borrowing are too large, too small or just about right. What is an acceptable level and structure of public finance for Neo-Liberals will be deemed excessive by Libertarians and insufficient by Collectivists.

Although apparently purely ideological, these differing philosophical views are based on rational arguments about the impact (positive or negative, actual or potential) of public finance on society and economy. It is here that principles and pragmatism interact. Propositions about what relative scale of public finance is appropriate in terms of national income (GDP) can only be understood and challenged by recourse to rational argument, both a priori and evidence-based. Those arguments revolve round whether there should be more or less state intervention (and therefore public finance) than is currently the case in a given country and, in particular, whether more state intervention is beneficial or harmful to economy and society. These arguments fuel the political debate underpinning elections at all levels of government. Those arguments ultimately boil down to deciding who should receive various forms and levels of state assistance, how effective is that assistance, and how should the voted-for public interventions in support of positive and/or negative rights be financed.

The apparent recent shift in the scale of public finance deemed acceptable by most developed countries reflects a move away from dominant Collectivist philosophies towards dominant Neo-Liberal approaches to the organisation of economy and society. Communist regimes have collapsed and socialism appears to be on the wane. Governments have increasingly adopted Neo-Liberal policies such as privatisation and conditional (that is, work-based) welfare. These reforms to the nature and relative scale of public finance reflect an increasingly accepted view that, whilst it can deliver a more equal share of national income and wealth, a relatively large scale of public finance may actually reduce national prosperity. Such a reduction may not be in absolute terms but, instead, relative to what prosperity would have been in the absence of such a relatively high level of public finance. It would result if higher levels of income support and taxation created substantial disincentives to self-support through productive employment and/or disincentives for companies to invest in the economic infrastructure.

Therefore, guaranteeing positive and negative rights to a fair share of the economic 'cake' may come at the cost of a smaller 'cake' or one that is smaller than it would otherwise have been. If so, then principle is tempered by pragmatism. Potentially significant trade-offs between equity, efficiency, economy and effectiveness mean that the net benefits of additional public finance may be small, perhaps even illusory. Whether incremental changes in public finance have net benefits or net costs is the fundamental strategic issue. The fact that the Neo-Liberal political philosophy is increasingly dominant at a global level reflects a more questioning appreciation of the effectiveness of increased levels of state intervention, certainly of the traditional direct-provider tax-financed form.

Nevertheless, there is still a widespread belief that governments generally act in the 'public interest'. That term is broad and vague enough to encapsulate changing perceptions of the 4Es and the changing balance of emphasis between them. As perceptions of what constitutes equity, efficiency, economy and effectiveness change, so governments have to reconfigure property rights in delivering objectives for those 4Es. Those property rights relate to negative and positive rights, not just to ownership of physical property. They include access to services such as health care and education. Property rights may therefore have to be reconfigured for equity reasons, for example ensuring that those in need of medical care have access to it, irrespective of their age, ethnicity and ability to pay for care.

Property rights are so configured for some services that the individual is unable to access them unless they are financed collectively by the state. Consideration of the degree to which property rights are enforceable and sustainable allows a distinction to be drawn between pure public goods, pure private goods and mixed goods, the term 'goods' also referring to services. Chapter 2 demonstrated that, in principle, public finance is required for efficiency purposes for pure public goods such as national defence, the benefits of which are non-rival and non-excludable, and for rival but non-excludable mixed goods such as municipal or regional country parks. In these cases sustainable provision solely by means of private finance (that is, market prices) is simply not possible because the providers of those services cannot recover payment from those who use or benefit from them. The resulting market failure means that these types of services can only be financed collectively by compelling citizens to make payments (that is, pay taxes).

Such services require public finance to cover their costs if they are to be provided. However, they do not typify the majority of public services, only a minority. Most services provided by the public sector have the same characteristics as those provided by the private sector in terms of being rival and excludable in use, for example health care and education. Their costs are therefore capable of being recovered by charges, although there may be efficiency reasons for subsidising their provision, such as the wider benefits to economy and society of a well-educated labour force. Nevertheless, such wider social benefits typically only justify partial subsidy of costs in efficiency terms, not full subsidy.

Public services are capable of being fully financed by user-charges when property rights are enforceable and usually only need partial subsidy of costs when they are not fully enforceable. Only pure community-level services and rival but non-excludable mixed goods need be fully funded by taxation because payment of user-charges cannot be enforced. This property rights analysis makes clear that user-charges should be the primary (not residual) source of public finance.

In principle, equity issues can be resolved by a comprehensive system of means testing. Pursuit of greater equity via public services provided free at the point of use may be at the cost of lost national output because of the consequently high levels of taxation. Provision of services free to all users, whether rich or poor, may mean that equity is achieved only at the cost of making the average citizen poorer than they would otherwise have been – the 'diminished cake' analogy.

Justifying the use of public finance in terms of efficiency and/or equity criteria justifies neither public property rights nor public sector provision of services. The private sector is capable of delivering most public services to socially optimal levels as long as public finance is used to complement (rather than replace) private finance. Therefore, to say that all public services must be publicly owned and fully funded by public finance is based on an incomplete logic. Public sector provision of services free at the point of use results in the relative scale of both the public sector and public finance being higher than necessary to secure the particular levels of negative and positive rights thought appropriate in individual countries.

The analysis in Chapter 3 found that there is a relatively high scale of public finance within West European countries, especially EU and Scandinavian countries. Moreover, that scale increased substantially over the last 40 years of the twentieth century, in terms of both government expenditure/GDP ratios and tax/GDP ratios. The Libertarian, Neo-Liberal and Collectivist philosophies cannot themselves explain the rising trend in public finance within GDP because they only philosophise about negative and positive rights. They do not determine levels of entitlement to particular services. Nor do they consider how the economic, social and political restructuring that accompanies economic growth impacts upon negative and positive rights. Thus, the different political philosophies provide no practical guidance in respect of the optimal level of public finance, whether in absolute terms or relative to GDP.

Whilst the theory of property rights can be used to provide a more objective approach in assessing the optimum level of public finance than can political philosophy, its practical use in policy-making is also severely constrained. This is because of the difficulties in identifying and measuring both direct and indirect costs and benefits to both the individual service user and society as a whole. Nevertheless, whilst acknowledging this indeterminacy, efficacy in the use of public finance can be improved (perhaps substantially) by paying attention to how it is raised and spent. Whatever its relative scale, the ways in which public finance is raised and spent crucially determine whether it has adverse or beneficial effects.

The detailed analysis of the main components of public expenditures in developed countries in Chapter 4 made clear that relatively high levels of public finance are largely and increasingly accounted for by current expenditures. Growth in current expenditure/GDP ratios has been almost wholly accounted for by the growth of social security transfers, most notably in EU countries. Provision of public sector services (as distinct from welfare payments) has generally only kept up with the growth of GDP. This changing composition of public expenditures increasingly led to questioning the legitimacy of redistribution through social security transfers. Irrespective of one's political philosophy, it is not clear how those growing social security transfers can be financed without adverse effects on economic growth. If they create dependency cultures by creating disincentives to self-sufficiency through paid employment, then such trends in public finance will not be sustainable over the long term.

Thus, spending public finance is not a simple task if value for money is to be achieved. Strategic decisions have to be made regarding achievement of the 4Es. Their outcome objectives have to be specified in operational terms and the services needed to deliver those outcomes must be identified. Whatever those outcome objectives, their achievement depends crucially upon both cost containment and the degree to which the use of public finance results in truly additional expenditures on services.

Cost containment requires a judicious mix of political, economic and administrative control over public spending. Political control requires effective democratic processes, an effective top-down process of priority-setting and accountability of service providers. Economic cost controls include payment at point of use, competition in the supply of services and grant mechanisms for local governments and other public sector bodies that encourage control of costs. Administrative cost controls generally control inputs and processes, as distinct from outputs and outcomes. Maximising the additionality of public finance requires avoidance of deadweight loss (that is, avoiding subsidising a level of activity that would have occurred even without public subsidy) and displacement of public funds to unintended uses.

However, spending is only half the picture. The ways in which public finance is raised also has to be considered. In particular, raising public finance is not simply a matter of levying taxes, as made clear by Chapter 5. The ways in which public finance is levied is a strategic issue, not a purely financial or administrative one. Each possible source of public finance has different implications for achieving the 4Es. The possibility of disincentive effects in relation to work and investment due to high rates of tax means that public finance should also be raised from other sources, charges being another potentially significant source of revenue. Nevertheless, it would appear that many European countries have relied too heavily on taxation to raise public finance. Furthermore, they have been too inclined to raise taxes on employment rather than on pollution and other such socially and economically undesirable activities. In particular, the simple tax and spend model of public finance is increasingly open to question.

Considering both halves of the public finance picture, in other words the combined effects resulting from both the raising and spending of money, makes clear that, ultimately, there is a limit on the additional benefits to be achieved by an ever-higher relative scale of public finance. Most people would probably accept the notion that there is some level of spending where additional public finance for a particular service results in additional costs beginning to exceed additional benefits. Thus, there exists an optimum level of public finance used to support a service, namely that at which the additional benefits just equal the additional costs. Just as benefits include those conferred on society as well as on the individual service user, so the costs include not just the direct financial costs but also any other (indirect) costs resulting from behavioural responses to high taxes and high levels of state intervention more generally. If the balance between those benefits and costs changes over time, then so does the optimal level of public finance. Public finance should therefore be viewed in dynamic rather than static terms. What was judged right for times past is no guide to what is right for the present or will be for the future.

Chapter 6 made clear that, inevitably, as public spending and revenue accounts for an increasing share of national income, the direct and indirect costs of ever-higher levels of public finance rise faster than the direct and indirect benefits it delivers. Ultimately, therefore, incremental costs exceed incremental benefits. Implementation of cost-containment measures and ensuring the net additionality of public finance slows down the rate at which costs catch up with benefits. Nevertheless, at some point the combined effect of the aggregate of public expenditure and taxation may create a profound dependency culture. In other words, public finance must be considered in its totality as well as in terms of the services and welfare benefits on which it is spent and the sources from which it is raised.

Taking such a broad view of the totality of the public finances suggests that many developed countries have developed increasingly unsustainable means of paying for public services. Structural gaps between expenditures and revenues occur when the latter are lower than the former year after year. Structural gaps seem increasingly prevalent and increasingly large within Europe and North America, this scenario being identified by the analysis of Chapter 7. Structural gaps were disguised in the past by high inflation reducing the real values of public sector debt and also by the very low, sometimes negative, real interest rates paid on that debt. Revenues raised from privatisation during the last couple of decades have had the same effect.

Nonetheless, current generations of service users and taxpayers are increasingly living at the expense of the future generations who will have to repay public sector debt. This is especially the case if borrowing is used to finance current consumption (that is, current expenditure) rather than long-lived infrastructure (that is, capital expenditure). These structural gaps have arisen because there is no symmetry between decisions to spend and decisions to raise public revenues from sustainable sources. The logic of collective action results in politicians and bureaucrats pursuing their own self-interest by serving the special interests of lobbies and pressure groups. Taxpayer resistance to higher levels of taxation is easily avoided by borrowing, leaving future generations to pay the higher public sector debt that results. Future generations of taxpayers are not represented in the current generation's decision to increase levels of debt and so are unable to protect their property rights. Thus, the logic of collective action results in chronic government failure being manifested in structural gaps in the public finances.

This theoretical explanation of structural gaps shows how they occur, irrespective of whether the overall political philosophy of any one country is Libertarian, Neo-Liberal or Collectivist. However, the greater the ratio between public finance and national income, the greater the potential structural gap. This is because there is more public expenditure and its associated benefits to be 'captured' by pressure groups, those elite groups being able to pass much of the burden of financing onto other, less politically mobilised groups. Thus, the greater is the relative scale of public finance, the greater the impact on property rights, this serving to exacerbate the logic of collective action in leading to a structural gap.

Whilst practitioners believe that structural gaps can be remedied by higher taxes, the logic of collective action makes clear that such expectations will ultimately be dashed. Structural gaps re-emerge following the adverse impact of high tax rates on economic growth and therefore on the tax bases to which tax rates are applied. Once again, public expenditures rise faster than public revenues. Fairly draconian cuts in public expenditure are also required to remove structural gaps. Hence, prevention is better than cure. Avoiding structural gaps requires a long-term strategic approach to public finance, controlling its growth relative to that of GDP. This means restricting the role of the state to core functions, levying charges for public services whenever possible, borrowing only to finance economically productive capital expenditures, and maximising the scope for political devolution.

Devolution of political decision-making from national to local government is recommended in order to match more closely willingness to pay taxes with decisions about service provision. This closer matching of public service expenditures with their financing is a way of constraining the emergence of structural gaps arising from the logic of collective action. As long as municipalities are largely self-financing, devolution from central to local governments achieves greater symmetry between decisions relating to expenditures and those relating to revenues than does central government. Symmetry is even more closely achieved if municipalities make as much use as possible of direct charges for service use, instead of financing services by local taxation.

Ironically, the analysis of Chapter 8 suggested that there is a general tendency for central governments to finance from national taxation increasingly large proportions of local government expenditures. As local governments' service responsibilities increase over time, their autonomous revenues rise more slowly than their expenditure commitments. Thus central governments pay intergovernmental grants to municipalities. However, this only serves to recreate asymmetry between decisions to spend public money and decisions to pay for public services.

A strategic approach to local government finance therefore attempts to match as closely as possible expenditure liabilities with locally autonomous (that is, locally exclusive) revenue sources. This allows payments of intergovernmental grants to be minimised by reforms to local government size and structure designed, as far as possible, to minimise fiscal disparities in municipalities' taxable resources and expenditure needs per capita. Any remaining fiscal disparities can be removed by a Robin Hood system of financial equalisation, taking from the 'rich' to give to the 'poor' and so minimising the need for additional public finance.

Even more radically, local governments should make much greater use of user-charges, regarding them as the primary (rather than the residual) source of their finance. This would bring more symmetry between those who vote for, those who pay for and those who use municipal services, so constraining the logic of collective action. Ability-to-pay issues are more effectively addressed through national income support arrangements, rather than by municipal services being provided free to all users irrespective of income. Where national social security systems are considered inadequate to achieve equitable outcomes in terms of access to municipal services, local authorities could use voucher schemes to bring a closer match between payment for and use of services whilst meeting equity objectives.

Vouchers could be used to promote greater economic and social equality by basing both their allocation and their value on ability to pay and medical and/or social need. Of course, voucher schemes have to be carefully designed if social objectives are to be met, as made clear by Chapter 9. The potentially beneficial changes resulting from the introduction of vouchers are primarily linked to the change in the role and status of the recipient as a customer with inalienable property rights in terms of access to services. Thus public service vouchers are much more than simply income transfers. They can more effectively match provision of service with user preferences and ability to pay. They can also encourage greater efficiency in the production of services. They are just one particular example of the scope for innovation in the delivery and financing of public services.

A STRATEGY FOR PUBLIC FINANCE

The above integrative summary of the themes analysed in this text makes clear that, whatever the dominant political philosophy at any one point in time, a strategic approach to public finance attempts to maximise the benefits to be gained from both private choices and public choices. Such a strategic approach avoids the worst manifestations of market failure and also government failure. An optimal outcome is not static, however. As economic, social, cultural and other contexts change, so there is a need to continually reappraise the financing, operations and outcomes of state activity. This ongoing reappraisal can be undertaken within the 4Es analytical framework. Strategic public finance is therefore necessarily dynamic and evolutionary, a perennial issue of public policy, practice, outcome and sustainability.

Whilst attempting to secure 'the public interest', a strategic approach to public finance has to recognise that it is more appropriately viewed as the outcome of competing group interests, the balance between them reflecting the degree of political mobilisation of each group. A strategic approach to public finance has to take account of the logic of collective action because it compromises the sustainability of public finance by leading to structural gaps in the public finances. Therefore a strategy for public finance has to be developed independently of political philosophy so as to ensure sustainability. It will not be possible to satisfy the objectives for the 4Es without sustainable levels of public finance.

The sustainability of arrangements for public finance can be judged in terms of the following checklist of strategic points. It is based on the 4Es and broadly follows the sequence of the preceding chapters and the above integrative summary of those chapters. It is intended only as a rather crude rule of thumb to assist a deeper strategic consideration of public finance. It cannot be used effectively without a deep understanding of the broad multidisciplinary nature of public finance. Nevertheless, it highlights the diverse and wide-ranging nature of public finance and provides a useful framework by which to ensure the adoption of a truly integrative, strategic and sustainable approach to public finance. It can also be used to identify the need for reform of the current system of public finance in any one country by drawing attention to strategic issues that may have been neglected thus far:

- *Consider the possible impact on the constitutional relationship between the state and the individual* whenever taking decisions about public finance
- *Bear in mind that successive cumulative changes in public finance can have potentially large positive and/or negative effects on society and the economy.* It would be unwise only to be concerned with whether the net effect is positive because the net effect will be highly volatile if it is the residual outcome of two very large and unstable opposing gross effects
- *Be pragmatic and realistic* about what can actually be achieved by public finance
- *Recognise that public finance need not be synonymous with public provision:* the private sector can be used to deliver many public services
- *Pay attention to long-term trends in the four public finance/GDP ratios*, so that the relative scale of public finance does not increase by default rather than by design
- *Maximise the net additionality of public expenditure*, wherever possible using public finance to complement rather than replace private expenditure that would have taken place anyway
- *Implement cost-containment measures*, there being considerable scope for reducing costs in the public sector without compromising service objectives
- *Undertake more evaluation studies* of the use and effectiveness of public finance in achieving clearly specified outcome objectives

- *Undertake more international comparisons* of raising and spending public finance to try to learn lessons and best practice from other countries
- *Avoid competition by subsidy*, for example for mobile industrial and service sector investments, essentially a zero-sum game at the expense of taxpayers
- *Seek to improve the targeting of subsidy*, avoiding middle-class capture of subsidy intended to benefit low-income groups
- *Minimise the potential for the fraudulent use of public monies* paid as social security, agricultural subsidies and so on
- *Shift the balance of taxation away from 'goods' to 'bads'*, avoiding as far as possible taxing socially beneficial activities generating incomes and wealth
- *Minimise the scope and incentives for tax avoidance and tax evasion* by simplifying the tax structures and avoiding punitive rates of tax
- *Avoid fiscal drag* by increasing tax thresholds and so tax bases each year in line with inflation of the relevant tax bases (for example by index linking personal income tax thresholds to growth of earnings – linking them to retail prices still results in fiscal drag, albeit reduced, since earnings typically rise faster than prices)
- *Widen tax bases so as to be able to reduce tax rates* for a given tax revenue, so minimising any disincentive-to-work and disincentive-to-invest effects
- *Make use of a plurality of sources of public finance* in order to minimise the adverse effects of any one source
- *Make more use of user-charges*, avoiding any adverse equity effects through the use of means testing or exemptions and discounts for specific groups of user such as children and low-income groups
- *Encourage income generation schemes within public sector bodies*, for example in seeking sponsorship from the private sector for equipment and encouraging donations and bequests. Such schemes should not compromise service objectives: they are a means to an end, not an end in themselves
- *Reduce the need to borrow* by requiring public sector organisations to keep inventories of the capital assets they own and to sell underused capital assets, using the capital receipts to finance new infrastructural investments or repay debt
- *Consider how changes in public finance may affect peoples' incentives to work and companies' incentives to invest*, in particular considering how the combination of taxation and social security benefits affects decisions to work
- *Make unemployment benefits conditional*, recipients having to undertake training for employment
- *As far as possible, make social security budgets balance*, that is, contributions equal to transfers

■ *Prevent the emergence of structural gaps in the public finances*, prevention being much less traumatic and more practical than cure

■ *Devolve public finance decisions to the lowest possible level of government* in order to match as far as possible the areas benefiting from services with the areas from which tax payments are collected

■ *Minimise the need to pay intergovernmental grants to lower tiers of government* by ensuring they have sufficient autonomous revenues and using Robin Hood systems of fiscal equalisation

■ *Subsidise service users instead of service providers as far as possible*, for example by using vouchers to increase the scope for choice on the part of service clients.

Not all elements of this strategic checklist can be adopted immediately and some will most definitely require pilot tests (for example for user-charges and voucher schemes). Nevertheless, it is clear that there is considerable scope for more effective and discriminating use of public finance. Public finance is definitely not simply a matter of tax and spend or vice versa.

Ultimately, whatever the political philosophy underpinning public finance, this checklist emphasises the need to use public finance sparingly and judiciously. Policy-makers should always question the need for more public finance and consider whether ongoing expenditures are still as effective as they could be. Hence, the strategic checklist outlined above assumes the need to be prudent with public finance, not profligate. Only by adopting such an approach will the public finances be sustainable in the long term.

CONCLUSION – THE HOLISTIC NATURE OF PUBLIC FINANCE

Hopefully, the reader now appreciates the all-encompassing nature of public finance. It is not just about financial flows, about how to finance spending on services. Even recognising the need to pay attention to raising as well as spending money, public finance is about much more than budgeting.

Instead, public finance is a manifestation of the interface between the state and the citizen. It reflects the dominant political philosophy in any one country and the consequent entitlements to state assistance as well as responsibilities for self-support. It supports the pursuit of objectives in respect of equity, efficiency, economy and effectiveness. It impacts upon the rate of economic growth and so affects not just the distribution of income and wealth but also the absolute level of material standards of living.

Put simply, public finance is synonymous with public policy writ large. A strategic approach to public finance requires the analyst to take a holistic view, recognising that the whole is greater than the sum of the individual parts. Public finance has to be considered in the round, not just in the detail. Whilst policy-makers, practitioners and subject specialists usually consider only their particular specialisms, a strategic approach to public finance must be holistic, encompassing all the issues covered in this book. To neglect any one of them may lead to unintended and unwelcome outcomes and compromise the sustainability of public finance. Even though, in practice, the reform of public finance may have to be incremental and gradual, those ongoing reforms should be in pursuit of a strategic sustainable vision in terms of what public finance can potentially deliver to the benefit of the economy and society. Those who complain about 'the dead hand of public finance' have clearly failed to appreciate the vibrant, contentious and evolutionary nature of the subject. Rather than being dull and moribund, the study of strategic public finance is both fascinating and intellectually demanding.

Index

A

ability-to-pay, 231, 233
additionality, 108–9, 114, 116, 246, 250, 277
allocative efficiency, 224, 226, 231
Aristotle (384–322 BC), 5, 29
Austrian/Hayekian School of Public Choice, 209

B

balanced budgets, 56
benefactions, *see* donations and bequests
Bentham, Jeremy (1748–1832), 7
black economy, 77, 172
borrowing, 144–5
burcaucracy, self serving, 14

C

capitalism, 15
categoric exemptions, 140
centrally planned economy, 15–16
charges, 138–41
collective action, logic of, 209–13, 278–9
collective goods and services, *see* public goods
communism, 15
contingent valuation methods, 33
correlation v. causation, 171
cost containment, 116, 119–25, 277
counterfactual, 83, 111, 164
cream skimming, 260
crowding in v. crowding out, 116, 165, 170
    see also disincentives to work/enterprise

D

data problems, 58, 77
deadweight subsidy, 28, 110
decentralisation principle, 224–5
    see also devolution
deficits v. surpluses, 184–92
democratic deficit, 235
demographic restructuring, 216
demutualisation, 32
dependency culture, 8, 173, 176, 277
dependency ratio, 216
development charges/fees, 149, 150
devolution, 279, 283
direct democracy, 75
direct provider state, 4, 5, 259
diseconomies of scale, 123
disincentives to work/enterprise, 166, 176
    see also crowding in v. crowding out
displacement, 110, 114
disposable income, 166
distributional coalitions, 14, 221
    see also pressure groups
donations and bequests, 147–8

E

economic cycle, 56, 72
economic restructuring, 215
economies of scale, 122, 215, 227, 259
economy, 20–1, 28, 140
    see also the 4Es
effectiveness, 20–1, 88
    see also the 4Es
efficiency, 20–1
    see also the 4Es
enabling state, 4, 5, 9, 242

entrepreneurial government, 3
equality of opportunity, 8–9
equality of outcome, 9–10
equity, 20–1, 136, 230, 236
    see also the 4Es
ERDF, 109, 112, 113
EU accession countries, 62
European Charter of Local Self-
    Government, 30, 225
exactions, 149
exit, 107–8, 225, 264–5
external markets, 225
    see also quasi-markets

F

financial equalisation, 236–7, 241, 280
fiscal crisis *see* fiscal stress
fiscal drag, 168, 203, 282
fiscal illusion, 75, 208
fiscal stress, 179, 206, 236
fiscal substitution, 110
freeloaders, *see* free riders
free riders, 38, 210
Friedman, Milton, 13, 247

G

Galbraith, John Kenneth, 11, 14
GDP, definition of, 54
globalisation, 14, 214
golden rule, 56, 145, 204, 219
government expenditure, definition of,
    61
government failure, 22, 28, 34
grants, 113–15, 121–2, 233, 236–41
Great Depression, 11, 13

H

Hayek, Friedrich August von
    (1899–2002), 13
health care, demand for, 117
    see also social benefits
households, restructuring of, 19, 134,
    215

human capital, 9, 16, 89, 228
Hume, David (1711–76), 7

I

impact fees, 149
income effect, 115
institutional sclerosis, 14, 217
interest rates, positive v. negative,
    201–3
intergenerational (in)equity, 55, 144,
    145, 149, 219
intergovernmental transfers, *see*
    grants
internal markets, 225
    see also quasi-markets

K

Keynes, John Maynard (1883–1946),
    11
Keynesian approach, 12

L

laissez-faire, definition of, 8
levelling down, 13
levelling up, 237
liberalisation, definition of, 16
lifestyle restructuring, 216
lotteries, 145–7

M

Maastrict debt/deficit ratios, 56–7, 72,
    144, 219
market failure, 22, 44
Marx, Karl (1818–83), 7
Marxist theory, 15
means-testing, 139, 140
middle class capture, 139, 207
Mill, James (1773–1836), 7
Mill, John Stuart (1806–73), 82
mixed economy, definition of, 15
mixed goods (and services), 41–3
moral hazard, 8, 173, 176

N

nanny state, 175
national debt, 68, 192–204
negative rights, definition of, 7
Niskanen, W. A. 14
not-for-profit sector, examples of, 26

O

obesity, 216–17
OECD, country sub-groups, 62
Olson, Mancur, 14
opportunity cost, 27, 56, 139, 163
organisational slack, 107, 138, 167
Orwell, George (1903–50), 12

P

Paine, Thomas (1737–1809), 247
patents, 35–6
payments in-kind, 148–50
philosophies, taxonomy of, 6
planning gain/obligations, 149
Plato (429–347 BC), 5
political lobbying/mobilisation,
    210–13, 221
positive rights, definition of, 9
post-tax income, 167
poverty trap, 169, 173, 215
pressure groups, 75, 210–11, 221, 279
    see also distributional coalitions
private affluence v. public squalor,
    204–6
private finance, definition of, 4
private finance initiatives, 4, 141
private goods (and services), 40–1,
    43, 243–4
privatisation, 16, 18, 141–3, 150, 268
property rights, 26–52, 275
public choice theory, 210
public expenditure
    definitions/categories of, 90, 93,
        95
    theories of, 74–7, 78–9, 208
    see also government expenditure

public finance
    definition of, 3
    causes of fluctuations/trends in,
        72–7
    models of, 80–4
    philosophical views of, 7–9, 23
public goods (and services), 37–9, 43
public interest, definitions of, 27–8,
    274
public–private partnerships, 4, 141
public v. private provision, 47
purchaser–provider split, 121, 124,
    268

Q

QALYS, 113
quasi-markets, 247, 258, 264
    see also external markets, internal
        markets

R

ratchet effect, 97, 117, 176
rational ignorance, 211, 212
recession, impact on public finance,
    69
reinventing government, 80
representative democracy, 75
research methods, 111–12, 114
Robin Hood system, see financial
    equalisation
rolling back the frontiers of the state,
    16, 80, 253
Rousseau, Jean Jacques (1712–78), 82

S

St Thomas Aquinas (1225–74), 29
service-level agreements, 124
Smith, Adam (1723–90), 7, 247
social benefits
    of education, 30, 46–7, 226
    of health, 30
social insurance, 12
socialism, 14

social justice, 10, 27
social security contributions,
      definition of, 153
Socrates (469–399 BC), 5
special assessments, 150
spillovers, 228, 230, 234
Stability and Growth Pact, 219
stakeholders, 108, 113
standard deviation, meaning of, 63
state, stereotypes of, 12, 13, 17, 175
      see also enabling state, direct
            provider state
statutory monopoly, 107, 138, 142,
      149, 254
structural gaps, 179, 207–17, 278
subsidiarity, 28
subsidies, production v. consumption,
      261
      see also ability-to-pay, allocative
            efficiency, grants
substitution effect, 115

T

taxation, 132–8
      burden of, 134
      compliance costs of, 137, 159
      definitions of, 66, 153, 155, 156,
            157
      globalisation and, 133
      invisible, 76
      local government, 206, 233–4,
            240
tax avoidance/evasion, 171, 174, 214
tax base, erosion of, 133, 214
tax competition, 133
tax deferment, 150
tax expenditures, 125–8, 147
tax exporting, 228, 230
tax harmonisation, 133, 214
tax havens/shelters, 214
taxing 'bads' v. 'goods', 137

tax relief, 118, 121, 125, 147
      see also tax expenditures
tax thresholds, 168
the 3Es, *see* the 4Es
the 4Es, 19–22, 27–8, 87–90, 136–7,
      139–40, 142–9, 150, 272
totalitarianism, definition of, 14
trade cycle, *see* economic cycle
tragedy of the commons, 31–2,
      48–50, 220
transaction costs, 255, 258
transition economies, 16
trickle down, 13

U

undeserving poor, 135, 174
unemployment trap, 168–9, 173, 215
usufruct, 36, 49, 250

V

value for money, 86–8, 105–6, 129
      see also the 4Es
Virginia School of Public Choice, 210
voice, 107–8, 264–5, 269
vouchers, 243–71

W

weighted averages, calculation of, 61,
      63
welfare
      conditional, 19, 71, 274
      cradle-to-grave, 12
      dependency, 169
      measures of, 172
      unconditional, 19
      work-based, 19, 274
      workless, 19
willingness to accept, 33
willingness to pay, 33